Knowledge and Skill Develop

in Nonprofit Organizations

Roger M. Weis
Murray State University

Vernon W. Gantt
Murray State University

eddie bowers publishing co., inc.

<u>*Special thanks to:*</u>

Dr. Robert F. Long of the W.K. Kellogg Foundation
and Jerome and Jeanette Cohen for grant support for this textbook.

Editing: Katharine W. Cohen

Cover and Interior Layout/Design: Linda M. Pierce

Exclusive marketing and distributor rights for
U.K., Eire, and Continental Europe held by:

Gazelle Book Services Limited
Falcon House
Queen Square
Lancaster
LA1 1RN
U.K.

eddie bowers publishing co., inc.
P. O. Box 130
Peosta, Iowa 52068-0130 USA

www.eddiebowerspublishing.com

ISBN 1-57879-058-1

Dedication

This book is dedicated to colleague and friend, Dr. Robert F. Long of the W.K. Kellogg Foundation, who has encouraged and supported our collaborative projects and publications for a number of years.

It is also dedicated to Jerome and Jeanette Cohen, whose kindness and generosity have been instrumental in the successes of thousands of people over the years, including each of ours.

Roger M. Weis

Vernon W. Gantt

Authors

Roger M. Weis

Roger Weis is Campus Director and Associate Professor for the American Humanics/ Youth and Nonprofit Leadership program at Murray State University, where he has twice been selected as student advisor of the year. He has published numerous journal articles and manuals regarding character development, career development, and service learning and has written four books, including three textbooks on various aspects of leadership in nonprofit organizations.

As director of the AH program at MSU for the past fifteen years, he has served as the chair of the American Humanics Director's Association for two terms and as a member of the National AH Board of Directors for two terms and he was the first recipient of the AH National Award of Excellence in Leadership. He is the founding chair of the local Campus Connection Volunteer Center and the Big Brothers Big Sisters program, and the founding co-chair of the Service Learning Scholars program. Prior to working at MSU, he was a program director and director for the Boys and Girls Clubs of America in Norfolk/Virginia Beach, Va., and the Chief Executive Officer for the Leukemia Society of America for the state of Virginia.

He presents service learning workshops nationally and internationally, and has done consultation with school systems, the Boys and Girls Clubs of America, the Big Brothers Big Sisters program, the YMCA, and the United Way of America.

Weis received his B.A. and M.A. from Marshall University and his Ed.D. from the University of Kentucky.

Vernon W. Gantt

Vernon Gantt is Professor Emeritus of Organizational Communication from Murray State University and previously served as chair of the department. He is an award- winning teacher, busy consultant, and author. He has published a number of articles regarding communication and mentoring, and this is his third book publication. He taught interpersonal and organizational communication for over thirty years before his retirement in June 2000.

For over seventeen years, he has served as a Trustee for American Humanics and chair of the Murray State University Advisory Council. He makes regular presentations at the American Humanics Management Institute. His volunteer efforts include service to Boy Scouts, Red Cross, Rotary International, American Cancer Society, and his church.

His consulting clients include state and local government agencies, schools, national and international professional associations, Ingersoll-Rand, Briggs and Stratton, AE Staley, Tennessee Valley Authority, and General Tire. He is also a trained Mediator.

Gantt received his B.S. from Murray State University, and his M.A. and Ph.D. degrees from Ohio University.

Preface

According to most reports, there are more than 1.5 million nonprofit organizations in the United States and over 50,000 new positions open in youth, human service, and other nonprofit organizations each year. The main purpose of this introductory text is to present information relevant to a number of competencies required to be leaders in these organizations. Another purpose is to provide opportunities to develop skills in these competency areas through classroom activities, simulations, and service learning projects. The competencies selected for discussion in the chapters to come were selected through surveys developed by the American Humanics program. American Humanics is an alliance of colleges, universities, and nonprofits preparing undergraduates for careers with youth, human service, and other nonprofit organizations. The organization headquarters is located in Kansas City, Missouri.

The first chapter of the text discusses the history, purpose, and importance of the nonprofit sector throughout history. The next chapter presents theories, models, and studies on leadership and leadership development, as well as discussing the connection between leadership, character, and ethics. Following this, Chapter 3 is an in-depth look at staff, board, and volunteer development. Chapter 4 includes information on various theories of human development essential to future leaders in the nonprofit sector, and presents information on a number of trends and issues--important information to have prior to designing programs. Developing programs from beginning to end is covered in Chapter 5 and includes information on marketing and promotion of programs. Chapter 6 presents an overview of financial processes including accounting, budgeting, and financial development. The importance of risk management and developing a risk management plan, along with a discussion on the importance of insurance is covered in Chapter 7. Chapter 8 discusses the best ways to address the needs of constituents and ways to deal with customer concerns effectively. The final chapter, Chapter 9, provides information on assessing oneself relative to a career in the nonprofit sector and information on developing effective resumes, cover letters, interview and networking techniques.

The authors would like to acknowledge and thank a number of individuals who made a contribution to this book. These include Christopher R. Edginton, Susan D. Hudson, and Phyllis M. Ford, who authored *Leadership in Recreation and Leisure Service Organizations*, which served as a model for a portion of this text. Another author, Thomas Wolf, provided a significant foundation for some of the financial aspects of this text with his book *Managing a Nonprofit Organization*. Special thanks go to Susan Ellis and Katherine Noyes for their book *By the People: A History of Americans as Volunteers*, which served as a foundation for Chapter 1. Acknowledgment also goes to personnel at the Independent Sector for providing statistical information and to various individuals with the Nonprofit Risk Management Center for their assistance with risk management and insurance. And recognition goes to Holly Brandon Shoemake, who researched and prepared Appendix A.

Again, we would like to thank Dr. Robert F. Long, of the W.K. Kellogg Foundation, along with Jerome and Jeanette Cohen, for their support. Many thanks to Dr. Barbara Keener, of the American Humanics program for connecting us with the Cohen Grant.

And thanks to our editor, Katharine Cohen, and our layout specialist, Linda Pierce, for their expertise and commitment to the project.

Last, we would like to express our appreciation to those closest to us, our family members: Stefani Weis, Clint Weis, and Loretta Adkins, as well as Dolores (Dee) Gantt, Michelle Gantt, Darren Gantt, and Virginia Gantt for their never ending support and encouragement.

Contents

1 Understanding the Nonprofit Sector: Purpose and History

Throughout time, communities have developed systems to address the needs of the young, the old, the weak, the sick, and the disabled. In centuries past, families and neighbors were often responsible for the care of these individuals. But as time advanced, and individual needs became more and more specialized and complex, families and neighbors could no longer address these needs effectively. In many countries, the government has provided for such needs as education, health care, and retirement, to mention several. In other countries, these needs are met through a network of private, charitable organizations. And in still others, like the United States, various needs of the citizenry are addressed through a complex combination of government programs and private, nonprofit organizations with public purposes.

There is a Middle Eastern legend about a sparrow lying on its back in the road, when a journeyman comes along and asks the sparrow what he is doing. The sparrow responds that he has heard that the heavens were going to fall on that day. The journeyman looks at the sparrow and asks the sparrow if he really thinks he can hold up the heavens with his spindly little legs, and the sparrow responds, "One does what one can, one does what one can" (Ellis and Noyes 1978, 31). There is a tremendous gap in what the government can do in the way of various services for citizens, and private, nonprofit organizations do an amazing job of filling that gap.

There are at least 1.5 million nonprofit organizations in the United States, and the first section of Chapter 1 offers an operational definition of nonprofits and provides several explanations for their tax-exempt status. This chapter includes a number of examples of different types and categories of nonprofit organizations, along with a list of criteria characteristic of these organizations. The history of the nonprofit sector is rich and diverse. The remainder of the chapter deals with an exploration of philanthropy and service, from its early colonial beginnings involving the Pilgrims, patriots, and Native Americans, to its involvement with relief efforts for the victims of the horrendous terrorist attacks of September 11, 2001. Included in this section is the sector's involvement with various areas of American life: health care, education, recreation, politics, social welfare, conservation, and religion, to mention several. The nonprofit sector has been an integral factor in a number of turning points in the history of the United States, including the colonization of the country, the Great Awakening, and the American Revolutionary War. The establishment of private institutions of higher education, the Civil War, child welfare, women's suffrage, World War I, the Great Depression, World War II, civil rights, the Korean War, the Vietnam War, Desert Storm, and 9/11 are all examples of important historical events in which nonprofit organizations have played a significant role.

■ What is the Nonprofit Sector?

The **nonprofit sector** is often the name used to describe agencies that are private, nonprofit entities with public purposes. These organizations are neither government, nor businesses incorporated for a profit. The sector is also referred to as the **voluntary sector,** the **not-for-profit sector**, the **third sector**, the **independent sector,** the **charitable sector,** the **philanthropic sector** and **non-governmental organizations (NGOs),** for those organizations outside the United States (Independent Sector 1997). There are at least 1.5 million organizations in this country that belong to this sector that have made the enhancement of the lives of people in their community the sole purpose of the organization. These privately incorporated organizations range from educational, cultural, and religious institutions, to recreational, service, and character development organizations, to hospitals and wellness centers, and many others.

The term **nonprofit organization** signifies that the organization can charge fees for memberships and services, but cannot make a profit for owners or investors. In other words, these organizations are committed to programs to meet specific missions, and any revenue

that is generated above expenses must go back into supporting the operation of the organization. The million and a half nonprofit organizations have combined annual revenues of approximately $670 billion, making the sector an integral part of the country's overall economy. About one in twelve Americans work in a nonprofit or-

ganization and over fifty percent of American adults volunteer in a nonprofit organization each year (Independent Sector 2002). A list of some of the leading organizations, along with a brief history, purpose statement, various programs, career opportunities, and contact information can be found in **Appendix A.**

Nonprofit organizations have received a limited **tax-exempt status** throughout history for several reasons (Independent Sector 1997):

- **They provide assistance in place of government.** The thousands of day-care centers, hospitals, schools, and shelters that nonprofits offer relieve the government from providing these services. Government, in turn, provides a tax-exempt status for the many benefits nonprofits offer. Nonprofits also provide services that governments wouldn't be required to provide anyway, such as encouraging civic involvement and other community enrichment activities.
- **The taxation process would be problematic.** According to lawyers and economists, deciding what income would be taxable would be difficult, and taxation would make it even more difficult for nonprofits to operate efficiently.
- **Tax-exemption for religious organizations protects separation of church and state.** Making religions tax-exempt prevents government from using taxation as a way of favoring one religion over another, or of putting one religion out of business. The tax-exempt status of nonprofit organizations will be discussed in more detail in the section below.

Some sample nonprofit organizations are listed in Figure 1.1.

Figure 1.1
Sample Nonprofit Organizations

AFL-CIO	National Collegiate Athletic
American Cancer Society	Association (NCAA)
American Heart Association	National Geographic Society
American Humanics, Inc.	Planned Parenthood
American Red Cross	Pop Warner Little League
Boys and Girls Clubs of America	The American Civil Liberties
Ford Foundation	Union (ACLU)
Girl Scouts of America	The Brookings Institution
Jewish Community Centers	The National Rifle Association
Metropolitan Museum of Art	W.K. Kellogg Foundation
National Association for the Advance	Yale University
ment of Colored People (NAACP)	YMCA
	YWCA

∎ Characteristics of a Nonprofit Organization

Most nonprofit organizations have similar characteristics or meet a number of criteria (Weis and Gantt 2002).

- **Maintain a legal, incorporated status.** Although some nonprofit organizations exist as ad hoc, informal groups, most nonprofit organizations have a legal designation as a corporation chartered under state laws. This is significant in that it allows the organization to enter contracts and frees the officials of the board from financial entanglements and personal financial responsibility of the organization's obligations.

- **Private but provide a public service mission.** Private, nonprofit organizations are institutionally separate from government, but may still receive significant government support. The general purpose of all nonprofit organizations is to serve the public in some manner. Because the purpose is often very broad, nonprofits designate a number of **goals** to accomplish as part of the mission. Organizational goals often have a number of **objectives** or outcomes within the framework of a goal. For instance, a nonprofit that has as its mission the enhancement of the lives of children in the community could have educational enhancement as a major goal, and literacy improvement as an objective beneath that goal. Private citizens or community organizations initiate and develop nonprofit organizations to serve the public good. Nonprofits attempt to fill the huge gap between services provided by public organizations and those provided by businesses for profit.

- **Governed by a voluntary board of directors.** In order to keep cost down and maintain expertise in a number of different areas, nonprofit organizations enlist the help of volunteer staff members and consultants. Key volunteers for a nonprofit organization are often referred to as the board of directors. Boards act as a governing body for nonprofits and their function and purpose will be discussed in detail in Chapter 3. Organizations such as the National Charities Information Bureau and the Council of Better Business Bureaus' Philanthropic Advisory Service are charged with monitoring the activities of nonprofits, while a division of the IRS (the Tax Exempt/Government Entities division) is responsible for insuring that organizations comply with the requirements for maintaining their tax-exempt status.

- **Funded primarily through individual and corporate fees and/or contributions.** Financial support for these organizations comes through a variety of measures. Individual and corporate donations make up a significant portion of the funding for nonprofits. Allocations from the United Way, membership fees, program fees, special events, and grants and governmental contracts are additional ways in which these agencies are funded.

- **Operate under a financial system without profit.** Although hundreds of billions of dollars are exchanged each year within nonprofit organizations in the form of fee payments or contributions, revenue that exceeds expenses cannot be used for personal profit, but must go back into the support of the organization. Revenue above expenses may be used as a **contingency fund** for special situations or emergencies, or it may be placed in a **reserve fund** that can be used for the purchase of new equipment, renovations, or growth of any kind. Sometimes these funds are combined and labeled as either contingency or reserve.

- **Possess a tax-exempt status from the IRS (Exp.: 501 (c) 3)** Nonprofit organizations are exempt from federal corporate income taxes and most are exempt from state and local property and sales taxes. Because of the great diversity of this sector, there are at least twenty-six different sections under which nonprofit organizations can claim exemption from federal income taxes. They are not exempt from withholding payroll taxes and they must pay taxes on income that is not directly related to their mission, such as the income from a university owning a retirement home and receiving revenue from that home. This exempt status can be traced back through medieval England to ancient times. Various types of tax-exempt organizations operating in the United States are included in Figure 1.2.

- **Conduct an annual, independent audit.** Conducting an annual, independent audit by a competent, certified accounting firm provides insight for nonprofits to operate efficiently, ethically, and legally. The *independent* aspect of the audit signifies that the audit is done by accountants without close ties to the organization being audited, thereby avoiding the possibility of a conflict of interest. The annual audit provides valuable information to the organization, its members, potential donors, and accrediting organizations.

■ Sub-categories of Nonprofit Organizations

Charities. Nonprofit organizations that are exempt under Section 501 (c) (3) of the income tax law are sometimes referred to as charities, although they offer a lot more services than sheltering and providing food to the poor. These organizations include hospitals,

Figure 1.2
Types of Tax-Exempt Organizations in the United States

Tax Code Number	Type of Tax-exempt Organization
501 (c) (1)	Corporations organized under an act of Congress
501 (c) (2)	Title-holding companies
501(c) (3)	Religious, charitable, educational, etc.
501 (c) (4)	Social welfare
501 (c) (5)	Labor, agriculture organization
501 (c) (6)	Business leagues
501 (c) (7)	Social and recreational clubs
501 (c) (8)	Fraternal beneficial societies
501 (c) (9)	Voluntary employees' societies
501 (c) (10)	Domestic fraternal beneficiary societies
501 (c) (11)	Teachers' retirement fund
501 (c) (12)	Benevolent life insurance associations
501 (c) (13)	Cemetery companies
501 (c) (14)	Credit unions
501 (c) (15)	Mutual insurance companies
501 (c) (16)	Corporations to finance crop operation
501 (c) (17)	Supplemental unemployment benefit trusts
501 (c) (18)	Employee-funded pension trusts
501 (c) (19)	War veterans' organizations
501 (c) (20)	Legal services organizations
501 (c) (21)	Black lung trusts
501(d)	Religious and apostolic organizations
501(e)	Cooperative hospital service organizations
501(f)	Cooperative service organizations of operating educational organizations
521	Farmers' cooperatives

Source: Internal Revenue Service, Annual Report

art centers, schools, advocacy groups, public radio and television stations, wellness centers, disaster relief organizations, various recreational centers and many others (Independent Sector 1997).

In 2000, more than 720,000 public charities registered with the IRS. An organization must have a broad base of financial support to be considered a public charity before applying to the IRS for tax-exempt status. Individuals and corporations may receive tax deductions for making contributions to public charities, but an accountant is generally consulted regarding any possible deductions.

Foundations. Over fifty-thousand individuals, families, corporations, and/or communities have established foundations for the purpose of providing funding for support of various causes while operating as a 501 (c) (3) entity and receiving tax breaks. Some of these foundations are subject to strict regulations, being required to contribute at least five percent of investment assets each year and being required to pay approximately two percent excise tax on net earnings. Some common types of foundations are listed below:

Private foundations are typically funded by an individual, a family, or a business and use investment income to make contributions to nonprofit organizations. Good examples of private foundations include the W.K. Kellogg Foundation, the Ford Foundation, and the Carnegie Corporation.

Corporate foundations is a type of private foundation that receives funding from and make grants on behalf of a corporation. Many corporate foundations provide grants to community organizations, as well as to employees and their family members, for educational and other purposes. The Metropolitan Foundation and the Starbucks Foundation are examples of corporate foundations.

Operating foundations are yet another form of private foundations that use the majority of their resources to fund their own service programs, rather than funding other programs. Examples of operating foundations include the Carnegie Endowment for International Peace and the J. Paul Getty Trust.

Community foundations receive income from a number of contributors and then direct their grants on specific cities or regions. Community foundations are classified as publicly supported charities by the IRS and are therefore not subject to excise taxes or distribution restrictions like private foundations. Individual donations to community foundations are generally tax deductible. The Cleveland Foundation and the New York Community Trust are examples of community foundations.

Nonprofit organizations such as hospitals and colleges often create related 501 (c) (3) organizations, referred to as foundations, whose sole purpose is the support of the parent or sponsoring organization. These foundations are fund raising in nature, and all of the proceeds go toward the parent organization.

Social Welfare Organizations. Advocacy organizations, such as the NAACP and the National Rifle Association (NRA) are exempt entities under Section 501 (c) (4) of the tax code. Social welfare or advocacy organizations have greater freedom in legislative advocacy, lobbying, and political campaign activities so contributions to 501 (c) (3) organizations are generally not tax-deductible.

Professional and Trade Associations. Organizations that promote business or professional interests, such as chambers of commerce, usually qualify for tax exemption under 501 (c) (6) of the tax code. Donations to these organizations are not tax-deductible, but membership dues should qualify as a business expense.

In addition to donations, United Way allocations, special events, grants, program and membership fees, nonprofit organizations can also receive funding from the government in the form of grants or as contracts for providing services.

One of the most important and distinctive aspects of the United States is the important role that has been left to private, nonprofit organizations and the way in which these organizations have changed and benefited the American way of life. Millions of Americans have learned to swim, received blood transfusions, turned their lives around at "safe" houses, learned a trade, developed character, been rehabilitated, or just had fun at one or more of the hundreds of thousands of nonprofit organizations across the land. But how did all this begin? The history of the nonprofit sector is rich in detail and scope and certainly worth examining.

■ How Did the Nonprofit Sector Begin?

The concept of American benevolence or **philanthropy**, as it is often called, is generally considered to be an imported product originating in Europe before the colonization of America began. However, the concern for the well-being of others in the United States stretches all the way back to the seventeenth century, when no one individual could overcome the harshness of the new land. White settlers received enormous assistance from Native Americans, and this cooperation often meant the difference between life and death. In the winter of 1620-21 in Plymouth, Massachusetts, one Indian in particular, Squanto, proved to be especially helpful when he taught the weary Pilgrims how to plant corn, where to fish, and how to procure other commodities that were necessary for survival. Squanto also guided the Pilgrims in their exploration of the new land and stayed by their side until his death. Many Native Americans followed in Squanto's footsteps, assisting the settlers in adjusting to conditions that few had ever encountered before. American benevolence was influenced by European experience and theory, and for many years American institutions practically mirrored those of Europe. These institutions also sought and received financial support from abroad. American philanthropy took root almost immediately and grew rapidly, probably because the colonization of America coincided with one of the greatest periods of European philanthropy. A number of missionary enterprises, a renewed interest in charitable works, and the development in England of tax-supported poor relief in the seventeenth century all inspired similar goals in the New World.

A more detailed account of the history of philanthropy and the nonprofit sector follows and is derived primarily from several sources, including *Historical Perspectives on Nonprofit Organizations* by Hall, and *Leadership and Program Development in Nonprofit Organizations* by Weis and Gantt. Ellis and Noyes conducted unparalleled, historical research regarding nonprofit organizations in this country and much of what follows is a selected chronology of their work, *By the People: A History of Americans as Volunteers*. More information on each of these references and others can be found in the reference section at the end of this chapter.

New Beginnings and Colonization:
Philanthropy and Service Take Root in the 1600-1700s

In 1620, the Pilgrims developed the **Social Compact** as a declaration of their determination to achieve mutual, civic goals. This document resulted in a covenant that tied the Pilgrims to the mutual care of other community members. This covenant was supported by the doctrines of **Puritanism** that consisted of a strict moral code and an active concern for the members of the church and the community. According to the tenets of Puritanism, man was born evil, but could obtain Grace by positive actions and deeds. These doctrines had a profound influence on the behavior of the settlers. Farmers often combined their efforts to clear land, plant crops, build barns, and to defend against any and all assaults by nature or man. While the men did most of the strenuous work, the women and children assisted and also prepared communal meals.

The largest church in a particular area often directed the social welfare activities of the community. For example, the **Quakers** in Pennsylvania would hold meetings that dealt with both church and community issues; the tradition was referred to as **Meeting Day**.

Members of the church would prioritize what needed to be done for the poor, for the maintenance of the city, and for other community needs, and volunteers from the church would initiate appropriate action. In most cases, even the church buildings were built by voluntary community effort. A religious revival referred to as the **Great Awakening** swept the colonies between 1740 and 1760 and was as much a social and political revival as a religious one. The evangelicals promoted liberties and organized voluntary associations such as the **Sons of Liberty**, which eventually played a role in resisting the British. With the support of Benjamin Franklin, secret organizations like the **Juntos,** artisans who met weekly to discuss politics and other issues, and the **Freemasons,** a club formed for mutual improvement, began to establish themselves as leaders in the collective movement for independence from Britain (Hall 1994).

During the colonial period in New England, the strong, Puritan ethic maintained that individuals were first responsible for their own well-being, and there was often a lack of "organized charity" (Ellis and Noyes 1978). Alms giving to the poor was looked down upon, and people who provided handouts were considered to be fools. In spite of this culture, the need for an occasional charitable act was recognized, and families were considered the first line of assistance for members, poor relatives or close friends. These activities were not necessarily voluntary actions, since the colonies eventually adopted the provisions of the **Elizabethan Poor Law** that framed these activities and others as requirements of the citizenry (Hall 1994).

Oftentimes the elderly and those with serious illnesses were kept in private homes, and the host families were paid through tax collections. In some communities, families would take turns taking care of indigents and the infirm for a couple of weeks each year; a term referred to as **taking in.** When the population grew in the cities, these informal systems of care became less and less effective and **almshouses** were initiated to assist the poor and the needy, the first in Boston in 1662 and in Philadelphia in 1732. In addition to almshouses, clubs, societies and fraternal orders began to develop with the primary purpose of providing assistance to others.

Medical care was also important during colonial days, the quality of which left much to be desired and the few doctors that were available were much in demand. In an effort to establish medical standards, the **Weekly Society of Gentlemen in New York** was formed in 1749, and it later evolved into the **Medical Society of the State of New York** in 1794. Colonies did not have health organizations, as such, but when a medical crisis did occur, a committee of citizens with a physician at the head was appointed to address the situation; these committees were usually referred to as **boards of health.** When epidemics occurred, individuals or families were treated in **pest houses**, which were little more than shelters built in a remote area because of the need to quarantine. The first colonial hospital was the **Philadelphia Hospital**, built in 1751 as a nonprofit, philanthropic enterprise.

During the period when the colonies were developing, most educational institutions in Europe were supported by the church, and few were actually state supported. Accordingly, the first educational institutions in this country were initiated and developed by the churches. Children, however, were often put to work at home or in industries, and when educational activities did take place, they occurred in log cabins, in seacoast churches or in sod houses along the prairie. The first schoolhouses were generally built through a cooperative effort, such as the "Old School House" in Mount Holly, New Jersey; constructed in 1759 by a group of citizens who also bought the land the schoolhouse was built on (Ellis and Noyes 1978). In 1794, the **Society of Associated Teachers** was formed in New York City to improve the education of teachers and to set and regulate standards for teaching. This prompted some of the initial instructional activities for teachers in the early part of the 1800s.

Advanced degrees were also desirable, but candidates were forced to consider expensive, European universities until 1636, when a group of clergy founded the first college in the New World. The success of this college was insured when John Harvard left the developing college a large sum of money and hundreds of books from his own library; the school honored Harvard by naming the institute **Harvard College**. Following this, a group of Connecticut clergy founded **Yale University** in 1700 by offering books from their own, personal libraries and embarking on a successful fundraising campaign; hence two of America's most prestigious, private, nonprofit institutes of learning were firmly established (Ellis and Noyes 1978).

As the population expanded in the cities the potential for fire and the need for effective fire fighting equipment and personnel became more and more important. In 1736, Benjamin Franklin in Philadelphia pioneered the first voluntary fire department that became an immediate and extraordinary success and the idea spread quickly through the colonies. It was not until the late 1700s that fire departments started to become staffed with professionals as well as volunteers.

In the eighteenth century, America was mainly an agricultural society and it was important that farmers understood the most efficient methods of farming and had the most modern equipment. To this end, voluntary organizations such as the **Society for the Promotion of Agriculture** were formed in 1785. This organization provided farmers with the latest results in agricultural testing and supported them with reports regarding other activities. In 1786, the **Patriotic Society in Virginia** began which combined agricultural activities with political initiatives; such as blending different methods of fencing with the preservation of timber (Ellis and Noyes 1978).

There was such a strong emphasis on farming and farming societies and associations, that business and trade associations didn't fully develop until the mid-1800s, with some exceptions. Two noteworthy exceptions were the **New York Chamber of Commerce** established in 1792 and the **New York Stock Exchange** initiated in 1792.

For obvious reasons, these organizations were primarily concerned with economic profit and activities designed to enhance commerce but were also actively involved with civic and community enrichment.

A Century of Paradox:
Service Opportunities Abound in the 1800s

The end of the Revolutionary War brought a great number of opportunities and challenges; a unified government was formed and the original frontier was moved further and further west. In spite of the development of a unified government, there were many limits to what government could accomplish, and social welfare, education, the arts, and many other local issues often had to be handled by local citizen groups and community organizations.

Small towns expanded into cities, and as factories and industrial trades grew, labor organizations were created to provide sick benefits and voluntary assistance to widows and orphans. In the early 1800s, a number of these **benevolent societies** began in the state of New York. In 1811, child labor had not yet become a major issue, but the **Manumission Society** was organized with the primary function of encouraging legislation that would regulate the horrible working conditions for chimney sweeps, who tended to be juvenile boys.

A different form of assistance for children began to form in the mid-1800s: **day nurseries**, which are now referred to as children's day care centers. Organizations such as the **Children's Aid Society** and the **National Conference of Charities and Correction** worked diligently to develop an effective structure for child care. These nurseries were usually located in large, urban centers and were sponsored by the wives of wealthy men, who could plan charity balls, fairs, and other activities in support of the nurseries. Nurseries usually employed a large number of women and were sometimes part of settlement houses, churches, or adjuncts of family welfare agencies, and they were almost never publicly supported. In addition to providing child care, day nurseries offered a number of services including employment and training. Staff from the nursery would match individuals looking for domestic work with some of the local, wealthy families, and individuals would train to be domestic workers or child-care providers under the supervision of more experienced staff members.

It was also around this period that a concern grew for the separation of the juvenile court system from the adult justice process. Volunteer associations, such as the **Cook County Woman's Club** in Illinois, lobbied with parent-teacher associations and many other such associations across the country, and in 1899 the first juvenile courts were established in Chicago and Denver. These were typically staffed by volunteers until the early 1900s.

Prior to the turn of the century, **free schools** did not exist for poor children, most of whom were laboring at home or in an industry. This problem was particularly true for children in urban areas who did not have the time for or the money to pay for private schooling. This problem was also prevalent in Europe, where they began the first **Sunday Schools** established for reading and religion. They were held on Sunday, when children did not labor in the factories. This idea soon spread to the United States, where citizens volunteered their time and their money to provide educational experiences for the poor. **School societies** began forming throughout large cities and on the East Coast, providing educational opportunities for children. They were supported completely by voluntary contributions and voluntary instruction. These societies became the basis for tax-supported, public school systems that made their appearance around 1840.

Another popular and successful method of instruction was the **Lancastrian** method, named after Joseph Lancaster, who developed the system in London in the late 1700s. This system was brought to this country around 1800, and it involved teachers teaching a lesson to older students, who would then present the lesson to their younger classmates. This method of using students as resources was highly successful and cost effective and thrived between the early 1800s and 1825.

In the early 1800s, private, nonprofit institutions of higher education came under attack by members of the Jeffersonian party who wanted to convert the privately founded **Dartmouth College** to a state institution. In 1816, the New Hampshire legislature passed a bill reorganizing the college under state control (Hall 1994). The old trustees of Dartmouth, represented by Daniel Webster, appealed to the United States Supreme Court in 1818 and won on the basis that property and money had been contributed to the trustees for the purpose of establishing a private college; the Constitution prohibited states from passing laws breaking contractual agreements (Hofstadter and Smith 1961).

The education of slaves in the 1800s was extremely limited. In spite of the fact that teaching slaves to read or write was illegal, many individuals would risk being arrested. Family members of the master's house would sometimes teach slaves to read and write, and in turn the educated slaves would teach others. A strong interest in adult education also developed in the 1800s and the **Lyceum Movement** began in 1820. This was a fairly formal way of educating the adult population in which philanthropic, humanitarian organizations and corporations would sponsor libraries, museum collections, seminars, and debates for self-improvement.

Between 1862 and 1877, the war between white settlers and Native Americans reached a fever pitch which led to the federal government taking over Indian land and forcing entire tribes to live on reservations. A number of whites were so affected by this injustice that they formed the **Indian Rights Association** in 1882. This organization joined with the **Women's National Indian Association** and lobbied successfully for educational centers for Native Americans. Boarding schools were instituted on most reservations, first run by missionaries and then by government-contracted instructors.

In the late 1800s, education underwent a significant renaissance, public school systems began to out-number private educational systems, and the demand for adult educational opportunities increased. As a result of this demand, there was an increased need for efficient public libraries, and in 1876 the **American Library Association** began in Philadelphia. Members of this group initiated the cataloguing and circulation systems that remain in existence today and began raising funds to build and start more libraries.

The system of higher education also went through a number of changes in the late 1800s due in large part to a committee of university presidents who worked together to change what they considered to be an already inefficient higher education system in America. Working individually and collectively, these presidents brought about revisions in curriculum and then founded universities supported by state funds. They established technical and professional schools, graduate education, co-education, and education for blacks. They also encouraged philanthropic gifts that led to creating laboratories, purchasing new equipment, and building libraries and museums. This period of growth encouraged scholars to form nationwide associations in many branches of research, including the **American Chemical Society**; the **American Ornithologists' Union**; the **American Catholic Historical Association**; the **American Climatological Society**; the **Association of Economic Entomologists**; and the **American Psychological Association** (Ellis and Noyes 1978).

Several events late in the century led to the encouragement of increased contributions to private colleges, universities and other nonprofit organizations and to a support system for college-educated women. In 1874, **Harvard** defended its tax exemption to the Massachusetts General Court so eloquently that the court raised the ceiling on the amount of property that could be exempted from taxation, and it expanded exempt institutions to include educational, charitable, benevolent and religious organizations (Hall 1994). This was great news for nonprofit organizations, which grew at an enormous rate in the latter part of the nineteenth century. Then, in 1882, a group of the first college-educated women joined together to form the **American Association of University Women**. Still in existence today, this association supported other women in seeking college degrees and worked diligently to make colleges co-educational.

Religion continued to be a significant part of the lives of the early citizens, and the Protestant dominion was preserved through collaborative participation in various causes. Organizations made up of different denominations, such as the **Connecticut Moral Society**, also began to appear throughout New England and the Midwest in the early 1800s with purposes such as moral development, missionary pursuits and educational activities.

Early missionary societies served the American family, settlers, and the Native Americans. Missions were established throughout the Midwest and the Southwest, with a primary purpose of converting Indians to Christianity. This was usually a dangerous mission with little progress, until Congress authorized ten million dollars to fund religious groups working with various tribes. As a part of these missionary activities, thousands of Bibles were distributed and an outgrowth of this movement was the establishment of the **American Bible Society** in 1815 with chapters beginning in hundreds of locations in just a few years.

Religious growth was also occurring in the south, where preachers would hold services for slaveholders and their families in the morning, followed by similar services for their slaves on Sunday afternoon. Sometimes even the master of the plantation would hold services, but eventually black religious leaders began to emerge and mostly black churches began to come into existence. A similar occurrence began with urban slaves who became very active in religious life, taking on more leadership roles with the churches. Free blacks and slaves also combined forces to develop associations, such as the **Free African Society** in Philadelphia, for the purpose of developing leadership in black churches and other cities soon followed suit.

In spite of the fact that religious freedom was a legal right in most states, prejudice, particularly against atheists and Jews was rampant and organizations such as the **Native American Party** began in the 1830s and reflected hatred and divisiveness for anyone who was different. But most religious organizations had much more positive purposes. For instance, following the Civil War, the American missionary movement grew rapidly and contributed evangelical efforts, humanitarian aid, and commercial ventures throughout Latin America, the Middle East, Africa, Hawaii, and the Far East in the 1880s and 1890s.

In the early part of the 1800s, medical practices were relatively unstructured, with few standards, and doctors often served as druggists and visiting nurses as well. Initially, women provided medical assistance in most areas and often prescribed and even formulated their own remedies. Most wagon train leaders also served as surgeons as pioneers headed westward and the need for removing bullets and treating snakebites became prevalent.

Local counties were allowed to institute boards of health to coordinate efforts regarding matters of health. As a result, free vaccination clinics begin to form, and New York established a **Vaccination Institute** in 1802, with Boston following in 1803. These clinics provided essential services and were generally staffed with volunteer doctors. The first visiting nurse service in the country, called the **Ladies' Benevolent Society**, was established in 1813 in Charleston, South Carolina, with medical care primarily for the sick poor. Volunteers established specialized institutions, such as the **Asylum for the Deaf and Dumb** in 1827, the **New York Institute for the Blind** in 1831, and the **New York Ophthalmic Hospital** in 1852. In 1892, the **Pennsylvania Society for the Prevention of Tuberculosis** was created and became the first organization in which lay and medical persons worked together toward the prevention and cure of a specific ailment. Medical societies played a significant part in establishing standards for medical practice and the **American Medical Association,** started in 1847, was at the forefront of this movement. Its purpose was to insure the quality of licensure and to improve instructional methodology.

Although the Civil War had been tremendously divisive, it also united citizens of the North and South as never before. Northern women organized themselves into **Ladies' Aid Societies** to assemble bandages and other items of medical aid. Several of these societies were eventually merged into the **Women's Central Relief Association for the Sick and Wounded of the Army.** The association encouraged the formation of the **U.S. Sanitary Commission**, which soon became the largest private relief organization of the war. This organization stockpiled huge warehouses of food, clothing, and medical supplies for future distribution, and it maintained houses where traveling federal soldiers could find meals, rest, lodging and comfort. Following the war, the commission also found jobs for soldiers who returned disabled and for their wives and mothers. Another commission, the **Christian Commission**, was established in 1861 in order to present evangelical opportunities to soldiers, distributing Bibles and religious tracts, and providing food kitchens.

Black contributions to both sides of the war were numerous and invaluable. Although some slaves remained loyal to their masters even after the Emancipation Proclamation, records indicate that thousands of slaves helped the Union cause by engaging in work slowdowns, serving as spies, and by not participating in the Southern Army. They also provided food and shelter to Northern soldiers whenever possible. The **Loyal League**, for instance, helped escaped slaves and spied for the North. The **Underground Railroad**, used primarily by runaway slaves to escape from the plantations, was also used by Northern soldiers as an escape route from Confederate incarceration.

The 1800s were such a turbulent time, and the population of the country was growing so rapidly, that a staggering number of associations and nonprofit organizations came to be following the end of the Civil War. One of the first of these organizations was the **Freedmen's Bureau**, established in 1865 to coordinate the monumental mitigation efforts for former slaves. The bureau's main concern was to make emancipation a reality through programs of education, employment, and land acquisition. The Freedmen's Bureau joined with other such organizations to recruit teachers and acquire school buildings for providing educational opportunities for the newly freed Southern blacks. It has been estimated that about 90,000 black men, women, and children attended 1000 schools supported by the bureau in the year 1866 (Ellis and Noyes 1978).

Manufacturing flourished following the Civil War, and new production methods for steel and oil added to increased jobs and consumer demand. As manufacturing increased, so did the demand for stronger and stronger unions to address issues such as unfair wages, lack of benefits, and unsafe working conditions. Groups such as the **Sovereigns of Industry**, the **Industrial Brotherhood**, and the **Knights of Labor** came to the forefront of workers' rights and made their demands felt through strikes and other work stoppage methods. It was out of this support for the labor movement that the **Young Women's Christian Association (YWCA)**, established in the mid-1800s, grew much stronger in the late 1800s. Churchwomen in cities throughout the East developed more YWCAs to provide housing, recreation, and training for women, particularly women who were working in the sweatshops in the Eastern cities. This organization continues to empower women through health, education, and enrichment programs and operates in all fifty states.

Because of the proximity of some manufacturing companies to one another, competition existed for raw materials and customers, and trade unions were founded to fix prices and discounts, and to allocate materials. The first such recognized union was the **American Brass Association**, founded in 1853 in Connecticut. Since local efforts were not always enough to manage business problems, trade associations began to create national ties. Local Chambers of Commerce joined together in 1868, forming the **National Board of Trade** to represent this country's business interests nationally and internationally. And by the end of the century, other business groups were coming together for the purpose of economics and professionalism, such as the **American Association of Public Accountants**, established in 1887, and the **National Association of Life Underwriters**.

Farmers also felt a need to organize, and the **Grange** association was established in 1867 in Washington, D.C. The Grange was supported by the Department of Agriculture. The Grange provided opportunities for forums on new scientific agricultural techniques, recreational activities, and other communication opportunities for farmers and their families to share their knowledge and interest. Grange organizations had a tremendous impact on formal education and lobbied for more curricula relevant to farming. A Cornell University professor initiated a process of naturalist pamphlets for young people in country schools in 1898 and assisted in organizing nature studies. This eventually led to the formation of the **4-H** organization in partnership with the U.S. Department of Agriculture. The purpose of 4-H is to help young people acquire knowledge and develop life skills and it has served over 40 million boys and girls nationwide.

Another group that was feeling the need to organize during this period was women. Women had always worked together before and during the Civil War, and women's associations of one kind or another had existed for a long time. Women's groups began to develop strong interests in child welfare, public education, divorce reform and other civic concerns. The **Women's Christian Temperance Union** sought legislation prohibiting the sale of alcohol, and the **General Federation of Women's Clubs** became a strong force for a number of social issues. The **National Woman Suffrage Association** was considered a radical group devoted to women's rights at almost any cost, and the **American Woman Suffrage Association** developed as a more conservative group devoted to women's issues. Women's rights, particularly for the working class, became of paramount importance, and feminist leaders urged the formation of independent unions, such as the **Working Women's Association** and the **Protective Association for Women**.

One woman in particular who made a big difference during this time was Clara Barton, a Civil War battleground nurse who founded the **American Red Cross (ARC)** in 1893. Barton thought there should be an organization with volunteers trained to handle disasters during war as well as during peacetime and trained to prevent, prepare for and respond to different kinds of emergencies. Devastating forest fires in Michigan and floods along the Ohio and Mississippi provided the Red Cross its first tests, tests that the organization handled wonderfully. Congress chartered the Red Cross in 1905 (Boylston 1955).

Philanthropy in general was undergoing change in the 1800s, and contributing money to charities had reached monumental levels, but it was unorganized and highly competitive. Eventually, the **American Charity Organization Society** was established in Buffalo in 1877 to provide an organized system of fund raising and by 1893 there were dozens of similar organizations across the nation. In addition to fund raising, the society established a process referred to as **friendly visitors**, in which volunteers would interview individuals and families to determine eligibility for charitable funds. This process evolved into the profession of **social work**, and individuals received training and payment for their investigative efforts.

Following this, the **Young Men's Christian Association** and the **Jewish Federation** joined in 1887 in conducting fundraising activities that eventually led to the formation of the **United Way of America**. Initiated by four clergymen in Denver, the idea of a coordinated, unified, fundraising campaign for nonprofit organizations spread across the country, and there are currently over two thousand United Way offices nationwide. In the last quarter of the nineteenth century, wealthy citizens such as Andrew Carnegie and John D. Rockefeller were looking for ways to more effectively use money to get at the real root of problems, and the concept of **grant-making foundations** was born. Instead of operating programs, foundations would fund organizations that were addressing the issues that interested the foundations. However, while Carnegie and Rockefeller were sold on the concept, they were slow to move, and credit for establishing the first foundation went to a lesser-known individual, Margaret Olivia Slocum Sage (Hall 1994).

Another organization active in the late 1800s was the **Salvation Army**, which originated as an integral part of the **Social Gospel** doctrine and was first involved with evangelistic efforts. It then expanded to operating shelters, food warehouses, and employment agencies. Organizations were also formed for the care and prevention of cruelty to animals, and in 1873 the **Society for the Prevention of Cruelty to Animals (SPCA)** was established, and volunteers for the organization distributed millions of pamphlets nationwide. In its early days and in a dramatic and unusual act, the SPCA brought a beaten child to court in a case that spurred the formation of the first **Society for the Prevention of Cruelty to Children** in New York in 1875.

Recreational and cultural activities increased following the Civil War with the advent of playgrounds, recreational centers, community centers, music and drama groups, theaters, bands, and orchestras. Recreation was becoming more and more a part of church related activities and the **YMCA**, first founded in England in 1844 and then established in the United States in 1852, became a leader in offering organized sports. The first **Girls Club** came to be in 1854 in Connecticut, with the purpose of providing safe havens and social and educational centers for workers in northeastern mill towns during the industrial revolution. The Girls Club would change its name to **Girls Incorporated** in 1990 and maintain its purpose of empowering girls and young women to be self sufficient and personally fulfilled. The **Boys Club** was established in the late 1860s in New England as a place for boys to be able to get off the streets and to have a safe and inviting place to play. The idea spread quickly, and by 1906 there were fifty clubs nationwide that banded together to become the **Boys Clubs of America**. The Boys Clubs gradually began inviting girls to participate in their programs, finally becoming known as the **Boys and Girls Clubs of America** in the 1980s.

As the industrial, urban lifestyle increased, so did the interest in outdoor activities, and camps began springing up across the country. YMCAs, settlement houses, and private individuals founded a number of camps in the late 1880s and the YMCA established itself as a leader in outdoor activities. A conservation movement also developed and grew during this time. The **American Forestry Association** was formed in Chicago in 1875 by a committee of horticulturists and concerned community members. This first organized conservation initiative was not able to have much influence with Congress at the time, but it did manage to have an impact on the public's perception of conservation. These energies also led to the establishment of **Arbor Day**, a national day of planting trees. To foster geographic knowledge, thirty-three men who had occupations ranging from explorer to meteorologist founded the **National Geographic Society** in 1888. The Society promotes research projects and then disseminates information about the physical and social world through publications. The **Sierra Club** was founded in 1892 to protect California's forests and wildlife. It soon became clear that there were limits to what local actions could achieve, so eventually the Sierra Club became a national venture. The **Audubon Society** was established in the late 1800s with a mission of conserving wildlife; colleges and universities soon began offering classes in forestry.

National and International Challenges: The 1900s and Beyond

The depression of the 1890s was a devastating period, but individuals, families, and communities seemed to bounce back quickly. The citizens of the United States entered the twentieth century with a great deal of optimism, and the country established itself as an industrial leader at home and overseas. While the country as a whole was prospering, wages, benefits, and working conditions were still problems for the urban poor, and middle-class, progressive, social reformers began to organize groups into coalitions to bring about change.

Not all voluntary organizations had socially redeeming intentions. One group that opposed this progressive movement was the **Ku Klux Klan**. Having been organized in the 1800s and then disappearing into the background for a while, the Klan re-emerged in the 1900s. First operating as vigilante groups to protect the tobacco farmers in Kentucky and Tennessee, the Klan became a national, fraternal order made up of men who believed in protecting the "Anglo-Saxon" way of life and who set themselves against Catholics, Jews, blacks and foreigners. World War I briefly interrupted the growth of the Klan, but in the 1920s the Klan made a second re-birth in the North, the Midwest and the Southwest and actually organized some charitable activities in places where they were present. Southern Klans often participated in vigilante activities and used lynching as a deterrent to those they opposed. The **Southern Women for the Prevention of Lynching** organized interracial committees in the 1930s, and by 1933 the **National Council of Women**, representing twenty different women's groups and totaling five million women, held the **International Con-**

gress of Women, which worked to abolish lynching.

Women began to develop a collective social conscience for various concerns, and the **General Federation of Women's Clubs** emerged, with an interest in child welfare, public health, the protection of women in industry, growth of educational institutes, and the reform of civil service. The question of women's suffrage was a continuing issue and women's clubs began educating women regarding the need for change and the importance of the vote. In 1913, the **National Women's Party** was established and led the movement to introduce the first **Equal Rights Amendment** in 1923.

The issue of child welfare was another major issue for women and men and the **Big Brothers Association** began in 1903 in Cincinnati, with the purpose of matching adult mentors with needy boys, many from single parent families. Soon afterward, the **Big Sisters** program was formed in 1908 in New York City, with the mission of working with court-referred, delinquent girls. Volunteers first operated both organizations, but social workers were eventually hired to manage the matches and other administrative duties. These two organizations would later merge to become the **Big Brothers Big Sisters of America**. The **National Child Labor Committee** was formed in 1904 and worked both to prohibit children under fourteen from working and to limit the hours and time of day that fourteen- and fifteen-year-olds could work.

In 1912, the **Children's Bureau** was initiated by a group of women concerned with the welfare of mothers and infants, and it was placed under the control of the Department of Labor. The organization grew rapidly and was designed to assist poor mothers in finding adequate shelter and work. Another nonprofit organization began in 1919, **Junior Achievement**, with the purpose of providing young people with economical education programs and experiences in the competitive private enterprise system (Weis and Gantt 2002). This program has provided tens of thousands of children with opportunities to create and develop products and to learn effective ways to market and sell the products they have developed. And in 1939, **Little League Baseball** was organized to teach the game of baseball and the value of sportsmanship to youngsters. It would go on to exist in all U.S. states and territories as well as twenty-nine foreign countries.

Blacks were also looking for a voice in the early 1900s, and in 1905 a group of college-educated blacks formed a coalition to encourage brotherhood and end racism that was to become the **Niagra Movement**. Although this movement lasted only a few years, it laid the foundation for the creation of the **National Association for the Advancement of Colored People (NAACP)** in 1909. The organization was interracial and was established to address discrimination. A conference held in 1910 specifically to address issues pertaining to blacks living in New York City eventually led to the formation of the **National Urban League**. The National Urban League was also an interracial organization and often joined with the NAACP in the battle against unfair practices of discrimination.

Health and social welfare issues were of paramount importance in the early years of the 1900s; there were a number of discoveries made in medical science and a number of national voluntary health organizations began to form. **Goodwill Industries** began in 1902, with the purpose of assisting and enriching the lives of the disabled, and the **National Association for the Study and Prevention of Tuberculosis** was formed in 1904 by a group of doctors dedicated to the elimination of tuberculosis. As tuberculosis was brought under control, the organization expanded its work to fight other lung diseases and pollution and adopted the name **American Lung Association.**

Maryland Association for the Colored Blind was formed in 1913 for the purpose of assisting and enriching the lives of the disabled, and. the **American Foundation for the Blind** was established later, in 1921, and was recognized as Helen Keller's cause. When Edgar Allen's son was injured in a trolley car accident in Elyria, Ohio, and died from lack of sufficient medical help, Allen vowed to never let anyone die from lack of care in his hometown again. He quit his job and began raising funds that led to the establishment of the Elyria Memorial Hospital in 1908. He soon began raising funds throughout the state and enlisted the aid of the local Rotary Club to form the **Ohio Society for Crippled Children** in 1919, which evolved into the **Easter Seals Society**.

Cancer also caused increasing concern, and the **American Cancer Society** was formed in 1913 by a group of doctors and concerned citizens. The organization joined forces with women's clubs across the country and raised public awareness of the disease and promoted interests in finding a cure. Also concerned with health-related issues, John D. Rockefeller, financier, and Frederick T. Gates, Baptist minister, joined to establish the **Rockefeller Foundation** in 1913. The foundation began funding millions of dollars for medical research and soon became a model for well-organized, effective philanthropy. The numbers of those suffering from the disease of alcoholism grew steadily, following the depression of 1929, and a New York stockbroker and an Ohio surgeon, who had been hopeless alcoholics for years, founded **Alcoholics Anonymous (AA)** in 1935. It grew from two members to over 2,000,000 members today and is the largest self-help group for alcoholism in the country.

The **Leukemia and Lymphoma Society of America** was established in 1949 as the Villiers Foundation and was later renamed. The organization is dedicated to eradicating leukemia and related cancers and improving the lives of patients and their families. Another national health organization, the **Juvenile Diabetes Foundation** began in 1970 with the purpose of providing funds for research for the cure, treatment, and prevention of diabetes and its complications.

Social welfare organizations also continued to increase, and one result of this growth was the **Junior League**, which began as a way for girls to learn about charity and community responsibilities in their neighborhoods. A national school lunch program was initiated in the early part of the century, and the **Parent Teacher Association (PTA)**, the **Junior League**, and the **American Legion** joined forces to provide volunteers and equipment; a decade later the program was providing a hot meal a day to over nine million school children. **Catholic Charities USA** began in 1910 with the goal of reducing poverty, supporting families, and building healthy communities throughout the country. Today, Catholic Charities USA serves approximately ten million people in need.

Camps and public parks increased in the early part of the twentieth century, and the Sierra Club and similar organizations encouraged the growth of the National Park Service and the Forest Service. The **National Conservation Commission** was established in 1908 to influence legislation that would protect environmental interests. The **Boy Scouts of America** was the primary boys' organization at the start of World War I, with over 300,000 scouts and 8,000 volunteer Scout Masters (Ellis and Noyes 1978). It began as an organization to develop character and practical skills with a membership made up mostly of middle-

and upper-class boys, but later its members included immigrant and Native American youth, as well. Both the **Girl Scouts of America** and the **Camp Fire Girls** began in the early part of the 1900s with similar purposes as the Boy Scouts. The **National Collegiate Athletic Association (NCAA)** would form in 1906 and serve young adults by setting guidelines and fostering sportsmanship for collegiate athletic competition. Other youth-serving, recreational organizations appeared on the scene later, such as the **Ski Patrol** in 1936, the **Cub Scouts** in 1937, and the **Little League** in 1939.

World War I brought tremendous collaborative efforts among the nation's major nonprofit organizations. The **YMCA, YWCA, National Catholic War Council (Knights of Columbus), Jewish Welfare Board, Salvation Army** and the **American Liberty Service** all worked together to assist soldiers overseas and at home, as well as the general public. The **American Red Cross** was recognized as the preeminent disaster-relief organization in the United States in the early 1900s and had begun to develop nursing programs and training for first aid. At the start of WWI, the Red Cross organized fifty-eight military hospitals overseas and managed forty-seven ambulance companies to transport injured soldiers. The Red Cross also handled the assignment of thousands of nurses, provided field directors for counseling, served as a communication link between servicemen and their families, and maintained over 700 canteens where servicemen and women could shower, use a telephone and generally relax.

With WWI at an end, the nation entered a period of prosperity. Employers and employees began a time of relative harmony, and farming cooperatives and agricultural youth programs grew in popularity. Such organizations as the **Young Farmers**, **Junior Farmers**, and **Future Farmers of America** provided information, activities and support for young people who were interested in agriculture. Businesses also begin to organize around the common cause of safety of all kinds—home, industrial, and automobile. The **National Safety Council** took the lead in educating the public concerning safety issues and organizing community committees around the country to meet and develop action plans for implementing safety plans.

When the stock market crashed in 1929, the nation experienced a nearly devastating depression, and soup kitchens and bread lines were established by a number of charitable organizations. To offer cooperative help for citizens, many of the national service and religious organization joined forces just as they had done during WWI. The Catholic Church, in particular, fared very well during this period, forming the **National Catholic Welfare Conference** to increase the parameters of its secular services. Ecumenical organizations such as the **Committee on Religion and Welfare Activity**, made up of churches of different denominations, joined forces during this time to provide a coordinated effort of services for citizens affected by economic hardships. And private, charitable think tanks, like the **Brookings Institution**, played a pivotal role in public initiatives by helping to draft the Social Security Act. Although unrelated to the depression, the **National Wildlife Federation** began in 1936 with the purpose of educating and inspiring individuals and organizations to conserve wildlife and other natural resources and to protect the Earth's environment.

As the Second World War in Europe began to heat up, communities all over America initiated steps to prepare citizens for conflict. Many community businesses subsidized young men who joined the National Guard or participated in some other government sponsored military endeavor. The **Green Guard**, an all female militia organized to defend the homeland, was initiated in North Carolina, and the **Military Training Camps Association** offered military training to middle-class professionals and business people who would be good candidates as officer reserves. The **American Women's Volunteer Service** was founded and had over 200,000 members who assisted with military activities at home, such as driving trucks and chauffeuring Army and other military officers and instructing house-wives and others how to cope in case of an air-raid. A number of women, however, became involved in the pacifist movement, and even the Girl Scouts changed their uniform color from military khaki to a neutral green as a means of protest.

Prior to entering WWII, many Americans felt compassion for the French and English, and the American Red Cross raised over seven million dollars in aid money. Employees at Lockheed donated their own time and used their own money to construct and pay for a new Hudson airplane as a Christmas gift to the Europeans. As America entered WWII, a massive shortage of farm workers ensued, but thousands of volunteers from the **YWCA**, the **High School Victory Corps**, and the **American Women's Voluntary Service**, pulled together to operate the farms successfully. Many farmers cooperated with the **Farm Security Administration** in a movement called "An Acre for a Soldier," in which a farmer would donate the money raised from an acre's crop to the war effort.

In 1942, a nonprofit organization called the **Seaman's Service** was founded, and it collaborated with the **YMCA**, **Travelers' Aid Society**, and the **Red Cross** to provide housing, medical care, counseling and recreation to seamen stationed on shore. American business was actively involved in supporting war efforts, and the **American Society of Association Executives** was created to coordinate activities such as selling war bonds as a funding source, encouraging gasoline conservation, and providing technical assistance to government agencies that needed help. The **American Red Cross** recruited over 71,000 nurses for military duty and provided volunteer staffing for a number of military hospitals, clubs, and mobile club units for servicemen abroad in rest and recreation areas. Americans supported the Red Cross by donating more than $785 million for these efforts (Ellis and Noyes 1978).

Following WWII, the country became forever linked to the world community as witnessed by the creation of the **United Nations** in 1945, and one voluntary organization, the **General Federation of Women's Clubs**, was recruited for input. Urged by the Federation, the **Commission on Human Rights** was included in the United Nation's Charter. Congress chartered the **Civil Air Patrol** in 1946 as a nonprofit organization with a humanitarian focus, and the **Red Cross**, the **Salvation Army**, and the **Veterans of Foreign Wars** agreed to a collaboration to provide disaster relief, air and ground searches, and instruction for aerospace. The business community encouraged the growth of **Chambers of Commerce**, and in a landmark decision in 1952, the New Jersey Superior and Supreme Courts declared that financial gifts by business corporations to institutions of higher education were legal and desirable and did not constitute an endorsement of the business on the part of the educational institution (Hall 1994). Business contributions to education were therefore sanctioned, and future involvement was insured.

A large number of nonprofit organizations established themselves or grew significantly in the 40s and 50s, and ninety percent of nonprofits currently in existence were established following WWII. The **School Safety Patrol** was formed with guidelines from the

AAA, National Committee on Safety, and the **National Safety Council**. The **Red Cross** assisted in pursuing those missing in action after the end of WWII and in helping families reunite in spite of political complications. This organization also began to coordinate large-scale relief operations following major disasters. The **American Heart Association** grew from a group comprised totally of health professionals to a voluntary health organization with community members, and the **National Association for Mental Health** was established in 1950. The **National Epilepsy League** began in 1948 (Ellis and Noyes 1978). That same year, H. Roe Bartle, the Mayor of Kansas City, Missouri, would initiate the **American Humanics (AH)** program. AH is an affiliation of colleges, universities and partner organizations that prepare students for leadership roles with youth, human service, and other nonprofit institutions (Taylor 1995). The **Muscular Dystrophy Associations of America** began funding research in 1950, and the **Fellowship of Christian Athletes,** an evangelical group associated with sports, started in 1954. The **Cystic Fibrosis Foundation** was organized in 1955 to provide support for researching a cure for cystic fibrosis**,** and **Parents Without Partners**, a self-help support group for single parents was established in 1957.

Another significant aspect in the growth of nonprofit organizations during this period was the role the government played. Prior to the 1940s, the government had already been the largest source of revenue for nonprofit organizations in the fields of culture, education, health, and social welfare. This role became enhanced when the **National Science Foundation** and the **National Institute of Health** made grants on a huge scale to private hospitals and universities. During this same period, the **GI Bill**, passed in 1948 and renewed in 1952, combined with the **National Defense Education Act** of 1958 to provide massive federal funding in the form of student aid to private colleges and universities (Hall 1994).

In the period between the 1940s and the 1970s, the civil rights movement became a major factor in the political landscape of the country. Thousands of volunteers joined in interracial activities, such as boycotts and sit-ins, and a visible militancy emerged. The Montgomery, Alabama, boycott of 1955 involved over 50,000 black residents who avoided using local busses in opposition to segregation and discrimination. This boycott was supported by the **Montgomery Improvement Association**, with Rev. Martin Luther King as the president. Other civil rights groups included the **Southern Christian Leadership Conference (SCLC)**, founded in 1957 by clergy members and committed to the concept that the church should provide key leadership in the civil rights movement, and the **Congress of Racial Equality (CORE)**, which was an interracial, urban group committed to civil rights for all.

In spite of the 1957 **Civil Rights Act**, white supremacy groups often intimidated black voters, and organizations such as the **Mississippi Summer Project of 1964** were created to conduct campaigns to build up voter registration for blacks. Following the march on Washington in 1963, things moved rapidly and a number of black student unions and heritage awareness groups began to form, such as the **American Society of African Culture**. Some militant groups, such as the **Black Panther Party**, advocated armed resistance as the primary method for achieving racial equality. On the other side, white supremacy groups, such as the **Citizens Council**, made up mostly of professionals and business groups, did everything possible to fight discrimination laws.

The Vietnam War also elicited strong sentiments from the majority of the population, and a number of protest groups formed all over the country. The **American Friends Service Committee**, for instance, advocated a pacifist stance and organized citizens to resist the draft. The **Women's Strike for Peace** and the **Veterans and Reservists to End the War** were other groups opposing the Vietnam War that organized citizens to oppose and demonstrate against the government's position. Local and national demonstrations proliferated, and some anti-war groups such as the **Students for a Democratic Society (SDS)** took a militant stand and even attacked Selected Service offices. There were also groups who supported the war, such as the **National Committee for Responsible Patriotism**, who organized demonstrations of loyalty toward the troops overseas and the cause they represented.

In the middle of the civil rights movement and prior to the controversy surrounding the Vietnam War, President Kennedy initiated a corps of dedicated and skilled Americans to volunteer for positions in the world's developing countries. The **Peace Corps** was established in 1961, and it provided idealistic Americans with productive outlets for their idealism. Though publicly funded, the Peace Corps sparked an interest in serving others. Another famous American, entertainer Danny Thomas, fulfilled a pledge to St. Jude Thaddeous, patron saint of the hopeless to whom he had prayed for direction, by establishing **St. Jude Children's Research Hospital** in 1962 in Memphis, Tennessee. This unique hospital is devoted to curing catastrophic diseases in children. Thomas almost single-handedly raised the money to build the hospital, and today it is the seventh largest health care charity in the country. The same year St. Jude's Hospital was founded, a migrant farm worker named Cesar Chavez organized the **National Farm Workers Association (NFWA)** to lobby for fair wages, benefits and shelter for the thousands of crop pickers harvesting grapes, apples, lettuce, oranges and other produce in southern California. Chavez incorporated nonviolent measures, such as fasting, picketing and boycotts, against the powerful Teamsters Union and the California Growers Association, and the NFWA was eventually victorious in the fight for fairness, thanks to Chavez's quiet resolve and determination (Weis and Gantt 2002).

A few years following the establishment of the Peace Corps, President Johnson initiated **Volunteers in Service to America (VISTA)**, a publicly funded organization that provided citizens opportunities to work in projects in the United States. These government supported volunteer programs have been hugely successful, in spite of some objections to the volunteers' receiving a basic subsistence allowance and a modest stipend. Another organization with a Kennedy name attached was founded in the early 1960s. **Special Olympics** was initiated by Eunice Kennedy Shriver to provide year-round sports training and athletic competition in a variety of Olympic-type sports for children and adults with mental retardation. Those who become involved in Special Olympics develop physical fitness, a sense of belonging and accomplishment, and friendships with fellow competitors and volunteers in their community. While the Peace Corps, VISTA, and to some extent, Special Olympics tended to attract young and often college-educated people, the **Serve and Enrich by Volunteer Experience (SERVE)** was developed in New York to attract senior citizens. This experiment grew to over forty-two pilot programs in New York and eventually inspired the creation of the **Retired Senior Volunteer Program (RSVP)**, which provided seniors with volunteer opportunities nationwide.

President Nixon sought to organize and stimulate the nation's volunteer efforts even further, so in 1971 he created **ACTION**, which was to serve as an umbrella organization for six volunteer organizations: the Peace Corps, VISTA, the Foster Grandparent Program, RSVP, the Service Corps of Retired Executives (SCORE), and the Active Corps of Executives (ACE). Founded during the presidency of Jimmy Carter, **Habitat for Humanity International** was organized by Millard and Linda Fuller in 1976 to provide affordable housing for families in need. This was a cause that President Carter later embraced, and he became actively involved in recruiting volunteers, raising funds, and assisting in the actual building of homes for people of low-income. This was also the decade that brought the **Independent Sector** into existence. The Independent Sector would become a national clearinghouse, of sorts, for information regarding all private, nonprofit organizations, and it would also serve to represent the viewpoint of the nonprofit sector to the public.

In the 1980s, President Reagan proposed that citizens rely less and less on the federal government and more on nonprofit, service organizations. In an economic, belt-tightening move, the president also cut a significant amount of funds for federal programs. This cut in funding had the opposite effect of supporting the efforts of nonprofit organizations, since a number of these organizations received federal support in the form of grants or contracts for performing program services. Ironically, the **Alzheimer's Association** was founded in 1980 to provide patient aid support and research for Alzheimer's disease, a disease that eventually afflicted President Reagan himself. Although federal dollars were less attainable during the Reagan era, the president's efforts to involve corporations with nonprofit work brought forth a tremendous amount of cash through the concept of **cause related marketing.** Cause related marketing involves tying in a nonprofit cause with a specific product. This produced and still produces hundreds of collaborations between the for-profit and nonprofit sectors, providing a great deal of publicity for for-profit businesses and millions of dollars for nonprofit entities (Hall 1994).

An area of service that found deeper roots in the 1980s was the area of service learning, in which students incorporate learning objectives in community service projects. National organizations such as **Campus Outreach Opportunity League** and **Campus Compact** took the lead in encouraging service on college campuses across the country, whether as extra-curricular activities or curriculum-based activities, such as with service learning (Weis and Gantt 2002).

Although there have been occasional scandals involving charities, they usually had no more than a local impact. This changed in the 1980s and 1990s with a series of breaches in trust. First, the **Covenant House**, which provided a safe haven for children, was rocked when the CEO and founder was found to be misusing funds and sexually abusing clients; then, the national **United Way** was besieged when the leading executive was accused of obtaining unreasonable perks and benefits; a series of scandals beset televangelists who had misused organizational funds for personal gain; and the **Blue Cross** experienced a number of different scandals across several states (Hall 1994). These breaches of trust sparked a series of laws that more closely regulated charitable giving and charitable organizations.

In the late 1980s and the early 1990s, President Bush encouraged national service with his **Thousand Points of Light** initiative, which led to financial support for thousands of community service projects across the country. President Clinton signed the **National and Community Service Act** in the early 1990s, which was followed by the creation of **Americorps.** Americorps provides thousands of citizens the opportunity to engage in community service across the country, while receiving financial assistance to register for college coursework. Although not as heralded as President Kennedy's Peace Corps, Americorps is much larger than the Peace Corps and has proven to be a valuable asset for fulfilling community needs, as well as for providing service opportunities and college tuition for citizens who may not have been able to afford college otherwise.

Following the controversial election of 2000, President George W. Bush took a strong and unique stand on involving citizens in community service by offering to fund "faith-based" organizations that fulfilled tasks that the federal government could not or would not be able to do. Though a number of politicians and citizens argued that this position endangered the separation of church and state, a number of eligible, nonprofit organizations actively sought funding to expand their service base. Following the unbelievably tragic terrorists attacks of September 11, 2001, a number of national, nonprofit organizations such as the **American Red Cross,** the **United Way,** and the **Salvation Army** took the lead to raise funds and provide services for the thousands of citizens that were affected by those events. Millions of citizens across the country contributed blood, money, and other support to the thousands of nonprofit organizations that bonded together to work cooperatively in support of the relief efforts following the terrorist attacks.

■ Summary

The nonprofit sector includes educational, cultural, religious, recreational, service, and character development organizations, along with foundations, hospitals, wellness centers, and other privately incorporated organizations that serve a public mission of some kind. These organizations can take in revenue, but any money over and above expenses must go back into the organization in some manner. Nonprofit organizations provide assistance to citizens that the government cannot or does not provide, and they receive a special tax-exempt status, which differs with the type of nonprofit organization. Other characteristics include being governed by a voluntary board of directors and conducting an annual, independent audit of financial processes and records.

The sector's roots can be traced back to the benevolence that existed between the Pilgrims, patriots, and Native Americans and to the importation of philanthropic ventures from Europe. The combination of a strong Puritan ethic of concern for family and community and the Elizabethan Poor Law, which framed some community activities as requirements, made for a fertile ground for service. For instance, the elderly and infirm were often boarded in private homes, for which families were paid through tax collections, and religious institutions were often the center of many other community service initiatives in Colonial times.

The end of the Revolutionary War brought a number of opportunities and challenges as the country pushed westward and towns became cities. Industrialization brought on the need for organizations that would encourage safe and fair working conditions for laborers, particularly children. Educational processes became more and more sophisticated, public education systems began to outnumber private ones, and adult education grew in importance. Health care also became more sophisticated with the founding of a number of private, nonprofit hospitals. The Civil War created a need for establishing a number of nonprofit organizations as support systems during the war and as relief organizations following it. Charitable giving became more organized and grant making foundations were born. Recreational activities and organizations increased significantly following the Civil War, as the industrial urban lifestyle involved more people.

Women began to develop a collective social conscience for various concerns, and a number of women's groups and associations began forming in the 1900s. Because child welfare was one of these concerns, a number of youth organizations were formed throughout the twentieth century. A number of discoveries in medical science were made in the 1900s, and a number of national health care organizations formed to support further research and patient aid. World War I brought tremendous cooperative action among the nation's major nonprofit organizations, as did the stock market crash of 1929. In the early 1940s the Second World War in Europe began to heat up, and a number of nonprofit organizations developed to prepare citizens for support efforts of the war. As America entered the war, support and relief efforts provided by nonprofit organizations were highly significant, and a large number of organizations established themselves or grew at an unparalleled pace following the war.

The passing of the GI Bill and the National Defense Education Act in the 1950s provided massive federal funding in the form of student aid to private colleges and universities. A large number of organizations were involved in the civil rights movement between 1940 and 1970. The Vietnam War evoked strong emotions from most citizens in the 1960s and 1970s, with a number of people and nonprofit organizations ending up on both sides of the conflict. The Peace Corps, which provided opportunities to volunteer for positions in the world's developing countries, and VISTA, which provided opportunities for volunteers to work in projects in the United States, were established by Presidents John F. Kennedy and Lyndon B. Johnson, respectively, in the 1960s.

President Richard M. Nixon put his own stamp of support on nonprofit organizations in the 1970s with the creation of ACTION, which was designed to bring a number of successful, nonprofit organizations under the same umbrella. In the 1980s, President Ronald Reagan encouraged citizens to depend less on government and more on nonprofit organizations. President George Bush established the Thousand Points of Light initiative that led to financial support for thousands of community service initiatives; President William J. Clinton signed the National and Community Service Act in the early 1990s, which led to the establishment of Americorps. Americorps provides thousands of citizens the opportunity to engage in community service across the country while receiving financial assistance from the government to register for college coursework. In 2001, President George W. Bush offered to fund faith-based organizations that fulfilled tasks that the federal government could not or would not be able to do.

This chapter addressed, in part, the American Humanics Certification Competency Requirements of Historical and Philosophical Foundations.

Two books that include a description of the history of nonprofit organizations are suggested:

- *By the People*, by Susan Ellis and Katherine Noyes, Prestegord and Company, 1978.
- *The Jossey-Bass Handbook of Nonprofit Leadership and Management*, edited by Robert D. Herman & Associates, Jossey-Bass, 1994.

■ Discussion Questions

1. What types of organizations are included in the nonprofit sector?
2. List and describe the characteristics of a nonprofit organization.
3. Why do nonprofit organizations receive a tax-exempt status?
4. How did the Social Compact of 1620, Puritanism, and the Elizabethan Poor Law affect the lives of the early settlers?
5. Describe medical care in the 1700s.
6. Describe some of the educational activities of the 1800s
7. What role did religion play in black churches in the 1800s?
8. Describe the role nonprofit organizations played during the Civil War.
9. What role did nonprofit organizations play during World War I? During the stock market crash of 1929? During World War II?
10. List and describe some of the nonprofit organizations that have been established since the 1950s.

■ Activities

1. Contact a select number of nonprofit organizations in the community to see if their characteristics parallel those listed in Chapter 1.
2. Select a nonprofit organization and research its history and purpose.
3. As a class project, research the different kinds of nonprofit organizations in your community and the services they provide.

■ References

Beard, M. R., ed. (1933). *America Through Women's Eyes*. New York: Macmillan Company.

Boylston, H. D. (1955). *Clara Barton: Founder of the American Red Cross*. New York: Random House.

Christenson, R. M. (1970). *Challenge and Decision*. New York: Harper Row.

Coalition of National Voluntary Organizations and National Council on Philanthropy (1979). *To Preserve an Independent Sector: Organizing Committee Report*. Washington, DC: Coalition of National Voluntary Organizations.

Croly, H. (1909). *The Promise of American Life*. New York: Macmillan Company.

Ellis, Susan J., and Noyes, Katherine H. (1978). *By the People*. Philadelphia: Prestegord and Company.

Epler, P. H. (1919). *The Life of Clara Barton*. New York: Macmillan Company.

Fosdick, R. B. (1952). *The Story of the Rockefeller Foundation*. New York: Harper Collins.

Hall, P. (1994). Historical perspectives on nonprofit organizations. In Robert Herman and Associates, eds. *The Jossey-Bass Handbook of Nonprofit Leadership and Management*. San Francisco: Jossey-Bass.

Hansmann, H. (1981). Why are nonprofit organizations exempted from corporate income taxation? In Michelle J. White, ed. *Nonprofit Firms in a Three-Sector Economy*. COUPE Papers. Washington, DC: The Urgan Institute Press.

Hicks, J. D. (1941). *The American Nation: A History of the United States from 1865 to Present.* Cambridge, Massachusetts: The Riverside Press.

Hodgkinson, V., ed. (1990). *The Nonprofit Sector (NGOs) in the United States and Abroad: Cross-Cultural Perspectives – 1990 Spring Research Forum Working Papers.* Washington, DC: The Independent Sector.

Hodgkinson, V., Weitzman, M., Toppe, C. M., Noga, S. M. (1992). *Nonprofit Almanac 1992-1993: Dimensions of the Independent Sector.* San Francisco, CA: Jossey-Bass.

Hofstadter, R. and Smith, W., eds. (1961). *American Higher Education: A Documentary History.* Chicago: University of Chicago Press.

Hopkins, Bruce, R., (1989). *The Law of Tax-Exempt Organizations.* 5th ed. New York: John Wiley and Sons.

Hunt, G. (1914). *Life in America One Hundred Years Ago.* New York: Harper and Brothers.

Independent Sector (1998). *America's Nonprofit Sector: Facts and Figures on the Independent Sector.* Washington, DC: Independent Sector.

_____(1990). *Giving and Volunteering in the United States, 1990.* Washington, DC: Independent Sector.

_____(2002). *The New Nonprofit Almanac In Brief.* Washington, DC: Independent Sector.

Independent Sector and National Center for Nonprofit Boards (1997). *What You Should Know About Nonprofits.* Washington, DC: Independent Sector.

Lacour-Gayet, R. (1969). *Life in the United States Before the Civil War.* New York: Frederick Ungar Publishing Company.

Laidler, H. W. (1968). *Boycotts and the Labor Struggle.* New York: Russell and Russell.

Levy, J. E. (1975). *Cesar Chavez: Autobiography of La Causa.* New York: W. W. Norton and Company, Inc.

Lundberg, E. O. (1947). *Unto the Least of These: Social Services for Children.* New York: Appleton-Century-Crofts, Inc.

Macleod, C. W. (1928). *The American Indian Frontier.* New York: Alfred A. Knopf.

McMaster, J. B. (1884). *A History of the People of the United States.* New York: D. Appleton and Company.

O'Connell, B. (1983). *America's Voluntary Spirit: A Book of Readings.* New York: The Foundation Center.

O'Hare McCormick, A. (1956). *The World at Home.* New York: Alfred A. Knopf.

Renz, L. (1990). *Foundations Today.* 7th ed. New York: Foundation Center.

Salamon, L.M. (1992). *America's Nonprofit Sector.* The Foundation Center, John Hopkins University.

Salaman, L., and Abramson, A. (1981). *The Federal Government and the Nonprofit Sector: Implications of the Reagan Budget Proposals.* Washington, DC: Urban Institute.

Schlesinger, A. M. (1925). *New Viewpoints in American History*. New York: Macmillan Company.

Schouler, J. (1882). *History of the United States of America, Under the Constitution*. New York: Dodd, Mead and Company.

Starr, P. (1982). *The Social Transformation of American Medicine*. New York: Basic Books.

Sullivan, M. (1935). *Our Times: The United States, 1900-1925*. New York: Charles Scribner's Sons.

Taylor, J. B. (1995). *Down Home With the Chief and Miss Maggie*. Prairie Valley, KS: Leathers Publishing.

Van Dyke, H. (1910). *The Spirit of America*. New York: The Macmillan Company.

Veblen, T. (1918). *The Higher Learning in America*. New York: B.W. Huebsch.

Wade, R. C. (1964). *Slavery in the Cities: The South, 1820-1860*. New York: Oxford University Press.

Warner, A. G. (1908). *American Charities*. New York: Thomas Y. Crowell.

Weis, R. M. and Gantt, V. W. (2002). *Leadership and Program Development in Nonprofit Organizations*. Peosta, IA: Eddie Bowers Publishing Company.

Weisbrod, B. (1978). *The Voluntary Nonprofit Sector*. Lexington, MA: Lexington Books.

Wright, Louis B. (1955). *Culture on the Moving Frontier*. New York: Macmillan Company.

2 Foundations of Leadership, Character, and Ethics

Leadership is about guiding, directing, and influencing others to reach goals and to make a difference. This is certainly true in nonprofit organizations, where the purpose of the institution is to strive toward a mission, and individuals at every level—administration, board, program staff, support staff, volunteers, and organizational members—have an opportunity to be a part of this endeavor. Considering the fact that approximately twelve percent of the work force in the country work in a nonprofit organization and that more than fifty percent of all individuals spend some time volunteering (Independent Sector 2002), it could be said that nonprofit organizations are the country's largest employer, and effective leadership is essential

Leadership in the nonprofit sector means strengthening individuals and communities by developing influence through collaborative and trusting relationships. Leading others through influence inevitably involves skills, character and a good moral compass that includes an accepted system of principles and ethics. Personal character implies traits and values that make each person who he or she is. It is an essential ingredient in the formula for successful leadership, as is a personal system of ethics that helps an individual make effective moral decisions and commitments.

Since effective leadership is so essential to the success of nonprofit organizations, the first section of the chapter describes fundamentals of leadership, including relevant theories, models and studies. The next section of the chapter describes the connection between leadership, character, and ethics. The final section discusses ways in which leadership can be developed by looking at different leaders through the ages, and by understanding the processes of mentoring and service learning.

■ The Essence of Leadership

Leadership opportunities in the nonprofit sector are diverse and exist at many different levels. Consider the fitness director, community outreach coordinator, Girl Scout field director, social activities director, tutoring coordinator, YMCA executive director, American Red Cross CPR trainer, and others. In all of these areas, leaders in one capacity or another are the essential individuals responsible for providing people with services and supporting those services once they are established.

> **REGARDING LEADERSHIP**
>
> *Begin where you are*
> *And do what you can.*
>
> **Arthur Ashe**
> Tennis great and Philanthropist

Good leaders provide expertise, direction, guidance, support, enthusiasm and motivation needed for successful experiences in youth, human service, and other nonprofit organizations. In many instances, effective leaders arrive at a **shared vision** as to the best direction a group should go to reach their goals and they invite ideas and suggestions from others. If skills and character can be developed, as is the belief of the authors, then individuals can develop as leaders when they see needs that should be addressed and aspire to acquire characteristics and skills that are important in influencing others to meet those needs.

Effective leaders know that they are strengthened by their followers, and therefore they work hard to **empower** others by providing them with training, support, and encouragement. By providing others with opportunities to lead and have influence themselves, a leader can provide perhaps the strongest base for success, a base of **empowerment**. Individuals who are empowered can operate confidently and competently, especially when they are encouraged to use their own initiative. Bennis and Townsend (1995) suggest that when these individuals are encouraged to operate with a degree of autonomy and freedom, a motivated and empowered work force ensues.

One aspect of empowering individuals is the aspect of **delegation**, or providing individuals with opportunities to share in responsibilities and authority. Out of both necessity and trust, leaders realize they must share responsibilities and authority in order for the organization to succeed. Good leaders then monitor the progress of individuals who have been delegated responsibilities and make adjustments when necessary; a process referred to as **responsible delegation**. There has been a long-running discussion regarding the differences between managers and leaders. In most cases, **managers** are considered to be individuals who direct, control and organize tasks and people within organizations, whereas **leaders** may be considered individuals who inspire others to reach toward a vision and are willing to accept the risks involved in being at the forefront of reaching toward that vision. Hitt (1988) proposes that organizations try to develop **leader-managers**, individuals who have the knowledge and ability to organize as well as the ability to inspire individuals to realistic, yet challenging, heights. This is sometimes a necessity in smaller organizations that do not have the resources for a large, diverse staff.

■ What is a Leader?

A **leader** can be considered "an individual who guides, directs, and influences the attitude and behavior of others" (Edginton, Hudson, and Ford 1999). A leader may provide guidance for individuals to meet their goals as a part of the mission of the organization. For example, a leader in a performing arts setting can offer suggestions on various classes that individuals could consider in order to develop competencies in the arts. Once a person becomes involved in a program, a leader can offer directions and instructions on how to learn and perform in a particular artistic area. For instance, a dancer might be directed in various movements or exercise techniques. Lastly, a leader may use his or her influence to motivate and encourage individuals to continue learning or to perform at higher levels, or to persevere in their calling. As a matter of fact, many authors equate leadership with **influence**, or the ability to affect the behavior of others through the rela-

tionship. Leaders recognize an opportunity or a need that should be addressed and are willing to accept the responsibility and risks involved in leading and influencing others to meet certain challenges.

What are some characteristics necessary for successful leadership? Handy (1996), Hesselbein (1996), and others have suggested that a combination of **characteristics** is necessary for effective leadership:

1. **A belief in oneself and a decent doubt.** It is important that leaders have a vision of what needs to be done and some ideas on how to reach that vision. Many world athletes and business leaders visualize and virtually experience their goal before even attempting it. And leaders develop a sense of confidence by practicing this kind of process. At the same time, good leaders are confident enough and flexible enough to remain open to ideas from others and to the possibility of going in different directions if the need arises. Hesselbein (1996, 4) states, " . . . leaders succeed through the efforts of other people . . . . [T]hey build bridges, invest in relationships, . . . are healers and unifiers."

2. **A passion for the job and an awareness of other worlds.** A leader must have a strong commitment and belief in what he or she is doing in order to have passion. Passion provides strength and energy to lead and to reach goals. Leaders should also be open to other perspectives and interests.

3. **A love of people and a capacity for aloneness.** Successful leaders are often oriented toward people and working with others. They are interested in the well-being and success of other individuals and are generally good motivators. Leaders are often on the cutting edge of new ideas and ventures and must bear many burdens alone. Leaders must become comfortable with the aloneness that can accompany being out in front.

4. **A vision.** Good leaders are able to think conceptually and often arrive at a shared vision of where an organization should be headed. They also have a structure or process for reaching toward that vision and are willing and able to involve others in their plans.

Because of the increased complexity of operations and programs in the nonprofit sector, it is particularly important that leaders in this area meet certain **criteria** (Weis and Gantt 2002):

1. **Commitment.** The focus of a nonprofit organization should be on the purpose or mission of the organization. The mission becomes a beacon of light for the public and members of the organization toward which all activities and energies should be directed. In other words, all activities are directed toward the perceived organizational purpose. Leaders of nonprofit organizations must have a strong belief in the purpose of their organization and must guide others to the realization of that purpose.

2. **Concern.** Leaders of nonprofit organizations must have a genuine interest in the well-being of the people in their community. Members of nonprofit organizations describe effective leaders as individuals who express a real interest in their lives and demonstrate that interest through programs and other actions.

3. **Competence.** Nonprofit leaders must have competence in human relations and

in technical and conceptual skills in order to provide effective programs and services as well as the support for these programs and services.

4. **Flexibility.** Because of the complexity and difficulty of tasks involved, non-profit leaders must be able to coordinate a number of different tasks, often at the same time. They must be able to able to develop and utilize a variety of resources, and they must be able to coordinate and sometimes initiate change.

5. **Determination.** Staff and volunteer members are faced with a number of hurdles on a daily basis. By focusing on the mission of the organization, staff members and volunteers need to work together to overcome whatever obstacles develop in working to fulfill that mission.

6. **Integrity.** Establishing a tradition of trust and responsibility encourages confidence from members of the community that is important for successful practices and programs.

7. **Communication.** Understanding what the community needs in relation to the organization's mission and then communicating the organization's intentions to the community is essential for the realization of goals and mission. The purpose and intent of the organization must be continually monitored and communicated to members of the community.

8. **Motivation.** It is important that nonprofit leaders understand the nature of human motivation. Understanding motivational concepts can lead to the establishment of a **motivational environment**. Staff, board, volunteer and organizational members clearly expect something for their participation and performance, and an effective environment can provide positive reinforcement for all of these groups. This is particularly true of volunteers who are neither paid a salary nor receive services from the organization.

In addition to understanding characteristics and criteria necessary for leadership, it is also important to understand the **processes** and **responsibilities** that leaders become involved with (Sessoms & Stevenson 1981). Several of these are listed below:

1. **Building Camaraderie and Cohesiveness.** Leaders must help individuals feel they are a part of the group and help the group to feel like a cohesive unit.

2. **Identifying and Defining Goals.** Generally, leaders help groups define and clarify their goals as well as their own needs and desires.

3. **Developing Methods and Procedures to Achieve Goals.** Leaders work with members of the group to identify and develop processes of achieving goals.

4. **Organizing the Work of Others.** It is the responsibility of the leader to develop roles for others, along with some kind of organizational structure and a reward system. Additionally, a system of communication must be established.

5. **Motivating Others.** The leader is often the key individual who energizes the group and provides encouragement for group members to work toward goals.

6. **Evaluating the Work of Others.** The leader is generally the person who has the responsibility of determining whether the group has met its set goals. If a discrepancy exists between the standards set and the actual accomplishments, he or she must decide what action to take, if any.

7. **Representing the Group.** Leaders often represent the rest of the group to other

organizations in the community. To represent the organization effectively, a leader must be cognizant of the organization's general position.

8. **Developing Group Members.** It is the role of the leader to encourage individual growth in areas of competency and character, particularly with regard to the organization's mission.

9. **Establishing the Group Atmosphere.** One responsibility of leadership is to help in establishing a climate in which individuals can operate. Working toward goals can sometimes be stressful, and it is important to maintain as positive an atmosphere as possible.

10. **Promoting the Ideals of the Profession.** Nonprofit organizational leaders usually have numerous opportunities to promote the ideals of the profession, such as the ideal of providing people with a helping hand.

The processes and responsibilities involved with leadership are numerous and challenging. Most leaders in the nonprofit sector fulfill many of these responsibilities simultaneously, adding to the complexity of their position.

The question is often asked, **"How do individuals become leaders?"** Shrivers (1980) suggests that people become leaders by one of the following methods: by appointment, by election, by emergence or as a result of charisma. Each avenue is discussed next:

1. **Appointment.** Individuals often become leaders through an appointment based on their level of skills and knowledge. This type of appointment is usually sanctioned by the organization. The degree of leadership depends on the level of the position.

2. **Election.** In some cases, nonprofit leaders are selected through some sort of elective process. For instance, the officers of a board of directors or commissioners for an athletic league are often elected. Elected officials are generally people who are well-liked and respected and who are capable of fulfilling certain obligations.

3. **Emergence.** Emergent leaders become leaders when there is a void in the leadership position, and these individuals have the experience and motivation to fill a particular role. They usually recognize that there is some need for organizational structure to obtain goals, and they set about developing the appropriate structure.

4. **Charisma.** Sometimes individuals are so well-liked and respected that they are selected by group members to be a leader. These people lead with intangible qualities and a demeanor that is desirable to other group members. These individuals tend to be persuasive and influential in a likable way.

Each of these leaders can be found in the nonprofit sector. Individuals are often appointed to their position based on their skills and experiences. Others are elected to a position through a democratic process. Still others emerge to a position of leadership because of a leadership vacuum. And finally, individuals become leaders because of their personal charm and their ability to persuade and influence others because they are well liked.

■ Leadership and Power

A correlation exists between successful leadership and the use of powers to get things accomplished. Unfortunately, some people perceive power as a negative thing, but when it is equated with influence it becomes one of the most desirable aspects of leadership. Nonprofit leaders who understand this correlation and use powers to reach organizational goals are often very successful. Power can emanate from several different sources as identified by French and Raven (1959): referent power, legitimate power, expert power, reward power, and coercive power. The authors suggest these powers can be used individually or in combination. A discussion of each power follows:

1. **Referent Power.** Individuals sometimes arrive at a position of leadership based on their level of energy and desirability as perceived by others. These individuals lead through the strength of their personality and usually develop a loyal following.

2. **Legitimate Power.** Individuals often develop a foundation of power based on the position or office they hold. The importance of influencing others from an official position should not be underestimated. The authority that goes along with a position is particularly important in hierarchical organizations where there are pronounced superior-subordinate relationships.

3. **Expert Power.** Individuals who have significant knowledge and skills in particular areas are often influential, and their advice and counsel are highly sought after by other members of the organization.

4. **Reward Power.** Being in a position of offering rewards for desirable behavior can be very effective. Rewards can take the form of tangibles and intangibles; in nonprofit organizations, rewards can consist of salaries and benefits, but it can also take the form of appreciative gestures for a job well done.

5. **Coercive Power.** Leaders can and should incorporate the threat of punishment to get some things done effectively. This power can be particularly important in enforcing practices that have to do with safety and health or in dealing with areas of member or client confidentiality. This power, however, is sometimes misused, resulting in hostility, distrust, and turmoil.

These powers can influence behavior when used individually and/or collectively. Nonprofit leaders who understand and use these powers effectively have a greater potential for making a positive difference in people's lives.

■ Leaders and Followers

Leaders must aspire to develop certain characteristics and competencies in order to be effective. Good leaders also understand that the base of their support is from their followers; without followers there could be no leaders. As a matter of fact, some of the best training for leadership is to follow others. Individuals learn from modeling the behavior of successful leaders and also learn, in some cases, what not to do in particular situations from unsuccessful leadership practices. To be a good leader, it is important to understand some of the reasons that individuals follow others. Sessoms and Stevenson (1981) have theorized three explanations of why individuals follow others. These explanations are discussed below:

- **Efficiency.** Individuals sometimes follow others because it allows them more time to complete other activities and tasks. In other words, it is sometimes easier and more efficient for someone else to take on the job of leader.

- **Satisfaction.** When people are happy with the status quo, they tend to let things continue as they are. If the organization is running smoothly without major concerns, then individuals generally support the current leadership. It is usually when things become unorganized and goals are in jeopardy that leadership comes into question.
- **Experience.** Individuals who have had a positive experience in leading in the past are more likely to seek out leadership roles for the future. Similarly, individuals who have tended to be followers in the past and are comfortable with that role, often seek that role again.

Individuals become followers in certain situations because their needs are being fulfilled. Sometimes it is easier for an individual to be a follower; it takes less time and energy. At other times it is a matter of comfort with the current leadership, and at still others it may have something to do with comfort and previous experiences. Being aware of the different reasons that individuals become followers should help in making a leader more responsive and effective.

■ Leadership Theories

There have been literally thousands of books, articles, and other documents directed toward the study of leadership, and each one has a slightly different slant on what works and what doesn't work. Some theories of leadership maintain importance because they have withstood the test of time and are worthy of consideration by developing leaders. These theories will be discussed below:

Classical Organizational Theory

Frederick Taylor (1911) suggested that natural work, completing tasks in a natural manner, was uneconomical and inefficient; he stated that organizations needed to plan, organize, direct, and control in order to be successful. Taylor determined that there was really only one right way to complete a task and any other way was inefficient. Dividing tasks up into different processes, and training an individual for each part of the task seemed much more efficient to Taylor than having one individual complete an entire task alone. As the employee became more skilled at a particular task, according to Taylor, the more efficient production became overall. This theory was reinforced by the behavioral movement in psychology and by B. F. Skinner, who emphasized the importance of behavior alone in the work place.

Great Man Theory

This theory was developed by Eugene E. Jennings and is based on the idea that leaders develop in relation to the situations and the times with which they are confronted. According to Jennings, past leaders such as George Washington, John F. Kennedy, and Martin Luther King developed their platform for leadership and power because of specific circumstances they were passionate about and responded to. In the nonprofit sector there are a number of individuals throughout history who have recognized various needs in the community and have gone about initiating an organization of people to respond to those needs. Clara Barton recognized a need to respond to casualties of war and natural disasters, and she developed the American Red Cross. Mrs. Juliette Gordon Low thought young girls should have an opportunity to expend their energies in productive and character developing ways and founded the Girl Scouts of America. Sir Robert Baden-Powell believed these same kinds of opportunities should exist for boys and started a scouting program in England that eventually led to the Boy Scouts of America, founded in this country by William D. Boyce.

Sessoms and Stephenson developed the great man theory further by introducing categories of great men (1981, 23-26).

- **Princes.** These individuals tend to develop a strong base for personal power, often for their own self-aggrandizement.
- **Democratic Hero.** A democratic hero is someone who has been elected to a position of importance and draws their power from the support of the collective voters.
- **Great Average Person.** This is an individual who recognizes needs in his or her family and community and goes around quietly organizing support to meet those needs.
- **Receptive Person.** This individual perceives that there is a need for change and recognizes that he or she has the ability to make these changes and then takes advantage of the opportunity to lead others in making a difference
- **Eventful Person.** An eventful person will change the course of history by doing what he or she thinks is right, regardless of the consequences. These individuals lead with integrity and often by example.
- **Nietzsche's Superman.** This person is a self-starter who likes to develop power so that he or she does not have to depend on others. This individual is not a conformist and looks past society's constraints in order to develop to the fullest.
- **The Superior Person.** This individual has a high level of self-esteem and leads from a platform of personal strength and self-respect. Although leadership is based on the power of his or her will, this type of leader is prepared to return to the role of a follower, if it would be more beneficial.

When we consider some of the enormously complex situations that have occurred throughout history and the number of leaders who have risen to the occasion, the great man theory makes sense.

Group Theory

The primary basis for the group theory of leadership comes from the exchange theory of G.C. Homans. Homans states that before an individual seeks a leadership role in a group, the individual and the group members must perceive that the rewards for both the leader and the follower must exceed the costs. With this theory, the leader fulfills a role expectation and assists group members in reaching their goals. This relationship is reciprocal: the leader is rewarded with the status of being in charge, and progressing toward their goals rewards the group members. There are three interrelated factors necessary for the exchange theory to be successful:

- **Activities.** Tasks must be implemented with the help of the group members and the leader.

- **Interactions.** Interaction is considered the communication that occurs within the group when individuals reach goals, resolve conflict, and coordinate the work of the group.
- **Sentiments.** Sentiment has to do with the level of attraction and degree of bonding that group members develop for one another.

Homans suggested that the more interaction within the group, the stronger the bonding, and the stronger the bonding, the greater the sentiment among group members that would enhance the quality of activities. The group theory provides a link between group and leader effectiveness with overall satisfaction.

The Trait Theory

The trait theory attempts to identify and explain what traits might be helpful for individuals to be leaders. The great man theory of leadership provided the stimulus for this theory and a number of studies indicate that certain characteristics, such as intelligence and confidence, correlate with successful leaders. Traits that are considered important for effective leadership are listed below:

- **Intelligence.** Being able to think critically and creatively is important for successful leadership.
- **Desire for Achievement.** Good leaders have a need to achieve goals and will work tirelessly toward that end.
- **Decisiveness.** It is important for leaders to research issues thoroughly and then carefully weigh the pros and cons of an issue before making a decision.
- **Maturity.** Effective leaders are individuals who are responsible and trustworthy. They are leaders who can be counted on and have a great deal of knowledge to share.
- **Confidence.** Strong leaders project a sense of quiet strength without appearing overbearing or flashy.
- **The Ability to Work with Others.** Good leaders work cooperatively with others and provide support, encouragement and inspiration.
- **Initiative.** Initiating tasks and activities from an inner sense of what is necessary and appropriate, rather than from an outside source, is an important trait for any individual.
- **Flexibility.** Because of the constant changes that occur in organizations and all of society, leaders need to adapt to new trends, issues, activities, and individuals readily and effectively.

Behavior Theory

This theory had its origins in the 1950s and 1960s and focuses on the concept that leaders develop an understanding of what a group shares as its vision and then encourage group members to focus on and work toward that vision. Leadership is considered the way in which an individual behaves or acts in directing the group toward their vision.

Leadership is the pattern of interpersonal processes that occur between the leader and group members, and understanding the ways in which a leader influences group members in reaching their goals is the focus of the model. Leadership is understood to be the processes the leader uses to influence others in reaching their goals.

Situational Theory

Situational theory is based on the idea that the leader takes into account different aspects of a situation prior to deciding on a leadership style. A good leader will consider a number of variables, such as the skills and abilities of the group members and the kind of task involved, before deciding upon a particular strategy or leadership style. Additional variables, such as social, political, cultural, and financial considerations, may also be figured into decision making process.

Depending on the circumstances, a leader may decide to take a highly disciplined, authoritative style of leadership, if this style seems appropriate for the group in the context of the tasks at hand. Or in a different situation, the leader may take a more democratic approach to leadership and invite input from group members before making a decision on how to reach goals. According to the theory, the best style is the style that works best for a particular situation, and effective leaders are consistently successful at selecting which style works best for any given situation.

Humanistic Theory

Supported by the work of Douglas McGregor (Witherspoon 1997), this theory's underlying assumption is that all individuals naturally seek responsibility. Humanistic theorists are interested in developing organizations that are structured to motivate individuals to seek responsibility and to realize their full potentials. As individuals realize their full potential, they will invariably assist the organization in realizing its goals.

The humanistic leader's purpose, therefore, is to develop organizations that provide guidance, support, and encouragement for individuals to reach their full potential and to acquire expertise in various areas of importance. As individuals mature in the levels of expertise, the leader will provide less guidance but continue with support and encouragement.

Excellence Theory

This concept of leadership first appeared in the literature in the 1970s, but it was articulated further and brought to the forefront of leadership concepts in the next decade by the works of Peters and Waterman (1982). According to the theory, an organization can excel only when individuals aspire to individual and organizational excellence. The theory pulls from the transactional/transformational model of leadership, in which leaders and followers motivate each other to reach higher and higher levels of quality in service and products.

In this concept, a leader works actively with followers to complete tasks and reach goals. One way to do this is to incorporate a process referred to as **Managing by Walking Around (MBWA)**. This process can lead to a strong rapport between leaders and followers, it can ensure more effective communication, and it can assist in addressing problems before they become significant. If enacted effectively, it can build camaraderie and even increase morale for leaders and followers.

The Principle Theory

Character traits, such as honesty and patience, have often been mentioned as essential aspects of good leadership. Stephen Covey (1989) took this concept in a specific direction in the 1980s and 1990s with his idea that effective living and leadership could only be achieved if individuals integrated principles into character and led life through those principles. The principles Covey selected were based in all the major religions and include *integrity, fairness, honesty, service, human dignity, excellence,* and *potential*, among others. Covey believed people could develop and maintain these principles by processes he referred to as *habits*. He referred to habits as purposeful systems that involve knowledge, skills, and desires and once formed and practiced would be difficult to let go.

Incorporating habits based on principles, Covey thought people would be able to take charge of their lives; they would set goals and priorities based on what is truly important and act accordingly. This process would encourage all parties involved in situations to feel as if they are winning. It would also encourage leaders to listen and understand individual input from group members, provide a way to enhance collaborative creativity and energy, and give some direction on keeping that energy fresh.

∎ Leadership Studies, Styles and Models

The first classic study in leadership can be traced to a 1939 study by Lewin, Lippitt and White that laid the foundation for understanding leadership styles (1939).

The Lewin, Lippin and White Studies

A number of studies were conducted by Lewin, Lippin and White that involved young boys who were members of a hobby club. The boys took part in a number of activities involving different kinds of crafts, and the studies examined the effectiveness of various leadership styles. The styles that were identified as a result of the studies are explained below:

- **Democratic Leadership Style.** Members in this group are asked for their input on goals, processes, and even the individuals they may wish to work with. An attempt is made to treat individuals fairly and equally.
- **Authoritarian Leadership Style.** During this type of leadership, the leader directs group members toward the goals of the organization, the processes involved to reach those goals, and the individuals with whom members would work. The leader often maintains a distance from the group and can appear to be aloof, but not hostile.
- **Laissez Faire Leadership Style.** There is very little guidance or direction involved with laissez faire style of leadership. Although the leader may provide some of the supplies and materials, he or she does not provide guidance and support. There is also little monitoring or feedback provided by the group leader.

Comparisons were made among the different styles of leadership, and it was determined that members in the authoritarian-led group were more hostile and aggressive than the members of the democratic group. Members reported positive feelings toward the democratic and laissez faire leaders when compared with the authoritative leader. The Lewin, Lippitt, and White studies have been considered ground-breaking research into understanding the nature of leadership, and the results have been the foundation for training, teaching, and further research.

The Ohio State Studies

The Bureau of Business Research at Ohio State University initiated a series of studies on leadership in 1945 (Stogdill and Coons 1957). A group of researchers involved with these studies developed an instrument referred to as the Leader Behavior Description Questionnaire (LBDQ). The instrument was designed to assess a leader's conduct in a number of different work settings, including the armed forces, manufacturing, civil service, and education. Two important areas of leadership behavior were identified as a result of the studies, *initiating structure*, and *consideration*.

- **Initiating Structure.** This concept refers to the way in which the leader determines group goals, group structure, and role expectations.
- **Consideration.** This refers to the relationship that develops between the leader and group members regarding their ideas and feelings. This consideration may be weak or strong depending on the level of trust and respect that exists between the group leader and group members.

University researchers Halpin and Weiner conducted a study in which 83.2% of a leader's behavior was determined by combining these two factors (Stogdill and Coons 1957). Prior to this, it was thought that leaders were either task-oriented or people-oriented, but the results of the Ohio State Studies indicated both factors should be considered when examining leadership styles and models.

Figure 2.1 (at right) demonstrates the different combinations of the factors of *consideration* and *initiating structure*. *Initiating structure* has been designated as task orientation and *consideration* has been designated as human relations orientation. Each of the four quadrants represents a possible leadership style. For instance, a leader with a high human relations orientation and a high task orientation would be interested in doing a good job while at the same time establishing good relationships with employees. This study did not suggest which of the styles was most effective, just that the styles occurred under certain circumstances.

The New Managerial Grid

Robert R. Blake and Jane S. Mouton developed another leadership style model, the New Managerial Grid, in the 1950s. This model includes two dimensions: concern for production and concern for people. Concern for production might include completing organizational tasks and meeting various quotas. Concern for people would include developing effective employee benefits packages and activities to enhance employee morale.

**Figure 2.1
A Leadership-style Model Portraying the Ohio State Studies' Dimensions**

	Task Orientation	
High human relations orientation and low task orientation	**High human relations orientation and high task orientation**
Low human relations orientation and low task orientation	**Low human relations orientation and high task orientation**

(Human Relations Orientation: High / Low; Task Orientation: Low / High)

Reproduced by permission

Figure 2.2
Blake and Mouton's Managerial Grid

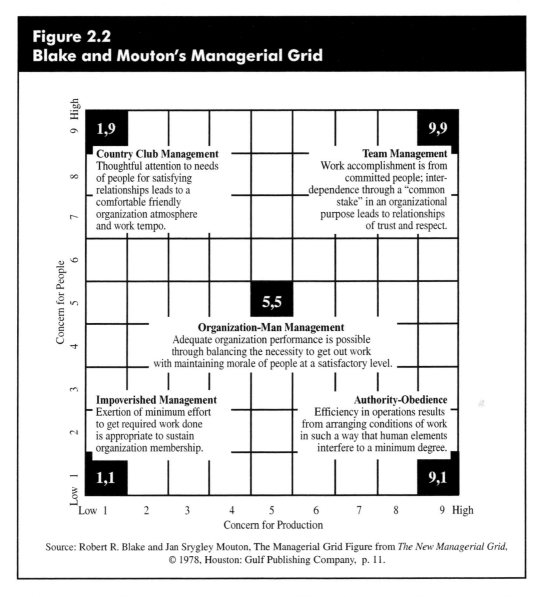

Source: Robert R. Blake and Jan Srygley Mouton, The Managerial Grid Figure from *The New Managerial Grid*, © 1978, Houston: Gulf Publishing Company, p. 11.

These two variables are placed along two axes (Figure 2.2, above). Concern for production is positioned along the horizontal axis, and concern for people is placed along the vertical axis. A high concern is represented by the number 9 and a low concern by the number 1. Blake and Mouton identified five different leadership styles using this grid (Blake and Mouton 1978).

- **1,1 Impoverished Management.** This individual has little interest in getting work done and little interest in developing relationships. This leader essentially manages in name only.
- **1,9 Country Club Management.** With a high concern for relationships but little concern for accomplishing tasks, this person would spend his or her time effecting positive relationships with others.
- **9,1 Authority-Obedience**. This individual would have a strong interest in com-

pleting tasks but little interest in the ideas or feelings of employees. This individual usually uses a leadership position within the organization to control others and to get the job done.

- **Organization-Man Management**. This person tries to take a middle-of-the-road approach to leadership, often compromising both production and employee needs.
- **Team Management**. This individual attempts to reach organizational goals through trusting and effective relationships with employees. Creating a sense of interdependence and commitment to organizational goals can do this.

Blake and Moulton suggest that the first four styles listed are ineffective. A leader can only be effective by concentrating on a high level of achievement and by developing trusting and respectful relationships with employees.

The University of Michigan Studies

The University of Michigan Survey Research Center started investigating leadership behavior in 1947, with a focus on determining factors that might lead to group achievement and satisfaction. The results of this study suggest that leadership behavior could be plotted on a continuum. At one end of the continuum, the leader encourages ideas from employees and includes these ideas in decision-making processes. This individual would be people-oriented and interested in the satisfaction of individuals in the organization. At the other end of the continuum, the leader is task-oriented and focuses on overall organizational achievement. This person would be more interested in achieving organizational goals and developing strategies for reaching goals.

Conclusions derived from the study indicate that employee satisfaction was contingent on the presence of an employee-centered leader and that the level of productivity was less important when compared to the importance of the relationship between employees and leader.

Tannenbaum and Schmidt's Leadership Continuum. Tannenbaum and Schmidt developed a leadership model that organizes leadership style along a continuum (1973, 166). At one end of the continuum (Figure 2.3), the leader would make decisions with little or no employee input and would direct most of the actions of his or her subordinates. At the other end of the continuum, the leader would encourage employee input in decision-making, planning, and other aspects of the organization. The leader would allow a certain range of freedom of action based on pre-established agreements.

A leader may select the style of leadership based on any number of variables. For instance, if the leader has faith in the abilities and motivational level of the employees involved in a task, a democratic style of leadership might be selected for that task. On the other hand, if the leader is unsure about the skill or motivational level of employees, and if time is a consideration, then he or she may choose a more autocratic style.

The authors of the study suggest that leaders remain flexible regarding which style to select, and they state that no style is necessarily better than another; the best approach depends on the situation and circumstances involved.

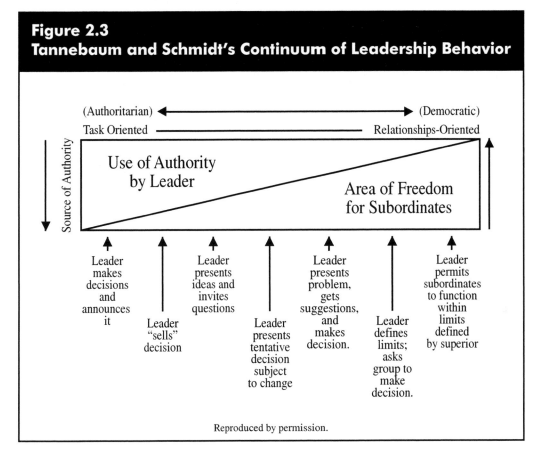

Figure 2.3
Tannebaum and Schmidt's Continuum of Leadership Behavior

Reproduced by permission.

Transactional/Transformational Leadership

Burns (1978) incorporated the social exchange theory developed by Hollander (1978) to advance the concept of transactional/transformational leadership in the 1970s. Burns used the exchange theory as a foundation, stating, "Leadership occurs when one person takes the initiative in making contact with others for the purpose of an exchange of valued things. The exchange could be economical, political, or psychological in nature" (156). Burns thought that leadership involved mutually shared influences as perceived by followers.

Transactional Leadership. This type of leadership involves the exchange of something of value between the leader and someone who may be thought of as a follower. For instance, a leader may exchange a salary for an employee's time and expertise in a particular area. In a nonprofit setting, individuals often exchange money for the opportunity to participate in a program, to develop a skill, to learn something, or experience something else of significance.

At one level, a transaction may seem like a practical and effective exchange process, but it can also have a negative connotation if more meaningful processes are not present. Exchanges that do not involve other meaningful processes can lead to a "carrot and stick" mentality where individuals are rewarded if they provide the right exchange, but might be punished if the exchange is inadequate. This process could lead to a "wage mentality" in a work environment where individuals compete solely for the highest salaries at the expense of feeling proud of accomplishing something worthwhile. The process of treating people according to their productivity can also lead to a negative environment of hostility between employees and between leaders and employees.

Transformational Leadership. Burns suggested that individuals could motivate each other toward higher levels of job satisfaction and wrote that transformational leadership occurs "when one or more persons engage with others in such a way that leaders and followers raise one another to higher levels of motivation and morality" (1978, 20). Authors Peters and Waterman proposed that leadership is a system of transforming individuals and organizations to pursue excellence (1982). Using the transformational model, a leader would empower employees and inspire them to work together to achieve greater heights.

Transformational leadership assumes that individuals need commitment and self-fulfillment, which might actually enhance personal productivity. It is a leadership process that is based on fairness and trust and as Burns wrote, "Transformational leadership is elevating" (1978, 455). This type of experience "can take place in many aspects of our personal, professional, and moral lives. These transformations can be physical, intellectual, aesthetic, psychological, social, civic, ecological, transcendental, moral, spiritual, and holistic" (Rost 1993, 126). With this process, individuals are important in and of themselves and are encouraged to pursue a more visionary approach to productivity. As Peters and Waterman (1982) noted, individuals will commit a great deal of themselves to efforts they deem worthwhile.

Tri-Dimensional Leader Effectiveness Model

Hersey and Blanchard (1977) incorporated elements of the Ohio State Studies (human relations orientation and task orientation), in developing a situational leadership theory called the **Tri-Dimensional Leader Effectiveness Model.** This model is based on the idea that leadership style should be determined based on two variables: (1) the level of maturity of group members, and (2) the demands of a particular situation. A mature individual is described as someone who sets high goals, accepts responsibility for attaining those goals, and has the knowledge and skills to realize those goals.

Leadership styles, then, would vary according to the maturity levels of group members (Figure 2.4). Four different leadership styles are suggested: telling (S1), selling (S2), participating (S3), and delegating (S4). The telling quadrant involves a high task and low relationship orientation. Selling involves a high task and a high relationship orientation. Participating includes a high relationship with a low task orientation, and delegating involves a low relationship with a low task orientation. As an individual progresses in their level of responsibility, knowledge, and skills, they would move from a low level of maturity to a higher level, resulting in a leader changing styles accordingly.

An example of how this process might work would be an employee who is relatively new to an organization and who has not had a great deal of practice in using skills relevant for a particular project. A leader using this concept might adopt an S1 or S2 style of leadership while the individual is developing competence and confidence. As both competence and confidence are enhanced, the leader might assume an S3 or S4 position, encouraging the employee to take more initiative while still monitoring his or her progress.

An employee who reaches a high level of maturity in one project may not reach the same level under different circumstances, and it is important for a leader to adjust leader-

Figure 2.4
Situational Leadership

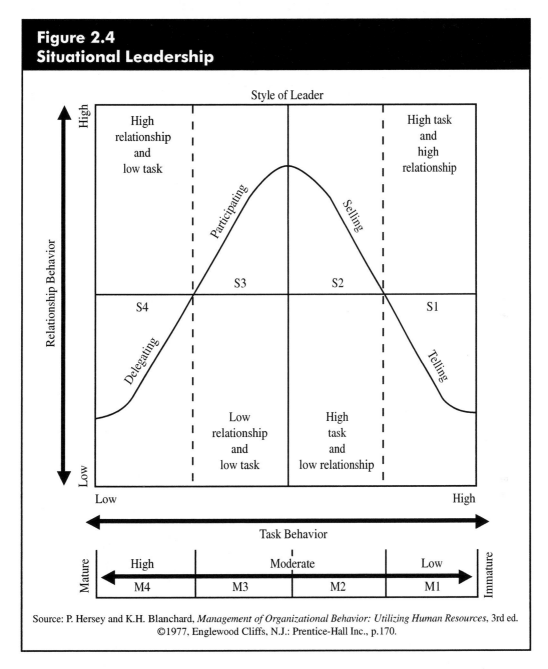

Source: P. Hersey and K.H. Blanchard, *Management of Organizational Behavior: Utilizing Human Resources*, 3rd ed. ©1977, Englewood Cliffs, N.J.: Prentice-Hall Inc., p.170.

ship styles accordingly. The bell shaped curve running through the quadrants is a continuum, and a leader can go back and forth on this continuum, depending on the circumstances and the maturity level of the employees.

Hitt's Model of Leadership

Hitt (1988) proposed a simple model of leadership in which a leader would create a vision for an organization and then develop a plan of action to reach that vision. The process of leadership, then, would be in creating a desirable vision and developing an effective plan for people to follow to achieve success.

Hitt suggested that the leader must both create a vision **and** develop an effective plan to follow in order to motivate others, and he refers to these qualities as dreaming and doing. In the two-dimensional model at right (Figure 2.5), Hitt designates the four possible types of leadership styles:

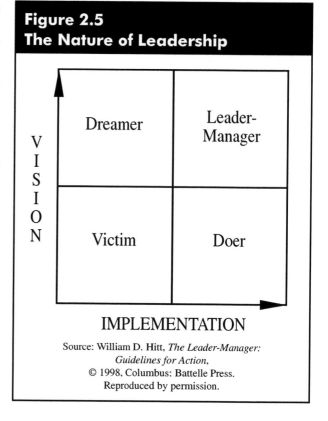

**Figure 2.5
The Nature of Leadership**

Source: William D. Hitt, *The Leader-Manager: Guidelines for Action,* © 1998, Columbus: Battelle Press. Reproduced by permission.

- **Victim.** This person has little vision or initiative and often complains about unfair practices within the organization.
- **Dreamer.** The dreamer has a lot of vision but few implementation skills.
- **Doer.** This individual will work hard at implementing the vision of others.
- **Leader-Manager.** This person is high on vision as well as implementation.

The victim is someone with little motivation and vision and remains happy regarding almost everything within an organization. The dreamer is an individual who has high goals but little ability to reach those goals. The doer will work diligently to reach the goals of others. The leader is someone who can create an exciting and worthwhile vision and can motivate group members toward a plan of action to reach goals.

Collaborative Leadership

Collaborative leadership involves bringing people together to build trust, cooperation, and communication. This is a contemporary style of leadership in which the leader brings people together in a synergistic mode to develop leadership in groups who are working together to make decisions and solve problems.

This style of leadership emphasizes sharing ideas and listening, understanding, and often acting on the input of those involved. Collaborative leaders are empowering leaders who bring people together for discussion and reflection; then they encourage individuals to accept responsibilities, depending on situations and levels of professional expertise.

According to Eisler (1995), collaborative leaders avoid dominating and directing approaches and develop a nurturing environment of unconditional support. This is a similar concept to the Christian theology of "agape love," which can be considered unconditional love or support. Leaders work to bring people together in groups and treat members as important and worthwhile individuals.

In their book, *The Flight of the Buffalo,* Belasco and Stayer developed an interesting model of collaborative leadership based on analogies to geese. Belasco and Stayer (1993) describe the way geese communicate with each other and change leadership positions in flight when one becomes tired or the situation changes in some other way. Accordingly, in the discussion presented by the authors, effective communication and trust is encouraged as is the sharing of leadership. Individuals are encouraged to accept positions of leadership at opportune times. This sharing of leadership responsibilities results in a strong commitment for the goals of the group.

Comprehensive Approach to Leadership

For a leader to be effective, he or she should be aware of important variables associated with a particular project or activity. Consideration of factors such as the particular situation, group members, and the leader are important in the selection of a leadership style and are depicted in Figure 2.6. These three factors are interrelated and are discussed in detail next.

Situation. The term *situation* has to do with the task at hand and the process involved in accomplishing the task.

- **External Forces.** External forces are those forces that individuals have little or no control over, such as weather conditions, political conditions, cultural preferences, customs, and traditions. Knowledge of these circumstances can help in the selection of a leadership style.
- **Group Goals.** Having a clear understanding of organizational goals can be helpful in selecting a leadership style and determining the process for reaching those goals.
- **Methods and Procedures.** There are a number of different methods that a leader can choose from to achieve results. For instance, programs can take the form of leagues, special events, seminars, classes or workshops. Different situations call for different approaches.
- **Type of Environment.** Environments can be more or less stable, depending on circumstances. A more stable environment calls for a more task-oriented leadership style, whereas a less stable environment might call for a more people-oriented style.

Group Members. Understanding the background and qualifications of each group member is essential in selecting a style of leadership. A number of factors should be considered.

- **Knowledge, Skills, and Abilities.** A leader must have an understanding of individual areas and levels of expertise in order to match this expertise with specific, correlating tasks.
- **Needs Disposition.** Group members are each motivated differently, so a leader must have knowledge of individual interests, needs, and desires prior to developing a plan of supervision.
- **Experience.** Members of a group who have had a broad range of experience may require a less direct approach than members with minimal experience.
- **Task-relevant Maturity.** Individuals who have proven to be responsible and/

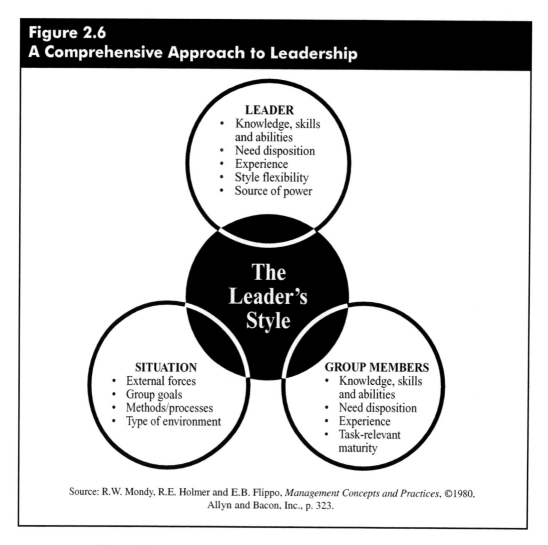

Figure 2.6
A Comprehensive Approach to Leadership

Source: R.W. Mondy, R.E. Holmer and E.B. Flippo, *Management Concepts and Practices*, ©1980, Allyn and Bacon, Inc., p. 323.

or high achievers may require less supervision than individuals with less task-relevant maturity.

 The Leader. The leader is the key in pulling all of the elements together for successful programs and organizations. Some of the factors important in the development of a successful leadership style are detailed below.

- **Knowledge, Skills, and Abilities.** Being aware of one's own strengths and weaknesses is important when selecting a leadership style.
- **Needs Disposition.** The leader's own interests, needs, and desires are significant factors, since a leader operates according to his or her own motivational factors and comfort levels.
- **Experience.** The leader who has had previous experience working with group members can use this experience in making decisions in the future.
- **Style Flexibility.** The degree to which a leader can adapt to different leadership styles should also be a factor in selecting a style of supervising.
- **Source of power.** The ability of a leader to incorporate sources of power (men-

tioned previously in this chapter) is important in selecting leadership style. A leader who is charismatic may need to take a more relaxed style, while an individual who is comfortable with a legitimate or authoritative style may be more directive in supervising others.

Being able to evaluate each of these areas effectively – the situation, group members, and the leader – will provide the leader with valuable information in selecting the best leadership style.

■ The Connection between Leadership, Character and Ethics

Too often, leadership models fail to include the importance of character and ethics in the overall scheme of leading and influencing others. Aristotle identified *ethos* as a central element in understanding how one person influences another. He contended that our perception of another is based heavily on our perception of that person's virtues, wisdom, and good will (*On Rhetoric*, 2.1.-6). **Character** includes the beliefs, traits and values that distinguish one person from another. It is being true to a standard or standards a person has set to govern his or her life (Weis and Gantt 2002). **Ethics** is a system of moral principles and values and moral duty and obligation; it not only deals with what people believe about how they should act, but what they *should* believe (Jeavons 1994). Leaders must have the kind of character it takes to represent the organization effectively and the type of ethical system that would allow them to lead with a strong moral compass. First, we'll look at a leadership model that includes character at the center, and then we'll look at a concept for maintaining ethical standards in nonprofit organizations.

The Integrated Leadership and Character Model

The Integrated Leadership and Character Model (Figure 2.7, page 51) has been developed to discuss the importance of character in leadership (Weis and Gantt 2002). The model identifies critical skills and knowledge areas and illustrates the central function of personal character.

According to the model:

- To be successful, organizations must have leaders with traits, values and ethics (personal character) that are important to the overall development of the organization.
- Leaders must also possess or develop an effective level of conceptual, technical, and human relation skills.
- The interaction and effectiveness of these three skill areas is dependent on the personal character of individual leaders within the organization.

To develop and implement effective programs in a nonprofit organization, a leader must have an idea of what individuals need and want (conceptual skills). He or she must have competent skills in planning and implementing programs (technical skills), be able to inform and motivate staff members to implement programs, and know how to encourage constituents to participate in the programs (human relations skills). The more determined an individual is to make a program work, and the more trusted the leader is (personal character), the more likely the program is to succeed.

This same concept would work for any procedure in a nonprofit organization. For instance, in developing and implementing a budget, a leader must have an understanding and a vision of financial matters. He or she needs to be knowledgeable and skilled in developing the technical aspects of the budget and the budgeting process, along with being able to communicate budgetary procedures effectively to others. Personal character is critical in making certain all of the skill areas are working effectively and that the processes are moving along smoothly.

There are three important **implications** to consider in the context of this model:

- First, it is important to consider the model in the context of oneself. It provides a framework for individuals to go by to assess and develop their own character and skills.
- It also provides a framework for individual leaders to use in selecting and Training staff and volunteer members.
- Finally, it can be a frame of reference in determining the types of programs that may be helpful for organizational members.

Recognizing that individuals need to be competent in these three skill areas and that character is the key element in the overall scheme of things provides nonprofit leaders with guidelines for personal development, staff and volunteer development, and the development of constituents.

Realizing that character consists of traits, values, and ethics, it is important to examine these attributes to discover how they enhance character. First, we'll look at traits and values. While each person might identify a slightly different list of **personal traits** and **values** that make up character, **Character Counts!** (http://www.charactercounts.org/) a nonpartisan, nonsectarian coalition of 454 schools, communities and nonprofit organizations, works to advance character education by teaching what it calls the **Six Pillars of Character:** *trustworthiness, respect, responsibility, fairness, caring and citizenship.*

Trustworthiness implies that an individual can be depended upon. When a person is considered to be trustworthy, his or her word means something. He or she can be expected to do everything possible to assist the organization and the individuals in the organization in succeeding. It is important to be able to work alongside people we believe in and that we can trust.

Respect includes valuing the contributions, the differences, and the feelings of others. It is only possible to value someone else's ideas and feelings through a genuine effort of understanding. Understanding means making an attempt to gather as much information as possible regarding another person in order to empathize and collaborate with that person.

Responsibility means accepting a degree of ownership for all areas of an organization and accepting strong ownership for particular areas of an organization. Accepting responsibility is important for the overall health and success of an organization. Leaders of good character do not waste time blaming others, but rather work cooperatively to ensure success.

Fairness involves full consideration of all information to assure that all parties in a situation are listened to and dealt with without favoritism. Being fair is not always popular or necessarily expedient, but it is always just and equal. Fairness is a trait that, when perceived, brings with it the trust and loyalty of others.

Figure 2.7
Integrated Leadership and Character Model

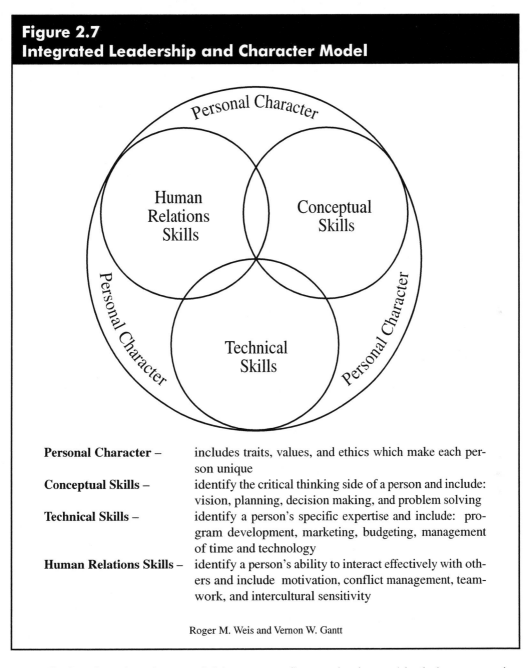

Personal Character –   includes traits, values, and ethics which make each person unique

Conceptual Skills –   identify the critical thinking side of a person and include: vision, planning, decision making, and problem solving

Technical Skills –   identify a person's specific expertise and include: program development, marketing, budgeting, management of time and technology

Human Relations Skills –   identify a person's ability to interact effectively with others and include motivation, conflict management, teamwork, and intercultural sensitivity

Roger M. Weis and Vernon W. Gantt

Caring for others is essential in a nonprofit organization and includes compassion and concern for others. Members of nonprofit organizations report that good leaders are those who care about their needs, concerns, and feelings. Members are not so concerned about the behind-the-scenes activities of organizations, but they are concerned about leaders who exhibit a genuine interest in their well-being.

Citizenship means taking an active and thoughtful interest in the community. Leaders of nonprofit organizations have an opportunity to incorporate their position to make things happen in the community. They also have the opportunity—and perhaps obligation—to involve staff, volunteers, and members in community action, when appropriate.

Organizations such as the YMCA, Boy Scouts of America, Girls, Inc., and others often have other traits and values they associate with character, and these traits and values may differ from individual to individual and from culture to culture. The important consideration is that character is critical to effective leadership, especially in the nonprofit sector. Greater attention should be given to the role character plays in leadership, regardless of context. Doing the right thing for the right reasons as opposed to doing what works is the subject of the next section, ethics.

The Role of Ethics in Nonprofit Leadership

Staff members, volunteers, and constituents often look to leaders to set the standards for moral thought and behavior in the nonprofit sector. One way to address this would be to establish an ethical culture within an organization that includes a number of ethical *obligations* that organizations should embrace and pursue. Jeavons (1994) suggests five such obligations necessary for developing an **ethical culture**: *integrity*, *openness*, *accountability*, *service*, and *charity*.

> *We are discussing no small matter, but how we ought to live.*
>
> **Socrates**
> - as reported by Plato in the *Republic* (ca.390 B.C.)

Integrity implies that the organization and individuals within the organization can be depended upon to do what they have stated they intend to do. In other words, their deeds match their words. Integrity is critical for establishing trust within the organization and between the organization and the community. Integrity can be demonstrated in a number of different ways. Organizational literature such as promotional brochures, fundraising materials, and other reports should match actual situations. In other words, documents should never be embellished for organizational gain. If actual performance in an area does not match the degree to which it is billed, then a wedge of distrust develops between the organization and its constituents and other members of the community.

Another way integrity can be demonstrated is to have leaders who represent the values and mission of the institution effectively. In other words, trustworthiness can and should be demonstrated on a daily basis. In 2001 the American Red Cross generated hundreds of millions of dollars to assist the victims of the terrorist attacks of September 11. When it is was revealed that a small portion of the money contributed would go elsewhere, the public was outraged and the ARC quickly reverted to its original plan. Nonprofit leaders have an obligation to be as honest as possible with the public as well as with their own staff members. Attempts to disguise facts or offer misleading information can create dramatic results often with far-reaching consequences.

Openness may not accurately qualify as a "moral" value, but for organizations operating in the public sphere, maintaining openness to public observation and scrutiny is certainly virtuous and even practical. For organizations that provide public services or advocacy and have impact on community life, operating in secrecy would arouse skepticism regarding motivation. Part of this skepticism is historical in nature, since a small number of service organizations from time to time have operated with ulterior motives. The most successful nonprofit organizations operate effectively and welcome inquiries regarding any area of their operation.

Organizations that are concerned with maintaining a culture of interest and excitement realize that maintaining a climate of trust is essential to this interest and excitement and that operating openly is the best way to develop trust. Another reason to maintain openness is that many nonprofit organizations began as volunteer associations with a rich, populist, democratic background, and maintaining openness and democratic ways helps to insure that tradition. Maintaining openness in decision making, programs, financial matters and other issues relevant to the overall operation of an organization is key to maintaining the trust of the community.

Accountability means that not only should organizations maintain an openness regarding all operations, but they must also be able to explain and be accountable for their activities. Nonprofit organizations often receive the right to solicit tax-deductible contributions, or at least receive a tax-exempt status, and with that they have an obligation to perform public service as effectively and as efficiently as possible. These tax statuses are contractual in nature, and that obligates organizations both ethically and legally to perform according to promise and to be evaluated accordingly.

By accepting the privilege of tax-exempt status or the opportunity to solicit tax-deductible contributions, organizations inherently accept the obligation to be evaluated not only by their constituents but also by the public at large. This also obligates organizations to pursue the stated mission and purpose of the institution and to be accountable to the membership in working toward that end. The need for accountability has motivated more and more states to pass laws mandating financial disclosures and regulating fundraising activities for nonprofit organizations. Additionally, "watch-dog" groups such as the National Charities Information Bureau and the Better Business Bureau's section on nonprofit organizations are taking a closer look at organizational finances and other operations. Nonprofit leaders have an obligation to insure that the organization and all individuals within the organization—are accountable to their constituents, their board members, and to the broader public.

Service is similar to accountability in the sense that nonprofit organizations exist, and are granted special privileges, because of their commitment to serve the public, or at least the membership, in some way. The social contract they receive, which provides them with special privileges, obligates them to work toward a mission of public good; the membership dues, program fees, special event money, contributions, volunteer time and other resources these organizations receive also obligate them ethically toward service.

This service ethic must also be manifested in the leaders of nonprofit organizations, who can certainly work toward their own advancement, but, without sacrificing personal well-being, they must always place the cause of the organization and the well-being of the people the organization is serving uppermost in their priorities. The idea of leaders seeing themselves as servants for the cause of the organization and for their constituents is critical in focusing others within the organization on the needs of the members. Nonprofit organizations are by nature altruistic, and it is therefore necessary for the leaders of these organizations to lead with a philosophy of selflessness and service.

Charity is one of the most important ethical obligations of all, since the word "charity" comes from the Latin *caritas*, which means more than giving to those in need (Jeavons 1994). Originally, the translation of the word "charity" was "love," but not romantic love. Rather, it meant the kind of love a neighbor shows for another neighbor in need. It also meant to be caring, putting the welfare of others above one's own, and sharing one's resources with others out of a sense of concern and social obligation rather than a sense of pity.

From an organizational standpoint, an ethical obligation to charity is derived in part from reciprocity. In other words, nonprofit organizations benefit from the generosity of others and are therefore obliged to express generosity themselves. The motivation of the supporters of many of these organizations comes from the idea that the organization is committed to caring for others. Additionally, individual service recipients often indicate that they believe they will receive more personable and more caring service from private, nonprofit organizations than from public entities. The leaders of these organizations must be selected for their character traits that include a caring and respectful nature. Leaders often set the tone for all operations within the organization and a caring and giving person will be reflected in the way the organization operates.

Leadership Development

Former White House Fellow, Thomas Cronin, has written that leadership cannot be taught, as such, but that individuals can learn in their own minds the strengths and limitations of leadership (Wren 1995). Examining leadership theories, studies, and models provides a theoretical and academic foundation for learning about leadership. Assessing the actual lives of leaders can provide understanding and inspiration for self-development (Immegart 1988). Another process, mentoring, allows current leaders opportunities to pass on their knowledge of leading to the next generation. And finally, service learning, a field experience that combines community service with specific learning objectives, provides individuals with opportunities to perform meaningful service while developing knowledge, skills, and character, all important for effective leadership (Weis and Gantt 2002). These aspects of leadership development will be discussed in the next three sections.

■ Leaders through the Ages

Lao-Tzu was a Chinese sage who lived in sixth century B.C. and described leadership as providing a service in a selfless manner. According to Lao-Tzu, a leader should place the well-being of others above oneself and accordingly, these acts of selflessness would actually enhance oneself. He compared an enlightened leader to water that "cleanses and refreshes all creatures without judgment (Wren 1995)." A leader is yielding, like water, and if a leader does not push forward too severely, group members will not resent or resist being led. He thought leadership should be a nourishing experience and that leaders should be humble and direct credit for successes to others. He imagined leaders as facilitators who would lead with as little direction as possible.

Lao-Tzu also compared the process of leadership to being a midwife, in which the leader is merely facilitating another person's process. The leader needs to be reminded that it is basically someone else's process and that the leader should guide the process with as little intrusion as possible. If the leader trusts the other person in the process, according to

Lao-Tzu, that person will also trust the guidance of the leader. Just as a midwife assists at someone else's birth, a leader should facilitate what is happening, rather than what he or she thinks should be happening. And if the leader must take the lead from time to time, the leadership should be such that the group member is assisted, yet still feels a sense of autonomy.

Plato lived between 428-347 B.C. and was a student of Socrates. He founded the Academy in 387 B.C., and this was the first permanent institution in Western civilization completely devoted to education and research (Wren 1995). Plato often expressed disappointment in the excesses of liberty and democracy and, writing in his *Republic,* suggested these excesses often led to tyranny and anarchy. He thought wise philosophers, selected for their love of philosophy and knowledge, should lead the state. These philosopher-kings should rule the state based on their natural inclinations and should set themselves apart from their followers in order to rule more objectively with their intellect.

Plato thought these philosopher-kings would be discovered as individuals who naturally wished to study philosophy and who would also exhibit leadership qualities. These individuals would be intelligent, noble, gracious, courageous and temperate, and they would therefore appear different from the rest of the citizenry. These philosophers would be able to focus on the eternal nature of truth and justice without varying from generation to generation and without being led astray by corruption.

Aristotle (384-322 B.C.) was the gifted student of Plato, yet he disagreed with his teacher and mentor regarding the selection of philosopher-kings as leaders of the state (Wren 1995). Aristotle believed all citizens should have an opportunity to govern and to be governed. He believed that all men should experience being governed in order to be more effective as leaders themselves. Aristotle thought all men should be treated equally by the state and that all men should have an equal chance to govern. These were concepts he believed to be essential in order for the state to survive. Anything else would lead to anarchy and revolution and the demise of the state.

Aristotle stated that it was impossible for any one class or group of citizens to assume a place of superiority over another. According to Aristotle, it was the charge of the state, therefore, to provide education that would allow a citizen to learn to be a good citizen, to learn obedience and at the same time to learn to command. Obeying and commanding were both honorable in themselves, as long the intentions and the end results were good.

Niccolo Machiavelli (1469-1572) was trained as a humanist and served as a diplomat for Florence prior to being exiled (Wren 1995). While in exile, he wrote his infamous *The Prince*, which addresses the idea of gaining and maintaining individual power by any means. Although *The Prince* describes the importance of individual power, his other famous work, the *Discourses*, describes the important aspects of a republic. In *The Prince*, Machiavelli suggests that individuals should be merciful, gracious, upright and religious, whenever possible, but should revert to trickery and deceitfulness whenever it is necessary to gain power and to maintain authority.

Machiavelli postulated that individuals who used cunning measures when necessary to reach their goals accomplished more and would win over individuals who incorporated honesty in their dealings. He believed that men were generally dishonest by nature, and therefore a leader should not keep his (or her) word when it becomes advantageous to do otherwise. According to Machiavelli, whenever a leader succeeds in establishing and maintaining authority, regardless of the means of accomplishment, the leader will be judged honorable and be approved by all. Although this philosophy was timely for Machiavelli's day, its treatise resonates to present time and *The Prince* remains a classic in the study of leadership.

 **Thomas Jefferson** (1743-1827) was a brilliant statesman, scientist, architect, inventor, educator and public servant. He was the author of the Declaration of Independence, the founder of the University of Virginia, and the third president of the country. He was born into a Virginia family of means; his father was a wealthy plantation owner, and his mother was of distinguished English and Scottish pedigree. He took advantage of the opportunity for a formal education and eventually earned a law degree from William and Mary College in 1762.

Jefferson's interest in politics led him to become an accomplished statesman. His southern, aristocratic background and culture generally served him well, and he incorporated his vast knowledge and statesmanlike abilities to move the country toward the birth of its independence from England. This same culture, however, led to a contradiction for the man who wrote, "We hold these truths to be self-evident, that all men are created equal, that they are endowed by their Creator with certain unalienable Rights, that among these are Life, Liberty, and the pursuit of Happiness" in the Declaration of Independence. At the same time he bought, sold and owned slaves, and did so even later when he became president. In spite of this contradiction, Jefferson continues to be revered as one of the greatest leaders of the country and a champion of democratic ways.

 **Harriett Tubman** (1820-1913) was born into a slave family in the Eastern Shore section of Maryland on a plantation owned by Edward Broadas. Growing up, Tubman learned what it meant to be a slave and was taught to say, "Yes, Missus," "No, Missus," to white women and "Yes, Mas'r," "No, Mas'r," to white men (Petry 1955, 21). At nighttime she would sometimes hear the hoofbeats of horses as slave owners would ride up and down the dirt roads looking for runaways. Runaways would sometimes be brought back shackled in chains and beaten, or worse, "sold South," a term that meant a slave was sold to a plantation in the deep South (Petry 9). As a young girl, Tubman worked in the fields of the plantation, often from dusk to dawn, but when hard times came to the plantation, she was sometimes hired out to other families for cleaning, weaving, watching trap lines and caring for their children.

Tubman later married a freed slave named John and was allowed to live in his cabin with him. But Tubman feared being sold South, and she plotted running away to the North. When John refused to accompany her, she left anyway. On her escape North, she was befriended and supported by people along the way. This assistance came to be known as the

Underground Railroad, but it was little more than a loosely organized group of people who offered hiding and food. She soon found herself a free person in Pennsylvania, but missed her family and friends and made the dangerous journey back and forth to Maryland numerous times, always guiding a group of slaves North with her. Later in life, Tubman became a scout and a spy for the North, but she is remembered most as a conductor for the Underground Railroad. In later years, she had a difficult time financially and even sold produce door to door. In 1913, she died penniless, but free.

Clara Barton was born on Christmas day in 1821 in an unpretentious farmhouse in Oxford, Massachusetts. Barton was a shy student as a youngster but was something of a tomboy and relished the idea of jumping on a wild colt and racing across the Massachusetts countryside. It was during her early years that her younger brother David was injured in a fall, and she was asked to assist in his care. Barton was a natural nurse and completely took over the care of her brother until he was well. Later, she became a teacher, winning the admiration of her students for her caring ways and her ability to keep up with them in recreational pursuits. After teaching for a number of years, Barton left to work in the U.S. Patent Office in Washington, D.C. While she was there, war broke out between the states, and Barton accepted a nursing position and was able to go to the battlefront, where most of the casualties were. As a nurse, Barton saved countless lives, often working from daybreak to long past dusk.

Following the war, President Lincoln recruited Barton to assist in locating 22,000 missing soldiers, which she did for four long years. Afterward, tired and ill from her efforts, she sailed to Europe to recuperate. While in Europe, Barton learned of the International Red Cross (IRC), an organization designed to provide relief for people during a time of war. Upon returning from Europe, she began forming the American version of the IRC. In no time at all, Barton's organization was providing relief services for flood and fire victims, and in 1882 President Arthur appointed her as the first president of the National Red Cross, which later came to be known as the American Red Cross. Her desire to help others has changed the lives of millions, and in so doing helped to change the shape of an entire nation.

Geronimo (1829-1909) was born in the mountains of Arizona into a Bedonkohes Apache family. As a young man, Geronimo was very athletic. He played games that prepared him for a rigorous adult life, which often involved raiding the enemies of his people and then fleeing to the mountains for weeks at a time. He was considered stronger and wiser than his years and was admitted into the council of warriors for his skill and knowledge in battles at the early age of seventeen. He experienced a great personal tragedy a little later in life, when his entire family—mother, wife, and three children—were slain by the members of the Mexican Army. From that day forward, he vowed never to be killed by a Mexican bullet, and he managed to live to be over ninety and died of natural causes.

Geronimo became one of the most feared Indians ever and could ride a horse, handle a lance, and shoot a rifle better than anyone. Once with Geronimo at the lead, he and eighteen Apache warriors were able to confront and deter the forces of 5000 U.S. Troopers. Since there was no formal leadership structure with the Apache Indians, Geronimo led by example and was admired by his fellow warriors for his independence, integrity, courage, determination and ruthlessness. He was often very persuasive and led through this skill as well as by being trusted by the other Indians. He was a highly religious man, and his sense of honor and courage had been observed in battle on numerous occasions. They earned him the respect of friend and foe alike. Although Geronimo had been lied to many times by his enemies, he never broke his own code of honor. In fact, it could be said that the Apache culture itself was the style of leadership adopted by Geronimo.

George A. Custer was a West Point graduate who served as a general and became a true hero in the Civil War. As one of the leaders for the Michigan Wolverines, he and his troops defeated the Confederate cavalry General Jeb Stuart at Gettysburg and defended the Union Army from attack by General Pickett and over twelve thousand Confederate infantrymen. He and his troops also dogged General Robert E. Lee in his final retreat and eventually forced Lee to surrender. He was described by his superiors as a warrior who fought with audacity, courage, and an unparalleled fury and focus on winning. He was revered by most and considered to be one of the greatest military leaders of his time. In fact, had it not been for a place in Montana named Little Big Horn, Custer could very well have become President Custer.

Following the Civil War, millions of Americans moved West in search of cheap land and encountered nearly 200,000 Indians, many of whom were determined to defend their territory. The dashing Civil War hero, Custer was sent along by his government to protect the pioneering Americans. Custer and the U.S. Army adopted a tactic referred to as total war, which meant that all Indians were viewed as dangerous and were to be attacked wherever and whenever possible. He again became a national hero for the successes of this tactic and planned his next attack against the Indians at Little Big Horn. But Little Big Horn was to be his undoing, and Custer and all of the men in his unit were killed by an enemy enraged by past brutalities. Brimming with confidence from his successes, he had tragically underestimated the spirit and experience of his enemy, and overestimated his own ability and the will of his troops.

W.E.B. Du Bois (1868-1963) was one of the founders of the National Association for the Advancement of Colored People (NAACP) and is considered one of the fathers of the modern black militancy movement. His involvement in militancy came about, at least partially, as a reaction to the conciliatory methods of Booker T. Washington. Du Bois was also the founder of the Niagara Movement and wrote extensively, his most memorable work being *The Souls of Black Folk*. The first black man to receive his Ph.D. from Harvard, he believed the Negro race, as he referred to it, could only be saved by the Talented Tenth. This was the term given to exceptional blacks who needed to be selected from the population for their intellect, charisma, and potential and who would then be educated and developed into leaders, who in turn would provide direction and education for the masses.

Du Bois believed that the only way the Negro race could rise above the shame and degradation that slavery had brought them was to find exceptional blacks who would educate other blacks. He believed that only by being educated in a culture with its own thoughts, its own ideals, and its own leaders could the masses of Negro people flourish and rise above the history that had been forced upon them. He thought that if blacks did not furnish these leaders to be trained to educate and lead others within the race, then chaos and misdirection would abound. Du Bois also believed that if this group of talented individuals did not come to be, the Negro race would become a lost cause and would pull down other races of men with it. His idea was that his fellow blacks would be lifted up through education and work, and he believed that education should not only provide work-related knowledge, but it should provide knowledge in life skills as well.

Mohandas Gandhi (1869-1948) was educated in law but devoted his entire life to helping the disadvantaged. He worked to bring an end to discrimination against the lower orders of India, known as the untouchables, he helped establish Hindu-Muslim unity, and he was instrumental in securing independence for his native India from Great Britain. But it was not so much the issues he was involved in but the method he used that brought him fame and the honorable title of Mahatma, which meant Great Soul. His use of passive resistance to organize his countrymen in the wake of overwhelming British odds is legendary. He believed that passive resistance should only be used for just causes, and individuals espousing passive resistance must be willing to suffer to the end for those causes.

For Gandhi, evil was only to be overcome by good, anger by love, and untruth by truth, and always through peaceful means. He believed that only the courageous could be passive resisters and that, in the long run, both the individuals involved in resistance and the individuals who were being resisted benefited from the process. Gandhi thought that men of integrity would disregard unjust commands from leaders, even if it meant putting their lives in jeopardy, and that in defying death they freed themselves from fear. He believed there was no one in the world so bad that they could not be converted by love. His example of practiced non-violence inspired millions of people to emulate his example for decades.

Helen Keller was born in the small town of Tuscumbia, Alabama, in 1904 and had a pretty normal childhood until she reached the age of nineteen months, when she developed a fever that left her blind, deaf, and unable to speak. Because this left Keller with limited opportunities for effective communication, she became something of a behavior problem. Her parents were encouraged to take her to Dr. Alexander Graham Bell, a prominent teacher of the deaf and inventor of the telephone. Dr. Bell recommended that Keller receive schooling from Anne Sullivan, who had become nearly blind herself and had overcome many obstacles to become a teacher of the blind, the deaf and the mute. Under Sullivan's care, Keller began to read and write by using braille and became calmer as she grew in her communication skills. By the age of seven, Keller had mastered four alphabets: the manual one for the deaf, the square pencil script, raised letters, and Braille dots.

Eventually, Keller wrote her own story about growing up with so many complications and the story became a book, *The Story of My Life*, which was printed in fifty different languages. Sullivan went on to encourage thousands of others with similar afflictions and was deeply involved in what was then a new organization, the American Foundation for the Blind. She also wrote *Teacher*, a tribute to her teacher and mentor, Anne Sullivan. Keller, with the unparalleled assistance of Sullivan, had overcome incredible obstacles to become a source of inspiration for millions of people worldwide.

Cesar Chavez grew up in the small town of Gila Bend, Arizona, where his father and grandfather were local business and landowners. The depression of 1929 left the Chavez family nearly penniless, however, and they had to leave their home and begin a life of crop picking. The conditions in the labor camps where the Chavez family had to live were horrible; there was no heat, sanitation system, running water, or electricity. The school system where Chavez and his brother and sister attended was racist, and children were punished if they spoke Spanish during school hours. Outside of school their life consisted of picking walnuts, cherries, cotton, potatoes, apricots, melons, and grapes for meager wages and for labor contractors who often cheated the growers regarding the weight of their daily production.

Following a stint in the United States Navy during World War Two, Chavez began working for the Community Service Organization (CSO). His job was to register people to vote, and he learned about power, organizing agencies, and organizing sit-ins. Later, Chavez's determination and personal involvement was critical in organizing the National Farm Workers Association to work for better wages and conditions for crop pickers. He successfully incorporated nonviolent strategies, such as boycotts and picketing, against the powerful California Growers Association, represented by the Teamsters Union and the AFL-CIO. When the Teamsters began physically attacking NFWA members, Chavez adopted the Hindu concept of fasting, which encouraged other NFWA members to commit to his nonviolent movement, and the NFWA was eventually victorious in its fight for fairness with the growers in California. Like Ghandi before him, Chavez put his beliefs and his life on the line again and again in support of the culture and people he loved.

These individuals represent a wide range of philosophies regarding leadership and provide insight for a variety of approaches. Aspiring nonprofit leaders should assess these approaches when developing a philosophy of leadership.

■ Using Mentoring to Develop Leaders

U.S. tennis great Althea Gibson once said, "No matter what accomplishments you make, somebody helped you." This statement is the starting point for discussing **mentoring** – people helping people. Some of the more positive terms associated with the term mentoring include *counselor, consultant, expert, referee, advocate, motivator, guide,* and *teacher.* Applebaum, Ritchie, and Shapiro (1994) point out that there is a close relationship between mentoring and leadership, but the defining characteristics are elusive. Mentoring provides opportunities for seasoned leaders to counsel and guide aspiring leaders in the nuances of successful organizational processes. Nonprofit organizations that provide successful mentoring activities can benefit immensely from the results. Perhaps mentoring is best understood in terms of the relationship that exists, or should exist, between or among organizational members. For effective mentoring to occur in an organization, four desirable qualities must exist: **caring**, **sharing**, **correcting**, and **connecting** (Gantt 1997):

- **Caring** involves a genuine concern for the well-being of others. For true mentoring to occur, the individual being mentored should feel that the mentor is highly concerned for his or her growth as a person and a leader. Successful mentors accept individuals for themselves, but recognize their potential and will work with them to achieve high results.

- **Sharing** suggests helping a person to become knowledgeable in any and all areas relevant to the successful operation of the organization. This might also include the sharing of information that could help an individual avoid making mistakes. While learning from mistakes is important, it can also be detrimental if those mistakes are significant. Sharing some information can be risky, and the information could be used against the mentor, or in some other harmful way, so the mentoring process should be undertaken carefully.

- **Correcting** implies that a mentor should be able and willing to point out mistakes, misperceptions, and incorrect assumptions. Since correcting is sometimes associated with criticizing, it must be handled carefully. The way in which situations are addressed may be just as important as the subject matter addressed, and an employee being mentored should feel that the mentor is addressing a specific situation for the benefit of the organization and the development of the employee. Correcting is about helping a person change, not about punishing someone for making a mistake.

- **Connecting** means having an active level of consideration for whom a mentee needs to know or meet in order to be successful in the organization and which activities an employee should be involved in for professional growth.

When all four of these qualities exist in an organization, learning can best occur. When learning occurs, the employee is actively developing, and the organization benefits from this development, as do all of those served by the organization. According to Appelbaum, et al. (1994,6), "First, a positive correlation exists between mentoring and career commitment. Second, a negative correlation exists between mentoring and dissatisfaction manifested in absenteeism, turnover and plateauing." These statements imply that everyone benefits from the process of mentoring.

In one CBS television series, "The District," the main character, Mannion, is a modern, technology-savvy police chief in Washington, D.C. He begins his new job as chief by demanding professionalism and the use of modern technology for a troubled and traditional police department. Although Ella, the person he hires to develop and run his new technology, is very capable, she lacks confidence and is burdened with personal problems. Mannion supports her and assures her she is critical to the success of the department. Ella begins to trust his confidence in her, and grows in competence and confidence herself. She comes to accept the fact that when Mannion corrects her, it is because he cares about her and about her advancement within the organization.

Mentoring is a highly important companion to leadership. A leader must be able and willing to provide mentoring to aspiring leaders for the sake of their development and for the continued growth of the organization.

■ Developing Leaders through Service Learning

Another way of developing leaders is by providing individuals with activities that offer the opportunity for skill and character development through an experiential learning process. **Service learning** is a field experience that combines community service with various learning objectives (Weis and Gantt 2002). It is a way in which individuals can perform meaningful service to the community while incorporating theoretical constructs that can include skill and/or character development. It is a process that combines community service with personal growth, learning, and civic responsibility. Individuals learn and develop by using newly acquired knowledge and skills in actual community situations; this helps them develop a sense of caring and responsibility for others.

One example of a service learning project might involve a college class that is learning about program development and financial processes in nonprofit organizations. As a service learning project, the class members could incorporate what they have learned in class to plan a college day event for 8th grade students to attend college for a day and thereby begin to understand better what college life is like.

Another example might involve teenagers in a YMCA leadership club who have had workshops on responsibility and caring, followed by participating in a clean-up day for senior citizens.

In each of these activities, individuals take information that they have learned in a classroom setting and put it to use in a community service setting. The individual recipients of the service benefit from the activity, the service providers benefit from an enhanced learning process, and the community in general becomes stronger.

A slightly different version of a service learning project would take place when nonprofit staff members incorporate what they have learned as professional staff members to participate as board members or in other service capacities with various nonprofit organizations.

Research on the effects of service learning indicates a number of positive benefits, several of which are included below (Cairn and Kielsmeier 1991).

- **Personal Growth.** Individuals who participate in service learning activities exhibit an increased sense of self-esteem and self-efficacy (the feeling that you are making a difference in someone's life).
- **Career Development.** Participating in service learning activities increases understanding of the world of work, as well as providing a familiarity with and knowledge of specific job skills. This exploration may provide individuals with greater confidence when making a career choice.
- **Social Development.** Service learning offers numerous opportunities for interacting with others, therefore enhancing interpersonal skills. Working with people from different backgrounds may also increase tolerance and support for diversity.
- **Cognitive/Academic Development.** Service learning provides individuals with situations to practice problem solving and critical thinking skills. Grades often improve in academic settings and individuals generally believe service learning is a positive learning experience.

Most studies regarding service learning have been conducted in an academic setting. One such study involved 24,000 K-12 grade students participating in the Learn & Serve

America program in Florida. In this study, GPAs improved for most of the students, attendance improved and disciplinary referrals declined during the program period (Follman and Muldoon 1997).

In another study at the University of Michigan, political science students in an experimental group with twenty hours of service to the community earned better grades than students in a similar class, but without the service requirement (Markus, Howard and King 1995).

A study at Murray State University compared students in a service learning experimental group with a control group who were not involved in service projects and found the students in the experimental group felt a stronger sense of achieving something important in their lives as well as a stronger sense that they had made a positive contribution to the community. The service providers felt that what they did made a difference for the population they served and for the community, as well as for themselves (Weis 1998).

The many benefits derived from service learning can be very useful in developing skill areas as well as character attributes important in leadership development. Introducing service learning projects into an organization or educational institution can be both exciting and challenging. Although there is not a definite set of criteria, guidelines developed at the Lowell Bennion Community Center at the University of Utah reflect classic service learning components and are listed next (Lowell Bennion Community Service Center 1996).

- Service should be directed toward an understandable need in the community.
- The service learning experience must involve learning components.
- Service providers should have a chance to learn from each other, as well as from the instructor, during the experience.
- In an academic setting, students can be evaluated on their experience through journals, papers, or other methods of assessment. Credit should be given for the learning as well as for the service component of the experience.
- Service recipients can also be given an opportunity to evaluate the service project.

Service learning is like a laboratory in which character and skills relevant to effective leadership can develop under supervision, while important needs in the community can be addressed.

∎ Summary

Leadership in the nonprofit sector means strengthening individuals and communities by developing influence through collaborative and trusting relationships. Good leaders guide, direct, and influence others to reach higher and higher goals. A combination of characteristics and criteria is necessary for successful leadership. Leaders become leaders by a number of methods including appointment, election, emergence, and charisma. It is suggested that one way that leaders influence the behavior of others is by using personal powers, including referent power, legitimate power, expert power, reward power, and coercive power. To be a good leader, it is important to understand some of the reasons that individuals follow others. Reasons such as efficiency, satisfaction, and experience are worth examination.

For a better understanding of the concept of leadership, the authors have incorporated a framework of classic theories, beginning with the Classic Organizational Theory that is based on a scientific approach to getting things done. The Great Man Theory suggests that leaders emerge and develop as a product of the times in which they live. The Group Theory states that there are roles to be filled and specific traits that are important for effective leadership to occur. The Trait Theory includes a list of personal traits necessary for successful leadership, and the Behavior Theory implies that leadership is a pattern of interpersonal processes with a goal of influencing the group. The Trait Theory implies that individuals should take situational variables into account when selecting a leadership style. Another important theory, the Humanistic Theory, signifies the leader as someone who encourages others to reach their full potential. The Excellence Theory implies that individuals and organizations can be transformed to higher levels of excellence, and finally, the Principle Theory is a values-centered concept for effective leadership.

Over the years, large numbers of studies have been undertaken to explain leadership more fully. The Lewin, Lippit, and White studies were helpful in determining classic styles of leadership such as Authoritative, Democratic, and Laissez-Faire. The Ohio State studies identified two different dimensions of leadership – initiating structure and consideration. The New Managerial Grid places achievement and people along two axes. The University of Michigan study places the same two components, achievement and people, on a continuum relevant to the situation.

The Transactional Leadership Model is based on the social exchange theory, and the Transformational Leadership Model suggests that leaders can work with others in such a way that both leaders and followers are transformed to higher levels of achievement and morality. The Tri-Dimensional Leader Effectiveness Model combines the level of maturity of the employee with the demands of the situation. Hitt's Model of Leadership combines the importance of leadership and vision, and Collaborative Leadership implies team-building and turn-taking in various situations. Finally, the Comprehensive Approach to leadership is suggested in considering differing styles of leading, depending on the circumstances.

Too often, leadership models fail to include the importance of character and ethics in the overall scheme of leading and influencing others. The Integrated Leadership and Character Model was developed to discuss the importance of character in leadership. The model emphasizes the importance of three interrelated skill areas—conceptual, technical, and human relations—and the significance personal character has in the effectiveness of these three areas. Personal character is made up of traits and values, including trustworthiness, respect, fairness, caring and citizenship. Putting values to work is the role of ethics, and it is suggested that an ethical culture can be created in a nonprofit organization by emphasizing five ethical obligations: integrity, openness, accountability, service, and charity.

It has been stated that leadership cannot be taught, but must be learned by individual examination and experience. Several ways to accomplish this would include studying the lives of leaders through the ages, being a part of a mentoring program, and participating in service learning activities. Studying leaders such as Lao-Tzu, Plato, Aristotle, Niccolo Machiavelli, Thomas Jefferson, Harriett Tubman, Clara Barton, Geronimo, George A. Custer, W.E.B. Du Bois, Mohandas Gandhi, Helen Keller, and Cesar Chavez can provide insight for a variety of leadership approaches.

Being a part of a mentoring plan can encourage aspiring leaders through qualities of caring, sharing, correcting, and connecting. And finally, service learning, a field experience that combines community service with various learning objectives, provides individuals with opportunities to practice skills and develop character while addressing important needs in the community.

This chapter addressed, in part, the American Humanics Certification Competency Requirements of Personal Attributes, Human Resources Development and Supervision, and General Nonprofit Management.

∎ Discussion Questions

1. Describe your concept of leadership.
2. What is the significance of a leader-manager?
3. Why is empowerment so important? Have you empowered someone? Has someone empowered you?
4. List individuals who have influenced you. What were some of their characteristics?
5. Discuss ways in which leaders become leaders.
6. Explain the Classical Organizational theory of leadership? Great Man theory? Group theory? Trait theory? Situational Theory? Principle theory?
7. How do Transactional and Transformational leadership differ?
8. Describe how you might incorporate the Collaborative Leadership concept in your overall style of leading? The Comprehensive Approach?
9. What is the significance of the Integrated Leadership and Character models?
10. What are some characteristics of Geronimo you might incorporate in your leadership style? Tubman? Keller? Chavez?
11. What is one characteristic of Custer you liked most, and least? Explain.
12. Why is mentoring important in leadership development? Service learning?

∎ Activities

1. Ask each person in class to select someone who has influenced his or her life; then discuss that person's leadership characteristics.
2. Discuss "powers," and then ask each person to consider a supervisor they've had, and list that person's powers in the order of use. Assess each profile. Ask each person to list his or her own powers in order of priority and explain. List each power and identify a U.S. president who has led with that particular power. Rent the movie "Dave," and then show the class scenes from when Dave meets the little boy in the homeless shelter to the scene where the president's wife is interrupted by his security guard (approximately 14 minutes). Ask class members to identify Dave's use of different powers.
3. Develop a scenario in which you incorporate the Comprehensive Approach to Leadership.
4. Select one of the leaders from the section on biographies and do an in-depth Critique, incorporating leadership concepts in the critique.
5. Develop a "mentoring" program, and incorporate the concepts from this chapter.
6. Design and develop a service learning activity as a part of the class.

■ References

Belasco, J. A., and Stayer, R. C. (1993). *Flight of the Buffalo*. New York: Warner.

Bennis, W., and Townsend, R. (1995). *Reinventing Leadership*. New York: Morrow

Blake, R. R., and Mouton, J. S. (1978). *The New Managerial Grid*. Houston: Gulf.

Boylson, H. D. (1955). *Clara Barton: Founder of the American Red Cross*. New York: Random House.

Burns, J. M. (1978). *Leadership*. New York: Harper and Row.

Connell, E. S. (1984). *Son of the Morning Star*. New York: Harper and Row.

Constantinides, H. (2001). The duality of scientific ethos: deep and surface structures. *Quarterly Journal of Speech*. February 87(1).

Covey, Stephen R. (1989). *The Seven Habits of Highly Effective People*. New York: Simon and Schuster.

Debo, A. (1976). *Geronimo: The Man, His Time, His Place*. Norman: University of Oklahoma Press.

Edginton, C.R., Hudson, S.D., and Ford, P.M. (1999). *Leadership in Recreation and Leisure Service Organizations*. 2nd edition. Champaign, IL: Sagamore Publishing.

English, Fenwick W. (1992). *Educational Administration: The Human Science*. New York: Harper Collins Publishing Company.

Epler, P. H. (1919). *The Life of Clara Barton*. New York: Macmillan Company.

Fiedler, F. (1967). *A Theory of Leadership Effectiveness*. New York: Macmillan Company.

French, J. P. P., Jr. and Raven, B. (1959). *The Basis of Social Power*. In D. Cartwright, ed. *Studies in Social Power*. Ann Arbor, MI: Institute for Social Research.

Gantt, V. W. (1997). Beneficial mentoring is for everyone: a reaction paper. Paper presented at the November 1987 National Communications Association Convention Chicago.

Hardy, J.M. (1984). *Managing for Impact in Nonprofit Organizations*. Erwin, TN: Essex Press.

Hersey, P., and Blanchard, K. (1977). *Management of Organizational Behavior-utilizing Human Resources*. 3rd edition. Englewood Cliffs, NJ: Prentice-Hall.

Hesselbein, F. (1996). A star to steer by. *Leader to Leader* (Premier Issue).

Hitt, W. D. (1988). *The Leader Manager: Guidelines for Action*. Columbus, OH: Battelle Press.

Holander, E. P. (1978). What is the crisis of leadership? *Humanitas*. 14(3), 285-296.

Homans, G. C. (1950). *The Human Group*. New York: Harcourt, Brace and World.

Horwitt, S. D. (1989). *Let Them Call Me Rebel*. New York: Alfred A. Knopf.

Independent Sector (2001). *What You Should Know About Nonprofits*. Washington, DC

Independent Sector (2002). *The New Nonprofit Almanac In Brief*. Washington, DC

Jeavons, T. H. (1992). When management is the message: relating values to management practice in nonprofit organizations. *Nonprofit Management and Leadership*.

Jeavons, T.H. (1994). Ethics in nonprofit management: creating a culture of integrity. In *The Jossey-Bass Handbook of Nonprofit Leadership and Management*. R. Herman, ed. San Francisco: Jossey-Bass.

Katz, D., Maccoby, N., and Morse, N. C. (1950). *Productivity, Supervision, and Morale in an Office Situation*. Ann Arbor: Survey Research Center, University of Michigan.

Koch, A., and Peden, P. (1993). *The Life and Selected Writings of Thomas Jefferson*. New York: Random House.

Kouzes, J., and Posner, B. (1995). *The Leadership Challenge: How to Keep Getting Extraordinary Things Done in Organizations*. San Francisco: Jossey-Bass.

Levy, J.E. (1975). *Cesar Chavez: Autobiography of La Causa*. New York: W.W. Norton and Company, Inc.

Lewin, K., Libbin, R., and White, R. K. (1939). Patterns of aggressive behavior in experimentally created social climates. *Journal of Social Psychology*, (May).

Luthans, F. (1967). *The Human Organization*. New York: McGraw-Hill.

Mason, D. E. (1992b) Ethics and the nonprofit leader. *Nonprofit World*.

Parkinson, R. (1980). *Zapata*. New York: Stein and Day Publishers.

Peters, T. J., and Waterman, R. H. (1982). *In Search of Excellence*. New York: Harper and Row.

Petry, A. (1955). *Harriett Tubman*. New York: Thomas Y. Crowell Company.

Reddin, W. J. (1970). *Managerial Effectiveness*. New York: McGraw-Hill.

Richards, N. (1968). *People of Destiny. Helen Keller.* Chicago: Children's Press.

Rost, J. C. (1993). *Leadership for the Twenty-first Century*. Westport, CT: Praeger.

Sessoms, H. D., and Stevenson, J. L. (1981). *Leadership and Group Dynamics in Recreation Services*. Boston: Allyn and Bacon.

Shivers, J. S. (1980). *Recreational Leadership: Group Dynamics and Interpersonal Behavior*. Princeton, NJ: Princeton Books.

Stogdill, R. (1974). *Handbook of Leadership: A Survey of Theory and Research*. New York: Macmillan Company.

Stogdill, R., and Coons, A. (1957). *Leader Behavior's Description and Measurement*. Columbus: Bureau of Business Research, Ohio State University.

Tannenbaum, R., and Schmnidt, W. H. (1973). How to choose a leadership pattern. *Harvard Business Review*, (May-June).

Taylor, F. W. (1967). *The Principles of Scientific Management*. New York: W. W. Norton and Company, Inc.

Utley, R.M. (1988). *Cavalier in Buckskin*. Norman: University of Oklahoma Press.

Weis, R. M. (1996). *A Lifetime of Making a Difference: A Student Manual for Career Planning in Youth, Human Service and Other Nonprofit Organizations*. Kansas, City, MO: Clevenger and Company.

Weis, R. (1998). *Service Learning Training Manual for Faculty K-16*. Murray, KY: American Humanics, Murray State University.

Weis, R., and Gantt, V. (2002). *Leadership and Program Development in Nonprofit Organizations*. Peosta, IA: Eddie Bowers Publishing Company.

Wolf, Thomas (1999). *Managing a Nonprofit Organization*. New York: Prentice Hall Press.

Wren, J. Thomas (1995). *The Leader's Companion*. New York: The Free Press.

3 Staff, Board and Volunteers: Leading Agencies Effectively

Many people look at nonprofit organizations and see small for-profit organizations and try to suggest that nonprofits need to be organized and run in the same way as a for-profit. While all organizations share many qualities and characteristics, there is a vast difference between the nonprofit and for-profit worlds. What is successful in one world will not automatically succeed in the other. What is good for General Motors may not be good for the American Red Cross. Much, if not most, of the product or service delivered by the for-profit organization is "created" through advertising and marketing. In the nonprofit world, most, if not all, of the services delivered result from an individual or community "need." The very assumptions about why organizations exist and the core values are very different. For-profit organizations exist, first and foremost, to make a profit. They are profitable or they die. Nonprofit organizations exit to help people. They help people or they die. While this characterization is really an oversimplification, it is necessary to set the stage for viewing the similarities that matter and the differences that matter when it comes to staff, board and volunteer fundamentals.

All organizations depend on the successful integration of three key components: people, resources, and a service or product. No matter how important or needed the product or service of an organization, the absence of appropriate resources or qualified and motivated people will cause the organization to struggle and ultimately to fail. It might help to visualize any organization as a stool sitting on three legs (one for people, another for resources, and another for the product or service). The seat represents the organization's mission or reason for being. If one leg is missing, weak, or flawed, the seat of the stool will be adversely affected. Ultimately, it will fail to support its share of the weight of the mission. A successful nonprofit organization, like any organization, must have three strong legs for its stool to do the job for which it was intended.

Within the people component, for nonprofits, there is another three-legged stool. Those legs consist of the **staff**, the **board** and the **volunteers**. If any group is ineffective, less effective than needed or just not willing to live up to its potential, the whole organization is at risk.

When looking for answers, people often turn to principles that stand the test of time: Choose a busy person to get the job done. Do to others as you would have them do to you. Walk softly and carry a big stick. While each of these statements has value, no one time-tested principle works in every case. One reason for this is that psychologists tell us that every person is unique. There is no one exactly like us! With 5 billion unique human beings in the world, what is a person to do? People do fall into general categories when it comes to the type of interaction they desire when interacting with others, desired working conditions, and reactions to very stressful situations. There are many tools that help supervisors understand the general categories. One of those tools is the **Personal Profile Preview™** (1994). The research by the developers of the Personal Profile shows that people fall into four general interaction styles with all four styles interacting to produce a highly predictive tool for what happens when people interact at work, at home or at play. The four styles are these:

- **Dominance** – People who emphasize this style like to solve problems and get immediate results, question current methods, and enjoy independence and varied tasks.
- **Influence** – People who emphasize this style enjoy persuading and influencing others, are highly verbal and open to expressing feelings, and prefer to work with others.
- **Steadiness** – People who emphasize this style prefer a stable and organized work climate, usually are patient and listen well, and enjoy working in groups more than directing others.
- **Conscientiousness** – People who emphasize this style want to achieve high personal standards, carefully weigh all sides of an issue, are diplomatic, and desire clearly defined expectations with no surprises.

The implications for working relationships as they relate to these four styles will be discussed later in this chapter.

It is possible that the greatest risk of all is to offer suggestions as to how others can best do their jobs. It always seems easy to give advice to others. The advice tends not to work in the real world, however. The best way to view suggestions from others is to consider the suggestion as a choice rather than an answer. There is a line in the 2002 movie "Solaris," when the lead character is trying to determine whether his true love is real or a figment of his imagination. He is told by a space station veteran that "There are no answers, only choices."

In this chapter, we will examine each group of people – staff, board, volunteers (their roles and how to recruit the best people); make suggestions as to how best to assure the success of each group (how to integrate the roles of each group and how to evaluate each group); and explore the communication skills needed by an executive director or supervisor to insure a solid, effective stool (through evaluation and re-direction).

First, we will discuss the role of the Executive Director (ED) /Chief Executive Officer (CEO) in selecting and leading people. Leadership is much more a matter of character than a matter of certain qualities (Weis and Gantt 2002). Leadership qualities are critical, but leadership qualities alone cannot do the job without character. In the nonprofit arena, anyone can be a true leader. Martin Luther King, Jr., put it this way, "Everyone can be great because anyone can serve. You don't have to have a college degree to serve. You don't even have to make your subject and your verb agree to serve. . . .You only need a heart full of grace. A soul generated by love." However, not everyone who serves effectively can lead a nonprofit agency. What is expected of the ED/CEO?

Even with regard to great character, experience and research teach us that certain skills, strategies and attributes help define what employees consider to be a successful leader. A better word for leader, in this context, might be mentor. Being a good boss, someone that people enjoy working for and with, should be the goal of every ED/CEO. How can an ED/CEO get the job done for the agency, the board, the clients, the staff and the volunteers? There are six key qualities:

- **A person who works to ensure a feeling of inclusion** – The "good" boss treats people fairly but not necessarily the same. He or she seeks feedback, rather than just accepting it graciously, and encourages innovation and creativity as long as it is true to the agency's mission. An ED/CEO should want all staff, volunteers and board members to be engaged and feel as though they are a part of the "business" of the agency. People don't feel included or think they have voice (being heard) in an organization by accident. A feeling of inclusion is produced for staff, clients, volunteers, and board members by action, by effort. Inclusion is felt when there is an environment of trust and respect where every effort is made to treat people fairly.

- **A person with a sense of mission** – Every agency needs to do something well. The ED/CEO should set the agenda for what the agency wants to be known for in the community. It may be a service – hot meals, on time by Meals on Wheels. It may be an attitude – compassion and caring from Hospice. The ED/CEO must be a good "business" person, but to be known only as a person who runs a "tight" ship is not inspirational for staff and volunteers. Organizational skills are crucial for agency leaders, but there must be a touch of humanity and compassion. People want to work with and for someone who goes about doing the "right thing."

- **A desire to learn and promote learning** – The freedom to make mistakes is a powerful freedom. The ED/CEO who allows staff and volunteers to learn from their own mistakes is a person who will go a long way toward his or her own success. We grow as we learn. To stop learning is to stop growing and eventually to die professionally and intellectually. An ED/CEO must be willing to learn in order to encourage learning. New ideas and new technology are not just for the new employees; they are for everyone, even the volunteers. True learning can't be forced. It can be encouraged and rewarded.

- **A coach, counselor, mentor** – The very best ED/CEOs are the ones who **help** staff, volunteers and board members become the best they can be. It takes less time to help a person grow than it does to correct errors, smooth over hurt feelings or repair damaged relationships. In the long run, an ED/CEO must view coaching, counseling and mentoring as *investment time*, not lost time.

- **A person who helps everyone position for advancement** – A successful leader understands the rewards of helping another person to succeed. He or she should avoid any suggestion of jealousy or any actions which would hold someone back or slow someone else's career development. If every person in an agency is prepared to advance, the agency will have a great pool of qualified and motivated people for its future. If only select people are prepared, the agency suffers. People may not be ready to advance when they are needed. Also, if there is no clear career path, the best people will find another agency to work for. They will find a way to succeed in spite of all efforts to hold them back.

- **A person who personally learns from mistakes** – The best way to demonstrate that an agency values learning from mistakes is for the ED/CEO to learn from his or her mistakes in a very public way. He or she should admit mistakes, talk about what was learned and encourage others to talk about what they have learned from their mistakes. This is a sign of strength and not of weakness.

With the qualities of an effective ED/CEO in mind, what is the nature and function of those who make up the rest of the organization – staff, board and volunteers?

■ Human Resource Management

In the world and work of a nonprofit agency, people make or break the organization. Without good people, the most needed service can be underutilized. A great vision can be thwarted by an ineffective board. A visionary executive director can be undermined by a staff unwilling or unable to keep pace with the changing nature of a dynamic community. A committed and dedicated staff can be frustrated and rendered impotent by an agency head who will not allow them to do their job. It is easy to identify what can go wrong. How can all these very different and very capable human resources be melded together to produce a useful, dynamic, vision-driven nonprofit organization that can make a difference in the lives of people who need help? See **Appendix D**, 335, for a sample organizational chart.

Staff

The **staff** of any organization often has more to do with the ultimate success of the organization than does the designated leader. While the vision and direction of the organization are the responsibility of the leader, it is the day-to-day function of any organization that determines its success. The key to day-to-function is the quality of the work of the paid staff. Fully developed **job descriptions** must exist for every paid position in the organization. All job descriptions should consist of **seven elements** – *position title, purpose of the position, credential requirements, individual to whom the position reports, responsibilities of the position, specific duties of the position, and evaluation timetable along with the criteria for that evaluation.*

The **seven most critical issues** with respect to staffing an organization are *recruitment, selection, hiring, training, evaluation, termination, and retention.*

- **Recruitment**

    This step involves positioning the agency to be seen as a desirable place to work. If the agency image in the community is positive, it is much easier to attract the best applicants for positions. Every action of an agency is part of this activity of positioning. Positive activities produce positive perceptions by the community and potential employees for the organization.

    First, the best source of the "right" person for the position is people who know the organization and what is required for the position – other staff, board members, satisfied clients, and financial supports. The only danger here is that some of these people may recommend people based on their relationship with the person, rather than what is best for the agency. This type of recommendation should not necessarily be rejected, without considering the suggestion on the basis of its merit.

    Second, it is a good idea to network with other nonprofit professionals and ask for any suggestions they may have. Often, a person who is not "right" for one agency is perfect for another. Networking can extend beyond the immediate community to surrounding communities and can include contacts within for-profit organizations. At times, highly qualified people want a change of scenery and will trade the for-profit world for the nonprofit world. People who are burned out should be avoided, but those who want to "make a difference" in the world should definitely be considered.

Third, advertising within agency publications—newsletters, job listings, and journals—is often very successful. Local newspapers, radio and television all help to get the word out.

Fourth, the whole community contains prospects and recruitment possibilities. It is easy to learn about new companies coming to the community by reading the newspaper, listening to the radio, and watching television. It is also helpful to watch the performance of volunteers in other agencies. A good volunteer for one agency could be an even better paid staff member for another agency.

- **Selection**

    The next step is to select the persons who will be interviewed. Each candidate's credentials should be compared with the requirements listed in the **job description**. If no one has the credentials to do the job, the search must continue. A position should never be filled with an obviously inadequate candidate. Instead, the organization should cover the position as well as it can until a suitable person is found.

    Before a careful selection can be made, **three criteria** must be clearly determined: what training/education is required, what level of experience is required, and what personal qualities are required. These three should be a part of the **credential requirements** listed in the job description.

    All necessary background checks should be completed at this stage. A careful check of references can be a significant factor in making the "right" choice and reducing risks. The general process of **risk management** is discussed in detail in **Chapter 7**. Selecting the wrong person can be very costly to an agency. Risk reduction is a critical consideration. No agency wants to risk exposing its clients to potential physical harm, and no agency wants to risk being accused of unfair or biased hiring practices. Every applicant deserves full and fair consideration, but the agency must also protect its clients and itself.

- **Hiring**

    The best indication of future behavior is past behavior. The interview must be constructed to determine **three** things: *Are the credentials accurate? Will the person fit with others in the agency? Does the person's work experience predict success in the position being filled?*

    The more care taken at this stage, the more likely it is that the new employee will become an old employee. Mistakes made by not being careful here tend to turn into bigger problems as time goes on. Firing someone is never easy. It is much better to hire well.

- **Training**

    Organizational training should be considered an investment, not a cost. An organization should hire for attitude and train for skills. The time spent and possible expenditure of funds involved for new and continuing staff training is essential for any agency to continue to deliver effective service.

    Training new staff in the "agency way" helps everyone understand and adjust to the changes that will occur when a new person or new people enter an agency. Training must be presented to employees in such a way as to enhance productivity or to meet legal requirements. Training for the sake of training is rarely useful. People must find training useful for it to be worthwhile.

    When training is built into a mentoring process, it is often more effective and more relevant. Training inside the mentoring process tends to be delivered when and where it is needed, not on an arbitrary time schedule that meets the agenda of the trainer.

- **Evaluation**

    In the ideal world, evaluation should be an ongoing **process**. When evaluation is treated as an event, rather than a **process**, problems tend to arise. Even when a person is given a six-month probation period, he or she should not have to wait six months to learn that there are performance problems. **Evaluation** is the comparison of expectations to actual performance. Assessment should occur daily.

    With a well-written job description and daily interaction about expectations and observed performance, evaluation is simple. If problems arise that are not covered by the job description, they must be addressed immediately and agreement reached as to how the issue will be addressed.

- **Termination**

    Anyone associated with an agency can be asked to leave. While an agency leader is well advised to work to get the best out of everyone – staff, board members and other volunteers, some people are just not right for some organizations. When a person is asked to leave an agency because they can't get along with others, it can reflect very badly on a leader's ability to mentor and monitor staff or volunteers.

    Effective leaders must find a way to help all agency personnel do the best they can to meet the mission of the agency. When that is done, everyone benefits. The payoff is worth the effort.

    Anyone can be terminated for any reason if there is no employment agreement. However, everyone from staff to volunteer should know that there is a problem and efforts should be made and sufficient time spent to correct problems. No person should ever be surprised with a notice of termination, regardless of the seriousness of the reason.

If termination is necessary for someone who has an employment agreement with an organization, there are **three justifications** for ending an employment agreement: *incompetence, violating agency rules, and violating local, state or federal laws*. A person who cannot perform the required task after due training and coaching may be dismissed. A person who violates agency rules by leaving young children unattended in a dangerous location may be dismissed. A person who traffics in drugs or firearms may be dismissed.

- **Retention**

Efforts made to retain effective staff are never wasted. The key is to give people meaningful work to do, appreciate them for what they add to the success of the agency, and reward them for a job well done. Retention is also an issue for board members and volunteers.

The relationship an ED/CEO establishes with each staff member, each board member, and each volunteer is critical to the success of the agency's mission. Since human beings are so adaptable and resilient, the importance of relationship is often downplayed. A positive relationship with a staff member is icing on the cake, not a paramount goal. Few people enjoy cake without icing. True? Why, then. would an ED/CEO or any supervisor consider "icing" as unimportant?

Naisbitt and Aburdene (1985) report research that points to a view of "icing" that is a little different from the way many people view it. They report ten qualities that people want in their work – for-profit or nonprofit. High pay, good benefits, and job security are not in the top ten. They are in the top fifteen. Here is what research suggests that people want from their work and workplace:
- to work with people who treat them with respect
- to have interesting work
- to receive recognition for good work
- to have a chance to develop skills
- to work for people who listen if they have ideas about how to do things better
- to have a chance to think for themselves rather than just carry out instructions
- to see the end result of their work
- to work for efficient supervisors/managers
- to have a job/task that is not too easy
- to think they are well-informed about what is going on (85-86)

While the order of these qualities could vary among staff and volunteers, all ten represent what people want to see if they are to consider their work rewarding and meaningful. Can a person do well without these qualities? Certainly. The better question is what kind of organization would want to be known as an organization that provides for its staff the kind of environment where these qualities are absent. In fact, Levering and Moskowitz (2003) write in the January 7 issue of *Fortune* that the one hundred best companies to work for are expanding and increasing benefits, in spite of difficult economic times.

What is the proper way to establish an **appropriate relationship** with others? An appropriate relationship is open, honest, caring and genuine. Appropriate relationships are professional. They are two-way, joint ventures. Both parties must desire to participate and see reward from participation. Openness includes the opportunity to talk freely and express feelings and ideas. Honesty requires that each person be willing to discuss difficult issues and share views even when different, but this must be done with compassion and sensitivity. Caring is best shown by attentive listening to another and especially listening to how a person feels, not just to what a person thinks. Being genuine is shown by actually living the other three, and this is best shown by taking time to learn about and from another, admit mistakes, enjoy common good times, and share times of sadness or disappointment. A healthy relationship requires frequent and focused work to keep it going.

How does a person know if a relationship is decaying? While each relationship will have its own unique qualities and characteristics, signs of decay can help anyone take stock of any relationship so that discussion can occur. If a relationship appears to be changing, one might ask some questions: Is the change a natural and maturing progression? Is it really changing? Is the change comfortable? Is it uncomfortable?

Here is a list of "signs" of a decaying relationship. These signs can be adapted and applied to any relationship – personal or professional:
- Shorter encounters
- Increasing physical distance between parties
- Increasing time between interactions
- Less personal information exchanged
- Less relationship talk
- Fewer favors given and/or asked for
- More negative evaluations and absolutistic statements and fewer positive superlatives
- Less nonverbal immediacy – less eye contact, colder vocal tone
- Increasing concern for self, rather than for the other person or the relationship
- Less compromise due to increasing win-lose orientation
- More individual activities, rather than mutual activities
- Return to more formal language and formal etiquette, instead of comfortable, informal language and action

If relationships are sound and appropriate, an organization will prosper. If relationships are neglected or ignored, an organization will suffer. This is just as true of board relationships and volunteer relationships as it is of staff relationships.

Board of Directors

A board of directors, board of trustees, or administrative committee, hereafter referred to as the **board**, is common to nonprofit and for-profit organizations. The board serves to monitor organizational operation, set and adjust policies, and assure the financial support for the programs and personnel of the organization. The board is responsible for approving the direction, mission (or vision) of the organization; assessing the fit of programs with the organizational mission; approving budgets; and evaluating the effectiveness of the organization's programs in meeting the organization's mission (Widmer and Houchin, 2000).

Since these individuals work without pay, usually, they are volunteers. They are, in fact, key volunteers. Their role is important, but not more important than any other group in the agency – staff or other volunteers. They, in fact, need to be examined for inclusion on the agency team in the same way as would be done for staff and other volunteers.

All boards have legal responsibilities, represent an interested community constituency, monitor agency operations, and assist in raising necessary funds. We will examine each of these four broad categories in more detail.

Legal and fiduciary responsibilities include attending to local, state and federal laws that impact the operation of the agency. Board members must also guard against misuse of the assets of the organization. If something goes wrong in either area, a board member cannot claim ignorance as a defense. The law assumes the individuals will exercise due diligence when making decisions that contain legal or financial stewardship implications. In legal terminology, all board members have the ***duty of care*** (due care) which is usually defined as the "care that an ordinarily prudent person would exercise in a like position and under similar circumstances" (*Black's Law Dictionary* 499).

Representational responsibilities include acting in the best interests of all who receive benefit from the agency. Each board member should give **voice** to one or more of the groups or viewpoints served by the agency. In addition to a particular expertise (financial, visioning, advocacy, etc.) that a board member brings to the group, members should represent and give voice to those served. Great care must be taken to make sure the board members have the skills necessary for a board to do its job well. Every board should have members who have strong financial backgrounds, others who have knowledge of the laws governing nonprofits, others with strong programming experience, and others with fund raising skills—all with strong ties to the community and genuine interest in the agency's success. A board member is never to receive personal benefit from board membership. This is a part of a board member's ***duty of loyalty***, which is the legal standard of fairness. Said in another way, a board member must be true to the interests of the organization when making decisions that affect that organization.

Monitoring duties include assuring that the organization is effectively and efficiently run. This is part of the board member's ***duty of obedience*** in terms of each member's legal duty to be faithful to the organization's mission. The board is responsible for hiring and firing the agency head. It is also responsible for evaluating the agency head periodically and providing him or her with constructive feedback. If changes need to be made, the board must clearly spell out what action is expected and in what time frame. The board must then follow up on the action plan and timetable for improvement.

Financial support responsibility does not mean that board members must fund the organization personally. They should only be asked to participate on the board if they have already demonstrated their belief in the mission of the organization by offering some financial support. Their most important role, aside from making sure the organization adheres to local, state, and federal legal requirements and remains solvent, is to be a lightning rod for donors. In other words, the board must set an example for the community and help those responsible for fund raising to make contact with community members who are capable of making meaningful contributions. It must also support and speak for the organization's mission in such a way as to generate a positive image for the organization among potential donors.

The members of the board represent various groups and constituents from the community. They are further assigned specific roles on the board as officers or committee members. Most often, there are four board officers: **president, vice-president, secretary, and treasurer**. The duties of each office are the same as they would be for any organization. Specific or special responsibilities may be added due to the nature or mission of the organization. Officers should be eligible for re-election, but there should be some reasonable term limits or rotation of members through offices. This is not always practical. For example, the skills of the person who serves as treasurer or secretary may not be shared by all members of the board. Whatever system is chosen, a board does not need to be taken hostage by one or a few members and controlled for satisfaction of their egos over the best interests of the agency. A dominating board leader can destroy the effectiveness of an agency.

The **president** is responsible for running meetings, assuring that board members receive the information to discharge their duties, appointing committees as prescribed in the organization's governing documents, presiding over executive committee meetings, speaking for the organization as is appropriate and leading the annual review of the executive director.

The **vice-president** assumes the duties of the president when he or she is unable to discharge those duties. The vice-president serves on committees as appointed by the president and represents the agency at public meetings, when appropriate. This person is often the next one to serve as president of the board. Such a process allows a person to prepare for the position of president with proper orientation and training. This process is often employed by civic organizations, such as Rotary Clubs, to ensure a smooth transition of leadership.

The principle function of the **secretary** of the board is to maintain accurate minutes of all board meetings. This is critical, since in legal terms a board speaks through its minutes. The signed minutes must report all significant actions of the board. These minutes must be prepared in a timely fashion and distributed to all board members and other affected parties. Taking attendance for all meetings is also the secretary's duty, as is the responsibility for the safekeeping of all official board records and documents.

The **treasurer** monitors the financial business of the agency to assure that sound and accepted accounting procedures are adhered to and that annual, external audits are conducted and reported to the board. This officer must keep in touch with day-to-day fiscal activities of the agency. Legal and governmental regulations must be observed with respect to payroll and other financial obligations of the agency.

An effective board is organized into **committees** to divide the workload and assure proper monitoring of agency operations (Hardy 1990). These committees keep an eye on the "big picture" for the agency. It is a serious mistake for the board or its committees to become involved in micromanagement of the agency. At the same time, the board must be interested in and aware of the day-to-day activities of the agency. Typical board committees include:

- **Executive Committee** – This committee usually consists of the officers of the board. It can be expanded to include the chairpersons of standing committees or anyone else the board designates. Size is always an issue. An executive committee of more than seven would be large and potentially difficult to assemble for important functions. This committee makes recommendations for board action. It only has authority as authorized by the board. The board president serves as chair of the executive committee and calls necessary meetings between the regular meetings of the full board. The agency ED/CEO should be an ex officio member of this and all other committees.

- **Budget and Finance Committee** – This committee works with the ED/CEO to prepare and monitor the annual budget of the agency and it includes the board treasurer. If necessary, the committee recommends adjustments in the agency budget throughout the year. It oversees agency fund raising and provides liaison with external funding sources such as the United Way. In addition, the budget and finance committee plans capital campaigns, usually with the help of a consultant, and planned-giving programs to benefit the agency and its loyal supporters.

- **Strategic Planning Committee** – This committee should be an on-going committee and not just one that functions every five years or in times of crisis. This is the vision-monitoring and adjustment committee. Members of the committee should not be distracted by day-to-day issues. They must always be looking to the horizon to recommend needed change. They must watch for community changes, need for program modification, trends in funding, facility needs, personnel issues, opportunities for expansion and growth of the agency mission, and board issues.

- **Program Committee** – This committee monitors the programs of the agency for effectiveness and recommends changes and updates after appropriate consultation with clients and community representatives. It should consist of the ED/CEO and appropriate program staff, along with one or two board members to serve as liaison with the full board. The committee should also prepare a calendar of activities for each year. This can be distributed to board members, clients, media or any interested person.

- **Facilities or Property Management Committee** – This committee keeps track of needed repairs and renovations. Its members need to assure that all facilities meet or exceed local codes and that all risks associated with agency facilities are addressed in a timely fashion. It should monitor the agency inventory of equipment and facilities.

- **Human Resource Committee** – This committee is charged with developing appropriate written personnel policy for board approval. These written policies, practices and procedures outline a number of important items: affirmative action compliance, conditions of employment, probationary period, job descriptions and classifications, performance review criteria, working conditions and hours, benefits, vacations, expense reimbursement, promotion options, training and conference attendance requirements, termination of employment and severance pay, and leave policies for such things as family concerns, illness, or military service. The committee must also insure that meaningful and timely evaluation of all staff and volunteers occurs on a regular basis. Additionally, this committee must insure that appropriate training exists for all employees, volunteers and board members. Effective training is not an agency expense; it is an investment. A critical function of this committee is to assure the agency maintains a benefits and compensations package for all positions that is competitive with like agencies.
- **Marketing and Advertising Committee** – This is a year-round functioning committee charged with the promotion and marketing of all agency programs and works with the ED/CEO and appropriate staff. It insures that all activities of the agency are exposed to the community by using appropriate newspaper, radio, television, and magazine media to tell the story of the agency through press releases, flyers and the annual report. This committee works in consort with the local Chamber of Commerce to increase the visibility of the agency in the community.
- **Legal Issues Committee** – This committee monitors all issues related to risk management policies and insurance programs for employees and activities involving clients. The use of legal counsel from outside the agency would be recommended by this committee if the situation warranted it.
- **Board Recruitment and Recognition Committee** – This committee should search the community constantly for potential board members who could make a positive contribution to the mission and vision of the agency. It also prepares a process for member evaluation and recognition. It is responsible for preparing a slate of officers for annual elections, and it recommends term limits and rotation of board members through appropriate board positions. Finally, it formulates and recommends to the board policies for filling expiring terms of officers and other members. Committee members should be sensitive to the representational charge of the board.
- **Activities or Special Events Committee** – This committee may not exist in every agency, since its work would be handled by staff and volunteers. Its activities could include an annual banquet to honor clients and volunteers, a Soap Box Derby, a fishing tournament, a golf tournament or any other event outside the work of other committees.

Boards may have fewer committees or may have more committees or specialized committees to meet charter requirements. The number and size of committees is largely determined by the size and complexity of the organization. Too many committees can get in the way of organizational effectiveness. Committees of more than nine people can become unwieldy and ineffective. In short, a board needs the committees required to make it effective, not a long list of committees in order to look as important as other agencies.

Volunteers

Volunteers are critical to most nonprofit agencies. Volunteers can save an organization or kill it. The key is how clearly the organization defines the role of each volunteer, evaluates each volunteer, and rewards each volunteer. The word "each" is very important here. While it is always important to understand that each person is an individual with unique qualities, needs, drives, abilities, interests and skills, this recognition is critical when working with volunteers. Remember, board members are key volunteers.

Why do people volunteer to work for no pay? The answer is, they never do! While it is true that people who volunteer do not expect to receive money for their efforts, they do expect to get *something* for their experience. Basically, volunteers are drawn to an organization because they see a need or they need to be involved. These altruistic motives help agencies fill positions without having to hire full-time people.

An agency wants to find people who agree with Sarah Bernhardt, an early 1900s international silent film star who said, "Life begets life, energy creates energy. It is by spending oneself that one becomes rich." Another person might agree with Marian Wright Edelman, founder and president of the Children's Defense Fund when she said, "Service is the rent you pay for being." In either or both cases, the ideal volunteer wants to help and is willing to accept no salary for the service he or she renders. Is that enough?

Staff members are hired for a position and can be fired. Most agency executives find it more difficult to terminate a volunteer than to terminate a staff member. Since this tends to be true, great care must be taken when selecting volunteers and matching them to tasks within the agency. **Three broad categories** must receive special attention: *planning*, *recruitment*, and *integration*.

Planning is certainly the first step in the process of meaningful use of volunteers for any agency or organization. While planning comes first, it must also be viewed as a continuous process for the life of the organization. The initial stage in planning is assessment of needs. What positions can be filled by volunteers? How many are needed? How much supervision or oversight is required? How will the time required for oversight impact staff time constraints? Is the use of a volunteer of real value or just a way to hold down the number of paid staff? Once the assessment is complete, the results must be discussed with all staff, not just those who are most directly affected. A common mistake in any agency is to assume that only those most directly affected by an organizational change need to know what is happening. In truth, if organizational leaders only share information with people who are affected by a decision, people can infer that information is being hidden, and this may give rise to mistrust and feed the rumor mill. When the assessment results are discussed openly and honestly, the agency can secure staff concurrence. The time spent at this stage is time well spent. If the staff does not agree with or understand the need of volunteers, it is a waste of time to look for them.

The final stage in the planning step requires great care. Clear and thorough **job descriptions** for each volunteer position are paramount to the meaningful utilization of any volunteer. All job descriptions should include these items: the position title, a reporting line, clear details as to how the position fits into the organizational pattern, an outline of essential duties, training requirements/plans, expected time contribution, and benefits to the agency and volunteer.

Recruitment is almost as important as planning. In addition to organizational needs, agency leaders must consider what motivates people to volunteer. People seek to volunteer for the same reasons that everyone seeks to be a part of any group or relationship. Humans have four impulses that cause them to seek the companionship of other humans: to receive stimulation, to share experiences, to assert oneself, and to increase the enjoyment of certain activities.

People are attracted to each other much as a volunteer is attracted to an agency.

- **Reward or punishment** – The volunteer gets something from the relationship. The person may feel good about what he or she does for the agency or its clients. On the other hand, the volunteer may be compelled by guilt or some other motive that is a form of punishment for the person. In either case, the volunteer is getting a return on his or her investment.
- **Proximity** – An agency is close to the volunteer and is easily accessed, or an agency is distant enough to remove the volunteer from some undesirable condition or influence.
- **Similarity or dissimilarity** – Volunteers may turn to an agency because they see themselves and the agency as traveling the same road, wanting the same things in terms of helping people. On the other hand, they could see the agency as doing something they have never done but want to try. It may be that they see the agency going in the opposite direction from the one they have personally chosen.
- **Physical attractiveness** – The agency may be the place to be. It may be the one that all the best people choose to associate with. It may be the community "golden child." Some volunteers may conclude that association with a particular agency will improve their community standing or make them attractive to other agencies.

Whatever a volunteer's motive, the agency can benefit or suffer. The agency must have volunteers who have motives which blend with and support the mission of the agency. All volunteers must be driven by service to the agency and not by service to self.

In addition, due diligence must be taken in selecting volunteers, as with staff, in order to reduce any risk for the agency. General guidelines for **risk management** are discussed in some detail in **Chapter 7**.

Integration is the third consideration in the effective utilization of volunteers. The agency can have a great plan for the use of volunteers and recruit only people with motives that support the mission of the agency and still fail to retain the best or make optimal use of each person if the agency does not properly integrate the volunteer with its programs and paid staff.

Volunteers must have meaningful work, appropriate recognition, helpful feedback as to the effectiveness of their contribution to the agency's mission, regular opportunities for input based on their experience and wisdom, and the chance to expand their skills, if they so desire.

■ Communication

How can the different groups be developed to reach their potential and meet the needs of the organization? While this appears to be a question that can be easily answered, it has frustrated many leaders for centuries. What seems to work for one group brings limited success with another and fails miserably with still another. The answer is, in fact, simple – effective communication. The implementation of the answer is incredibly difficult. A leading author on the subject of people helping families get along puts it this way, "Once a human being has arrived on this earth, communication is the largest single factor determining what kinds of relationships she or he makes with others and what happens to each in the world. How we manage survival, how we develop intimacy, how productive we are, how we connect with our own divinity – all depend largely on our communication skills" (Satir 1988, xi).

If effective communication is so central to a productive life, why don't people naturally excel at communication? After all, we do other essential functions automatically—breathe, eat, sleep. The reason it is so difficult to achieve effective communication is that too many people assume that all one has to do is create clear and understandable messages. This is often referred to as the **conduit model**. The conduit model assumes that communication is the simple passage of messages from a sender to a receiver through a channel (or conduit). The **conduit model** is source oriented (Bokeno 2002). Sometimes the idea of feedback is added as a check device for the sender to verify if the receiver clearly and "correctly" received and understood the message. The **conduit model** often results from a misapplication of the Lasswell model of communication. Lasswell's model is a word model: "Who says what in what channel to whom with what effect." This view of communication puts emphasis on the sending of messages and their impact on the receiver. It identifies five components of a spoken or written message:

Who – *Source*
says **What** – *Content*
in what **Channel** – *Medium*
to **Whom** – *Receiver*
with what **Effect** – *Outcome*

Even when consideration of interaction or feedback is added, it is easy to see why people mistakenly oversimplify communication and reduce it to the sending and receiving of messages. If someone misunderstands, it is their fault; it is our fault; they didn't listen; we didn't check to see if they understood; and/or they had done it right before what happened this time. The list could continue for pages. The fault is not in the model. The fault is in the search for simple answers to difficult questions. The heart of the answer is in the question itself. Here is a poor question: "Why didn't you do what I asked you to do? " Here is a much better question: "Did you understand what I asked you to do?"

Effective communication is about understanding meaning. It is not just about sending clear messages. Satir (1988) offers a practical definition of communication that functions as well in the workplace as it does in a family setting. She contends that communication evolves from "the ways people use to work out meaning with one another" (4).

In order to be an effective communicator, one must understand the nature of interacting with another, understand the need to alter or adjust messages to achieve meaning, and understand that bridges must be built between and among individuals because of differences resulting from variables such as experience, culture, education, area of expertise.

The kind of communication which makes an organization succeed comes from genuine dialogue. It is a learned art. All humans have a natural desire to understand and be understood. What each of us must learn is that each person is a unique being. Therefore, when we consider individual communication styles, it becomes clear that generalizations about how, say, women, or Southerners, or African-Americans like to communicate are all but useless when it comes to trying to understand what an *individual* likes or wants. The most helpful way to learn to communicate more effectively is to observe and study individuals who are effective and then to ask questions, try different styles, and ask more questions.

In one's work and personal relationships, **four communication truths** can help prepare a person for daily interaction with people who are different from him or herself.

1. **Understanding must precede any agreement.** Understanding another is required if we are to agree with the person. Agreement implies that both parties are clear on each other's assumptions, values and positions.

2. **Agreement without understanding is usually meaningless.** In order for two people to agree to something, they must be talking about the same issue, idea, emotion, or relationship. To say we agree is without any substance unless we are talking about the same issues, idea, emotion, or relationship.

3. **We can't genuinely disagree with another without understanding why or how we disagree.** For disagreement to be genuine, it must be based on a clear understanding of the issue at hand—the other person's position, why he or she takes that position and the implication of that position for the relationship between oneself and the other person. Unless these conditions are met, disagreement is full of hot air. It is not based in substance, but is fueled by assumption, which may or may not be accurate. Understanding of another person does not require agreement with the person, but it does require a clear and accurate comprehension of the person's position.

4. **Disagreement without understanding is almost always meaningless.** As with statement number two above, there is no meaning or substance to a disagreement based on potentially inaccurate or unclear information. If there is clear understanding, there can be disagreement. If there is no understanding, there can only be shouting, anger, assertion, name-calling, or worst of all, violence.

Deetz and Stevenson (1986) describe **five assumptions about communication** that can help a person determine what can be done to modify and build useful communication skills for any workplace:

1. Communication skills are learned.
2. Interpersonal skill needs change over time and with the situation.
3. Personal, situational and relationship needs determine the usefulness of various skills.
4. Individuals can exert considerable control over their communication behavior and skill development.
5. Self-esteem and healthy relationships require successful skill development, or a

person will enjoy only very limited personal and professional accomplishment (3).

Below, we see how each of the assumptions aids a person in assessing and building useful communication skills for the workplace:

- **Communication skills are learned**. From the first day a person is born, he or she begins to learn the rules for communication, and if the "teachers" are effective, the greater is the chance that an individual will be successful and effective too. A person can practice communication skills in the same way one practices tennis or swimming. Practice can help a person improve or make the person less effective if good technique is not used. Just as a coach can help one become a better tennis player or swimmer, a "coach" can help improve communication skills. Learn what the effective skills are and ask people who can be trusted and who are effective communicators to provide constructive feedback.

- **Interpersonal skill needs change over time and with new situations.** A child is not expected to be as effective at communicating needs, wants and desires as is a college graduate. Nor is a nonprofit agency professional with five years of experience as effective as one with fifteen or twenty-five years of experience. As a person is assigned more and more responsibility, it is assumed (rightly or wrongly) that program and communication skills have been improving with the passage of time. Is that a valid assumption? Unfortunately, all too often, it is NOT a valid assumption. In many organizations, a person may have had to endure the same experiences and expectations each year for ten years, instead of experiencing a variety of activities and expectations in the organization over the same period. Einstein is reputed to have said, "Insanity is doing the same thing over and over again while expecting different results." As a person grows older, gains more experience in an organization, and is exposed to different program or leadership skills, his or her skill needs should and will change. It is good to be a continuous learner.

- **Personal, situational and relationship needs determine the usefulness of various skills**. A person may be very good at negotiating with used car salesmen, but that skill may not have anything to do with that person's position with the nonprofit agency which pays his or her salary. The agency may desperately need someone who can convince kids to enroll in an after-school physical fitness program. By the same token, a person may have great patience and listen well to elderly people, but have little or no patience with ten-year olds. If the agency serves ten-year olds, it needs a person who is patient and listens well to ten-year olds.

- **Individuals can exert considerable control over their communication behavior and skill development**. Each person must take leadership in identifying his or her own development needs. At the very least, when someone else identifies a need and is able to document clearly that need, one must be willing to get the recommended training or suggest an alternative that will achieve the desired outcome.

- **Self-esteem and healthy relationships require successful skill development,**

or a person will enjoy only very limited personal and professional accomplishment. Our relationships with others determine more than any other variable how high we climb or how low we fall within any organization. Each of us must understand our strengths and weaknesses. We must be confident, not cocky, with respect to our strengths. We must be accepting of our weaknesses, but not self-deprecating. We must be realistic and learn to accept constructive feedback and use it to improve.

Another factor in successful communication is the interaction environment. When we talk with another person, we use words that have meaning to us. Those meanings have evolved along with who we are. We cannot use a dictionary to find out what a word "means." We can, however, use a dictionary to find out how a word has been used throughout history. The *Oxford English Dictionary* is an outstanding example of the value of a dictionary. It illustrates that word meaning derives from people and cultures, not from books.

There are two factors affecting the interaction environment—the **cultural environment** and the **physical environment**. The **cultural environment** consists of the behaviors, attitudes and values which are shared by enough people to exert an influence on the messages we create. A person can begin to deduce the prevailing cultural factors by observing patterns of work, relationship styles, attitudes toward self-fulfillment and messages sent by the mass media.

The **physical environment** consists of the natural and human constructions that frame our conversations and relationships. These frames include a person's idea of what constitutes appropriate formality, warmth, privacy, familiarity, constraint and distance.
What are the essential communication skills and how does a leader use each one? There are **six skills** that are important for anyone working in nonprofit organizations: *listening, conflict management, decision-making, team building, coaching/counseling, and sensitivity to differences.*

Listening

Aside from our physical ability to hear sounds, perception is the most important variable in determining whether a person is an effective listener. Frequently, the mistake is made in equating hearing and listening. If we hear someone speaking to us, we consider that we are listening to him or her. Rarely is that true. Even the fact that a person does not respond as we expect them to does not mean that he or she is not listening to us. What is the difference between listening and hearing?

The first step in understanding the difference between hearing and listening comes from understanding the physical and psychological process of perception. There are **four stages** involved in the **human process of perception** of a person or a thing:

- **Sensation** is the process of receiving stimulation from the environment through the five human senses: sight, smell, touch, taste, and hearing. All five senses are involved in hearing, even though most people depend largely on two senses, hearing and sight. The next three stages influence and determine how this sensory data is used to change hearing into listening.
- **Selection** is the largely physiological process of deciding which sensory data to "pay attention to." All sensory data is received and stored in the brain. A person's

brain selects what data is the "loudest" or deserves the most attention. That selection will not always be based on the same criteria. Sometimes a person will notice something new, something familiar, the loudest, the softest, the most dramatic, the most sensational, or the most pleasing. The most important aspect of this stage is to remember that different people hearing the same sensory input may and probably will select different data to "pay attention to." Part of the reason for this is that, as a person selects which data to attend to, he or she begins to arrange that data into familiar patterns.

- **Organization** is the process of testing sensory data for recognition and arranging that sensory data into familiar patterns. This is both a physiological and psychological activity.
- **Interpretation** is the largely psychological process of determining what sensory data "means" to the person receiving it. This stage determines how and why a person responds as he or she does.

Listening, unlike hearing, which is a natural phenomenon, is a **learned skill**. Any person can listen more effectively by understanding and acting on the following information:

1. Effective, active listening is difficult for many people. Practice and training can improve one's ability to listen well.
2. There is no relationship between intelligence and listening skill. In fact, highly intelligent people are often very poor listeners because they jump to conclusions rather than hearing all that another has to say.
3. Listening is an active process. It requires a person's <u>participation</u> and <u>involvement</u>. Good listeners often notice a sense of fatigue after an intense listening experience.
4. Personality plays an important role in how well one listens. The more "other" focused a person is, generally, the better he or she listens.
5. Effective listening requires the whole body. Proper eye contact and body posture facilitate effective, active listening.
6. Feelings are often more important than the words spoken. People must look for the underlying feelings in any message. These feelings are often the <u>real</u> message.

The term *active listening* appears several times in this chapter. What is meant by active listening and how does one do it? Active listening involves listening for more than word meaning and includes listening for the feelings and emotions behind words or messages. There are **four** main **qualities of an active listener**:

1. Physical proximity or closeness
2. Appropriate, direct eye contact
3. An open mind
4. A demand for clarity as demonstrated by a willingness to ask questions to get at clear word meaning and to uncover underlying emotions and feelings

Conflict Management

Conflict is a naturally occurring phenomenon in the United States, indeed everywhere in the world. Hocker and Wilmot (1985) define **conflict** as "an expressed struggle

between at least two interdependent parties who perceive incompatible goals, scarce rewards, and interference from the other party in achieving their goals" (23). Why do many
people run from conflict? Conflict can, in fact, produce **positive rewards**. There are **four**:

- Conflict can produce a greater understanding by the parties in disagreement and
  clarify their relationship.
- Conflict can focus and clarify the similarities and differences between the parties in disagreement.
- Successful conflict management can help the parties in disagreement discover
  better methods for dealing with future conflicts.
- Conflict can expose areas where communication can actually be improved and
  strengthened.

The best way to look at the true value of conflict is to ponder the African proverb,
"Smooth seas do not make skillful sailors." People must be tested and trained on the seas of
conflict in order to know how to deal with it. A person cannot run from it, so he or she must
learn how to manage it.

Most definitions of conflict include reference to the inability to share scarce resources
as a common source of disagreement. This source of conflict occurs frequently in nonprofit
agencies. It will always be a source of conflict.

Another recurrent source of conflict in a diverse organization comes from the violation of communication rules. Communication rules define required, preferred and prohibited behaviors. The severity of the conflict often generates from the costs or rewards of rule
violation. Understanding the communication rules of others, as well as our own, helps to
reduce conflicts over violations of rules.

Writers often suggest that conflict resolution be a goal. In reality, conflict is rarely
resolved. One conflict leaves a residue, which is built upon for future conflicts. If that
residue is basically negative, the subsequent conflicts start in a hole and tend to become
more negative than the issue warrants. People typically choose from five options when
they are faced with a conflict: *avoiding, accommodating, competing, compromising, or
collaborating* (Borisoff and Victor 1998). While each has its place and each has its advantages, the first four usually lead to more conflict or at least to some unhappiness.

- **Avoiding** can be an appropriate approach to conflict if there is risk of harm.
  Otherwise, conflicts that are avoided tend to simply grow larger. On the surface,
  the only one gaining anything is the party who is avoided. Avoiding conflict
  doesn't solve anything and it typically produces little satisfaction for any of the
  parties, since nothing is resolved. The main residual of this style is to continue
  to avoid conflict even if it hurts to do so.
- The **Accommodating** style can be very appropriate when the issue at conflict is
  more important to one party than the other. If two co-workers are disagreeing
  over the best way to advertise a new program, and if one is insistent on the need
  for radio advertising while the other thinks newspaper advertising is enough, the
  one can accommodate the other by allowing radio advertising. It does not matter, and if there is enough money in the budget, why fight? This style involves
  one party giving in to the other. If a person uses this style too often, he or she
  may find others taking advantage to cut the person out of discussions where the

issue may matter a great deal.

- **Competing** is a common style in the United States and is a favorite of men. The objective is to win the issue and have the other party lose. This style can be effectively employed when there is a clear-cut solution with profound impact on an organization, or when critical information for decision-making is not fully available to all parties. If there is no real justification for the competing style, the result is stifled ideas, weaker solutions, hurt feelings, damaged relationships, and little teamwork. In fact, since competing is so dominant in the U.S. culture, it is rarely justified. The main reason for its ineffectiveness is that it tends to promote compliance with power more than it promotes open communication and effective conflict management.
- **Compromising** involves all parties giving some ground in order to move beyond the conflict. This style is very appropriate when there is no clear-cut answer to an issue and no one has cause to impose a solution on others. The worst effect of compromise is that everyone leaves the conflict with some dissatisfaction, which always dampens the victory achieved by the compromise.
- **Collaborating** promotes discussion pointing to the creation of a solution that can make every party's satisfaction maximized. It focuses on issues, not positions. All the other styles invite participants to adopt a position and stick to it. Collaboration, by its nature, invites all parties to look to the potential outcome— what will benefit everyone. This style usually requires more time and effort, but it has the potential to produce high degrees of satisfaction and more creative solutions. It also creates a residual of success, which in turn encourages those involved in a collaborative effort to have less fear of future conflict. There is a pattern of success to build upon. Collaborating is the most desirable style in most situations.

For that reason, we are discussing conflict management so we can talk about techniques that tend to improve a person's chances of reducing negative residue. While many approaches to conflict management improve the process, there are **three skill sets** which help people **focus on a win-win prospective**. These three tend to open a path to cooperation more than to competition:

- **See the disagreement from the point of view of the other person.** Recognize the other person's interest.
- **Actively listen to the other person; try to hear their emotions and their meanings.** Acknowledge the other person by valuing their views enough to work at understanding what they feel and believe.
- **Seek mutual problem solving with principled negotiation.** Endorse based solutions, ones that will last and be respected by others whom both parties admire and respect.

Decision-making

Decisions are easy to make but often difficult to live with. Why is this true? People often forget that decisions are best made using a process that considers not only the final decision but also the consequences of the decision. Research has suggested some models that help in remembering the nature of the decision-making process.

Tuckman (1965) introduced a very useful four-stage description of the typical process used by small groups when they initially come together or are assigned a task: *forming, storming, norming, and performing.*

- **Forming** – Another word to describe this stage is "confusion." Group members frequently have very different ideas as to why the group was put together and what it is to accomplish even when all have received the same written or oral instructions concerning the formation of the group. There are many questions at this stage. Why are we here? What do they really want? Are we going to have any real power? Can we select our own leader? Why am I here? Why are you here? When do we have to present our report? Who is going to prepare it? There is little attention paid to process or protocol. Members often test each other's tolerance and that of the appointed or emergent leader. At the other extreme there may be a great dependence on the leader, and no one will participate until encouraged or forced to do so. This is particularly true when there is a high level of anxiety or suspicion among group members.

- **Storming** – Another word for this stage is "uncertainty." While clarity of purpose and task direction improves, people have difficulty working together at this stage because they are positioning for power, influence and recognition. Power struggles may appear, as well as alliances or factions. Relationship and emotional issues tend to take center stage. A clear focus on the task at hand is very important if the group is to continue to mature and begin to move toward a meaningful outcome. The leader may need to suggest compromise or encourage members to look for win-win solutions to conflict.

- **Norming** – The one word to describe this stage is "stability." Work is now directed toward the goal(s) agreed to by the group. Decisions are made within the context of guidelines, and processes are understood and accepted by the members. Some decisions are made by the group as a whole, while others are delegated to teams within the total group. The group may now take time for some fun or social outings to build esprit de corps. Respect replaces uncertainty and suspicion. The uncertainties which still remain will usually be focused on the task and not on relationship or emotional issues. These uncertainties are understood as a natural part of group process and viewed as challenges that can be overcome.

- **Performing** – The word for this stage is "productivity." The group has now answered most of the questions that arose in the first stage (forming). They now know why they are doing what they are doing. The group shares a vision of the desired outcome and is able to act without supervision in completing its assigned task. When disagreements occur, they are now processed within an understood process and managed according to accepted guidelines. The group finishes its task.

The time spent in each stage is not important. The style of leadership employed by the appointed or emergent leader will largely determine how quickly and how well the group proceeds through the stages to become an effective, performing group. The more quickly a group can move to the performing stage the better, if they have satisfied all the behavioral obstacles inherent in the preceding stages.

One time-honored tool for groups is the **reflective thinking agenda**, promoted by John Dewey in the early 1900s. The **five step agenda**, when applied thoughtfully, can ensure higher quality decisions:

1. **Clearly describe the problem.** Without a clear sense of what must be done, a solution will have no value.
2. **Analyze what is causing the problem.** Understanding the cause or causes often suggests a solution.
3. **Establish criteria for solving the problem.** What must the solution do?
4. **Brainstorm solutions that match the criteria.** This step is critical. All possible solutions must be aired without evaluation. Then each unevaluated idea can be subjected to a careful analysis against the established criteria.
5. **Pick the solution or solutions that best fit the criteria.** Careful completion of the four preceding steps makes picking a solution simple and straightforward.

Elizabeth Dole, former president of the American Red Cross, demonstrated her understanding of effective decision-making when she outlined the steps for making and selling decisions. She observed, "What you always do before you make a decision is consult. The best public policy is made when you are listening to people who are going to be impacted. Then, once policy is determined, you call on them to help you sell it." Her insight for public policy is just as applicable to any decision made by any agency, at any level, with respect to any issue.

Team building

Many people grew up hearing the expression, "Two heads are better than one." In the twenty-first century, this expression was replaced with the word "teamwork." A very good website for resources on teamwork can be found at www.teambuildiginc.com. In addition to articles on important variables, there are links to other
sources, a bookstore, teambuilding exercises, assessment tools and more.

Observers of nature discovered the classic illustration of teamwork by documenting the behavior of geese as they fly south in the fall and back north in the spring. Here is what observers have documented:

- As each bird flaps its wings, it creates uplift for the bird following. By flying in a "V" formation, the whole flock adds seventy-one percent greater flying range than if one bird flew alone.
- Whenever a goose falls out of formation, it suddenly feels the drag and resistance of trying to fly alone and quickly gets back into formation to take advantage of the lifting power of the bird immediately in front.
- When the lead goose gets tired, it rotates back into the formation and another goose flies at the point position.
- The geese in formation honk from behind to encourage those up front to keep up

their speed.

- When a goose gets sick or wounded or shot down, two geese drop out of formation and follow it down to help and protect it. They stay with it until it is able to fly again or dies. Then they launch out on their own, with another formation, or they catch up with their flock.

What can be learned from geese? It seems obvious that working together improves productivity, discourages less productive activity, gives everyone an opportunity to get some of the glory, and provides encouragement and protection when someone makes a mistake or is simply discouraged.

Recently, the saying has emerged from the teamwork literature, "There is no 'I' in team." This does not mean there is no room for individual achievement, since most of what a team is able to accomplish is magnified if all individuals are striving for what Senge (1990) calls personal mastery. As individuals work to be the best they can be, everyone they work with is made better. "Organizations learn only through individuals who learn" (Senge 1990, 139). Personal mastery is not achieved at the expense of another; it is achieved at the expense of personal effort.

Several concepts relate directly to successful team building, team success or teamwork. Zoglio (1993) identifies and describes seven keys for a successful team effort. They are *commitment, contribution, communication, cooperation, conflict management, change management and connections.* Let's examine each of these briefly:

1. **Commitment** – In order for a group to become a team, the members must understand what they are doing and why they are doing it. Putting people together and telling them they are a team does not make them one. It is little wonder that so many "teams" fail to achieve what is expected. They were never more than a "team" in name.

   To achieve commitment, people must be given the opportunity to develop a mission for the team, a vision, and value statements that fit with the agency mission, but reflect the individual nature of the group. They must be allowed to develop their measures of success and to celebrate their accomplishments.

2. **Contribution** – Everyone must contribute to the team effort, but it is not necessary that they all contribute in the same way or the same amount. All members need strong technical and interpersonal skills and must be willing to learn new skills or improve current skills for the benefit of the team effort.

   Balanced contributions are more easily obtained when team members think they are included, have confidence and are empowered. A person who is reluctant to volunteer can be included when he or she is encouraged to talk or asked to provide input. A person's confidence can be enhanced through encouragement and coaching and by keeping past successes in front of the group. Empowerment comes from getting appropriate training, having sufficient resources, showing respect, and involving members in decisions that affect the team (not waiting to inform them until after a decision has been made.)

3. **Communication** – In order for a team to succeed, the most important key is the freedom to communicate openly and honestly. Members must be able to ask for help without feeling inferior, offer ideas that may appear to be off the wall with-

out being laughed at, think out loud without being scolded for not considering the feelings of others, and risk making a mistake without be held up to ridicule. Members must be able to ask for forgiveness for mistakes or careless words and receive forgiveness without reservation. Trust must be built and maintained above all else.

To improve communication, emphasize the importance of listening actively, using language with sensitivity, giving and receiving feedback with consideration for others, showing trust, and using meeting time efficiently. If some team members need training in interpersonal skills, it should be provided as enhancement, not as punishment.

4. **Cooperation** – In today's world very few programs or projects can be successful unless there is a great deal of interconnectedness. From for- profit to nonprofit, the information age relies on people sharing information and working together to meet goals and achieve organizational missions. The lone wolf is an endangered species.

   An effective leader can stimulate cooperation by demonstrating and rewarding behaviors that facilitate cooperation among staff and volunteers. These behaviors include doing work accurately, doing it on time, keeping in touch with others who need to share information, being creative enough not to fear doing something a new way, and promoting a healthy, open, trusting esprit de corps (spirit of the group or team).

5. **Conflict Management** – Conflict happens! It is natural. It is inevitable. It is often good. If conflict is managed well, it can, in fact, stimulate creativity and keep teams and individuals from becoming stale. If conflict is not well managed, future conflicts will be more intense or avoided all together, and neither response is ultimately constructive for individuals or an organization.

   Leaders can help team members to reduce the damaging potential effects of conflict by teaching members not to avoid conflict, and by simultaneously teaching members ways to manage conflict in order to produce constructive outcomes.

6. **Change Management** – For-profit organizations thrive and survive on the basis of their ability to "stay out front" in their area of business. They must stay ahead of the competition to do well. Nonprofit agencies that best satisfy community and individual needs learn to act, not react. Change happens! The best way to survive change is not to try to avoid it and hold on to the past, but to manage it.

   Leaders can help team members manage change by modeling a positive attitude toward any change and by continually supporting team efforts to change with resources and encouragement. Freedom to make a mistake or fail in a change effort is critical if leaders want team members to believe that change is truly expected and desired.

7. **Connections** – It is important for any team to take a systems view of its own work and consider how its work is connected to the mission of the agency, the work of other teams in the organization and the issues and concerns of its own team members. The operative word here is *networking*. Two critical connec-

tions must be monitored continually. First, how does our work connect with the mission of the agency? Second, how does our work connect with the feedback the agency receives from its clients?

Leaders can support connections by helping to keep communication lines open to all levels of the organization and to clients. If people are rewarded for helping each other, they will tend to continue to help each other. If there is no recognition or reward for helping each other, people will tend to do their own work and not help each other. Why should they do more work if there is no recognition or no reciprocation?

Alexander Graham Bell put it this way, "Great discoveries and achievements invariably involve the cooperation of many minds." If this is true for "great discoveries," how much more can people accomplish with respect to ordinary problems if they are approached with "many minds." Henry Ford described the value of teamwork and cooperation this way, "Coming together is a beginning, staying together is progress, working together is success."

Coaching/counseling

People frequently know they need to learn new skills to survive in their work, but they often don't know how to do it or just need a little help. Helping individuals succeed at work helps any agency succeed at its mission. If a person is unwilling or unable to do what is necessary for an agency to fulfill its mission, that person should be *freed* to find another job. If, however, a person is willing or able to improve, an agency should protect its investment and help improve the person's skills.

Very often skill improvement or enhancement can be achieved through the use of organizational training programs or training available through commercial vendors. When a person needs substantial help that can be provided by outside vendors or even through national affiliate agencies, the local agency must invest in its people and cover the cost of the training.

When the improvement or enhancement needed can be addressed by local staff, it should be conducted at the local level. This assumes that someone is capable of helping the employee in need. This is a coaching/counseling task.

The most powerful coaching and counseling tool is **mentoring**. Mentoring is a process that occurs in the context of a relationship. To be successful, a mentoring relationship is best built from a base of genuine dialogue (Gantt and Bokeno 2000). Genuine dialogue is characterized by open interaction, a problem-solution mindset, an effort to generate new ideas (not just to choose the best from the past), and a joint-venture thought process. Mentoring is characterized by **caring, sharing, correcting,** and **connecting** (Gantt 1997).

Mentoring is *not* a program to be implemented, an initiative to be started, or an assignment to be discharged. Mentoring only works well when people have a trusting relationship in which there can be sharing without fear of punishment or sabotage, where refinement or correction can occur without defensiveness and where genuine attempts are made to provide appropriate access to networks that will lead to advancement, development or improvement. Other-centered communication is the basic building block of mentoring relationships. This simply means that all parties in mentoring relationships use communication skills and techniques designed to understand others, rather than techniques or strategies intended to promote self-interest.

Mentors should collaborate, not tell another what to do. Mentors should seek to construct solutions by working together, not by recycling past solutions that seem to fit the situation in question. Mentors should engage in critical reflection by "thinking out loud" and risking mistakes by openly discussing concerns, problems and issues, not by trying to make new problems fit old solutions or using past analysis as a standard for new solutions. Mentors fully and openly participate in dialogue; they do not sit back and wait until they are "needed." Mentors give voice to their protégé (Bokeno and Bokeno 1998).

George Bernard Shaw provides a nice illustration of mentoring in his play *Getting Married*. He writes, "I am not a teacher, only a fellow traveler of whom you asked the way. I pointed ahead – ahead of myself, as well as you." Thus, mentoring, coaching and counseling, in their best form, become a joint venture between two persons growing with the help of the other.

If the person does not respond well to mentoring, the best way to proceed is to define clearly what behavior(s) is/are deficient; explain why change needs to occur; stipulate the consequences of a failure to change or improve; detail a plan for the person to demonstrate progress; and specify appropriate rewards for achieving agreed-upon goals. If change does not occur, it is time for a change of personnel.

Sensitivity to Differences

The mere mention of adapting to differences or valuing diversity sends some into a fit of rage. "Why can't **'they'** be like the rest of us?" The truth is, **"they"** are like us in more ways than **"they"** are different. William Schutz's theory of interpersonal needs (1966) identifies **three basic needs** all humans share:

- The need for **inclusion** is satisfied by a person's joining a civic club, church, fraternity/sorority; deciding to marry; attending a family reunion. What a person *wants* from others is *acceptance*. What a person *expresses* to others is *interest.*
- The need for **control** manifests itself in the choices a person makes in interactions with others. It is shown in our attempts to influence others, positions of authority taken, or choices made which involve others. What a person *wants* from others is *guidance*. What a person *expresses* to others is *leadership.*
- The need for **affection** is defined as caring and respect for others. A person receives care and respect from others when he or she shows care and respect for another. What a person *wants* from others is *closeness*. What a person **expresses** to others is *liking.*

How each person behaves or shows these needs is indeed influenced by age, gender, nationality, race, ethnicity, religion, and other factors. While we share the needs, we behave in different ways to tell people what we want and how we want it shown.

Very often a person's failure to be sensitive to people who are different can be traced to one or more of the following misconceptions about communication in relationships. Any one of these false assumptions can inhibit the formation of a successful relationship with a person who is different because of age, ability, culture, education, ethnicity, experience, race, or sexual orientation. A person is asking for difficulty in any relationship when he or she assumes that:

- **Communication in a relationship is consistent**. Just as people change over time, so does the need for different communication skills and different sensitivities with respect to others. The journey from the first meeting to working together occasionally, to working together regularly, to a deep, genuine friendship requires very different skills as two people progress. How any person thinks and feels about this type of relationship changes as the duration and depth of the relationship changes.

- **Communication has simple meaning**. The fact is that any interaction with another person is never simple, even if it is with someone we know well. How much more complicated interaction can become if it is with someone we know only at work. Psychologists established many years ago that human brains react to sensory stimulation in three domains: the affective or feeling domain, the cognitive or intellectual domain, and the behavioral or action domain. Interactions with another person, then, are based on predictions we make based on psychological data, which comes from how one **feels** about the person, the situation, self, past interactions, or potential for future interactions. Interactions with another person are also based on our intellectual abilities or what we **think** we know, can understand, or can explain. Finally, interactions with another are based on personally established rules for what is right and wrong or appropriate and inappropriate.

- **Communicators are independent**. Every person is connected to each and every person he or she has ever met, talked with, worked with, dated and so on. No relationship is ever truly ended, except by the death of one or both of the parties. Every communicator is influenced by others and influences others.

- **Communication behaviors have obvious causation**. Nothing is ever obvious. Some things appear to be obvious. It is human nature to try to explain everything we see. If someone smiles, most people want to know why. If someone yells, we think they must be angry with us. Since there are many possible explanations for the smile or the yell, it is very dangerous to assume that the reason for any communication behavior is obvious. There is nothing wrong with speculating and trying to think of causes. The error is not in speculating; it is in being convinced that we *know* the *correct* cause.

- **Communication interactions have a final point**. Interactions may have a temporary end or pause, but not a final point. With every interaction, there is a residual, something left over, something unfinished, something to build on for the future. If there were a true final point to interactions, everyone would have to start all relationships and interactions from the beginning each time there was a new contact. All interactions are built on previous interactions.

Having sensitivity to diversity is not just the politically correct thing to do; it is necessary. The arrogance of one race, one generation, one nation or one group of like-thinking people believing that they have the best answers to all the important human questions is not only very narrow and limiting, but it can lead to the virtual ineffectiveness or death of any organization or culture. Successories offers a motivational post card featuring a jigsaw puzzle background with the faces of several very different-looking people. One piece missing and is inscribed, "Great achievements are not born from a single vision but from the combination of many distinctive viewpoints. Diversity challenges assumptions, opens minds and unlocks our potential to solve any problem we may face." What a great justification for collecting differing points of view when faced with a problem or opportunity. Being sensitive to diverse people and ways of thinking enriches anyone's life.

Valuing diversity comes from seeing individuals as individuals, not as groups. In fact, the only way to have unity is to appreciate diversity. If a group is bound together by its sameness, it is a living stereotype—everyone looking, acting and believing like the others. If a group or staff is unified, it is capitalizing on its diversity with everyone adding his or her unique perspective—way of thinking and way of acting—to each and every challenge faced by the agency or organization. Being sensitive to differences is good business and even better human nature.

■ A Final Thought:

These words attributed to Mark Twain provide the best concluding thought for this chapter, "I can live for two months on a good compliment." Indeed, everyone— Executive Director/Chief Executive Officer, staff, volunteers and board—does better work and enjoys that work more if they always know they are appreciated for what they do.

■ Summary

Effective leadership is no accident. All organizations live or die based on their use of three key components: people, resources and service or product. The people component of an organization is the heart of successful leadership. Character is the variable that separates the effective leader from the merely efficient one. Effectiveness is much preferred in the nonprofit sector.

The agency leader (ED/CEO) must manage well the staff, the board and the volunteers. In each group clear expectations are essential. Meaningful work is required. Regular and appropriate feedback is indispensable. Reward for a job well done is appreciated.

The glue that holds the work of the ED/CEO together and makes him or her successful and effective is communication. The goal of all interactions should be to understand and then to be understood. In order to do that an agency leader must develop, refine and hone skills in attentive listening; fair conflict management; meaningful decision making; cooperative team building; compassionate coaching; counseling and mentoring; and, authentic sensitivity to differences.

This chapter addressed, in part, the American Humanics Certification Competency Requirements of Communication Skills, Personal Attributes, Board/Committee Development, Human Resources Development and Supervision and General Nonprofit Management.

■ Discussion Questions

1. Why are nonprofit organizations such a significant part of the culture and local communities in the United States?

2. What is the difference between what volunteers can do for an organization and what they should do?
3. What are the positive aspects of people in an organization having different interaction styles, as opposed to most people have the same style?
4. How could an ED/CEO or supervisor use the signs of decaying relationships to repair a relationship with a volunteer, a client or staff member before it goes beyond repair?
5. Why are the legal responsibilities of a board important?
6. Which is the most important board committee?
7. Why is it important for an agency to have "good" volunteers?
8. Why is understanding such an important variable in communication?
9. What communication skill is the most important one to master?
10. What can be learned from someone who has different values, different goals, different ways of thinking, different ways of behaving or a different sense of what is right and wrong?
11. Which American Humanics Certification Competency Requirements are best illustrated in this chapter?

■ Activities

1. Find an Internet site to help you define the nature and role of nonprofit organizations and the nature and role of nonprofit boards. (Hint: Look for your answer among the list of American Humanics Collaborating Professional Organizations.)
2. Write a 4-7-page paper describing the difference and similarities between for-profit and nonprofit boards.
3. In groups of 4-6 members, discuss the importance of staff, board and volunteer recognition and evaluation. Be sure to discuss similarities, as well as differences, among the three groups.
4. Write job descriptions for three different positions you would be willing to apply for upon receiving your degree.
5. Considering the differences and similarities between staff and volunteers, discuss the implications of the statement, "Interpersonal skill needs change over time and situation." Also identify which interpersonal skills are most critical for each group to effectively serve their agency at five, fifteen and twenty-five years of service.
6. How can an executive director use the information from the DiSC™ survey to build an effective staff and volunteer team? How can he or she use the DiSC™ survey information to work more effectively with an existing board or use it to create the core group for a new board?
7. In groups of 3-5, discuss how knowledge of cultural environment can be used to train volunteers to have a greater sensitivity to differences among staff and constituencies served. Design a half-day training segment to implement what you have discussed in your group.
8. Discuss your personal experience with the statement, "Word meaning is in people."

■ References

Black's Law Dictionary. (1990). 6ᵗʰ ed. St. Paul, MN: West Publishing.

BoardSource. (2002). Path <http://www.boardsource.org>

Bokeno, R. M. (2002). Communicating other/wise: a paradigm for empowered practice. *Reason in Practice: The Journal of Philosophy of Management* 1(2): 11-23.

Bokeno, R. M., and Bokeno, J. K. (1998). The cultivation of participative change: managerial development influences on employee communication practice. *Compendium of Winning Papers from the IABC Research Foundation 1997-1998* 37-67.

Bokeno, R. M., and Gantt, V. W. (2000). Dialogic mentoring: core relationships for organizational learning. *Management Communication Quarterly* 14(2): 237-270.

Borisoff, D., and Victor, D. A. (1998). *Conflict Management: A Communication Skills Approach*. 2ⁿᵈ ed. Boston: Allyn and Bacon.

Caputo, J. S., Hazel, H. C., and McMahon, C. (1997). *Interpersonal Communication: Using Reason to Make Relationships Work*. 2ⁿᵈ ed. Dubuque, IA: Kendall/Hunt Publishing.

Certification Competency Requirements Handbook. Kansas City, MO: American Humanics.

Deetz, S. A., and Stevenson, S. L. (1986). *Managing Interpersonal Communication*. New York: Harper & Row.

DeVito, J. A. (1998). *The Interpersonal Communication Book*. 8ᵗʰ ed. New York: Longman.

Gantt, V. W. (1997). Beneficial mentoring is for everyone: a reaction paper. Paper presented at the National Communication Association Convention, Chicago.

Hardy, J. M. (1990). *Developing Dynamic Boards: A Proactive Approach to Building Nonprofit Boards of Directors*. Erwin, TN: Essex Press.

Hocker, J. L., and Wilmot, W. W. (1985). *Interpersonal Conflict*. 2ⁿᵈ ed. Dubuque, IA: William C. Brown.

Levering, R. and Moskowitz, M. (2003). How companies satisfy workers. *Fortune* January 7.

Levering, R., Moskowitz, M., and Katz, M. (1985). *The 100 Best Companies to Work for in America*. New York: Plume

Maxwell, J. C. (1999). *The 21 Indispensable Qualities of a Leader: Becoming the Person Others Will Want to Follow*. Nashville, TN: Thomas Nelson Publishers.

_____(2001). *The 17 Indisputable Laws of Teamwork*. Nashville, TN: Thomas Nelson Publishers.

Moore, L. F., ed. (1985*). Motivating Volunteers: How the Rewards of Unpaid Work can Meet People's Needs*. Vancouver, B.C., Canada: Vancouver Volunteer Center.

Naisbitt, J., and Aburdene, P. (1985*). Re-inventing the Corporation*. New York: Warner Books.

Satir, V. M. (1988). *The New Peoplemaking*. Palo Alto, CA: Science and Behavior Books.

Schutz, W. (1966). *The Interpersonal Underworld*. Palo Alto, CA: Science and Behavior Books.

Senge, P. M. (1990). *The Fifth Discipline: The Art and Practice of the Learning Organization*. New York: Currency Doubleday.

Tuckman, B. W. (1965). Developmental sequence in small groups. *Psychological Bulletin* 63:384-399.

Weis, R. M., and Gantt, V. W. (2002). *Leadership and Program Development in Nonprofit Organizations*. Peosta, IA: Eddie Bowers Publishing.

Widmer, C., and Houchin, S. (2000). *The Art of Trusteeship: The Nonprofit Board Member's Guide to Effective Governance*. San Francisco: Jossey-Bass.

Wood, J. T. (1995). *Relational Communication: Continuity and Change in Personal Relationships*. Belmont, CA: Wadsworth Publishing.

Wood, J. T., ed. (1996). *Gendered Relationships*. Mountain View, CA: Mayfield Publishing.

Zoglio, S. W. (1993). 7 keys to building great workteams. Available on-line. Path: <http//www.teambuildinginc.com> (select: "Articles"; scroll down and select: "7 Keys to Building Great Workteams").

4 Human Development, Competencies, Issues and Trends

Individuals go through an incredible range of developmental changes and situations throughout their lifetime, and it is critical that nonprofit leaders understand the nature of human development and various other issues in planning programs that enhance people's lives.

Understanding human development provides leaders with a foundation of knowledge about what most individuals are facing in terms of developmental stages and how best to address these stages with supportive programs. Knowing for instance, that adolescents between the ages of twelve and seventeen are searching for a positive identity is important in structuring programs that would help them find a sense of self-worth, self- knowledge and some direction. Similarly, being aware of important issues and trends allows nonprofit leaders to structure programs that address specific individual, family, and community situations.

The first section of Chapter 4, Human Development, provides the reader with insight into the ways in which people develop including specific areas of Competency Development. The next section, Issues and Trends, presents information on important issues and trends that are developing. All three sections are intended to provide guidance for setting priorities in program planning.

■ Human Development

The highest goal of any youth, human service, or nonprofit leader is to develop programs that enhance people's lives and to provide supportive relationships for members/clients. With that in mind, it is essential to understand the nature of human development as individuals progress through various life stages.

The changes that occur between birth and death contribute to an amazing odyssey, and the saying "change is the only constant" is particularly true as individuals pass from one of life's many stages to another. Young children, for instance, often view their parents' commands as pronouncements to be accepted as what is right, but within a few years they begin to believe their parents are not always right. Then, in adolescence, a child may begin to think his or her parents are rarely correct; this often changes yet again into an appreciation of the parents' viewpoints in late adolescence or early adulthood. Mark Twain once wrote, "When I was a boy of 14, my father was so ignorant I could hardly stand to have the old man around. But when I got to be 21, I was astonished at how much *he* had learned in 7 years" (Rees 1994, 337). Physical changes, health, attitudes, beliefs, values, and behavior are continually evolving from one experience to another and from one time of our life to another.

Most experts believe developmental changes occur as a result of the interaction of genetic and environmental influences. The term **maturation** is most often used to describe the unfolding of the genetic plan, such as the appearance of baby teeth, facial hair in boys, and the oncoming of menstruation in adolescent girls. The maturation process is determined by internal signals. The concept of **learning**, however, involves changes that occur as a result of interaction with the environment. **Development,** then, is the interaction of genetic and environmental influences. With this in mind, it is easy to understand the responsibility and opportunities nonprofit leaders have in shaping human development.

Development does not happen in isolation, but occurs in the **context** of various circumstances and situations. The most important context is the **family**, which has tremendous influence on individual development. Other important contexts for healthy development include **school** and **community experiences**. To a degree, individuals are products of their school systems and neighborhoods. The **media** is another significant influence on human development. People are greatly influenced by what they watch on TV or experience at the movie theaters. Since most people's days are centered on their jobs, **career paths** are another important context for individual growth. **Culture** also has a great deal to do with who we are and who we become. A child growing up in China will have different experiences and values than a child who grows up in the United States of America. Children in rural settings often have different challenges and activities than those growing up in places like New York City. In complex societies, groups exist that differ from the majority in areas such as beliefs, attitudes, behaviors, values and traditions. These **subcultures** also have a legitimate and profound effect on individual development.

Considering the contextual nature of human development, nonprofit leaders have a tremendous opportunity to enhance areas of family structure and support, individual growth, and community development.

■ Developmental Theories

Theories explaining human development are important because they help us to explain various processes and stages of human nature, and they assist us in predicting what might come next. They also help us develop the kinds of programs necessary to address individual needs in various life stages and situations. Good theories can enhance understanding, they can help us make accurate predictions, and they are testable. There are a number of developmental theories worthy of consideration (Kaplan 1998).

Freud's Psychoanalytic Theory

Sigmund Freud postulated that there were three levels of awareness: the **conscious,** which consists of immediate awareness; the **preconscious,** which consists of memories that can readily become conscious; and the **unconscious,** which is beyond normal awareness and which sometimes manifests itself in dreams and inadvertent actions or words. Freud argued that behavior and actions could sometimes be caused by memories that had been stored and forgotten in the unconscious.

Freud used three concepts to explain the workings of the mind: the **id**, the **ego**, and the **superego**. The id is the construct that controls wishes and desires. It expects instant gratification. The ego interacts with reality and satisfies the needs of the id in a socially acceptable manner. The ego grows in importance as a child develops. The superego is similar to the conscious. It contains principles and compares behavior with the **ego ideal**, which is what individuals think they should be. The ego ideal tries to maintain a balance between the desires of the id, the constrictions of the ego, and the restraints of the superego (Kaplan 1998).

Anxiety can develop between the desires of the id and the restrictions of the ego that may lead to the ego creating **defense mechanisms** to protect itself. These mechanisms take the form of behavior designed to relieve stress and create emotional peace.

Early experiences, particularly those between parents and children, were considered to be very important by Freud, who thought bad experiences in childhood left irreversible impressions on children. More contemporary experts believe that subsequent positive experiences can ease the trauma of earlier negative experiences.

Although some of Freud's other theories, such as the **Psychosexual Theory,** are not as respected by modern theorists, his overall impact is unmistakable, and his theories are still used by developmental psychologists in understanding human nature.

Erikson's Psychosocial Theory

A proponent of many of Freud's theories, Erik Erikson has had a strong influence on the study of human development. Erikson developed a theory that holds that individuals pass through eight different stages of life. At each stage, each individual encounters the possibility of a crisis. If the crisis at each stage is handled relatively well, a positive outcome occurs, and the person develops into a healthy individual. Few people advance through Erikson's eight stages with an entirely positive outcome, but a mostly positive outcome is critical for healthy development. Passing through one stage successfully makes the next stage easier, and so on.

- **Trust versus Mistrust.** When caregivers and others support infants by expressing love and protection, a child emerges from infancy with a sense of trust for people and for their surroundings. Children may become distrustful if caregivers are perceived as angry and stressed. Infants who develop a sense of trust will feel more comfortable in their environment and will be more likely to develop positive attitudes toward all of life.

- **Autonomy versus Doubt.** Young children between the ages of two and three begin exploring their world by practicing new physical skills. When this exploration process is encouraged and supported by caregivers, the toddlers develop a sense of autonomy. If, on the other hand, this exploration process is discouraged, a child may begin to question his or her abilities. It is important that caregivers reward and encourage youngsters to explore and practice new skills.

- **Initiative versus Guilt.** When children around the age of four are encouraged to develop plans and to carry out these plans, they begin to develop a sense of initiative and often become self-starters. When plans are not encouraged and actions are often discouraged, a child may feel a sense of guilt and develop a lack of assertiveness.

- **Industry versus Inferiority.** Children between the ages of six and eleven who are rewarded for developing skills in such areas as reading, math, and socializa-

tion begin to develop a sense of industry and feel that their efforts are worthwhile. Children who feel that their efforts are not appreciated or who are compared unfavorably with other children could very well develop a sense of inferiority.

- **Identity versus Role Confusion.** Adolescents involved in healthy experiences
  who receive encouraging feedback for their actions usually begin to understand
  who they are and develop a positive self-image. Self-knowledge and a positive
  self-image provide adolescents with a sense of security and confidence. Adolescents who have less self-knowledge may begin to feel confused regarding
  their identity and could engage in negative behavior just to be noticed.

- **Intimacy versus Isolation.** Young adults who have entered into positive activities and who have developed a strong identity are often ready to share themselves in relationships that require commitment and sacrifice, such as a healthy
  marriage and close friendships. Individuals who are unable to form close relationships may become isolated and lonely, even despairing.

- **Generativity versus Self-Absorption.** Middle-aged adults who invest in the
  future through children, grand-children and/or community involvement generally experience a sense of fulfillment and gratification. Adults who concentrate
  on the acquisition of material possessions and physical well-being may fail to
  develop a similar sense of gratification.

- **Ego Integrity versus Despair.** Older adults who look back on their lives with a
  sense of accomplishment and gratification develop a sense that their lives have had
  meaning. Individuals who realize they have missed too many opportunities and
  made a number of significant mistakes may experience depression and despair.

According to Erikson, the resolution of each stage depends on the interaction between individuals and their culture, their relationships, and the historical context in which
they lived. The development of identity, for instance, could be very different for someone
growing up in Hollywood compared to a child's development in Afghanistan. In a similar
sense, the development of industry for someone growing up in the industrial age would
vary significantly from someone growing up in the twenty-first century. Erikson's theories
have been difficult to test, but they are easy to understand, and they provide an excellent
foundation of concerns at each stage of life.

Piaget's Theory of Cognitive Development

Jean Piaget spent his entire adult life studying the cognitive growth processes of
children and determined that development occurs as people assimilate and organize their
lives in relation to their environment. Development, according to Piaget, is defined by four
principal factors: **maturation, experience, social transmission,** and the **process of equili-
bration.** Maturation involves the gradual unfolding of each person's genetic plan for life.
Experience includes the interaction of the child with his or her environment. The traditions,
customs, and information that parents and others pass on to the child make up social transmission or education. And the process of equilibrium occurs when children try to balance
what they have learned with what they have experienced. When a disequilibrium occurs
between what one has learned and what one has experienced, one develops abilities to deal

with situations differently and in a mature and sophisticated manner (Kaplan 1998).

Piaget created the term **functional invariants** to refer to the processes that individuals use to adjust to situations throughout their lives (Bjorklund 1995). He defined the two most important processes as **organization** and **adaption.** Organization refers to structuring knowledge in a way that makes knowledge helpful, and adaption means being able to use knowledge to adapt to the environment and to survive. Essentially, as the environment changes, individuals must change to meet environmental demands.

For Piaget, maturation was the result of experience, and he believed experiential educational processes were more important than formal education. Piaget's theories have been criticized because they were not proven in a controlled environment, but his theories include the most complete description of cognitive development from infancy to adulthood and have been very influential on developmental psychology.

The Behavior Theory

Behaviorists believe that behavior is determined in part by environmental influences and that when the environment changes, behavioral will change as well (Kaplan 1998). For instance, when a neutral experience, such as seeing someone in a white lab coat, is paired with pain, such as getting a shot with a needle, then the neutral experience may become associated with the negative feeling. Repeatedly pairing the neutral experience with the negative experience until a similar response is elicited from both is referred to as **classical conditioning**. The sight of the needle prior to the conditioning process may have caused concern and is therefore referred to as an **unconditional stimulus**, and a response to the needle, such as grimacing, prior to the conditioning is referred to as an **unconditional response**. A **conditional stimulus**, then, is the pairing of the neutral stimulus with the negative stimulus, and the **conditional response** would be the individual's concern about the person in the white lab coat.

This kind of conditional process may help us to understand some emotional responses. For instance, if a newly married stepfather begins to berate and criticize his new stepson, the stepson may begin to associate stress and anger with the sight of the stepfather, whom he may have previously trusted and been happy to be around. **Operant conditioning**, in which a behavior is either reinforced or punished following its occurrence, is also important in understanding human development. With operant conditioning, if a behavior is reinforced with a positive response, it will continue and possibly increase in occurrence; if the behavior is followed by a negative response, it will decrease in occurrence.

The behavioral view has been criticized by some theorists who believe it is too mechanical and fails to include conscious thought and subjective experiences in the overall scheme of things, but it can be helpful in understanding some behavior and successful in modifying behavior in a number of situations.

Social Learning Theory

Social theorist A. Bandura postulated that individuals learn by watching and imitating others and learn from examining the consequences of what they are observing. For example, a person who watches someone else pick up a hot pan and then flinch in pain does not need to replicate the event to understand that the pan is dangerous. Bandura organized his theory into a four-step process. First, an individual must concentrate on the model. Then the model must be retained in memory. Next, the stored information must be used in an attempt to replicate the action in the model. For instance, a person watching a baseball player at bat may try to duplicate a certain swing. Finally, motivation in the form of reinforcement must occur in order for the person to learn the behavior and use the behavior again and again in the future.

According to social theorists, behavior is divided into two processes: learning and performing. Learning can occur through observation and other activities, but performance depends partly on what Bandura calls **self-efficacy**, or the belief one has about his or her ability to do something in a particular situation (Schunk 1996). When individuals believe a task is within their capabilities, they will attempt to do it; when they doubt their abilities with various tasks, they are more likely to avoid those activities. The Social Theory is helpful in understanding behaviors that are learned and imitated from others.

Ecological Theory

Urie Bronfenbrenner formulated the Ecological Theory in order to expand the viewpoint that human development is contextual in nature, involving families, communities, culture and even historical periods. According to Bronfenbrenner, individuals are influenced by four different environmental systems: the **microsystem**, the **mesosystem**, the **exosystem**, and the **macrosystem**. The microsystem includes an individual's immediate experiences, such as a child's experiences at home with the family. As the child develops, additional settings emerge and the mesosystem involves the child in two or more settings such as a day-care center or school. This entry of a child into a new setting invariably has an effect on other major settings. For instance, a child's attendance at day care will have some effect on family activities at home.

The exosystem describes settings the child is not actively involved in, but that have an effect on the child and/or the family, such as the actions of the local school superintendent or a sibling's involvement with the local theater group. Although the child is not directly involved with these activities, the activities may have a direct effect the child. For example, the sibling's involvement in theater may affect the opportunities the child has to play and interact with his or her sibling. It may also affect the amount of time the parents have to spend with the child, since they may have to spend time transporting the sibling to and from theater practice and participating in related activities.

Finally, the macrosystem includes the belief system that is a part of the social institutions as well as the ethnic, cultural, religious, political, and economic processes of the country in which the child resides (Kaplan 1998). These differing ideologies can have a profound influence on the development of a child. For instance, the increased percentage of single parent families, the changes in the welfare system, and the increased numbers of disappearing dads, separately and/or together, could have a significant effect on a child's life.

An advantage of this theory is that it provides us with the idea that individuals are always moving between one system and another, and then back again. This information allows us the opportunity to assist in the transactions from system to system. The interaction an individual has with each of these systems has a profound effect on each person's life.

■ Developmental Competencies

Edginton and Edginton (1994) subscribe to five basic areas of importance for the development of youth (as adapted from Pittman 1991), and they include:

- **Health/physical competence.** Youth need to have good health and to maintain knowledge, attitudes and behaviors to ensure good health for the future. This includes exercising, maintaining a healthy diet, and being aware of nutritional requirements.
- **Personal/social competence.** It is important that youth develop several good *intrapersonal skills*. They need the ability to understand and deal with personal emotions and to maintain-self discipline; they need to develop effective *interpersonal skills*, including the ability to work with others, to develop friendships and to understand and empathize with others; they need *coping skills* and the ability to adapt and assume responsibility; and they need *judgement skills*, for making good decisions and solving problems.
- **Cognitive/creative competence.** Youth need to have a broad base of knowledge and the ability to appreciate and participate in creative expression, good oral and written *language skills*, problem solving and *analytical skills* and an interest in learning and achieving.
- **Vocational competence.** It is important that youth develop an understanding and awareness of vocational and avocational opportunities. It is also important for youth to grasp the function and value of work and leisure time and for them to learn how to prepare for both.
- **Citizenship competencies (ethics and preparation).** Youth need to understand their nation's history and values and develop a sense of personal responsibility for community and national enhancement.

As young people move toward these competencies they develop a sense of self-confidence and self-efficacy and feel good about being themselves. Leaders of nonprofit organizations need to understand and incorporate these developmental competencies and other developmental theories into goal setting, program planning, and other relevant aspects of organizational operations when appropriate.

Additional information regarding human development can be found in *The Human Odyssey: Life-Span Development* by Paul Kaplan, Brooks/Cole Publishing Company, 2000.

Understanding situations that people might face throughout their lives is equally important and will be discussed in the next section.

■ Issues and Trends

Over the centuries, life has become more complicated with each passing year. Individuals, families, and communities are facing unparalleled challenges and opportunities in areas of health and fitness, education, family structure and patterns, cultural diversity, communication, social interaction, and technology, to mention several. The leaders of nonprofit organizations must be well-versed in the issues and trends their members and clients are facing and be capable of shifting strategies and resources to address issues and trends as they become relevant to the organization's mission.

Households, Families, Children, and Youth

Households can be distinguished from **families** in that a household is considered to be a residential and economic unit, whereas families imply a construct of meanings and relationships (Osmond and Thorne 1993; Rapp 1982). The U.S. Census Bureau defines households as taking one of three basic forms: **family**, **non-family**, and **single-person** household. Family households are considered to be two or more persons living together who are related through marriage, birth, or adoption. The most common type of family household is a married couple with or without children. Non-family households consist of two or more unrelated individuals who are residing in the same living area. Single-person households are made up of those individuals who live alone in a residential unit.

U.S. households continue to change in important areas. For instance, the number of households is still growing, but at a much slower rate, and there were approximately 110 million households in the year 2000. Another important change is the average size of a  household which has gotten smaller and smaller over the last fifty years and now represents an approximate average of 2.6 individuals per household. Two trends that may work to counteract this are the growing number of adult children who are living with their parents, and the growing number of elderly mothers and fathers who reside with their children. There are more single-parent families, childless married couples, and people living alone than ever before, and no household arrangement can be classified as typical. A noteworthy trend is the percentage of households headed by married couples, which has declined from eighty percent in 1919 to fifty-three percent in 1998 (Caplow, Hicks, and Wattenberg 2001).

As with households, families have also changed in some important ways. For instance, there is a greater variety of family circumstances than ever before. **Traditional families**, in which there is a working father, children under the age of eighteen, and a mother who is not in the work force, have diminished in number. Social forces, such as high divorce rates, an increased number of women in the work force, and declining fertility rates, have added to the growing variety of family situations.

Some of these social forces have also added to the numbers of **single-parent families,** at least ninety percent of which exist with a woman as the head of the household. In spite of the fact that teenage pregnancies have declined in recent years, teen parents lead a significant percentage of single-parent families. Although a number of children from single-parent families become successful adults, children from single-parent families have comparatively poorer academic achievement and are more likely to drop out of school. They are more likely to be poor, to marry early and more likely to divorce. They are also more likely to become involved in criminal activity, including the use of illegal drugs. Since there is a strong correlation between single parenting and living in poverty, it is difficult to separate the effects of these two factors. In many single-parent families, the father is absent, and there is minimal interaction or financial support, if any. In families with **absentee**

dads, the children are at much greater risk of dropping out of school, getting in trouble in school and having poor grades.

When a parent cannot or will not take responsibility for a child, a **skip-generation** family often develops in which a grandparent becomes the primary caregiver. This can become emotionally and financially difficult for grandparents, who may have to raise two generations of children but be unable to receive public assistance because they often do not have legal custody of their grandchildren. A large number of skip-generation families have the mother living there as well, but not as the head of the household. Family court judges and social workers often link drug and alcohol abuse to the skip-generation phenomenon.

Children staying at home longer and aging parents living longer due to advanced health technologies indicate there will be more **multi-generational** families in which the parent or parents are wedged between at least one child at home and their own frail and elderly parents. This is also sometimes referred to as the **sandwich generation** and has become more intense since families are smaller and the burden of care giving falls on fewer siblings.

Less than half of all marriages end in **divorce** and that percentage has plateaued and even declined in recent years. The median duration of marriage before a divorce is about seven years, and over half of all divorces involve children who will experience a permanent disruption. Many divorces involve tremendous emotional, psychological, and financial up-heaval for everyone involved. A large number of divorced fathers will let this upheaval become a reason for them to become completely absent from the lives of their children. Fortunately, divorce is expected to continue to decline since it is viewed with less favor as its disruptive and damaging impacts, especially on children, are increasingly recognized. There is also an increased disenchantment with the single lifestyle and a continuing fear of sexu-ally transmitted diseases. One-fifth of all married couples with children make up **stepfamilies**, in which at least one child under the age of eighteen is involved. Stepfamilies often have their own special dynamics and provide unique challenges for parenting and developing relationships. Most stepchildren live with their biological mothers and stepfathers.

Another demographic with significant implications is the growing number of senior citizens over the age of eighty-five, which has increased at a rate three times that of the general population. These citizens seek to live independently, but the frailty that comes with old age catches up with them, and **elder care**, in which seniors require assistance to remain somewhat independent, is a growing consideration. Many of these citizens are cared for at home, but the main caregiver often works a full-time job and care giving can be difficult for the caregiver as well as for the recipient. Although nursing home care is a consideration, only a small percentage of seniors ever live in a nursing home. Adult home-care programs, foster-care, day-care programs, Meals on Wheels, and telephone reassur-ance are just some of the programs that provide seniors with the support necessary to re-main in their homes.

Most experts agree that the caregiving and educational preparation for children from birth to age eighteen in this country is too often inadequate. Youth face other challenges as well, such as alienation, loneliness, social depravity, and a lack of connectedness. Low-income families, in particular, face hardships that include inadequate health care, crime and drugs, lack of successful role models, financial hardships, and a sense of hopelessness. An incredible twenty percent of all children in the United States live in **poverty**, which is often due to parental job loss and to the increase of children living in single-parent families. These families, usually with a female at the head, have a poverty rate of approximately five times the poverty rate of married-couple families.

In order to escape poverty and low income, most mothers work out of economic necessity, and the lack of affordable and effective **day care** for children under the age of six has become a serious problem. Many studies, including a study involving Head Start enrollees and a control group, concluded that the children involved with Head Start were more likely to become high school graduates, enroll in college or be employed. And they were less likely to become involved in crime or be on welfare by the age of nineteen (Eitzen and Zinn 2000; United Way Strategic Institute 1992).

Each year, tens of thousands of infants die before they reach the age of one. The infant morality rate for the United States is one of the highest among the industrialized nations, and the main reason for this is **low birth rate**, often a result of inadequate prenatal care. A significant portion of these children will end up with permanent disabilities. Many other children will have chronic and disabling conditions as a result of being born **HIV positive** or as a result of **cocaine exposure.** Spiraling health care costs make it difficult for many families to receive proper care, let alone incorporate preventive measures. Another health concern is the immunization process for preventable diseases. Although the vast majority of children are immunized against measles, mumps, and rubella, there are still a significant number of children who are not, particularly in inner cities. For instance, there are still tens of thousands of measles cases reported each year, which in severe cases can result in death. In spite of numerous diseases and other conditions, the number one cause of death among children is **accidents**, which can also result in permanent disabilities.

Another serious health concern for children is the lack of **proper nutrition**, which often leads to iron-deficiency anemia and is closely associated with poverty. Proper nutrition for low-income pregnant women, new mothers and infants is critical. This is often provided by **WIC**, which was created to do just that, but WIC is seriously under-funded and cannot meet the needs of all of those who meet the criteria. Incredible as it may seem, **hunger** is another serious problem for children: between five and six million children will go hungry nearly every day, and the number could increase throughout the 2000s. The rate of hunger is closely related to childhood poverty.

Another area of risk for children is the area of **education**, in which American students often lag behind students in developed and developing countries, particularly in math and science. A significant percentage of students fail to graduate from high school, or they graduate without the knowledge and skills necessary for acquiring and keeping a job. There is a strong correlation between dropping out of school and crime and poverty. Factors sometimes associated with **dropouts** include being poor, belonging to an ethnic or racial minority, having limited English proficiency, and being a child from a single- parent family. Though often interrelated, any one of these factors can cause problems in school. Each year, about one million teen girls become **pregnant**, and a significant number of these will conceive again in one to two years. These young mothers are overwhelmed with responsibilities and are unlikely to finish high school and more likely to face a life of economic hardship and dependency. Statistically, the children of teen mothers are less likely to finish high school and more likely to achieve lower levels of education, become involved with crime and drugs, and to become teen parents as well.

Nearly one million children are considered **discarded**, which means they live in foster homes, detention centers, hospitals, and mental health centers. These living arrangements are necessary for a number of reasons, including family breakup, homelessness, child abuse, and alcohol and drug abuse. Teenagers are going through a rapidly changing period of life and require strong support. **Suicide** is the second leading cause of death among adolescents. Additionally, there are over a million **runaways** living on the streets or in less than desirable shelters, and tens of thousands of youth are classified as **lost, injured**, or **missing**. And in a country that prides itself on its diversity, about half of all teenagers have witnessed racist acts, and a significant portion of teens have been the victims of bias.

Although most families are healthy, functional units, researchers sometimes consider families to be the most violent social group, next to the police and the military, and **child abuse** is too often the result of this violence. Child abuse is an act carried out with the intent of injury or acts of omission that place children in danger. The incidents of child reported abuse increased in the 1980s and the 1990s. **Neglect** is another type of abuse directed toward children. Neglect includes inadequate feeding of children, poor sanitary conditions, and leaving children in a potentially dangerous setting.

Health and Education

Americans are living longer than anytime in history with **life expectancies** ranging from early sixties to high seventies, depending on race and gender. On the average, men die younger than women do, and African Americans die younger than whites, primarily due to cancer, heart attack, and strokes. **Heart disease** still causes more deaths than any other disease, with **cancer** second. One of the reasons that life expectancy rates are so high is that **infant mortality** rates have been reduced so significantly from the beginning of the century. Poor and rural communities maintain higher infant mortality than urban settings, and life expectancy is lower for racial and ethnic minorities, many of whom live in poor communities with inadequate medical care.

Acquired Immune Deficiency Syndrome (AIDS) is caused by the **HIV** virus which damages the body's immune system and leaves the body more susceptible to infections and cancer. AIDS is spread through sexual contact, needles or syringes shared by drug abusers, infected blood or blood products; it is also passed from pregnant women to their offspring. People who are at high risk for contracting AIDS include those who practice unprotected sex with infected partners and drug abusers who share needles. AIDS has also spread among groups not previously thought of as high risk, such as crack smokers, women, and teenagers. AIDS has also increased in rural communities, where residents are often ill-equipped to handle the disease medically or socially. African Americans and Hispanics are disproportionately affected by AIDS, and the estimates of those infected ranges from the hundreds of thousands to several million. **Sexually Transmitted Diseases (STDs)** such as syphilis, gonorrhea, and pelvic inflammatory disease (PID) remain serious health threats and can cause a great deal of suffering and even death.

Another disease, **tuberculosis**, was once the leading cause of death in the United States, but it has been in decline for decades. Unfortunately, it is making a comeback in major cities, and drug addicts, the homeless, and people with AIDs are especially suscep-tible to it. Airborne bacteria spread tuberculosis, which has led some cities to forcibly hospitalize patients and test schoolchildren. In the future, viral conditions that are not cur-able with conventional therapies are predicted to be on the rise as are bacterial infections that become resistant to commonly used antibiotics.

It has been suggested that as many as one in four American workers suffer from **stress-related** illnesses or **anxiety disorders**, and **depression** is thought to affect a similar number of individuals. Increasing competition, advanced technology, work-family issues, and job uncertainties are just a few of the variables contributing to these conditions. Elec-tronic monitors that count the number of keystrokes made by some computer operators and electronic surveillance of telephone conversations are also causing increasing stress in the workplace. Medical experts generally agree that workers who are under electronic surveil-lance suffer higher levels of stress-related medical problems such as fatigue, ulcers, depres-sion, and even heart disease.

Millions of Americans are addicted to **drugs** and millions more suffer from **alcohol-ism** or **alcohol dependence**. An estimated five to ten percent of the population have experi-mented with marijuana, the most popular illegal drug (Caplow, et al. 2001), and millions of Americans use or experiment with cocaine, heroine, hallucinogens and inhalants. Illegal drug use seems to have peaked in the 70s and 80s and has leveled off since. Factors contrib-uting to drug abuse and addiction include boredom, social and work pressures, and medical needs. In moderation, alcohol is considered to be relatively safe, but when abused it is the leading cause of accidents and accounts for about half of all traffic related deaths. Crimi-nals, prior to committing a criminal act, often use alcohol and drugs. There is a strong correlation between abusing alcohol and the overall suicide rate, and it is a big factor in drowning. Consumed in large quantities over long periods of time, alcohol almost always results in serious health consequences.

Although **tobacco** smoking has been on the decline for years, millions of Americans still use tobacco and there has been a disturbing, steady usage by women, young people, teens, pre-teens and minorities. Additionally, there has been a movement on the part of tobacco companies to market tobacco overseas, which increases health and financial prob-lems in other countries that result in global consequences for all of us. **Second-hand smoke** also causes significant health problems and deaths from cancer and heart disease for thou-sands of individuals each year. Premature deaths as a result of smoking are possibly the most preventable kind in the United States, and the cessation of tobacco use results in al-most immediate health benefits for individuals of all ages.

Alternative health care methods, such as holistic medicine and self-help groups, have grown in popularity in the United States. Some of these techniques include biofeed-back, acupuncture, chiropractic medicine, meditation, yoga, massage, hypnosis, and ho-meopathic medicine. Many experts define health in terms of mind and body balance or harmony.

Health care is one of the most complicated, highly political and emotionally charged issues our nation is facing. Health care costs represent a significant percentage of the gross national product (GNP) and are rising steadily. While most people look to job-related in-surance to cover the majority of their health costs, insurance costs reflect the increased rise in health care costs, and a significant portion of the population simply do not have insurance coverage. And while health care costs are spiraling upward, the availability of services (**health care delivery**) has declined, particularly in rural and poor sections of the country. The need for long-term care is increasing as American become older on the average. **Medicare** is the governmental health care program that assists senior citizens with these costs and others and **Medicaid** was implemented to address the health care needs of the poor. The level of support from Medicare and Medicaid varies depending on circumstances and current policy. Free clinics for the working poor, volunteer nursing visitations, and programs to help individuals save on medical costs are just a few of the ways nonprofit organizations are addressing needs that are not now or in the foreseeable future addressed through health insurance, Medicare, or Medicaid.

Education will remain one of the highest priorities on the national agenda, and the correlation between excellence in education and quality of life has been proven again and again. For decades, **educational reforms** have been taking place in school systems around the nation. The most recent wave of reforms includes the concept of **school-based management**, in which there is a transfer of decision-making power from a centralized authority to instructors, parents, and administrators of the schools. These decisions range from developing the curriculum to deciding how a school will spend its money. With reform in mind, many school systems are also incorporating **service learning** into the curriculum. Service learning combines community service with specific learning objectives and has proven to be an invaluable pedagogy for teaching values and character and for bridging the gap between theory and practice. Other school districts have adopted an option of a **choice** for parents as to which school their children will attend. This concept is designed to develop competition among schools and to stimulate curricula and facilities improvement. Still other educational systems have adopted **year-round school** programs in an effort to expand educational opportunities and provide additional support systems for students and parents the entire year. Having met with some opposition initially, this program continues to gain favor because of its flexibility and continuity of academics and extra-curricular activities.

A number of studies indicate that high quality early-childhood education programs make a significant difference for at-risk youth, and more and more experts are stressing the

importance of early-childhood education. **Preschool** has been integrated into many educational systems, and the majority of all three- and four-year-olds take part in some form of early childhood education. The federal preschool program **Head Start** has helped millions of children since its creation in 1965 and is regarded as one of the government's most successful programs. Enrollment in both elementary and secondary schools has steadily increased, and more opportunities will develop for after school activities. **Home schooling** continues to be on the rise as some parents contend that public schools have poor academic standards, poor discipline and crowded conditions. Post secondary enrollment has been up and down so far in this decade, particularly among eighteen- to twenty-four-year-olds, and the average age of college students continues to rise.

The American way of life is still highly valued by many worldwide. Consequently, immigration has led to a **mosaic classroom** in which a significant number of students have limited English proficiency. This generally makes instruction much more challenging, and the combination of language and cultural differences sometimes leads to clashes in the school system. Even when **bilingual-education** programs are introduced, it takes about seven years for a non-native to reach national norms on standardized tests. **English-as-a-Second-Language (ESL)** has also been expanded, and many non-English speaking students have been mainstreamed into regular classrooms with ESL-trained instructors. A major concern remains regarding the educational underachievement among minority racial and ethnic groups. The situation is critical, since approximately one in three elementary and secondary school children are minorities. Clearly, there are numerous opportunities for nonprofit organizations to step in and assist in developing foundations for academic achievement.

About one in four students **drop out** each year, and that number is often higher in urban centers (Eitzen and Zinn 2000). Dropout rates are costly for individuals and for society. Jobs require higher skill levels than ever before, unemployment rates are twice as high for high school dropouts as for graduates, and dropouts are more likely to become involved in crime and drugs. Dropouts are also more likely to come from a single-parent family, live in a household that is considered at the poverty level, and be at home alone more than three hours a day. Having limited skills in English and/or coming from a home where the parents are dropouts adds to the potential of dropping out. The nation's number of **illiterates** are in the millions and illiteracy is increasing at an alarming rate. Millions of Americans are classified as **functionally illiterate**, which means they are able to read at a fourth grade level; there are even more people referred to as **marginally illiterate**, who read at the eighth grade level. This is frustrating and demeaning for individuals; it costs them billions of dollars in unrealized earnings and costs the country billions of dollars in welfare and unemployment compensation each year. There are a disproportionate number of African American and Hispanic children living in poverty who also have trouble reading.

The ratio of computers to students in the classroom has moved ahead at a rapid pace and **technology** has made **distance learning**—video courses with a two-way hook-up between teachers and students—an established pedagogical method. **Global classrooms** in which students search the Internet for information and interact with individuals online could help develop technical expertise, cultural understanding, and knowledge.

Population and Aging

The American population has nearly quadrupled in the past century, and the number of people in the country has exceeded 270 million (Weis and Gantt 2002). The combination of falling death rates due to **medical advances,** massive **immigration**, and **increased birth rates** has led to significant population growth, although population has declined somewhat in percentage of growth over the last several decades. The 1990 Immigration Act led to significant increases in immigration, and medical advances have made it easier for women to become pregnant and for individuals to have longer, healthier life spans on the average. Approximately 600,000 individuals immigrate to the United States each year and an estimated 200,000 to 1,000,000 people enter the country illegally on an annual basis (Caplow, et al. 2001). This influx of immigrants creates a number of cultural, educational, vocational, and financial challenges as new citizens prepare for a life sometimes far different from that in their native land.

Fertility rates have increased due to a number of factors, including the increased number of women bearing children in their middle to late thirties, the increased number of female immigrants who have higher fertility rates than native-born Americans, and an increased number of unplanned and too often unwanted births. Minority birth rates exceed that of the population in general.

About a third of the overall population was born between the years 1946 and 1964. These individuals are usually referred to as **baby boomers**, since many were conceived following the end of World War II, when people were putting their lives and families back together. Over the past century, the proportion of children and adolescents in the population has decreased as the proportion of older Americans has increased. As people live longer on the average and the proportion of births decreases, the average age of Americans will increase. The percentage of people seventy-five years old and older has increased and the proportion of **centenarians** increased more than any other age group in the last two decades of the past century. This trend will create tremendous challenges and opportunities for the social security system, health care, families, and certainly for nonprofit organizations.

Social Security is a major source of income for most seniors, and in many cases it is the only source of senior citizens' income. But Social Security is coming under increased pressure by the growing number of applicants, and people in certain occupations, such as agriculture, are often exempt from the Social Security program. Additionally, women who have worked as homemakers receive no credit for their work, and a woman who is widowed will not receive benefits until she is sixty, unless she has a child under sixteen or a disabled child, or unless she herself is disabled.

Although the majority of older people are in good health, the elderly are more affected by poor health than any other group. Both physical and mental conditions affect older people, and **Alzheimer's disease** is the leading cause of dementia in old age afflicting millions of senior citizens. Older people usually have more contact with physicians than other age group. Their prescription drug cost represents the largest out-of-pocket health-care expense for the majority of the elderly and their medical expenses are three times greater than those of middle-aged adults, yet their incomes are significantly lower (Eitzen and Zinn 2000). When senior citizens need to be institutionalized, an affluent minority receives **therapeutic care**, an approach that focuses on meeting the needs of patients and providing for their treatment. On the other hand, homes with welfare recipients tend to provide **custodial care**, which too often focuses on meeting the needs of the institution, rather than those of the patients.

The majority of the elderly are not institutionalized, and since senior citizens are living longer, family members will spend longer periods of **elder-caregiving.** Because there are fewer siblings in families than in decades past, caretaker responsibilities will fall to a very few individuals, usually daughters or daughters-in-law. Although most of the elderly benefit from family caretakers, there can also be an increased likelihood of **elder**

abuse. Abuse can take a number of different forms. Physical abuse involves individuals being slapped, hit, or restrained. Psychological abuse includes verbal assaults or threats. Drug abuse may occur when seniors are encouraged to over-medicate. Material abuse includes theft or misuse of money. And a violation of rights occurs when an elderly person is forced into a nursing home against his or her will. Abuse may occur more often when the caretaker is overwhelmed physically, emotionally, and financially.

Poverty, Housing, and Homelessness

A family is considered living in **poverty** if their pre-tax income is approximately $16,000-$17,000 per year, which includes about fifteen percent of all families. A study by the U.S. Bureau of the Census found that families living in poverty were twice as likely to divorce than families not in poverty; thus poverty can be a significant factor in the break-up of some families (Eitzen and Zinn 2000). The picture is even bleaker for single-parent families, who often have to get by on the income from one parent when child support is not available for whatever reason.

The number of children living in poverty has more than doubled in the past several decades with approximately fourteen million children living at the poverty level. Child poverty has been reduced by other industrialized nations, but the United States has failed significantly in this regard. Poverty can effect health, physical and intellectual development, and a number of social conditions, and there is a growing number of children living in **extreme poverty**, in which the family lives at half or less of the official poverty level. Extreme poverty can put a child at serious risk of malnutrition or some other threat. It is estimated that as many as one in five children live in poverty.

Individuals between the age of nineteen and twenty-four are more likely to live in poverty than older individuals, and families with the head of the household under the age of thirty are more likely to live in poverty than families with older heads of households. Two out of three adults living in poverty are likely to be women. Poverty rates for minorities are disproportionately high compared to whites, but the overall number of whites living in poverty is still higher. Immigrants have a higher rate of poverty than do native-born individuals, and a larger percentage of rural families live in poverty than do people living in cities. With fewer business and commerce centers, it is difficult to move out of poverty.

The poverty rates for senior citizens over the age of sixty-five has improved significantly over the past several decades, as America has done a better job of re-training and supporting the older generation. However, there is a higher percentage of the elderly living just above the poverty level than those that are non-elderly. Senior citizens are therefore over-represented among the **near poor**. In spite of all of the improvements, the United States is still in the lower tier of success stories with poverty among senior citizens.

With more than forty million people in the United States living in poverty and another thirty million or so living just above the poverty level, more effort needs to go into eliminating poverty. Welfare reform, school breakfast programs, school reforms that include family resource centers, Head Start, the United Way's Success by Six program, job- and business-related investment initiatives, and other public and private assistance programs have made a marked impact on poverty. Still, America lags behind most of the other industrialized nations, and until national policies are changed to address poverty genuinely and effectively, the nonprofit sector must make a strong initiative to address the needs of the poor.

Most Americans cannot afford to purchase a home because of the often-required down payment (approximately twenty percent) and/or high mortgage payments that go along with **home ownership**. Individuals and families who own their home often develop a greater sense of personal and community pride and benefit financially from home equity and tax incentives. Some individuals are able to purchase a home only with the aid of governmental, private, or nonprofit programs that assist with the down payment, interest rates, or construction costs. A significant number, about one-third of all Americans, are **shelter poor**, which means they spend so much of their income on home ownership that paying for necessities like food, clothing, and utilities is difficult.

Poor families must often live in **public housing**, which is often substandard and inadequate, and housing for poor minorities, the elderly, and households with females at the head is twice the average of substandard housing in general. Nearly a fourth of all **rural poor** live in substandard housing, and even though the cost of rural housing is less than for urban housing, the income of rural families is typically lower.

Incidents in which senior citizens share their homes with unrelated people, referred to as **shared housing**, for the purpose of rent, companionship, assistance with daily living and/ or security, has increased and will continue to do so in the future. The government's definition of "disability" now includes the de-institutionalized mentally disabled, as well as some classifications of drug addicts and alcoholics, and public housing for the **disabled** has increased significantly. Advocacy groups often make a point of working for fair housing for the disabled, the homeless, and the very poor. These efforts often run counter to the unwritten policies of housing managers who prefer residents with more options for paying rent.

Homeless families have increased in number and will probably continue to do so in the future. About one-third of all homeless families include children. Homelessness may come about through a variety of causes, including low-paying jobs, terminations and layoffs, domestic problems, alcohol and drug addictions, old age, and disabilities to mention several. There can be a number of solutions that involve shelters, job training and retraining, support, and sobriety programs.

The World of Work and Technology

Changes continue to take place at a dizzying pace as a mostly **information-based** economy replaces an industrialized one, and technology becomes more and more integrated into the way we conduct business and our personal lives as well. Businesses and organizations that are designed to incorporate information resources and electronic networks into their operating procedures can be responsive to changing customer demands and will have a decided edge over less enlightened organizations.

Individuals with specialized skills are in greater demand to work in information-based organizations. People who are innovative in developmental and problem solving areas will continue to be sought after by organizations. Individuals with critical skills and innovative character will find the highest paying jobs in all areas of work.

One of the benefits of enhanced technology has been that organizations have developed **flexible working environments** for employees who are unable to work a nine-to-five schedule, or are unable to work at a corporate headquarters. This flexible workplace also includes **job sharing**, in which several people share the same position. Working a **compressed work week**, working forty hours in less than five days, has become more popular and seems to enhance morale and efficiency, while reducing absenteeism. **Telecommuting** via computers from home provides individuals flexibility and provides opportunities for productivity and collaboration they may not have otherwise.

Changing demographics have made **managing diversity** a critical concern for organizational leaders. The rising number of women, minorities, and senior citizens in the workplace has made it a mosaic of different cultures and has led to a need for programs designed to empower and enhance a culturally diverse work force. These types of programs are important and demand for them will continue to grow.

As an increasing number of mothers come into the workplace, there is a growing need for more high quality, yet affordable, preschool, before school, and after school **child-care** programs. A significant number of parents believe that present day affordable child-care is often inadequate in staffing and content, and a demand for better child-care will continue to grow. Organizations that recognize and address this need should be in great demand.

Employees can experience a sense of **alienation** when working conditions become such that individuals feel separated from others, from themselves, and even from the work they do, if there is a lack of satisfaction and personal accomplishment. Additional factors, such as the transition to an information-based economy, inadequate child-care, increased responsibilities, ambiguous job descriptions, and lack of security, have taken their toll on many employees who report significant **stress** and **fatigue** at the business site.

Unemployed workers whose skills are obsolete can be **trained** and **retrained** by companies who find themselves in partnerships with educational institutions more and more. Transitional approaches such as **school-to-work** initiatives can be critical for the millions of individuals for whom high school is the end of their formal educational experience. A number of programs including **cooperative education, monitored work experiences,** and **vocational education** are sometimes necessary for establishing important connections for this transition.

A wired world, in which machine-to-machine communication has become faster and less expensive, began to develop when telephone transmission was converted from analog to **digital** and **fiber-optic** phone lines were installed. The investment, transfer, and distribution of finances will occur more and more often through **electronic mediums** as will the design, production, installation, and sale of goods and services.

Computers will continue to become smaller and less expensive while providing more and more functions. **Artificial intelligence processes** provide support for human problem-solving processes, rather than mimic them and will continue to assist in analyzing complex data such as with space travel and medical diagnostic procedures. **Wireless phone service** is fast becoming the preferred communication process worldwide, and **multimedia technology** connects different technologies for use in business, entertainment and home.

Interactive design procedures have become a multibillion dollar business by making it possible to create **manufactured materials** for health care, agricultural, and other technologies that have completely revolutionized various problem solving processes.

Knowledge of and skills in technology are critical for success in nearly all aspects of work and many aspects of home as well. A schism already exists between the information-rich—those with access to electronic technology—and the information-poor, whose access is difficult at best. One way to manage the issue is to make it a national, even international, priority to encourage the establishment of **information utilities** to ensure equal access by everyone.

Crime

Crime, particularly violent crime among teenagers, grew in the past decade as family structure and support diminished. Children need role models and guidelines for values and behavior. This may be particularly true for teenagers who are attempting to understand the world around them and their role and purpose in the world. When these guidelines are not available through the family structure, individuals sometimes look elsewhere and **gangs** too often take the place of the family. Gangs provide security and a sense of belonging and are most often driven by drug sales as a means of financial stability. Gangs, who represent all ethnic and racial groups, recruit both male and female members.

Hate crimes related to race, religion, sexual orientation, and ethnicity, and organizations that support one group's beliefs and values over another have continued to flourish in spite of the great strides that have been made in equal opportunities and cultural diversity. **Family violence** remains a constant reminder for the need for family enrichment, support, and intervention programs. This can be one of the cruelest kinds of violence, since the individuals causing pain are those who are supposed to protect and support, and it can take the form of **child abuse**, **spousal abuse**, and violence against **elderly** relatives.

Only one country, Northern Ireland, has a murder rate comparable to the United States, making this country one of the most violent countries of all. **Homicide** is a part of both large cities and mid-sized cities, and gang-related crime continues to be a factor in almost all cities regardless of size. **Gun control** remains a volatile issue with individuals and groups taking a strong stance on both sides. State and local gun control bills are constantly being challenged and changed, and the issue will continue to remain volatile in the future. A disproportionate number of young African-American men between the ages of sixteen and twenty-four become the victims of crimes involving hand guns. Homicide is often the number one cause of death in this age group.

The production, transfer, and sale of **illegal drugs** is a crime, and there is a significant correlation between dealing in drugs and other criminal activities. Drug trafficking and sales has emerged as a huge business involving tens of billions of dollars in revenue annually and often including high-powered weaponry in the battle for control. There has been some shift away from imported drugs, such as **cocaine, heroin,** and **marijuana,** and toward more domestic drugs that can be made cheaply in home labs with easily available products.

A get-tough policy on crime as a way of **punishment** and **deterrence** by the United States has led to seriously overcrowded jails. America has the highest incarceration rate of any country, with a disproportionate number of those prisoners being African- American men. Nearly one fourth of all black men between the ages of twenty and twenty-nine are incarcerated or under some form of supervision from the criminal justice system, as compared to one out of every sixteen white men and one out of every ten Hispanic men.

Over four million people are being supervised in some way by the criminal justice system, and the cost for corrections is often the largest financial item in a state's budget. Alternatives to prison can be effective and less costly and include **half-way houses**, **community service programs**, **revised sentencing policies**, increased **electronic monitoring**, and a fairer system of **matching the punishment to the crime**.

Environmental Issues

Some environmental concerns, such as earthquakes and tornadoes are natural occurrences and beyond human control, but others, like water and air quality are very much a by-product of mankind and human interaction, with national and often global consequences.

The **biosphere** is made up of the surface of our planet and surrounding atmosphere. Together they provide the air, land, water and energy necessary for life. The **ecosystem** is the mechanism that supplies human beings with the essentials to sustain life and involves plants, animals, and microorganisms interacting with each other and the physical environment. These ecosystems are being disturbed by a number of forces. The tremendous growth in human population (approximately seven billion people) takes a tremendous toll on the supply of food, energy, and minerals. The concentration of so many people in urban areas makes it difficult for the air, water, and land to handle waste and other toxic elements. And finally, some environmental problems are the result of modern technology and its uses.

Pollutants are a major cause of various health hazards and are an example of how humanity is fouling up its world. Specific examples of mankind's polluting the environment include **chemical pollution**, in which toxic chemicals are released into the air, water, and land during the development of chemical products; **solid waste pollution**, which includes the disposal of billions of tons of glass, plastics, textiles, and other materials each year; **water pollution**, involving contaminants, sewage, and oil spills that pour into rivers, lakes and oceans; **radiation pollution,** which occurs through x-rays, nuclear fallout from weapons testing, and nuclear accidents; and, **air pollution**, which is caused primarily by automobile emissions and industrial plants.

The burning of fossil fuels and the destruction of tropical forests contribute to the **greenhouse effect**, in which harmful gases, such as carbon dioxide, nitrous oxide, chlorofluorocarbons, and methane accumulate and act much like the glass roof in a greenhouse. When sunlight reaches the earth's surface, this "roof" traps heat radiating from the ground and causes a warming of the earth, the melting of the polar ice cap, and other significant changes in climate. Although still theoretical, the greenhouse effect is supported by the fact that sea-level has risen gradually of late, indicating that the earth is warmer now than it has been in the past 6000 years.

Trends in Philanthropy

Americans are among the most giving people in the world. Approximately fifty percent of all American adults formally **volunteer** in a nonprofit organization each year. Nearly half of teenagers volunteer to provide service, usually through their school, church, synagogue, or mosque. Nearly forty percent of senior citizens volunteer their time, and an almost larger percentage are willing but have not been asked. Of those who volunteer, the majority take part on a regular basis, monthly or more often. This translates into more than ninety million individuals volunteering approximately twenty billion hours of service each year (Independent Sector 2002).

There is a correlation between being asked to volunteer and volunteering and a correlation between those who attend some kind of religious service and volunteering. Women are more likely to volunteer than men, and there is a correlation between volunteering and contributing financially to an organization.

People with certain values and attitudes, such as those who want to help the less fortunate, those who gain personal satisfaction from giving and volunteering, and those who want to increase opportunities for others, are more likely to contribute financially to a nonprofit organization (United Way 1992). Approximately ninety percent of all American households **contribute to charities** each year with an average household gift of over $1000. Individuals who volunteer and contribute generally give more than those who just contribute financially. A higher percentage of adults who become involved with volunteering and giving in their youth are more likely to continue that pattern later on than those who do not. Individuals who attend religious services on a regular basis give twice as much as those who do not. And family members who worry about the economy give about half as much as those who are not worried about the economy in general (Independent Sector 2002).

Religious organizations generally receive the greatest dollar amount in gifts. Education receives the second largest amount, followed by human services. These are followed by health, arts, culture, humanities, and public/society benefit groups. Americans have demonstrated a willingness to work together in addressing problems in their communities and nonprofit organizations need to tap into this spirit by implementing innovative volunteer programs and creative financial development plans.

■ Summary

The goal of most nonprofit organizations is to enhance the quality of life in communities, and understanding human development is important for effective program planning. Organizational leaders must understand that human development is contextual in nature, meaning that development occurs in the context of various circumstances and situations, and leaders must understand developmental theories as well. Developmental theories provide information on how individuals pass through various processes and stages and provide a foundation to develop approaches that will assist individuals in addressing life situations.

Nonprofit leaders must incorporate their knowledge of human development with their awareness of issues and trends that individuals and communities are facing and will face in the future. Educational concerns, such as illiteracy and technology in the classroom, and health problems, such as AIDS, STDs, drugs and alcohol, and the complexity of the health care system are staggering issues. A growing population and aging continue to present challenges and opportunities for nonprofit leaders. Children, individuals, and families are often devastated by poverty, housing costs, and homelessness that can and must be addressed effectively. Technology and other changes taking place in the workplace are occurring at a dizzying pace, leaving some employees stressed and feeling disenfranchised. Although aspects of crime have ebbed and waned over the last several decades, the family structure and support are too often diminished, creating opportunities for criminal behavior and leaving a huge gap for nonprofit organizations to fill. Environmental systems have suffered the consequences of human greed and thoughtlessness and will continue to require a special area of attention.

Throughout time, societies have been faced with challenging situations. There are no "quick fixes" to the numerous problems and situations that confront families, children, and individuals daily. Nonprofit organizations have a unique opportunity and responsibility to work with educational institutions and governmental agencies to address the needs of all citizens through programs.

This chapter addressed, in part, the American Humanics Certification Competency Requirements of Youth and Adult Development.

■ Discussion Questions

1. What is the relationship between human development and context?
2. Which developmental theories can you identify with, and why?
3. What is the connection between the id, ego, and superego?
4. Which of Erikson's stages can you identify with, and why?
5. Describe a situation in which you have incorporated the Social Learning Theory?
6. Which issue or trend is most important to you, and why?

■ Activities

1. Use your own experiences to relate to and explain a developmental theory.
2. Using Erikson's Psychosocial Theory as the foundation, develop an idea for a program directed toward individuals in a specific stage.
3. Select an issue or trend that is important to you and write a report on its importance, as well as ways you believe it should be managed.

■ References

Bronfenbrenner, U. (1979). *The Ecology of Human Development*. Cambridge, MA: Harvard University Press.

Caplow. T., Hicks, L., and Wattenberg, B. (2001). *The First Measured Century: An Illustrated Guide to Trends in America, 1900-2000*. Washington, DC: The AEI Press.

Edginton, C.R., and Ford, P.M. (1985). *Leadership in Recreation and Leisure Service Organizations*. New York: John Wiley and Sons.

Edginton, S.R. and Edginton, C.R. (1994). *Youth Programs: Promoting Quality Services*. Champaign, IL: Sagamore Publishing.

Edginton, C.R.; Hudson, S.D.; and Ford, P.M. (1999). *Leadership in Recreation and Leisure Service Organizations*. 2nd ed. Champaign, IL: Sagamore Publishing.

Ehrlich, P., and Ehrlich, A. (1991). *The Population Explosion*. New York: Simon and Schuster.

Eitzen, D. S., and Zinn, M.B. (2000). *Social Problems*. Boston: Allyn and Bacon.

Erikson, E. (1958). *Young Man Luther: A Study in Psychoanalysis and History*. New York: Norton.

_____(1963). *Youth and Society*. New York: Norton.

_____(1969). *Ghandi's Truth*. New York: Norton.

_____(1975). *Life and the Historical Moment*. New York: Norton.

Erikson, E. H. (1963). *Childhood and Society*. Rev. ed. New York: Norton.

Feagin, J. R., and Feagin, C. B., (1994). *Social Problems*. 4th ed. Englewood Cliffs, N.J.: Prentice-Hall.

Freud, S. (1923). *The Ego and the Id*. New York: Norton.

Independent Sector (2001). *The New Nonprofit Almanac*. Washington, DC

Kaplan, P.S. (1998). *The Human Odyssey: Life Span Development*. Pacific Grove, CA: Brooks/Cole Publishing Company.

Mills, C. W. (1959). *The Sociological Imagination*. New York: Oxford University Press.

Piaget, J. (1970). *The Child's Conception of the World*. Totowa, N.J.: Littlefield and Adams.

_____ (1972). Intellectual evolution from adolescence to adulthood. *Human Development* 15:1-12.

Pittman, K. J. (1991). *Promoting Youth Development: Strengthening the Role of Youth Serving and Community Organizations*. New York: Center for Development and Policy Research.

Rubington, E., and Weinberg, eds. (1995). *The Study of Social Problems: Seven Perspectives*. 5th ed. New York: Oxford University Press.

Spector, M. and Kitsuse, J. I. (1987). *Constructing Social Problems*. Hawthorne, N.Y.: Aldine de Gruyter.

United Way Strategic Institute (1992). *What Lies Ahead*. Alexandria, VA: United Way of America.

Weis, R., and Gantt, V. (2002). *Leadership and Program Development in Nonprofit Organizations*. Peosta, IA: E. Bowers Publishing.

5 Program Development, Marketing and Promotion

Programs developed by organizational leaders are the means by which organizations achieve many of their objectives and goals as they work to fulfill their mission. In addition to exploring program development in Chapter 5, we will also take a look at some classic approaches to marketing and promoting programs in organizations.

■ A Customer-Centered/Benefits Approach to Program Development

Programs communicate to customers what the organization is trying to accomplish. A **customer-centered/benefits** approach to developing programs implies that leaders strive to develop programs that not only meet the needs of their customers, but often exceed them and provide customers with some form of positive outcome or benefit. This approach to program development communicates a quality organization with quality staff members. Quality programs must be carefully planned, implemented, and evaluated. Programs of all kinds can be developed for organizational members as long as they fall under the umbrella of the overall purpose of the organization.

Staff and volunteer members who are responsible for developing programs should meet certain **criteria** that include (1) believing in and being committed to the purpose of the organization; (2) being knowledgeable and skilled in program development; and, (3) being aware of the situations, needs, and desires of the constituents of the organization (Weis and Gantt 2002). Programs should meet the needs of the organization's constituents in the context of the organizational mission or purpose.

In addition to meeting certain criteria, it is important that leaders in nonprofit organizations commit to developing programs of the highest quality. More and more citizens are relying on nonprofit organizations to provide services to assist them in reaching their goals or in times of need, and these individuals deserve program services of the highest possible quality.

Quality. Once the need for a program is established, it is time to turn attention to establishing programs of the highest quality. **Quality programs** are those programs that meet or exceed the standards and expectations set for program activities. They are programs of excellence that focus on the needs of the customers and make them feel as if they are valued members of the organization; such programs also provide members with a positive outcome or benefit (Edginton and Edginton 1994). Meeting and exceeding the expectations of the members of an organization is the hallmark of a competent, caring, and dedicated staff with the knowledge and skills to develop exceptional programs. Programs that meet or exceed expectations are rare, and customers take note when their expectations are exceeded.

Developing programs that meet and exceed customer expectations is the responsibility of the organization's leaders. These guidelines should include, but not be limited to the following (Walton 1988):

- **Innovation.** Programs should be developed that meet the changing needs of organizational members and remain fresh by offering new and interesting activities to keep them exciting.

- **Continual improvement.** Constantly looking for ways that programs can be improved keeps them fresh, energized, and meaningful. Program development is a dynamic process that should always be evolving toward relevant methods and processes.

- **Continuous Education.** Good organizations commit to continuous educational opportunities for staff members. College classes, seminars, and workshops should be supported and encouraged for staff members to ensure competency and effectiveness in program and administrative areas.

- **Attention to Detail.** Programs in which details are important are generally superior to programs in which details are not an issue. Paying attention to details helps to ensure quality and success. There is an old saying that goes, "The devil is in the details," which reminds us that problems can occur when details are not attended to.

- **Pride.** Staff and volunteer members must have a strong feeling about the programs they are planning and must work diligently to provide customers with the best services possible. Pride is contagious, and it begins when everyone in the organization prides himself or herself on what the programs are accomplishing for their members. Pride includes planning and implementing new programs with as few mistakes as possible and eliminating mistakes or unnecessary aspects from existing programs.

- **Anticipatory Planning.** Program developers must be proactive in the sense that they look ahead to program needs for the future as well those of the present. In order to do this, leaders must be on the cutting edge of program development and must maintain knowledge of issues and customer needs.

- **Teamwork and Responsibility.** Programs are by necessity developed and implemented in a cooperative process. Program leaders must have skills in developing effective teams of professional staff members, volunteers, invested staff members of other organizations, consultants and even program participants in the overall development of programs. Shared input and responsibility requires leadership that is competent in developing collaborative, successful ventures.

- **Performance Measurements.** Program successes and outcomes can and should be validated through an evaluation process. Interviews, focus groups, surveys, pre/post tests, and observation are all legitimate ways to determine whether programs are meeting their objectives and whether they are successful from the participants' standpoint. Evaluations can be time-consuming but the results can assist the organization in developing better, more effective programs. They help staff members determine whether they are meeting the needs of their members, and they provide useful information when seeking support from outside funders.

**Figure 5.1
Stages of Program Development:
Planning, Implementation and Evaluation (PIE)**

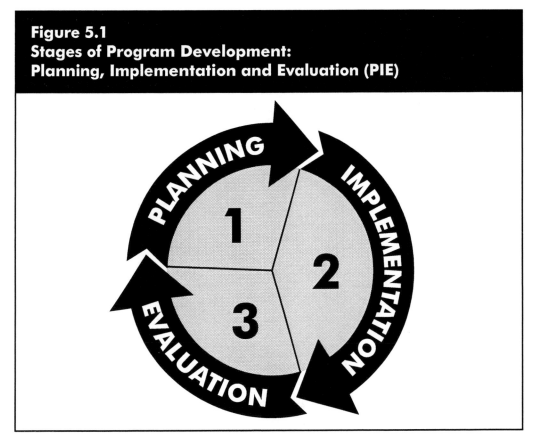

Providing programs of the highest possible quality that meet or exceed the expectations of customers is the only way to ensure that an organization maintains integrity in its mission while providing opportunities of enhancement for its members.

A commitment to programs of the highest quality is the responsibility of everyone in an organization, and once this commitment is established, the focus of attention turns to the developmental process itself. There are three major areas or **stages** of program development (Weis and Gantt 2002): (1) **Initial (Planning) Stage**, (2) **Middle (Planning/Implementation) Stage**, and (3) **Final (Evaluation) Stage** (See PIE, Figure 5.1 above).

■ Initial (Planning) Stage

Careful planning in this stage is important since it sets the groundwork for other activities throughout the program development process. Good planning should be a step-by-step process, although the sequence of steps and modification or simplification of steps depends on particular situations, and some steps may not even be necessary.

Action steps are specific work segments or activities that are necessary to accomplish program objectives (Hardy 1984). The development of action steps is the responsibility of the program or planning committee, and members of this committee are determined by the organization's leaders, usually a program director or another senior staff member. Action steps typically specify (1) which tasks are to be completed to accomplish program objectives, and in what order; (2) who is responsible for completing various tasks; and (3)

Figure 5.2
Program Planning Worksheet

Date____/____/____

Name of Organization _____

Name of Program/Project _____

Program Coordinator _____

Program Members:

	Name	Address	Phone Number	e-mail address
1				
2				
3				
4				
5				
6				

Program Objectives _____

_____

_____

Estimated Direct Expenses	Estimated Direct Income	Gain (Deficit)
Actual Direct Costs	Actual Direct Income	Gain (Deficit)

Action Steps or Work Tasks	Person(s) Responsible	Completion Dates

Evaluation Results _____

_____

Recommendations for Future Programs _____

_____

when these tasks are to be completed. Although tasks for specific programs may vary considerably, some standard tasks for consideration are listed below (Weis and Gantt 2002):

Step 1 – Selection of a Planning Committee. Groups often have greater potential for creativity and thoroughness than individuals because of enhanced expertise, synergy, and opportunity to attend to details. Selecting an effective planning committee to develop specific programs is essential for successfully meeting organizational goals and planning programs that meet and exceed the expectations of its members. Planning members should include:

- staff and volunteer members who have knowledge and skills in program planning as well as in the particular content area of the program.
- individuals with particular knowledge and skills in areas of specific expertise relevant to program planning, such as marketing, finances, and volunteer coordination and risk management when these are needed.
- individuals, such as the members of the organization, who will benefit from the program, since these individuals can often add insight into the needs and desires of the membership in general.

Planning committee members are *responsible* for the following:

- developing a schedule of program planning meetings
- identifying and prioritizing other tasks or action steps according to what needs to be done first, second, and so on
- assigning a responsible person or persons to accomplish each task
- recording each aspect of the program plan on a **Program Planning Worksheet (PPW)** (see Figure 5.2 on p. 128)
- implementing, monitoring, and reporting the progress of the program to the appropriate organizational leader(s)

Step 2 – Needs Assessment. The needs and desires of constituents should be identified and assessed so programs can be developed to focus on appropriate areas. **Needs** are usually considered as an individual *physiological, psychological, or social imbalance.* Edginton and Ford (1985) note that when an individual recognizes a deficiency in any of these areas, he or she has a need. Physiological needs might include deficiencies associated with the need for food, water, sleep, and sex. Psychological and social deficiencies might be harder to assess, but would include the need for companionship, social interaction, recognition, safety, love, achievements, and self- esteem.

A need, then, is the assessed difference between the ideal state of an individual and the actual condition of an individual as he or she is functioning in their environment. Communities, too, have needs as do states, nations, and all of society, and program planners should be aware of collective needs in developing programs. **Desires**, on the other hand, are considered wishes *that are perceived as something necessary* (Edginton, et al. 1998). In this context, desires are differentiated from needs in that they are not necessary to sustain life, but they can also be considered in determining future programs.

In the 1940s, Abraham Maslow advanced a general theory of human needs and motivation that still serves as a foundation and guide to understanding basic human needs. He identified physiological needs, safety needs, affiliation needs, esteem needs, and the need to become self-actualized. These needs are discussed in detail below:

1. **Physiological needs.** These include basic human needs for food, water, shelter, sleep, sensory gratification and could be satisfied by a supportive environment.
2. **Safety needs.** This category includes being relatively free from danger and might involve a safe home, neighborhood, or work environment.
3. **Affiliation needs.** These needs can be expressed in the desire to join with others in completing a project, making a family, or achieving a sense of belonging (fraternities or sororities). This need implores individuals to explore and develop relationships with friends, family, and co-workers.
4. **Esteem needs.** These needs are expressed in individual and collective desires for a sense of accomplishment or achievement. This satisfaction can be received externally, internally, or both. External esteem satisfaction comes from visible rewards such as a salary increase. Internal esteem satisfaction results when individuals realize a sense of accomplishment, success, and being counted on.
5. **Need for self-actualization.** Maslow described this need as a desire to become everything that one is capable of becoming. As self-actualization occurs, individuals reach out to assist others in becoming all that they are capable of becoming through empowering or mentoring activities.

(Maslow 1943)

Maslow posits that individuals will work to satisfy needs in that order and it is only when basic needs such as safety and food are met that higher needs for esteem and self-actualization can be considered. Although research has failed to conclude a clear separation between the categories and the validity of Maslow's theory in general, it remains a foundational treatise on human needs and motivation.

Programs should only be developed that address important issues and needs of organizational members and should take into account the various life stages that individuals may

L E V E L S	5	**Self-Actualization** Work which allows for independent decision making
	4	**Esteem** Internal: feeling good about how you help others External: bonus pay, family allowed at fun events
	3	**Affiliation** An organizational bowling or softball team
	2	**Safety** Working conditions which protect staff and customers
	1	**Physiological** Enough money to pay the bills – rent, food, health-care

Figure 5.3
Needs Assessment Survey

Kingston Community Center
Survey for New Programs

Please help the Kingston Community Center determine new program interests for the upcoming activity year. Complete the following anonymous survey and place it in the survey box located at the North entrance to the facility. Once you have done this, the front desk clerk will give you a coupon for 20% off any special class, workshop, or seminar. Thanks for helping your center be the best it can be!

PLEASE CHECK YOUR AREAS OF INTEREST:

☐ Aerobics   ☐ Bowling   ☐ Golf class   ☐ Trips
☐ Aquatics   ☐ Computer class   ☐ Karate   ☐ Softball
☐ Arts & Crafts   ☐ Culinary class   ☐ Racquetball   ☐ Volleyball
☐ Athletics/fitness   ☐ Cycling   ☐ Scuba   ☐ Youth activities
☐ Basketball   ☐ Education   ☐ Senior activities

Comments and other suggestions: _____

_____

---

be passing through. For instance, teenagers are passing through a very difficult stage of their lives as they struggle to develop and understand their identity, as noted in Erikson's Stage Theory in Chapter 4 of this text. At the same time, they are also often confronted with a number of issues such as smoking, alcohol and drug use, and premarital sex. A program that is designed to strengthen their system of values by offering them the opportunity to make a difference in someone else's life, for instance, could become a critical aspect to their personal development. These kinds of programs help teens develop a positive sense of **self worth** and the knowledge that they can and do make a difference (**self-efficacy**). Programs that also confront important issues head-on with facts, methods of handling situations, and the opportunity to teach these to others, such as younger children, can be an invaluable experience with lifelong implications. These experience can allow them to develop communication and teamwork skills and even provide insight into future vocational possibilities.

An **assessment of needs** should be made prior to further program planning, and that can be done in a number of ways: (1) Researching and assessing existing data, such as published reports in newspapers, magazines, journals, and institutional bulletins can be essential in understanding the needs of individuals in general. (2) Assessing the needs and desires of organizational members firsthand can and should be done through interviews, focus groups, and and/or surveys that can be implemented periodically or at set times throughout the year. Interviews can be face to face, or a sampling of telephone interviews can be initiated. Individual interviews provide a focus of insight that cannot be duplicated by other methods. On the other hand, focus groups sometimes provide collective information that cannot be found through an individual process. And surveys can provide confidentiality that is virtually non-existent with the interview and focus group format and may provide for more open and honest responses (an example survey can be found in Figure 5.3 above). (3) A third method of understanding the needs and desires of constituents is through information already gathered for organizations that are a part of a state-wide, regional, or national association. These organizations often receive pre-planned programs addressing the needs of the general membership, which can be valuable and time saving.

Step 3 – Review Developmental Theories, Competencies, Issues, and Trends. After assessing the needs of the constituents of an organization, it is also important to have an understanding of developmental stages they may be experiencing, along with an understanding of significant issues and trends that members may be challenged with (see Chapter 4). It is important to review developmental theories, competencies, and issues relevant to the needs of the membership and the mission of the organization. Although needs and desires are important, understanding developmental processes is equally important to crafting effective programs.

Maintaining an awareness of current and significant issues and trends provides program planners with the opportunity to address some of these issues through programs. Programs that address recognized needs, confront important issues, and focus on the overall development of individuals strike a chord with members who realize the organization is focusing on their situation and providing programs directed toward their well-being.

Step 4 – Incorporating Values and Character Education. Nonprofit organizations have a significant responsibility to assist members in becoming responsible individuals and citizens. This mandate dates back to the early part of the twentieth century when organizations such as the Boy Scouts of America, Girl Scouts of the USA, Boys and Girls Clubs of America, Camp Fire Boys and Girls, Girls, Inc., and the YMCAs and YWCAs focused a great deal of attention on character development, as they still do today (Edginton, Hudson, and Ford 1999).

Values can be thought of as principles that guide our lives and the constructs that are important in our lives (Edginton, et al.). **Values education** occurs when nonprofit leaders assist members in defining and developing their values through select, organized methods. Values education should reflect: (1) the basic values of the community and society; and (2) parallel the values of the organization, but they (3) should not impose values upon members. Values such as honesty, justice, equality, and freedom, to list several, are values that can and should be encouraged by organizations, but must be accepted freely by participants, not forced upon them.

There are several effective ways to introduce values in a program. In the **direct-programmatic approach** values clarification and development is the main focus of the program. In other words, the program is designed and promoted as a values clarification/development program. This can be a very honest and effective approach, although some participants may be hesitant to be open regarding their value system.

Another effective way to introduce values education is through an **integrated-programmatic approach.** In this approach, values are introduced as part of the structure of the program and occur more *naturally* within the program's framework. This makes this approach very functional and prevents compartmentalization. For instance, an indoor-soccer league might support the concept that all children make the team and there are no try-outs. It could also include the concept that all children will play an approximately equal amount of time and that all participants will shake hands with the opposing team members at the end of the game. Fairness, sportsmanship, and teamwork are just some of the values that can be presented within this framework. And finally, values are taught by **role modeling**. Organizational leaders inevitably provide examples of values for participants to consider through their decisions and actions, so it is important for these leaders to assess and monitor their actions in all facets of operational activities.

Another important concept to consider in program development is the concept of **character education**, or helping individuals internalize values such as honesty, integrity, equality, and fairness. It is one thing to clarify and develop a healthy system of values, but it is another thing to live one's life in accordance with that system of values. Nonprofit leaders have the opportunity to develop programs that allow individuals to internalize values by clarifying, using, and reflecting upon them over and over again in various situations. Clubs and organizations, service learning opportunities (see Chapter 2), and other programs that promote continual use and reflection of values are essential to healthy individual development.

Quality programs combine (1) constituent needs with (2) an understanding of developmental stages along with (3) a focus on important issues or trends, and include (4) values and character education which can have a powerful impact on the lives of the members of any organization.

Step 5 – Determine Program Objectives. Most nonprofit organizations have a **purpose** or a **mission statement** that spells out their reason for being in a general way (Weis and Gantt 2002). This statement usually refers to enhancing the quality of life of specific individuals in the community in some way, but it is so broad that organizations usually designate a number of definitive **goals** they plan to accomplish as a part of their purpose. For instance, an organization that plans to enhance the quality of life for socially/ economically disadvantaged children might have goals of helping children develop competencies in health, education, recreation, and vocations. More specifically, the organization could set a number of **program objectives** or outcomes for each of these areas (goals) (Hardy 1984). For instance, in the area of health, a program objective could include having children become competent in personal hygiene, or in nutritional guidelines of some kind. An objective for education could be to improve the literacy rate or the percentage of high school graduates in a particular community. Program objectives are both measurable and capable of being accomplished in a set amount of time.

Setting program objectives provides motivation and direction for the program staff, who can begin concentrating on developing action steps necessary for achieving set objectives. Having program objectives also provides a basis from which to measure whether or not goals have been achieved. The measurement process will be discussed in the evaluation phase of program development.

There are generally two types of program objectives: (1) **Qualitative.** This type of objective includes the various areas the program is designed to address or change, including needs, issues, situations, values, competencies, and/or life stages; and (2) **Quantitative.**

This type of objective includes areas of the program that can be counted and observed, such as the number of program participants, the length and meeting times of the program, and financial considerations. Both types of objectives need to be considered and documented on the Program Planning Worksheet prior to implementing a program.

Program objectives should be written in a certain way and include certain criteria (Edginton, Hanson, and Edginton 1992):

- **Specific.** Program objectives should be clear and succinct.
- **Measurable.** There needs to be a way in which to measure whether or not program objectives are met.
- **Reality-based.** Objectives should be challenging yet reachable.
- **Useful.** Objectives provide program staff with direction and therefore must be helpful in guiding staff members toward achieving the purpose(s) of the program.
- **Linked to Needs.** Obviously, objectives must be linked to the needs, issues, competencies, values and so on that the program is addressing and is designed to affect.

Inclusion of Program Concept and Format. Including the program concept or idea and the program format in the objective helps to connect the purpose of the program to the overall program process. The program concept and format will be discussed in Steps 6 and 7.

Setting purposeful objectives provides a foundation for the rest of the developmental process, and it is vital that objectives are well-written and defined. An example of a clear and effective **objective** follows:

> **The Teens for Seniors program provides teenagers in the Morganfield Boys and Girls Club opportunities to assist senior citizens attending the community center's day care program. Teens are trained to participate with seniors in social and recreational activities. Some of the intended objectives include:**
>
> **Involvement of a minimum of 10 teenagers in a program with 25 senior citizens meeting at least once a week for social and recreational activities for a three month period that results in**
> - **Improved inter-generational understanding**
> - **Increased flexibility on the part of senior citizens**
> - **Decreased depression on the part of senior citizens**
> - **Enhanced self-esteem of teenagers and senior citizens**
> - **Increased sense of responsibility and caring on the part of the teenagers**
> - **Improved teamwork, communication, recreation, socialization and leadership skills on the part of the teenagers.**

This kind of program provides opportunities for improving the overall health and well-being of both teenagers and senior citizens and allows the teenagers to develop a number of important skills and character traits that will be useful throughout their lives. This objective includes the program concept and format and addresses needs, issues, competencies, values, and life stages. The objectives for this program include both qualitative and quantitative areas that can be measured in various ways and the program is designed to be realistic, yet challenging in nature.

Step 6 – Selection of Program Concept. Once the program objectives have been established, a program idea or concept must be determined that results in an effective process for reaching objectives. There are a number of ways or program *approaches* that can be considered in determining the program concept (Edginton and Edginton 1994):

- **Traditional Approach.** Relying on past successes within the organization to determine a program concept is referred to as the traditional approach. Reviewing past programs to determine how they can meet current objectives can be valuable for two reasons: (1) Less time and energy needs to be expended on the planning process, since the program has been implemented previously; and (2) organizational members who have appreciated programs from the past often look forward to a repeat of those programs with anticipation.

    One disadvantage to planning programs from a traditional approach standpoint is that if current programs rely too heavily on past planning they may become uninspired by not taking into account changes in interests, issues, trends, and lifestyles. Taking traditional program ideas and adding new twists can help keep the program fresh and exciting.

- **Current Practice Approach.** Programs that are effective in one part of the country can often be effective in another part as well. Nonprofit leaders are usually open to sharing successful program ideas with each other in the field. This type of approach can save a good deal of planning time, and lends legitimacy to the future success of the program. One disadvantage, however, is that sometimes a program that works in a large metropolitan area of the country may not work in a rural area, or vice versa. In a similar manner, a program that succeeds in the northeastern part of the country may not be as acceptable in the southwestern part, and so on. Both sides of the situation to be taken into consideration before employing the current practice approach.

- **Expressed Desires Approach.** Offering members opportunities to express desires for program selection through surveys, interviews, and focus groups provides them with a feeling of involvement and may provide the program staff valuable insights for program development. This information can also be valuable in reducing risk of developing programs for which there is little or no interest. Information provided by members is important and should be weighed with other factors in determining the program concept.

- **Prescriptive Approach.** This approach is directed toward developing program concepts focused on members of the organization with special needs or special situations. This concentrated focus on specific individuals can have very important and far-reaching consequences and should always be considered in the overall scheme of program development. However, consideration should also be given to the fact that these programs are usually time-consuming and resource intensive and address the needs of only a select number of members and the approach may need to be used accordingly.

- **Innovative Approach.** Creating new programs from scratch can be challenging, exciting, and rewarding. Members of the planning committee should convene to discuss alternative program ideas in *brainstorming* sessions. These sessions include expressing any and all ideas without qualification, recording the alternatives, and returning later to discuss the feasibility of each idea. Each member of the planning committee should feel that his or her ideas are welcome while they are being expressed. The newness of the resulting program concept often creates a level of excitement and anticipation that other, more traditional program ideas may not incur. A possible disadvantage of this kind of program approach is that because of the newness of the program idea, more time and confusion in the planning and the implementation process may occur and some uncertainty may exist as to the potential outcome.

- **Combined Approach.** *Good organizational leaders incorporate some or all of the approaches above for creating options for program concepts.* Using successful program ideas from the past provides some continuity, certainty, and tradition. Incorporating program ideas that have been successful in other places may decrease the amount of time necessary for planning and provide a sense of certainty regarding the outcome. Inviting members of the organization to express their desires and needs gives them a sense of involvement while providing program staff members with valuable information. Developing specific programs for certain individuals in an organization indicates to those members that they are important and that their needs are being addressed. Finally, creating new program ideas can a sense of excitement throughout an organization. The combined approach to program development can be highly successful because it brings together information from numerous sources in making program decisions. Finding just the right approach to program development can be time-consuming, but being able to develop programs that create interest and excitement and that meet the intended objectives has a great deal of merit and is certainly worth the effort.

Step 7 – Program Format. The selection of a program format is important because different program structures or formats provide different kinds of experiences for individuals. The way in which a program is structured is linked to the likelihood that customers will achieve desired benefits. For instance, a program for self-improvement may be structured as a workshop or seminar. A program designed to include physical competition may take the format of a sports league. Farell and Lundegren (1991) posit that the program format chosen should be directly linked to the experience desired for the customers and suggest five program formats: (1) self-improvement, (2) competition, (3) social, (4) participant spectator, and (5) self-directed. A great deal has been written about program formats in the leisure services field and Russell (1982) suggests more common approaches to program formats: (1) clubs, (2) competition, (3) trips and outings, (4) special events, (5) classes, (6) open facility, (7) voluntary service, and (8) workshops, seminars, and conferences. Each of these formats vary in of general characteristics and provide for a wide selection on program structure. Yet another approach to categorizing program formats is offered by Kraus (1985), who identifies eight program structures to choose from in meeting customer needs: (1) instruction, (2) free play or unstructured participation, (3) organized competition, (4) performances, demonstrations, or exhibits, (5) leadership training, (6) special interest groups, (7) other special events, and (8) trips and outings. Most experts agree that the program format is the structure or form the activity takes and that the format is one of the key ingredients in meeting customer expectations.

Step 8 – Evaluate Resources. Another important consideration in the overall development of a program is the assessment of resources necessary for program delivery. Necessary resources may include any or all of the following:

- **Space availability.** One of the first things to consider regarding resources is determining what type of space is necessary and then exploring the use of existing space within the organization, or other areas and facilities.
- **Personnel.** Planners should develop a list of staff and/or volunteer members who are competent and available to develop a specific program. If an expert specific to a particular program is not already a part of the organizational team, one might be recruited as a volunteer or a part-time consultant or expert might be hired.
- **Finances.** Sometimes a program fee may need to be assessed to cover some expenses. It is also important to research the availability of sponsors to cover program costs.
- **Collaboration.** Some programs can be more successful if they are planned in collaboration with other organizations. Collaboration may take a little more time in the beginning, but often brings with it enhanced resources, increased services for more people, and more excitement and enthusiasm.
- **Supplies.** Planners must envision the supplies necessary for a successful program and develop a list. They must also determine which materials are already available and which materials can be borrowed, donated, or paid for through sponsorship. Businesses and service organizations often sponsor nonprofit organizations for several reasons: (1) it helps develop the community, (2) it enhances public relations, and (3) it builds morale among its members.
- **Equipment.** The equipment necessary for the program must meet the needs of the program and the participants, and must be in good, safe condition.

■ Middle (Planning/Implementation) Stage

This is also a vital stage of program development, since the steps necessary for planning and implementing the program are designated and developed further. This is also the stage in which a supervisory plan is selected and the program is actually implemented.

Step 9 – Risk Management is Priority #1. Risk management is the prevention, control, and handling of risk associated with programs. Because individual and group safety and health are at stake, it is the most important step in the implementation of programs and should be the number one concern of all staff and volunteer members. Anything that could involve a loss of resources is considered a risk. A **risk management plan** involves looking at potential problems before they develop, eliminating them if possible, or managing them through training, warning, controlling, and/or insurance; all of this is to prevent injury, illness, damage, or another kind of loss.

Risk management is the most important step in program development, and the risk management plan for the program must be carefully thought out and implemented with clear instruction and communication. The main focus of the plan is to protect the program participants and the organization and involves three essential components:

1. **Identification of Risks.** Each program should be examined carefully for conditions or situations that could present risks. Program staff and volunteer members should become aware of obvious risks as well as not-so-obvious risks. Risks can include potential losses, accidents, injuries, illnesses, health threats, or damages. For example, a service learning project that includes cleaning up a section of the shoreline at a lake could involve the risk of being around water as well as potentially dangerous materials along the shore.

2. **Evaluation of Risks.** All risks are relative in terms of importance, and two questions can be asked in determining this:
   - What is the probability that the risk will develop into an accident, injury, loss or damage of some kind?
   - If a loss of some kind occurred, how severe could it be?

3. **Handling Risk.** There are essentially three ways to handle risk:
   - *Prevention (Avoidance).* One of the first and most important areas of managing risks is to match participants with appropriate experiences. Following that, participant orientation, training, and appropriate communication and supervision are keys to preventing and avoiding risk.
   - *Risk Reduction.* Examples of risk reduction include clearly defined and communicated safety rules and well-thought-out procedures, including emergency procedures. In the case of the shore line clean-up, having water safety equipment readily available, including life jackets, and advising participants to stay away from potentially dangerous cliffs or deep areas of the water would be examples of effective risk reduction approaches.
   - *Risk Retention or Transfer.* This refers to how a loss will be handled should it occur. In other words, which entity is responsible for the loss and responsible for payment of any damages (Van der Smissen 1990)?
   There are a number of forms to be considered in various stages of program activities and throughout the risk management process. The organization's legal counsel must review all written forms. Some examples of forms are included below:
   - **Agreements** should be written between the organization and other community organizations that are involved with the program activity or where the activity may be conducted. This is done so that there is a clear understanding of expectations and roles between the sponsoring organization, the participant, and the community organization to which the service is provided, or for which an activity is conducted.
   - **Participant Agreements.** These forms can be used to document that the participant understands that risks might be involved in the activity, agrees to abide by set safety rules, and agrees to perform as trained or instructed. These forms are also referred to as *Assumption of Risk Agreements.*
   - **Waivers/Releases.** These two terms are often used interchangeably. Ordinarily, these forms state that the participant agrees not to hold the organization responsible if a loss of resource should occur. This kind of form is only valid if it is signed by an adult, and parents/guardians **can never legally sign**

the rights of children away (under the legal age of majority).
- **Insurance.** Maintaining effective insurance coverage is the standard way of handling risk to prevent excessive or even devastating financial loss to an organization or entity. Insurance policies should be checked carefully to determine coverage prior to each program or activity.

Managing and keeping risk to a minimum and being certain that liabilities are adequately covered through insurance should be the highest priority of each and every staff and volunteer member of the organization. Once risk management policies have been established by the organization, each individual **should make every effort to follow the risk management policies relating to program development and other activities.**

Managing risk is a fluid and ever-changing process, and risk management procedures should be reviewed periodically to keep them up to date. Experts in the field of risk management, legal counsel, as well as key board and staff members should be involved in the development and periodic review of risk management procedures. Further information on liability, risk management, and insurance relevant to nonprofit organizations can be found in Chapter 7 of this text. Additionally, the following references are suggested: *Leadership in Recreation and Leisure Service Organizations* (1999) by Christopher R. Edginton, Susan D. Hudson and Phyllis M. Ford, Champaign, IL: Sagamore Publishing; and *Legal Liability and Risk Management for Public and Private Entities* (1990) (Vol. 2) by B. Van der Smissen, Cincinnati, Ohio: Anderson.

Step 10 – Marketing and Promoting Programs. Bagozzi (1975) defines marketing as the facilitation of some form of exchange. Defined as such, marketing is an important process that can link nonprofit organizations with entities within their environment. These entities can include program participants, donors, governments, media, service collaborators, and others. Marketing is a vital process in a nonprofit organization because (1) the success of marketing campaigns often determines whether or not the organization will thrive; (2) it is not an optional process; whether it is done amateurishly or professionally, it inevitably will occur in some form; and (3) the exchange concept signifies that there is more to marketing than communication and that advantageous exchanges of something of value also occur (Moyer 1994).

In the context of nonprofit organizations, the something of value is usually a type of community service offered to the public. In conjunction, individual members of the community have something of value to offer nonprofit organizations: their membership and participation in programs. These individuals may also serve as volunteers from time to time, so there is an exchange of value when the organization needs assistance and offers the opportunity for individuals to assist through their specific expertise and involvement. Anytime two parties like this have something that might be of value to each other it is referred to as a **market exchange.** The process that brings these two parties together is usually referred to as **marketing** or **promotion** (Hardy 1984). The marketing and/or promotion committee of the board of directors should be involved in this process and should be able to be very helpful in developing strategies

Marketing and promotion are very important steps in the program development process, since programs are of little importance unless they are joined with individuals who need or desire to participate. In order to understand how individuals become attracted to particular programs, it is important to look at something commonly referred to as the four *Ps*, or the **marketing mix** (Wolf 1999):

- **Product.** One of the most important elements in the marketing mix is the product and the quality of the product. In nonprofit organizations this typically means a program or service. In order for a program or service to be desirable, it must meet or exceed the expectations of the participants for them to be willing to pay for and participate in it. Staff members focusing on developing programs that individuals need, want, and desire and then ensuring that those programs are of the highest quality possible helps to effect strong and continued program participation. The reputation of the organization and of the staff is another important consideration in order for the product to be successful. Since people often select programs from organizations with a history of success and quality, this may be the most important consideration in product selection.

- **Promotion.** Some of the best programs are often *best-kept secrets* as well when they are not promoted aggressively and effectively. Promotional material for programs should obviously be directed toward potential program participants, but it should also be directed toward other members of the public who may become interested in the organization as volunteers, potential sponsors, on in some other capacity. It is important to remember that some of the best potential program participants include current members. One of the most successful forms of promotion is to current members, and this is referred to as **market penetration**, since the promotional activities are designed to further penetrate an already established group. *This group is also an excellent group to ask to convey program information to others.* Promoting programs to individuals who are not already members of the organization is called **market development** and can also be a very successful process. Making promotional material available to target groups that have a high probability of participation and providing similar promotional material to groups that are less likely to become involved is referred to as the **80/20 principal.** In other words, significant time, energy, and money may be spent on getting results that can be counted on in a big way while also spending time, energy, and money on lesser results, because those results are also important. For example, meager results may occur by spending a good deal of time and money to place flyers promoting programs for children on the windshields of cars in a local mall parking lot. The same and possibly less money could be spent on flyers that are delivered directly to children at the local schools, churches, or youth organizations. Both methods can be successful, but one will be more successful and cost less and should be given a higher priority. There are a number of ways to promote program opportunities:
  - **Flyers.** Flyers need to be created that are attractive and appealing. They should contain appropriate information, graphics, and have some *open space* to make them easier to read and more appealing. Flyers should answer standard questions, such as (1) *What* is going to happen during this activity and *why?* (2) *Where* will the activity occur? (3) *Who* is organizing the activity? (4) *How* will it benefit the program participants? (5) *How much* will it cost?

**Figure 5.4
Promotional Flyer**

Make a Difference
in the life of a
Senior Citizen

You can make a difference in the lives of senior citizens in our community by joining the program at the Morganfield Boys and Girls Club. The Boys and Girls Club is located at 1618 Seawall Dr., behind the Southwest Cinema.

The teen program participants meet Thursday evenings from 7-8 p.m. to plan the project beginning April 19.

**TEENS
for Seniors**

The project includes recreational activities, crafts, health and fitness, and joint service outings. The project will last 6 months culminating with a big splashdown pool and pizza party.

There is no program fee, but you must be between the ages of 13 –17 and be a member of the Boys and Girls Club.

Call today for more information: Stefani Dowell, **762-3808**.

Morganfield Boys and Girls Club

Figure 5.5
Public Service Announcement

Morganfield
Boys and Girls Club
1618 Seawall Dr.
Farmington, DE 22904
Phone: 277-762-3808
E-mail: **MBCGA@ORG.COM**

N E W S   R E L E A S E

(For Immediate Release)

The Morganfield Boys and Girls Club is proud to announce the Teens for Seniors program beginning Thursday, April 19, 7 – 8 p.m., in the club facility located at 1618 Seawall Dr. just behind the Southwest Cinema. This program will involve teens between the ages of 13 – 17 spending quality time with senior citizens in local nursing homes and the community seniors center. The program will consist of recreational activities, arts and crafts, health and fitness activities, and a joint service project. The 6-month long project will conclude with a huge splashdown pool & pizza party at the Morganfield Boys and Girls Club swimming pool. There is no cost for the program, but you must be a member of the Morganfield Boys and Girls Club. For more information on the program and membership into the Boys and Girls Club, contact Stefani Dowell at 762-3808.

(6) *What* is the date and time(s) of the activity? (7) *Is there anything* the program participant should do in preparation for the activity? (8) Is *transportation* available for the activity? Any other questions that are applicable to upcoming events should also be answered. Graphics appropriate to the activity should be added, and sometimes a **registration form** may need to be added with spaces for appropriate information about when participants must register for an activity. Colored paper can be eye-catching and add to the appeal of a flyer. Most local printing companies can enlarge flyers to poster size when necessary. Flyers should be posted in highly accessible places well in advance of an activity, typically three weeks to a month. More advanced notice may be required for some programs. Members can be helpful in posting and passing out flyers in their neighborhoods, schools, or places of work. Contests and prizes for volunteers who bring participants in for program activities can also be effective. An example of a program flyer can be found in Figure 5.4, 141.

- **Public Service Announcements (PSAs).** Promotional announcements should be provided to local newspapers, television and radio stations with information regarding upcoming services and program opportunities. Including local media in the overall marketing and promotion strategies is an excellent way to promote opportunities and most media organizations are more than willing to assist in promoting community activities. It can also be advisable to include a member of the local media as a **media sponsor** for a program. As a media sponsor, a radio station for example, might agree do some extra on-air promotional spots and a live segment on the day of the activity. In return, the organization could mention the radio station as one of the sponsors on flyers, t-shirts (if there are any) and in public service announcements. The chances of an organization's programs being included in newspaper and radio spots depend on the excitement generated around a particular activity, the reputation the organization has for providing community services, and the relationships that have been developed with members of the media. The same type of appropriate information should be included in the public service announcement that would be included in a flyer (above). An example of a public service announcement is included in Figure 5.5, 142:

- **Displays, Exhibits, and Demonstrations.** Displays are generally two- dimensional, while exhibits are typically three-dimensional, and both can serve as a great way to let the public know about upcoming events as well as about the organization in general. They can be used to attract program participants, volunteers, donors, or other interested parties to the organization. A simple display could be a flyer in the form of a *tent* left on the table of a business, school, doctor's office, or other appropriate location. A more sophisticated display might include a Velcro board with attractive

Teens for Seniors

materials attached. An exhibit could include some of the equipment used in various programs, such as life saving apparatuses, and can be displayed appropriately on tables or floors. Demonstrations are a more dynamic approach and can include past program participants demonstrating something they have learned or experienced or it could be the program leader(s) demonstrating an aspect of the upcoming activities. Demonstrations should be rehearsed in order for them to be successful.

- **Newsletters.** Businesses, service associations, and other organizations will sometimes let nonprofit organizations include program activity information in their monthly, quarterly, or biannual newsletters for free. This not only assists the nonprofit organization, but it also provides an additional service to their members. By using publishing software or obtaining sponsors, nonprofit organizations can also develop their own newsletters, which can become excellent outlets for program and service information.

- **Advertising.** It may sometimes be necessary for nonprofit organizations to pay for advertisements in local newspapers and on radio and television stations. Media organizations typically assist the nonprofit organization with content and layout and often provide advertising for a reduced rate. Many media organizations will also provide advertising if they sponsor a particular event or they may provide a **gift-in-kind**, which means that the advertising is the media's way of contributing to the nonprofit organization.

- **Personal Contact.** One of the most effective ways of letting the public know what is coming up programmatically is by word of mouth. People who have had good experiences within an organization often willingly and voluntarily tell others about program opportunities. A more formal way of communicating program information is through a **speaker's bureau** made up of staff members and/or volunteers who present program information at club and organizational meetings. This process is an excellent way to provide program information as well as to recruit volunteers and financial support.

- **Informational Packets.** Information in the form of packets, brochures, or newsletters can often be left with the local Chamber of Commerce, United Way, Better Business Bureau, and other key places throughout a community where families and businesses that are new to the community can find out about the organization.

- **Web Site.** Creating and maintaining a web site with current program and organizational information gives both members and prospective members quick access to opportunities within an organization. Promoting the web site through informational packets, flyers, signs, and any other means available will provide the organization with a great deal of exposure.

Designing and implementing promotional material and promotional campaigns is often done by staff members in association with volunteers who possess expertise in marketing and promotion. Most nonprofit organizations have a board committee or group of volunteers created with the primary purpose of promoting the organization, program activities, and any other services. When effectively designed and implemented, promotional activities can be both fun and rewarding.

- **Price.** Price is a significant aspect in the selection process of choosing a particular program, and if all things are equal, price can be the determining factor. Generally speaking, individuals select the product, service, or program that is the least expensive if quality and other factors are fairly equal. However, cost is sometimes associated with value, and a program must be perceived to have *real value* in order to be desirable. So it is important for an organization to keep cost at a minimum in order to be competitive and be cost-effective for its members, while establishing a sense that the program is of *real value*. The cost of the program must also fit into the budgetary requirements established for programs. Staff members of nonprofit organizations usually set pricing for programs, sometimes with input from board members, and with the approval of the board of directors. Organizations with national and/or regional affiliations often receive assistance in setting fair and effective prices. Most nonprofit organizations set up scholarships, a sliding scale system, and/or payment plans for individuals who qualify for financial assistance.

- **Place.** The location of the facility or space where programs or services are offered is a significant consideration. The location must first be accessible to the targeted group of potential participants. Sometimes this means making programs and services *outreach* activities that are delivered to the targeted group through mobile or satellite units. The facility or space must be a desirable location for programs and services and, above all else, it must be clean and safe and be perceived as clean and safe by the community. Program space must also adhere to local health, safety, environmental, and fire codes.

Promoting programs and services for a nonprofit organization is a vital and exciting aspect of program development and must be well thought out, comprehensive, and focused both on the present and the future. Organizations with an eye toward quality, which are effective at program and service promotion, are generally successful in attracting participants, volunteers and financial support.

Step 11 – Program or Project Budget. Successful nonprofit organizations require a **program** or **project budget** prepared in advance of each activity. This should be a separate budget from the **operating budget**, the budget the organization uses to operate on for a **fiscal** or financial year, but it folds into the operating budget. The program budget includes a total of the **estimated expenses** and a total of the **estimated income** or **revenue.** Estimated expenses include any projected costs for a specific program. These expenses might include such items as supplies and materials, equipment, postage, food, travel, and personnel hired just for a specific program. Estimated income would include any fees or contributions that are received for the use of a specific program. Estimated expenses and income can be summarized on a PPW such as the one in Figure 5.2, 128.

Programs may be projected to have a **gain**, which means there is more income projected than expenses, or to have a **deficit**, which means the expenses are projected to exceed the income. Deficits are almost always listed in parentheses. Programs are usually planned to realize a gain or at least to break even, but some programs are considered so important

Figure 5.6
Program or Project Budget

Program Budget for Teens for Seniors

	Income	Expenses	Gain/Deficit
Estimated	$500	$300	+ $200
Actual	$580	$380	+ $200

they will continue to be implemented by an organization with the idea that the money will be made up in some other way. Once a program is completed there is a place on the PPW (see Figure 5.2) to include the **actual income** as well as the **actual expenses** and a space for the **actual gain** or **deficit.** This provides staff and board members with financial information regarding each program. For instance, the Teens for Seniors program mentioned previously might have an income based on projected sponsorships and expenses projected on the basis of planned activities. This would provide some budgetary guidelines for the program staff to work with. The actual income and expenses would be listed once the program was completed and would provide much-needed financial information for the program (See Figure 5.6 above).

Income and expenses can be broken down further on a separate ledger for a detailed analysis of costs versus revenue. Recording expenses and revenues for each program on the PPW as well as in a ledger also provides financial information if and when similar programs are considered in the future.

Some organizations also keep an accounting of how much time professional and volunteer staff members spend with specific programs, along with how much overhead expense, such as utilities and rent, is incorporated in each program. This is sometimes referred to as **indirect** or **functional** cost.

Step 12 – Walk-Through/Rehearsal. Before the actual implementation of any program or activity, it can be a good idea to do a visual and/or physical walk-through or rehearsal. This provides the program committee a chance to visualize and prepare for most aspects of the program, such as where equipment is to be set and where staff and volunteer members are to be stationed. It provides the committee with the opportunity to estimate spatial needs and examine equipment, materials, and supplies. A walk-through allows committee members an opportunity to review checklists and to become familiar with the layout of the program areas. Most importantly, it provides them with time to review the risk management plan and to be certain all aspects of the plan are in place.

Step 13 – Implementation and Supervision. The implementation step is the time in which the program or activity actually begins. The plans and steps that have been developed up to this date provide a structure and some guidelines on how to proceed with the program or activity. This is the time to follow carefully developed plans, monitor the progress of each aspect of the program, and make changes if necessary. Almost no program goes exactly according to plan, and ingenuity and flexibility are necessary character traits if and when things go awry.

Determining which leadership or supervisory style to adopt with specific programs is a lifelong endeavor (see Chapter 2). Studies indicate there is really no ideal leadership style for a given program (Edginton and Ford 1985), which means the leadership or supervisory style depends on the circumstances, the maturity of the staff and volunteers, and other dynamics that are involved with each activity. It means that individuals in leadership positions must develop leadership skills and knowledge and be flexible enough to incorporate appropriate concepts and actions when necessary. For instance, incorporating the Tri-Dimensional Leader Effectiveness Model (Situational Leadership), described in Chapter 2, Figure 2.4, as a supervisory strategy allows a supervisor to be flexible and lead differently under different circumstances. The same thing can be said of Collaborative Leadership, discussed in Chapter 2 along with Comprehensive Leadership, which is also outlined in Figure 2.6.

Good nonprofit organizations encourage leadership training for administrative program staff. These organizations typically provide training in the form of workshops, seminars, and conferences, sometimes offered as in-service opportunities. Some nonprofit organizations also support advanced, formal educational opportunities by offering financial assistance for tuition and/or rewards for advanced educational work.

Step 14 – Special Considerations. Staff and volunteer members should have training and should always be well prepared for special situations and individuals with special needs. Programs must be designed to meet the special needs of individuals, and often the diversity of individuals with special needs adds depth to program intent. Special needs may take the form of **medical problems,** such as diabetes, AIDS, or epilepsy. They could take the form of various **physical disabilities,** such as cerebral palsy and multiple sclerosis, or **psychological disorders** that include autism and psychosis, as examples. Severe **behavioral maladjustment** would include a condition such as attention deficit disorder (with hyperactivity). There are a number of **communication problems** that need to be considered, such as speech difficulties, hearing impairments, and language barriers (Weis and Gantt 2002). Some of these conditions may require staff and volunteers with specific training and qualifications. Others may require a certain staff-to-member ratio, and even special materials and equipment. Policies and procedures for handling individuals with special needs must be in place prior to program development. These policies and procedures must be inclusive, fair, effective, and within legal guidelines. They must be reviewed and approved by the board of directors of the organization.

Another special consideration when developing programs is the issue of **abuse** and **neglect.** In the course of offering programs and services, nonprofit leaders sometimes encounter children, senior citizens, spouses, and others who may have been or are being abused or neglected. Some **characteristics** of individuals who have been abused may include

(Weis and Gantt 2002):

- Feelings of inadequacy
- Listlessness and depression
- Lack of joy and excitement
- Unexplained bruises and abrasions
- Difficulties with relationships
- Aggressiveness
- Reluctance to receive praise and/or physical affection
- Thin or emaciated appearance

It is important to note that there might be other characteristics to suggest abuse or neglect and that the presence of any of the characteristics above doesn't necessarily mean that abuse or neglect is occurring. However, if a program leader suspects abuse or neglect he or she should follow the guidelines listed below:

- Report the suspected abuse or neglect to a supervisor.
- The supervisor should contact the organization's director.
- The director may decide to gather further information if further information seems necessary. Oftentimes, however, immediate action is called for.
- If abuse or neglect is still suspected, it must be reported to the local authorities as quickly as possible. In most instances, reporting possible abuse and neglect situations is a legal responsibility as well as being the right thing to do.
- An incident report should be completed documenting what occurred and what procedures were taken.
- Some organizations may require incidents of abuse and neglect be reported to a specific board member or committee.

If there is ever any question of abuse or neglect, it is imperative to follow the guidelines above and report suspected incident(s) without delay.

■ Final (Evaluation) Stage

The final stage of program development includes an effective and thorough evaluation process, which is important for a number of reasons: (1) it helps determine whether the program was successful and the program objectives were met; (2) the information is important in helping staff and volunteer members make constructive changes for the future; (3) it provides board members with the type of information important in determining if the organization is on the right track; (4) it gives program participants an opportunity to express their concerns, suggestions, and praise regarding activities that affect their lives; (5) the results may be reported to the media so that community members are kept abreast of the benefits of the organization; and (6) evaluation results are essential for accrediting bodies and financial sponsors, such as corporations or the United Way. This stage also includes the process of analyzing and reporting program results and making recommendations and changes for the future.

Step 15 – Evaluation Process. There are essentially four activities that need to occur in an evaluation process (Edginton and Edginton 1994):

- Determining which individual(s) should be involved in the process
- Determining what exactly needs to be evaluated

- Selecting the type(s) of evaluation
- Implementing the method(s) of evaluation

Which individuals should be involved in the evaluation process? There are a number of individuals who can and should be involved in the evaluation process. To begin with, the participants of the program are the primary individuals who need to be involved in the evaluation process because they are the individuals most affected by the program. If the participants are too young, or for some reason they are unable to respond to the evaluation, parents, guardians, or caretakers may be asked to assist. In addition to the participants, program staff, volunteers, collaborating agency members, sponsors, and anyone associated with the program can participate in the evaluation process.

What needs to be evaluated? Two major areas need to be measured regarding the success of the program to determine if the program met the program objectives and to what degree: **quantitative** measurements and **qualitative** measurements. In other words, did the program meet the numerical objectives, and did it make a difference and have a positive impact?

Numerical (quantitative) measurements could include the number of participants, the number of activities, and any financial objectives. Qualitative measurements help determine whether the program made a difference in specific areas such as knowledge, skills, health, and attitude.

In addition to providing information that helps to determine if objectives were met, evaluation processes can provide information regarding the overall quality of the staff, facilities, supplies, and materials. Other areas that can be examined include program accessibility and affordability, and any other aspect of a program that needs to be assessed.

Selecting the Type(s) of evaluation. In general, there are two major types of evaluation. The first type can be incorporated at various stages of the program; the second type is used at the end of a program:

- **Formative Evaluation.** A formative evaluation can be implemented at various stages while a program is being implemented to help determine whether changes need to be made while activities are in process. The advantage of this type of evaluation is obvious: constructive changes can be made before the program ends. The disadvantage is that it is one more task that can be time-consuming and therefore difficult to include.
- **Summative Evaluation.** This type of evaluation is done at the end of the program and provides feedback to determine whether the program met its objectives, and it provides information for making changes to a program in the future. Incorporating a summative or final evaluation at the end of a program is simpler and less time-consuming, but the disadvantage is that it will not help address changes that may need to be made during the implementation of an activity.

Implementing Methods of Evaluation. Programs can and should be evaluated incorporating a number of different methods. Select methodology is discussed below:

- **Observations.** Observation can be a legitimate form of evaluation that provides the evaluator with personal and immediate information. Although not as objective and often not as formal as other methodologies, observation provides a sensory assessment that cannot be duplicated.

- **Interview.** Conducting interviews provides the evaluator with a broad range of information. Questions should be designed from general to specific, and flexibility should be built in to ask other questions based on the responses. Interviews can be done in person, via telephone and e-mail or any other viable way, and the issue of confidentiality should be addressed up front. As an evaluation tool, interviews can be highly focused and valuable, but can be time-consuming. Example interview questions are listed in Figure 5.7. The evaluator should remember to remain flexible and to insert other questions based on the responses of the interviewees.

- **Focus Group.** Recruiting several people together at the same time for interviews provides the evaluator with a broad range of information and a synergy that is difficult to duplicate with interviews. Again, questions should be designed from general to specific, and flexibility should be built in to ask other questions based on the responses of the participants. Questions can be patterned after the interview questions in Figure 5.7

- **Evaluation Survey.** Providing program participants with a way to report their experiences and assuring anonymity with a survey increases the likelihood the responses will be objective and more honest. As with interviews and focus groups, questions should go from broad to specific and seek to assess any important aspect of a program. Questions can be turned into statements for use with the Likert Scale, and each statement should address only one aspect of the program. An example evaluation survey to be administered to the teenage participants is included in Figure 5.8.

- **Pre/Post Test or Survey.** Providing a pre-test to participants prior to a program and then providing the same test following a program is an excellent way of determining whether real changes and impact have been made. Knowledge, attitude, character, and skills are just a few areas that can be tested with a pre/post test to determine change. The pre-test and post-test must have correlative

---

Figure 5.7
Example Interview Questions

1. What did you think of the Teens for Seniors program?
2. Was the program beneficial? For whom?
3. What did you like best about the program? Least?
4. Was it offered at a convenient time?
5. Was the program accessible for you?
6. Were the trainers/counselors helpful?
7. What would you change about the program?
8. Would you recommend this program to others?
9. Is there anything else you would like to say about the program?

Figure 5.8
Example Evaluation Survey

Teens for Seniors Program Evaluation

In order to help us evaluate the Teens for Seniors program and plan for future programs, we would like you to complete the following survey. The survey is anonymous and no one will know the result of your responses. When you have completed the survey, please drop it in the box marked "Surveys" on the table near the exit. Thank you for participating in the Teens for Seniors program and for completing the survey.

Indicate the number that reflects your response to each statement based on the following scale:

	1 Strongly Disagree	2 Disagree	3 Undecided	4 Agree	5 Strongly Agree
1. The Teens for Seniors program was effective.	☐	☐	☐	☐	☐
2. I am now more comfortable with senior citizens.	☐	☐	☐	☐	☐
3. The recreational aspects of the program were successful.	☐	☐	☐	☐	☐
4. The crafts aspect of the program was important.	☐	☐	☐	☐	☐
5. The health and fitness aspects of the program were effective.	☐	☐	☐	☐	☐
6. The joint service outings were successful.	☐	☐	☐	☐	☐
7. The trainers did a good job in preparing us.	☐	☐	☐	☐	☐
8. The meeting location was convenient.	☐	☐	☐	☐	☐
9. I would recommend the program to a friend.	☐	☐	☐	☐	☐

Comments/suggestions: _____

_____

_____

Figure 5.9
Example Pre/Post Test

Teens for Seniors Program
Pre/Post Test or Survey

In order to help us determine various changes that might have occurred during the Teens for Seniors program, we would like you to complete the following Pre/Post Test. Be certain that your Pre-Test number correlates with your Post-Test number and thank you for participating in the survey and the program.

Indicate the number that reflects your response to each statement based on the following scale:

	1 Strongly Disagree	2 Disagree	3 Undecided	4 Agree	5 Strongly Agree
1. I am comfortable being around senior citizens.	☐	☐	☐	☐	☐
2. Senior citizens can make a positive contribution to their community.	☐	☐	☐	☐	☐
3. I am making a positive difference in my community.	☐	☐	☐	☐	☐
4. I am able to lead recreational activities with senior citizens.	☐	☐	☐	☐	☐
5. I am able to lead crafts activities with senior citizens.	☐	☐	☐	☐	☐
6. I can work effectively with senior citizens in making a difference in our community through service projects.	☐	☐	☐	☐	☐
7. I feel good about myself.	☐	☐	☐	☐	☐

Comments/suggestions _____

_____

_____

_____

_____

identification such as numbers and be completed by the same individual and scored accordingly. An example pre/post is included in Figure 5.9 at left:

The pre/post test above measures the participants' perception of knowledge, attitude, skills, and self-esteem regarding their experience and would be given to teenagers prior to the beginning of the program and again once the program was completed. The resulting scores will help the evaluators determine the degree of effectiveness of the program in a number of different areas.

Effective evaluation processes can be very helpful in determining whether or not programs are meeting their objectives and whether they are quality programs. The process also encourages communication between program staff members, volunteer members, and participants and provides helpful program information for the future. This information can also be used to develop funding, as a part of the promotion process, and for marketing processes as well.

Step 16 – Record and Report Results. Evaluation results need to be assimilated and recorded on the Program Planning Worksheet and maintained in a permanent file for future reference. This can provide invaluable information for future programs. The results of each program should be discussed by the program and volunteer staff members and with the participants when applicable. Program evaluation results are sometimes reviewed by the program committee of the board of directors and even by the entire board of directors. They may also be used as a part of personnel evaluations. The results of successful programs should also be reported to the media and included in the organization's promotional material.

Step 17 – Formulate Recommendations for Future Program. Program staff and volunteer members, along with a select group of program participants should discuss recommendations for future programs based, in part, on the resulting program evaluations. Recommendations for future programs will provide insight for the focus of programs and can be recorded on the Program Planning Worksheet and filed for future reference.

Providing programs that meet and exceed the expectations of customers and provide them with positive outcomes is both exciting and rewarding, and it requires a good deal of expertise in planning, implementation, and evaluation. This customer-centered/benefits approach to program development provides a step by step planning process intended to offer guidance and support for program development. Action steps or work tasks can be derived from the program planning steps. As mentioned earlier in this chapter, programs can and often do change directions in all stages for one reason or another, and flexibility and innovation are required characteristics for leaders in the nonprofit area. A simplified, simulated program plan is included in Figure 5.10, 154-155.

■ Summary

Programs should be designed to meet the objectives and goals of the organization and to meet and exceed the expectations of the customers while providing them with positive outcomes. This customer-centered/benefits approach to program development requires that staff and volunteer members be committed to the organization, to quality programs, and to the customers or members. Programs must be designed to meet and exceed the general standards and expectations of the constituents.

Figure 5.10
Simulated Program Plan (page 1)

Date 09 / 25 / 04

Name of Organization **Morganfield Boys and Girls Club**

Name of Program/Project **Teens for Seniors**

Program Coordinator **Julie Weston**

Program Members:

	Name	Address	Phone Number	e-mail address
1	Julie Weston	1407 Wall St.	762-4791	j.weston@b&gca.org
2	L.W. Perdue	131 Camile Dr.	762-0101	lw.perdue@bas.org
3	Vivian Perdue	7229 Opal St.	753-1098	v.perdue@bas.org
4	Virginia Kenova	1413 Carol Dr.	759-2038	v.kenova@lol.org

Program Objectives **The Teens for Seniors program provides teenagers in the Morganfield area opportunities to assist senior citizens attending the Westview Day Care program. Teens will be trained to participate with seniors in social, cultural, service, and recreational activities. Intended objectives include**

- A minimum of 10 teenagers involved in a program with a minimum of 25 senior citizens meeting once a week for activities

- Improved inter-generational understanding

- Increased flexibility on the part of senior citizens

- Decreased depression on the part of senior citizens

- Enhanced self-esteem of teenagers and senior citizens

- Increased sense of responsibility and caring on the part of teenagers

- Improved teamwork, communication, recreation, socialization and leadership skills on the part of the teenagers

Estimated Direct Expenses $340	Estimated Direct Income $500 (sponsorship)	Gain (Deficit) $160
Actual Direct Costs $270	Actual Direct Income $480	Gain (Deficit) $210

Action Steps or Work Tasks	Person(s) Responsible	Completion Dates
1. Formulate Committee	Weston	October 1
2. Conduct Needs Assessment	V.Perdue	October 9
3. Review Developmental Theories, Issues, and Values	Weston	October 11
4. Determine Program Objectives	Committee	October 13
5. Develop Program Concept & Format	Weston	October 14
6. Evaluate Resources	Committee	October 15
7. Identify Potential Program Risks	Committee	October 20
8. Prioritize Program Risks	Committee	October 20
9. Develop Plan for Handling Risks	Committee	October 21
10. Evaluate Insurance Coverage	Weston	October 22

Figure 5.11
Simulated Program Plan (page 2)

Action Steps or Work Tasks	Person(s) Responsible	Completion Dates
11. Prepare Participant Waiver Forms	Committee	October 23
12. Meeting to Develop Plan for Promoting Program	Committee	October 25
13. Develop Flyers & PSAs	L.W. Perdue	October 26
14. Develop Promotional Event	V.Perdue	October 27
15. Establish Program Budget	LPerdue	November 1
16. Plan for Special Considerations	Weston	November 5
17. Post Flyers	L.W.Perdue	November 9
18. Release PSAs	L.W. Perdue	November 9
19. Conduct Promotional Event	V. Perdue	November 9
20. Walk-Through/Rehearsal	Whole Committee	November 10
21. Participants Sign Waiver Forms	V. Perdue	November 15
22. Implement and Monitor Program	Whole Committee	December 1
23. Conduct Formative Evaluations	V.Perdue	January 15
24. Conduct Final Evaluations	V. Perdue	March 1
25. Record Results on PPW	Kenova	March 5
26. Report Results to Board & Media	Weston	March 6
27. Formulate & Record Future Recommendations (PPW)	Whole Committee	March 15

Evaluation Results   The Teens for Seniors program was evaluated primarily through observation and a final evaluation. A summary of the evaluation administered to the teenage participants follows:

Summary of Evaluation

Number of Respondents: 10

Statement	Average Score
1. The Teens for Seniors program was effective.	4.9
2. I am more now more comfortable with senior citizens.	4.5
3. The recreational activities were successful.	4.3
4. The crafts aspect of the program was important	4.4
5. The health & fitness aspects of the program were effective	4.6
6. The joint service outings were successful.	4.8
7. The trainers did a good job in preparing us.	4.1
8. The meeting location was convenient.	4.7
9. I would recommend the program to a friend.	5.0

Comments/Suggestions: I loved the program and would do it again!

Need more time for preparation.

Training could have been more comprehensive

Recommendations for Future Programs   Based on observation, informal interviews, and the final evaluation, it seems that the program basically met the objectives and in some cases exceeded expectations. It is recommended that the program be repeated annually or more often if appropriate. Suggestions for changes include a longer preparation time and a more thorough training period.

Program development can be divided into three interrelated stages: (1) Initial (Planning) Stage, (2) Middle (Planning/Implementation) Stage, and (3) Final (Evaluation) Stage (PIE). Each of these stages can be divided into specific steps that can be modified or simplified depending on the circumstances. The sequence of steps can also be changed if necessary.

The Initial Stage of program development is important because it builds the foundation for later stages. This stage includes selecting a program committee to organize the project, surveying membership needs, reviewing developmental theories and relevant issues, including values and character education, and then determining objectives for the program. Once program objectives have been decided, a program concept and format must be developed to ensure the objectives are achieved. This stage is concluded once resources necessary for the program, such as personnel, time, space, and money, are evaluated.

The Middle Stage of program development begins with the most important step in the whole planning process, developing a system to keep all risks involved in any program to an absolute minimum. The next step in this stage is to create a comprehensive marketing plan for generating promotional material. Another step in this stage is to design a Program Budget in order to record the estimated and actual expenses and the income for each individual program.

Conducting a walk-through or rehearsal for each program allows the program staff to visualize and prepare for most aspects of a program. Understanding leadership and supervisory styles is also important, so nonprofit leaders can incorporate appropriate concepts and actions when necessary in supervising others in program delivery. And finally, being trained and prepared for special situations and individuals with special needs is vital to the overall success of program development.

In the Final Evaluation Stage, the program must be evaluated to help determine whether it was successful and met its objectives. This information can also be helpful for staff and volunteer members in making changes for future programs as well as for sponsoring organizations to determine if their sponsorship is worthwhile. Some ways programs can be evaluated are through observation, interviews, focus groups, and surveys.

Program results should be recorded on the Program Planning Worksheet and reported as is appropriate. Reports might be made to a board of directors or to a committee within the board. Other reports may be presented to sponsoring entities, to the news media, and they may be included in the organization's communications materials. It is particularly important that recommendations for the future be recorded and kept readily available for future programming staff.

This chapter addressed, in part, the American Humanics Certification Competency Requirements of Nonprofit Program Planning, Nonprofit Marketing, and Nonprofit Risk Management.

■ Discussion Questions

1. Discuss different aspects of *quality* and its importance in program development.
2. List and discuss the importance of the steps involved in the Initial Planning Stage of program development?

3. Discuss the importance of the Middle Planning Stage as part of program development?
4. What is the significance of the Final Planning Stage in program development?
5. Explain the concept *customer-centered/benefits approach* to program development?
6. What are the advantages to this kind of approach?
7. Describe the various parts of a program objective?
8. What is the significance of program objectives?
9. What is the difference between a program concept and a program format?
10. How does a program budget fit into the fiscal, operational budget?

∎ Activities

1. Design a needs-assessment plan to develop a program scenario.
2. After developing a program scenario, design risk management plan.
3. Using the same scenario, develop a comprehensive marketing plan.
4. Finally, develop a plan to evaluate the program.
5. Develop a list of nonprofit leaders to interview regarding program development; then report back to class through a discussion or paper.
6. Using the same list, see about shadowing the staff during a day a program is implemented.

∎ References

Albrecht, K. M., and Zemke, R. (1985). *Service America!*. Homewood, IL: Dow Jones-Irwin.

Bagozzi, R. P., (1975). Marketing as exchange. *Journal of Marketing* 39:32-39.

Bush, P. (1972). *A Program Course for Writing of Performance Objectives*. Chico, CA: North California Program Development Center.

Covey, S. R. (1989). *The Seven Habits of Highly Effective People*. New York: Simon and Schuster.

Edginton, C.R., Ford, P.F., and Hudson, S.D. (1999). *Leadership in Recreation and Leisure Service Organizations*. Champaign, IL: Sagamore Publishing.

Edginton, C. R., Hanson, C. J., Edginton, S. R., and Hudson, S. D. (1998). *Leisure Programming: A Service-Centered and Benefits Approach*. Boston, MA: McGraw-Hill.

Edginton, S. R., and Edginton, C. R. (1994). *Youth Programs: Promoting Quality Services*. Champaign, IL: Sagamore Publishing.

Hardy, J. M. (1984). *Managing for Impact in Nonprofit Organizations*. Erwin, TN: Essex Press.

Jordan, D. J. (1992). Risk management guidelines. *Journal of Physical Education, Recreation, and Dance*. Cedar Falls, IA: University of Northern Iowa.

Kaplan, P. S. (1998). *The Human Odyssey: Life Span Development*. Pacific Grove, CA: Brooks/Cole Publishing Company.

Kotler, P. (1982). *Marketing for Nonprofit Organizations*. 2nd ed. Englewood Cliffs: N.J.: Prentice Hall.

Maslow, A. H. (1943). A theory of human motivation. *Psychological Review* July, 370-96.

Mohr, L. B. (1988). *Impact Analysis for Program Evaluation*. Chicago: Dorsey Press.

Purpel, D. and Ryan, K. (1976). *Moral Education: It Comes with the Territory*. Berkeley, CA: McCutcheon Publishing Corporation.

Rathmell, J. M. (1974). *Marketing in the Service Sector*. Cambridge, MA: Winthrop Publications.

Rea, L. M., and Parker, R. A. (1992). *Designing and Conducting Survey Research: A Comprehensive Guide*. San Francisco: Jossey-Bass.

Stern, G. J. (1990). *Marketing Workbook for Nonprofit Organizations*. St. Paul, MN: Amherst H. Wilder Foundation.

Thomas, J. C. (1994). "Program evaluation and program development." In *The Jossey-Bass Handbook of Nonprofit Leadership and Management*. San Francisco: Jossey-Bass Publishers

Van der Smissen, B. (1990). *Legal Liability and Risk Management for Public and Private Entities* (Vol.2). Cincinnati, OH: Anderson.

Walton, M. (1998). *The Demming Management Model*. New York: Perigee.

Weis, R. M. and Gantt, V.W. (2002). *Leadership and Program Development in Nonprofit Organizations*. Peosta, IA: E. Bowers Publishing.

Weiss, C. H. (1972). *Evaluation Research: Methods of Assessing Program Effectiveness*. Englewood Cliffs, N.J.: Prentice-Hall.

Wolf, T. (1999). *Managing a Nonprofit Organization*. New York: Prentice Hall.

6 Financial Processes and Financial Development

Individuals seek careers in the nonprofit field because they hope to make a difference in people's lives through the implementation of various programs and experiences. Few people enter the field because of opportunities to develop budgets, or to create financial development plans. Generally speaking, for individuals who consider this field as a career direction, financial matters are one of the last things on their mind and understandably so. The fact is that nonprofit organizations are businesses that provide services. And just like for-profit businesses, nonprofit organizational leaders have to be adept at financial processes in order to be successful and to provide the best services possible to members of the community. Another similarity between a nonprofit and for-profit organization is the fact they are both **legal entities**, usually in the form of a corporation. Too, they can both earn more revenue than expenses, usually referred to as a **profit** in for-profits and a **surplus** in the nonprofit world. For-profits may put the profit back into the organization or give some or all of it to stockholders. Nonprofit organizations must put all of their surplus back into the operation of the organization in some manner (Konrad and Novak 2000).

Although leaders at the administrative level are usually the financial managers in nonprofit organizations, leaders at the program level also have financial responsibilities, and it is important that all staff members have a working knowledge of financial matters. To assist the program staff in financial areas, many organizations also have bookkeepers, accountants, and/or consulting firms on staff. It is also important to note that most organizations receive a great deal of financial expertise from board members who are members of the financial community and who are ultimately responsible for the financial well-being of the organization. Much of what follows in the first two sections of this chapter is based on the work of Thomas Wolf and his book, *Managing a Nonprofit Organization*. More information on this book can be found in the reference section at the end of this chapter.

There are three major areas to consider in this chapter regarding fiscal matters: (1) financial management or budgeting, (2) financial statements, procedures, or accounting, and (3) financial development or fundraising. We will explore these three areas and how they relate.

■ Financial Management or Budgeting

Every nonprofit organization begins each year with a financial plan detailing how it will cover the cost of its operations. An **operating budget** is an organization's financial plan that specifies how much **income** or **revenue** an organization projects it will need to operate for a financial or **fiscal** year, and how much money it plans in the way of **expenses** for that same year (see Figure 6.1).

Figure 6.1
Simulated Operating Budget for a Fiscal Year

Income		Expenses	
Membership fees	$95,000	Salaries	$93,000
Program fees	27,000	Benefits	17,000
Special Events	20,000	Activity Supplies	14,000
United Way	15,000	Utilities	24,000
Foundation Grants	12,000	Facility cost	10,000
Annual Campaign	25,000	Telephone cost	9,000
Total	194,000	Postage	3,000
		Contingency/reserve	23,000
			194,000

A financial or fiscal year often runs with the calendar year, January 1 to December 31, but some organizations prefer the fiscal year to parallel the program year, the reporting year, or a period that correlates with major funding sources such as the United Way or a foundation. A nonprofit organization can select any dates for its fiscal year as long as it specifies these dates in its articles of incorporation.

The budget is generally divided into two major sections, **income** or **revenue** and **expenses**, and specific **income categories** and **expense categories** further divide each of these sections. Each specific expense and income category is listed on a separate line with a certain dollar amount to the side of it, and for this reason these categories are referred to as **line items.** It is up to the organization to decide which line items to include as categories. For instance, all salaries may go in one line item, with employee benefits making up another. In the income section, all membership fees may make up one line item while program fees may make up another.

Developing a Budget

Budgeting is a form of financial planning, and it is important to have specific guidelines to consider when developing the budget an organization is going to operate with for the coming fiscal year. The following steps are recommended in preparing a budget and are derived in part from Wolf (1999) and Weis and Gantt (2002):

Step 1: Develop a List of Expenses. Budgets need to be prepared months in advance of a fiscal year by the administrative staff, with input from the program staff and guidance from financial committee members of the board of directors. These individuals must consider and make a projection of all of the expenses necessary to operate the organization for a fiscal year.

Administrative staff members should (1) look at expenses from previous budgets to develop a sense of what costs have been in the past. They should (2) estimate any changes in those costs and (3) envision future needs and what those needs will cost the organization to operate effectively. To be as accurate as possible, leaders should seek input from all staff members of the organization, as well as from board members, before making projections about expenses. Expenses should be estimated on the high side, and room for unexpected expenses should always be considered.

Step 2: Determine Sources of Revenue. Once a list of projected expenses is determined, a process follows to determine sources of income. Administrative leaders, with input from the program staff and guidance and approval from the financial committee of the board of directors, develop a list of sources of revenue to pay for the projected expenses. This can be accomplished by (1) looking at revenue sources from previous budgets to get an idea of potential areas of income generation and by also (2) looking at new areas of financial development. Many organizations have a financial development committee comprised of staff and board members whose job it is to generate potential revenue sources. Income projections should be kept on the low side, and allowances must be made for possible discrepancies in income projections and lower- than-projected actual income outcomes.

Step 3: Comparing Expenses with Revenue. Once the projected revenue and expense lists have been developed, it is time for the administrative staff and financial committee members of the board to determine whether the projected revenue will cover projected expenses. If the projected revenue covers or exceeds the projected list of expenses, then the budget could move forward toward the approval phase of the budgeting process. If, on the other hand, the projected revenue does not cover the projected list of expenses, then a number of considerations can be undertaken.

First of all, each administrative and program need should be evaluated carefully. After close scrutiny, some of the expenses may be eliminated, or at least the cost of expenses reduced. One way to do this would be through a process referred to as **zero-based budgeting** in which no historical base is recognized for expenses and each expense line begins with a new slate. This process provides an opportunity to examine exactly what is needed to cover the cost of each organizational need. For instance, in looking at telephone costs, it could be advantageous to consider other, less expensive servers, provided the service is still effective. A change in servers can save an organization hundreds or even thousands of dollars each year.

The same process could be used in hiring a consulting firm for accounting and bookkeeping processes or any number of other organizational operations. Even though it is generally more time consuming, zero-based budgeting can be very effective in eliminating unnecessary expenses and should be considered when balancing expenses with income. Another way to meet organizational costs would be to look at the revenue side of the budget to determine other ways to enhance or develop new income lines to cover various expenses.

Step 4: Setting Administrative and Program Priorities. Once expense and revenue potential have been reviewed and assessed, organizational leaders should schedule a priority-setting session. This session should help in determining the need for specific programs and administrative operations. Several key questions need to be asked in this session:

1. Which programs are central to the purpose of the organization?
2. Which programs are cost effective and how important is this consideration?
3. Which administrative operations are essential to the overall success of the organization, and which ones can be altered or eliminated, if any?

When these questions have been addressed thoroughly, organizational leaders will be better prepared to select the best path for the organization to pursue for the coming fiscal year.

Step 5: Adjust and Balance. Once projected expenses and revenue potential have been carefully examined and a list of priorities decided upon, the next step involves listing expenses and income figures on a budget sheet and balancing those figures. Generally speaking, the projected expense side of a budget should balance with the total figure for revenue. Each program in a nonprofit organization may not be cost-effective, or even cover all of the expenses for the program, but the overall budget must balance.

The budget process so far has skewed the figures so that expenses are projected on the high side and revenue estimates are projected low. If the budget actually ended up as projected, the "extra" money for a fiscal year could not be used as a form of profit for anyone within the organization. This money must be used within the organization in some manner, so that the expense side of the budget balances with the revenue side. This is often done by incorporating this money in a contingency/reserve fund that will be discussed later in this chapter.

Step 6: Budget Approval. Following the development of a budget, only the board of directors can approve the budget of a nonprofit organization. This is often done by first having the finance committee of the board review a proposed budget and then forward their recommendation to the full board for final approval. Board members must be fully knowledgeable regarding any expenses that are to be incurred and confident about the revenue that is to be generated. Members should have an opportunity to ask questions about the legitimacy of any and all expenses and the accuracy and certainty of income projections. Board members are ultimately accountable for fiscal matters of an organization, and therefore they should challenge each line of the budget to be as certain as possible the organization is on a responsible fiscal path.

When they sign off on a budget, members of the board are exercising their fiduciary responsibility to set parameters for the budget and therefore for the staff and volunteer members. When they vote to approve a budget, they are implicitly agreeing to a level of financial development necessary to sustain expenses for programs and administrative operations.

Step 7: Monitor and Amend. Once the budget has been approved and put into place, it must be continually monitored. A budget is only a carefully thought out fiscal projection for the coming year, and a number of things can and often do happen to warrant monitoring and sometimes alteration. It is important that key members of the staff and board of directors monitor the budget at least on a monthly basis. It is also important that provisions are made to amend the budget when necessary and possible.

Most organizations have included in their constitution, charter, and/or bylaws policies as to when budget amendments can be made. Amending the budget once or twice a year provides an organization with some flexibility without necessarily going to extremes. Revisions should be carefully thought out and should reflect the changes that necessitated the revisions in the first place. "Revised budgets" must also be presented to, studied and approved by members of the board of directors, as designated by the policies regarding budget revisions.

Project or Program Budget

Developing a project or program budget for each project or program allows the organization to estimate income and expense lines for every project and then to analyze these income and expense lines once the project is completed (Hardy 1984; Wolf 1999). This is also known as functional accounting, or cost center accounting when referring to record-keeping procedures, and it allows an organization to assess income and costs on a project-by-project basis. Project budgets include the **direct income** and **direct expenses** associated with specific projects. This is income and expense directly associated with the project. For instance, certain classes such as CPR or swim classes require special instruction and equipment and are often paid for through a program fee of some kind. It is fairly simple to estimate the direct expense and income for these programs and to determine actual expenses, income, and gain or deficit once the classes are completed.

The projected income and expenses, as well as the actual income and expenses of each project, can be placed on a Project Budget (see Figure 6.2) and added or attached to a Program Planning Worksheet (Figure 5.2) with the total figures recorded on the worksheet.

Some administrators believe is it also important to represent management and support costs (administrative/overhead) for each project, and they often devises a formula to represent these **indirect costs** in each project budget. Costs can be calculated for the percentage of staff time, space and utility allocation, phone service, and other indirect costs and designated as indirect costs to each project. This information provides leaders with some idea of the indirect costs associated with each project and may help in determining the project's overall financial desirability.

Project or program budgeting has a number of benefits:

1. It provides a detailed analysis of each project for the purpose of cost effectiveness.
2. It helps determine the revenue-generating possibilities of each project.
3. It can be used as a tool to seek financial support from community service groups,

---

Figure 6.2
Project or Program Budget

Direct Income		Direct Expenses	
Registration fees	$13,000	Part-time salaries	$4,000
Concession fees	9,000	Materials and supplies	3,000
T-shirt sales	8,000	T-shirt costs	5,000
Total	$30,000	Promotion	3,000
		Total	$15,000
			$30,000
			-15,000
		Gain/(Deficit)	$15,000

foundations, and/or corporations if projects are determined to be important, but not necessarily cost effective.

4. It provides leaders of organizations with a project-by-project analysis of specific budgets and tells them how the estimates and results fit into the overall budgeting process.

Contingency/Reserve Funds

Nonprofit organizations should plan carefully to generate excess income that can be used for unexpected needs or expenses—the contingency part—as well as for new equipment, renovations, or growth of any kind—the reserve part (Wolf 1999). When heating units break down, roofs leak, and community outreach vans wear out, a contingency fund is vital to ensuring the continuation of needed programs, regardless of unexpected circumstances. Most organizations allocate a certain percentage, such as between five and ten percent of their annual income, to this fund, although it may be higher depending on the probability of need. This extra income is listed on the expense side of the budget and may be divided up as a contingency and a reserve fund or combined as in Figure 6.3.

Several factors need to be examined prior to creating a contingency/reserve fund:

• Probability of need. The larger and more intricate an organization, the more possible repairs or replacements will be needed.
• Probability of growth. The more probable some kind of growth is in the foreseeable future, the greater need for a significant reserve fund.
• Consistency of income or revenue. The less consistent income predictability is, the larger this fund should be.
• Cash-flow concerns. Organizations also may experience cash-flow problems when bills need to be paid before there is adequate income. With a reasonable reserve fund, an organization can borrow from itself.
• Relative stability of the organization. If the organization is constantly changing leadership and/or is a relatively new organization, the fund should be higher.

When an organization has what it considers to be an adequate amount of money in the contingency fund, it should allocate the rest to a reserve fund that is kept in a carefully selected interest-bearing account of some kind, approved by the board of directors. A num-

Figure 6.3
Contingency/Reserve Fund

Income		Expenses	
Membership fees	$430,000	Salaries	$520,000
Program fees	270,000	Benefits	213,000
United Way	128,000	Materials/supplies	119,000
Special events	96,000	Contingency/reserve	72,000
Total	$924,000	Total	$924,000

ber of organizations maintain as much as twenty-five to fifty percent of a year's budget in the contingency fund, and others maintain a good deal more. The reserve part of the fund may need a substantial amount if growth is on the horizon and if it is agreeable to the board of directors.

Sometimes an organization's reserve fund becomes significantly large and may become a disincentive to funders and supporters, inasmuch as it looks like the organization has more money than it needs. One way to manage this would be to allocate a portion of these funds in an **endowment** status, which consists of invested funds (principal) with special rules and restrictions. Generally speaking, only interest from this kind of investment can be used for operational purposes. This restricted, endowed money can usually be switched back into the unrestricted reserve fund by an action of the board of directors, if and when it becomes necessary.

Cash Flow

In the budgeting process, income and expense projections are made for an entire fiscal year. An annual budget can only indicate how things are supposed to come out at the end of a year, but it does not indicate how much money is needed or available at any given point in the year. Since organizations may incur more expenses in one part of the year than in another, and since the level of money coming into the organization may vary significantly from one month to another, it is important to know how much money is available for expenses throughout the year. **Cash-flow** projections, or projecting and maintaining an organization's expenses and income on a month-to-month basis, help to keep the organization solvent and able to cover its expenses.

To prepare a cash-flow analysis, both expenses and income are laid out on a computer-generated spreadsheet (if possible), with separate columns for each month. The first column lists the total yearly budget, and each horizontal row lists each budget item. Listed next to each item is the amount of expense or income expected for that item in each particular month. For example, if salaries for the organization total $360,000, and if that is consistent from month to month, then the line item for salaries would read $360,000 as the annual total, followed by the monthly totals of $36,000 for each month. The first three months would appear accordingly:

	Total	January	February	March
Salaries	$360,000	$30,000	$30,000	$30,000

On the other hand, if all the money for a special event came in March, the line item "Special Event" would look like this:

	Total	January	February	March
Special Event	$37,000	0	0	$37,000

A careful projection of cash flow requires that each expense item and each income item be calculated accordingly to determine the availability of money in relation to expenses for each month. There can be uncertainty regarding the exact amount of an expense

Figure 6.4
Cash-flow Analysis

Expected Income	January	February
Membership fees	$25,000	$25,000
Program fees	16,000	14,000
United Way	4000	4,000
Total	$45,000	$43,000
Expected Expenses		
Salaries	$31,000	$31,000
Benefits	6,000	5,000
Utilities	4,500	4,500
Facility rent	3,000	3,000
Total	$44,500	$43,500
Monthly net income (or loss)	$500	($500)
Cash-flow summary		
Opening cash balance	$200	$700
Monthly net income (or loss)	500	(500)
Ending (cumulative) cash balance	$700	$200

item, and it is best to be conservative and estimate on the high side. It is also advisable to be conservative with the income items, to underestimate the amount, and to estimate the time of the deposit later than expected.

Once all of the projected monthly income and expense items have been listed, a monthly net income (or deficit) is calculated by subtracting total expenses from total income for that particular month. For example, if the organization anticipates $45,000 of income for the month of January and anticipates spending $44,500, then there is a net income for January of $500. If in February the anticipated income is $43,000 and expenses are anticipated to be $43,500, then the anticipated net loss is $500 for the month of February (see Figure 6.4).

Monthly financial projections are important because each one affects a cumulative flow of cash. The cash-flow summary is indicated at the bottom of Figure 6.4 and begins with an opening cash balance or the amount of money on hand at the beginning of the month. The net monthly income (or loss) is added (or subtracted) from this amount for the ending or cumulative cash balance for the month. This bottom line indicates the amount of money the organization should have to begin the next month.

Developing cash-flow projections approximately six months in advance of the coming fiscal year helps to prepare for and prevent any potential shortfalls. If the organization still falls short at some point, money can be borrowed or moved from a liquid portion of the reserve fund. If this is not possible, money can be borrowed through a lending establishment. The board should take the lead in this process and seek a low or no-interest loan.

This chapter began with the idea that most people select a career path in nonprofit organizations to make a difference in other people's lives and not because of the opportunities in financial activities. Yet the fact remains that almost everyone who works in the nonprofit field has some level of fiscal responsibility, and it is important that all staff members have at least some knowledge of and input into financial matters. It is equally important that senior staff and board members are highly knowledgeable in the fiscal matters of the organization, particularly since senior administrators are responsible for preparing budgets and other financial processes and since board members are ultimately responsible for overall finances and the approval of finances. Delivering quality, effective programs from a financially sound foundation is a major factor in assuring organizational success.

■ Financial Statements and Fiscal Procedures
Accounting

Since so many people rely on nonprofit organizations for the delivery of important services and programs, it is essential that these organizations maintain financial records carefully and that these records be open for review and be examined annually by an independent auditor. **Accounting** is the term used for financial record keeping, and there are two main types of accounting methods. One is called **cash-basis accounting** and the other one is referred to as **accrual-based accounting.**

Cash-basis accounting may be the most familiar type of accounting, since most individuals employ this type of system with their personal finances. With cash-basis accounting, financial transactions are recorded only when cash changes hands. Records are made only when money is deposited in an account or when money is withdrawn from an account or a check is written from an account. This system is beneficial in its simplicity, straightforwardness, and quickness. It does not, however, take into account any bills that are outstanding, or any money that might be owed.

With an accrual-based accounting system, on the other hand, money that actually changes hand, whether through a deposit or a withdrawal, is recorded, and money that is owed to an organization and owed by an organization is recognized as well. The advantage of this system is that it represents an organization's actual financial status much more accurately (see Figure 6.5). The disadvantage is that it is a more complex and time-consuming process.

Figure 6.5
Cash Versus Accrual

	Cash	Accrual
Beginning cash in bank	$10,000	$10,000
Purchased materials (payable)	0	-500
Membership commitment (receivable)	0	5,000
Ending cash in bank	$10,000	
Net worth		$14,500

Still another option for an organization is to incorporate a **modified cash-basis accounting** system. With this system most accounts are kept on a cash basis with the exception of a few accounts that need to be monitored well. For example, an organization might incorporate a cash-basis system for all of its income lines with the exception of membership fees, if membership fees can be paid over a period of time. This system would provide information on memberships that have been paid in full, yet keep track of those that are being paid over a period of time. This same system can be used for paying bills. Bills that are paid in full using a cash-basis accounting system would be recorded, while select bills that may take some time to pay could be recorded through an accrual-based system. For instance, major equipment purchases that are being paid for over an extended time period could be recorded with the accrual-based system. This system is often used for paying federal and state taxes as well, which involves withholding money from employees' salaries and using that money for paying the appropriate taxes.

Fund Accounting

Income and expenses that are designated for the sole purpose of operating the organization are sometimes referred to as **operating funds** or **unrestricted funds**, which means they can be used for almost any aspect of the organization's operations. Some smaller organizations that operate exclusively on unrestricted funds are often able to develop a

Figure 6.6
Multiple Fund Budget

	Operating fund	Project fund	Grant fund	Total
Income				
Membership fees	$800,000			$800,000
Program fees	320,000			320,000
United Way	32,000			32,000
Annual campaign	64,000			64,000
Contributions		$87,000		87,000
Grant			$212,000	212,000
Total	$1,216,000	$87,000	$212,000	$1,515,000
Expenses				
Salaries	$720,000	$47,000	$132,000	$899,000
Benefits	253,000	24,000	43,000	320,000
Supplies	57,000	15,000	32,000	40,000
Utilities	66,000			66,000
Facility rent	47,000			47,000
Contingency/reserve	72,000			72,000
Total	$1,216,000	$86,000	$207,000	$1,509,000

budget for income and expenses on a simple format referred to as a **single fund budget.** Larger, more complex organizations have unrestricted operating funds and often have fund accounts that are used for a number of other areas as well. One such example might be a special project in which funds would be **restricted** just for that project. Another reason to have an additional fund account is to separate the accounting for grant funds from the accounting for operating and other funds.

Operating funds and additional funds can be recorded on the same budget sheet, which is referred to as a **multiple fund budget**. Each fund is separate from the other, each with its own categories of revenue and expenses (see Figure 6.6).

The operating budget is listed first on the left-hand side of the budget. A special project (restricted) is summarized in the second column, and the third column represents a project sponsored by a grant. The sum of the three columns is represented in the fourth column. A multiple fund budget is more beneficial than a single fund budget when more than one fund is necessary because it provides quick access to the records of separate funds at one time.

Financial Statements

Two types of financial statements provide information relevant to the financial well- being or financial condition of organizations, the **balance sheet** and the **income statement** (Wolf 1999). The balance sheet (see Figure 6.7) is like a snapshot of the organization's financial condition, providing information as of a particular date, and that date is usually the last day of the month of the last month of the fiscal year. Half of the balance sheet lists all of the organization's assets or those things it owns. The other half lists the organization's liabilities (all that it owes) as well as its net assets or fund balance. Each half adds up to the same total number, hence the term *balance sheet*

The **balance** exists between the assets on the one hand and the liabilities and net assets on the other. Mathematically speaking, it would look like this:
Assets equals Liabilities plus Net Assets, or A = L + NA
This formula makes calculating the **fund balance** easy, since it is determined by subtracting the amount the organization owes from how much it owns:
Net Assets equals Assets minus Liabilities: NA = A – L

Balance sheets may first appear to be complicated, but understanding each section helps to reveal the overall financial picture of an organization. Reviewing the **asset** section of the statement in Figure 6.7 indicates what the organization owns in terms of cash in the bank, land, buildings, and equipment, as examples. Since most balance sheets are prepared on an accrual basis, they also include all the money owed to the organization as an asset. These are often referred to as **accounts receivable** and might include money owed to the organization by way of membership payments that are on a schedule or grant money that has been committed but not received. The asset section may also indicate a line for **prepaid expenses** that might include expenses for an activity or event that is occurring in the next fiscal year or some other expense that had to be prepaid.

The asset section of the balance sheet is divided into **current assets** and **noncurrent assets**. Current assets include cash or any item that is expected to become cash within the next year; noncurrent assets are those items that are not as liquid and may not be paid for

Figure 6.7
Balance Sheet

Assets

Current Assets

Cash	$13,300
Accounts Receivable	15,200
Prepaid Expenses	16,300
Total Current Assets	$44,800

Noncurrent Assets

Fixed Assets (land, buildings)	$110,000
Grants Receivable	16,300
Total Noncurrent Assets	$126,300
TOTAL ASSETS	$171,100

Liabilities and Net Assets

Liabilities

Current Liabilities

Accounts Payable	$17,200
Deferred Income	10,500
Total Current Liabilities	$27,700

Noncurrent Liabilities

Mortgage	$91,000
Total Noncurrent Liabilities	
	$91,000

Net Assets

Unrestricted	$23,000
Restricted	$7,700
Net income/(loss) YTD	
	$22,000
Total Net Assets	$52,300

TOTAL LIABILITIES AND NET ASSETS	$171,000

two years or more in the future, like those from grants or contributions.

The other half of the balance sheet includes the organization's **liabilities**, or what it owes to others. This section is divided up as well, into **current liabilities** and **noncurrent liabilities**. Current liabilities include money that the organization owes in terms of unpaid bills (**accounts payable**) and any revenue or income that has been collected for activities that will not occur until the next fiscal year (**deferred revenue** or **income**). Longer-term obligations, such as **mortgages**, are classified as **noncurrent liabilities**, since they are not due in the next fiscal year.

Once all of the liability categories are totaled and subtracted from the total assets, the difference results in the **net assets**. Net assets are classified into one of three categories as established by the Financial Accounting Standards Board (FASB):

- **Unrestricted net assets** include income from contributions and grants and any other earned income or income from investments that is not restricted for use.
- **Temporarily restricted net assets** are those assets that are temporarily restricted by donors until that restriction has been met in the future.
- **Permanently restricted net assets** include donor-imposed requirements that will never be removed.

Looking at the total net assets in Figure 6.7, it would appear the organization is in good financial shape with a net worth of $52,300. But upon closer examination of the balance sheet, only $13,300 is actual cash in the bank and $15,200 is listed as accounts receivable. Also, a large portion of the asset section includes fixed assets such as land and buildings ($110,000), which is not liquid and would have to be sold to cover any debts the organization might have.

Since the balance sheet must include all assets and all liabilities an organization has, it is an excellent tool for board and staff members to have before major financial decisions are made. It is also an important barometer for prospective board members, funders, and regulators to determine the financial health of an organization prior to any commitments or designations. It is a much better indicator of financial health than a financial statement, which will be examined next, but because individuals are often mystified by all of the numbers and jargon, most people are content to review only the financial statement. But an organization can have a significant net worth and look healthy on a financial statement, yet have a large amount of money invested in a non-liquid asset, such as a building, and therefore appear less healthy on a more detailed balance sheet. This is why the balance sheet should be examined prior to any important financial decisions.

Whereas the balance sheet provides us with information about an organization's financial health at a particular moment in time, the **income statement** summarizes financial activity over a period of time, usually a month or a year. It contains historical financial information, and information as to sources of an organization's revenue and expenditures. Since revenue and expenditures are divided into sub-categories, it provides detailed information as to where revenue is coming from and where expenses are going. The income statement indicates whether an organization has a surplus or a deficit over a period of time, and it is calculated by subtracting expenditures from total revenue and is carried forward to the balance sheet. An income statement can include the fund balance at the bottom portion of the report, particularly in the case of year-end audited statements.

A monthly financial or income statement designed like the one in Figure 6.8 provides progress information on revenues and expenses, as well as activity for the month that was recently completed and all of the activity thus far this year, and it compares both to a monthly and annual budget. Looking at the statement, one can see that the organization is half way through the fiscal year, since the statement covers the period from July 1 through December 30. Focusing on the revenue half of the budget, it might be expected that approximately 50% of the budget would have been met half way through the fiscal year. The income or revenue that is indicated in Figure 6.8 for the first six months totals $144,000 of an annual budget of $264,000, which equals 54%. This is a good sign that the organization is pro-

Figure 6.8
Income Statement from July 1 to December 31

Revenue	Current Month		Year to Date	
	Actual	Budget	Actual	Annual Budget
Membership	$12,000	$12,500	$74,000	$125,000
Program	5,000	4,000	27,000	53,000
United Way	2,000	2,000	12,000	24,000
Annual Campaign	5,400	4,000	31,000	62,000
Total Income	$24,000	$22,500	$144,000	$264,000
Expenses				
Salaries & Benefits	$14,000	$13,700	$84,000	$171,000
Supplies/Telephone	700	800	4,200	9,000
Postage	1,600	1,200	8,800	15,000
Travel Expenses	1,100	1,000	7,000	16,000
Mortgage Interest	3,000	3,000	18,000	36,000
Contingency/ Reserve	0	0	0	17,000
Total Expenses	$20,400	$19,700	$121,000	$264,000
Net income (loss) YTD	$4,000	$2,800	$23,000	0

gressing well toward its overall goal of $264,000 in revenue for the fiscal year.

Looking at the expense half of the budget, the organization has spent $121,000 of an annual budget of $264,000 this equals 46% of the budgeted amount for the first half of the fiscal year. Based on the information provided by this financial statement alone, revenue seems to be accruing in a reasonable fashion, and expenses seem to be under control for the first half of the fiscal year. But a more accurate fiscal picture can be determined by looking "behind the numbers" at each category to understand the organization's fiscal status in depth. For instance, $74,000 has been generated in membership fees, which is 59% of what is budgeted in the membership line for the year ($125,000). This appears to be a positive figure, but what if the organization has completed a major membership campaign and expects far fewer members in the next half of the year? It still needs $51,000 in this category to meet the budget, and it needs to be certain that procedures are in place to generate this income. Similarly, the organization has only spent 46% of its allocation for expenses in the first half of the year, which is also a good indication of positive fiscal health. Key board and staff members need to monitor the expense side of the budget continually to be certain expenses are kept at the same conservative level for the remainder of the year to insure fiscal health.

Continually examining balance sheets and income statements provides board and staff members with the information they need to make effective financial decisions that often have a direct bearing on the overall success of the organization. Providing a narrative account with statements offers additional, in-depth information on financial categories and helps prevent any unwanted surprises down the road.

Controls

In handling money within an organization, a number of irregularities can occur, either intentionally or unintentionally. One of the most important responsibilities of the board of directors is to establish **fiscal controls** that protect individuals and the organization from fiscal irregularities. For example, it is generally accepted that fewer fiscal irregularities will occur if there are at least two people involved with financial transactions. Similarly, the board should design all financial processes and policies with a significant number of **checks and balances** to insure fiscal integrity.

One of the most important steps in establishing reliable financial procedures is for the board to require that two people be involved in processing all payments. A key administrator who is familiar with the budget and with specific financial expenditures should approve checks for payment. A board member involved with the financial committee should be responsible for writing checks and monitoring this procedure for other board members.

Each payment requires documentation, and one simple way of providing this effectively is to stamp each invoice with the following designations (Wolf 1999):

```
Date Received:
Date Paid:
Account:
Check Number:
Approved:
```

On the day invoices are received they should be recorded on the first line. The appropriate staff member then determines which line item the invoice is assigned to and records it on the third line. The board member assigned to this process writes the check and records the check number and the date it was written. All payment records should be systematically filed for future referral and review by an auditor.

Another important control on writing checks is to set a policy that checks cannot be made out to the same individual who is signing checks, or that at the least there must be a counter signature on those particular checks. This process—of having two people sign certain checks—could also apply to expenditures exceeding a certain amount, such as $1000, or whatever amount the board deems appropriate.

A system of careful controls must also be incorporated for the handling of incoming money so that both a staff and board member are included. Incoming money must be received, recorded, and deposited promptly. Deposit slips should be checked with records periodically, and any significant irregularities must be reported to the board.

The organization must be protected from loss of income through either intentional or unintentional irregularities. One way to do this is through the process of **bonding**, which is a form of insurance for fiscal matters. Because premiums for the bonding process vary with the amount of money under protection, careful consideration should be given to determine this amount. One way to designate this amount would be to determine the largest amount of money that could be in the bank at one point and increase that figure by twenty percent (Wolf). This amount should comfortably protect the organization, its staff and volunteers without an excessive bonding premium.

Physical controls and security measures are equally important in protecting organizations from financial loss, or worse. Financial transactions that are conducted with electrical or mechanical equipment, such as cash registers, have a small likelihood of error. Financial records should be kept in fireproof cabinets. Offices should have adequate fire and burglary protection and should install properly functioning security systems. If large amounts of money are expected to come into the organization at one time, as with a special event, hiring security police should be considered.

Reporting Requirements

Nonprofit organizations must file a number of reports each year to maintain their nonprofit status. Financial reporting procedures for organizations vary from state to state, and it is important that each organization check individual state regulations regarding reporting procedures.

Most nonprofit organizations are required to complete an **annual return** with the IRS that is called a **Form 990.** This form includes information on all income and expenses of the organization in support of its tax-exempt status. Failure to comply with this requirement could lead to significant civil and criminal penalties. If an organization receives income that is not related to the tax-exempt purpose of the organization (excluding income from investments), it must be recorded and filed on a **Form 990-T** if it exceeds $1000 and is submitted with Form 990. Determining which income this might include can be difficult and is best determined by the individual who does the annual audit.

All organizations that have employees must withhold income taxes, social security, and Medicare from pay and report this amount to the IRS. If a nonprofit organization is not a 501 (c) 3, it must also pay federal unemployment taxes (**FUTA**) on salaries that are reported on **Form 940.** Employers must prepare a **W-2 Form**, which is the annual wage and tax statement, for each employee. This must be mailed to each employee by January 31, and a copy must be filed with the IRS no later than February 28 of each year. Non-employee compensation paid in amounts exceeding $600 must be reported on **Form 1099-MISC**, filed with **Form 1096** and filed with the IRS annually. If an organization receives a gift of property, other than money or securities, it must file a **Donee Information Report Form 8282** with the IRS if the amount of the gift exceeds $500.

Recording and Reporting Systems

Prepackaged accounting software is readily available to handle accounting needs and even the smallest of organizations can benefit from these often-inexpensive programs. Customized accounting software packages that include links to membership and fund-raising packages can also be purchased through accounting or software firms with a specialty in nonprofit organizations. Affiliates of national nonprofit organizations may also be able to acquire software packages designed specifically for their organization from their national headquarters. Computerized spreadsheets are an important tool in recording and analyzing income and expenses, determining cash flow, and maintaining membership and fund-raising records. They are also readily available as prepackaged software, or they can be obtained in a more customized fashion.

Some organizations find it less expensive and/or more expedient to contract accounting procedures, payroll systems, and other record-keeping and form requirements to firms that specialize in these procedures. These firms are generally more accurate and can relieve the organization of unwanted and often time-consuming tasks.

Organizations with the best of intentions and purposes can help develop their effectiveness, in part, by maintaining appropriate financial records and reporting those accounts in a timely and appropriate manner. An effective accounting and reporting process adds to the overall success of the organization and helps to assure staff and volunteer members, participants, contributors and other community members of the organization's integrity.

■ Financial Development

The American people contribute tens of billions of dollars each year to private, non-profit organizations here and around the globe and may be the most generous people in the world. This spirit of giving evolved from the settlers who came to America from England and Europe and who built the first churches, schools, and colleges with their own money. The concept of giving became more sophisticated over the decades as paid solicitors began working for a fee, and the YMCA created a "campaign" process in which there was a fundraising goal and an organized system to reach that goal (Ellis and Noyes 1978). As the decades passed, the process of financial development or fundraising became more and more sophisticated and effective. As a result, universities have been founded, medical hospitals and treatment centers have been built, and many human service and cultural activities have come into being (Rosso 1991).

Modern nonprofit organizations must construct a thorough and comprehensive financial development plan in order to meet their financial needs successfully. Some pre-requisites for that plan include the following **criteria** (Weis and Gantt 2002)**:**

- *A clear and focused mission or purpose.* It is much easier to generate income for a nonprofit organization when the purpose of the organization is clear and highly desirable. The mission must be clear, understood, and important to community members.
- *An overall reputation for integrity.* Before any fundraising efforts are initiated, the organization must have developed a reputation for dependability and quality. For new organizations, the organizational reputation can be associated with that of the volunteer board members and staff members.
- *A history of program success.* Individuals like to support organizations that are successful and that enhance their communities. Some history of program success implies the probability of future success.
- *Professional staff members and committed volunteers.* Individuals like to support organizations that have competent and committed leaders. Proven leadership provides confidence in community support.
- *Clear and proven needs for financial support.* Community members are more likely to provide financial support to an organization that is generating money for specific needs that have been clearly established.

- *Administrators with experience and skills in financial development.* In addition to having clear needs for financial support, an organization must have individuals with specialized skills in developing support. Technical and people skills are essential in building a financial base.

There is some truth to the axiom "actions speak louder than words." Organizations with a proven record of success and with the potential to develop a financial base will have a much easier task developing financial support. In order to have organizational information readily available for fundraising activities, many organizations prepare a **case** or **case statement** in advance of such activities. Aspects of a case statement are discussed next.

Case Statement

The case statement is prepared information that can be used for public relations and/ or financial development activities. Any and all information can be extracted from the case statement to be used for appropriate purposes. Basically, the case statement includes (1) the history of the organization and what the mission of the organization is about, (2) what it plans to do or become, and (3) why it deserves support (Broce 1986).

The case statement should describe the importance of the organization and list some of its projects or activities that work toward its purpose or reason for being. It needs to include a specific list of projects that, with appropriate funding, could make further differences in the lives of individuals in the community. And it should include a list of program or project successes as proof of consideration for support.

Fundraising consultant and practitioner, Dan Conway, states that the case statement should answer these questions: Who are you? Why do you exist? What is distinctive about you? What is it that you want to accomplish? How do you intend to accomplish it? How will you hold yourself accountable (Rosso 1991)?

Whether the case statement is a written document or a data-base of information on the organization and the community, it should be a fluid instrument capable of being changed quickly as new data is revealed. It can save individuals within the organization a great deal of time searching files for effective information, and it provides potential contributors with invaluable assistance in making decisions for support. Extracts from the case statement can be used in annual and capital campaigns, grant proposals, special events, and in any other situation in which relevant organizational information would be helpful.

The Board's Role in Financial Development

The involvement of board members is critically important to the overall success of developing finances in a nonprofit organization. First of all, (1) as the primary stewards of the organization, board members have an overall responsibility for the management of the institution's resources. This is not a day-to-day assignment, but is generally realized by working through the ED/CEO or other top administrative leader. Additionally, (2) board members can play a key role in helping to determine the both kinds of fundraising activities that will occur and the goals of those activities. Organizations that do not include board members in revenue meetings are missing out on valuable resources and may be acting contrary to organizational bylaws.

Board members can (3) also provide key leadership in fundraising activities by their participation, guidance, and inspiration. Some board members are selected because of their experience and expertise in generating income and should be called upon accordingly. Other board members may not have significant financial expertise but (4) their connections with community leaders provides access to other potential donors. Board members can help identify donors and can serve as door openers for prospective gifts. With few exceptions, (5) board members should be asked to contribute financially to the organization and should be a part of the process in organizing and soliciting other contributions.

Although staff members have developed more and more expertise in generating funds in nonprofit organizations over the years, not involving board members in fundraising activities can leave a tremendous void in the overall development process. An explanation of the board member's role in financial development should be one of the first things the nominating committee provides for potential board members. Once a member has been selected, this same role must be reiterated in the board's orientation and training sessions. Committed and informed board, staff and volunteer members along with organizational integrity combine to make the best formula for financial stability.

The Development Committee's Role in Fundraising

One of the most important factors in contributing to sustaining, successful financial development is the creation of a cohesive development committee that has effective leadership, vision, and commitment (Rosso 1991). The complete *core* **development team or committee** is made up of board members that include members from the development and finance committees, the development committee chairperson, and the board chairperson. Other volunteers from the community may also be included on the development team. Key individuals from the staff side of the organization include the CEO, the development director, other professional and support staff members and paid consultants, when appropriate. Since all board and staff members are expected to contribute to financial development in one way or another, everyone needs to be involved in the development process at appropriate times.

The **development committee** works with the development director to (1) determine financial needs, (2) develop a fundraising plan, (3) implement that plan, and (4) monitor and amend the plan when necessary. This would often include financial plans for the short term such as a fiscal year as well as strategic, long-range development plans. The case statement, mentioned previously, can be an invaluable tool in assisting with all of the steps above.

Some organizations seem blessed with great leadership when it comes to matters of finance, while others struggle in their **recruitment** of quality staff and board members. Good leaders are generally attracted to an organization because of the mission or purpose and the organization's reputation for success and integrity. Recruitment of development committee members should be done just as it is with other board members, incorporating job descriptions and a matrix of specific skills and tasks. Once development committee

members have been recruited, they can be *empowered* by a number of strategies (Rosso):
- broad participation in the overall fundraising process, from , to setting goals, to implementation, to evaluation
- fundraising training
- coaching and practice
- clear and effective communication process
- providing experienced mentors with each team
- continually reminding team members of the importance of the fundraising activity to the overall mission of the organization

Because of the nature of their work, it is essential to organize the development committee into an effective team. Successful teams often demonstrate a number of the same qualities (Rosso 1996):

1. Highly productive teams have developed a similar vision and are able to share that vision with others.
2. Hierarchy is almost nonexistent, and communication is open and respectful.
3. The organization is highly supportive of the committee's work.
4. Team members rely on empowerment of each other and develop an effective level of synergy.
5. The team is open to new ideas and works hard to reduce misunderstandings.

Recruiting and maintaining a highly effective development committee needs to be one of the top priorities of the ED/CEO, development director, and the board chair. They must understand what kinds of individuals are important in building an effective development team, and they must be able to maintain that committee at the highest level of success. The development committee can and should be involved in one way or another in all of the activities discussed below.

Developing a financial base for any organization should be a comprehensive process involving the following possibilities, where appropriate: membership fees, program fees, special events, product sales, residential campaigns, United Way support, annual campaigns, capital campaigns, deferred gifts, and grant support.

Membership and Program Fees

Facility based and a number of non-facility based organizations require some form of membership fee to participate and sometimes another fee to be involved in certain programs. A membership fee (1) provides funds for operating the organization and (2) gives members the sense that they belong to the organization and are committed enough to pay a fee. It also (3) provides members with a sense that they are supporters of what the organization stands for. Program fees can be used to cover some of the direct expenses associated with certain programs. There are a number of questions that need to be asked regarding membership and program fees (Weis and Gantt 2002):

Who should make up the membership of an organization?

Membership in organizations is generally based on (1) the purpose of the organization and (2) the guidelines established by the board of directors in the bylaws and/or membership policy of the organization. For example, a nonprofit organization whose purpose it is to enhance the lives of children in the community should specify age, geographical parameters, and any other considerations.

How many members should an organization have?

Organizations generally set a limit on the number of members and program participants that can be served effectively:

1. **Space analysis.** The number of participants allowed for a given space is first of all determined by community policies, usually by the local fire department. Beyond this legal control, organizations may wish to limit the number of participants so there is adequate space for effective and safe program implementation.
2. **Resources.** An analysis should be done to determine an effective staff, faculty, and/or volunteer ratio with program participants. In most cases, a predetermined ratio of staff to program participants is set by organizational policy and in some cases, such as therapeutic settings, the ratio may be set by law. It is also important to assess the quantity of supplies, materials, and equipment available for adequate programming.
3. **Budgetary considerations.** It is also important to consider the number of members and program participants necessary to meet the specific line items of the budget dealing with membership and program participation.
4. **Tradition.** Some organizations have a tradition that limits the number of members and program participants and others have a history of including a larger number of members. Traditions can be changed, but they should at least be considered in the overall discussion to determine individual numbers for an organization and for specific programs.

How are membership and program fees determined (pricing)?

Determining the cost for memberships or a fee for a specific program in any organization is tricky, but a number of aspects should be considered:

1. **Mission and policy.** If the mission of the organization is to serve economically disadvantaged individuals, then this must be considered in establishing any fee, membership or otherwise. Many nonprofit organizations set some of their fees on a **sliding scale** basis, meaning that the fees for individuals who need assistance can be based on their income-to-expense margin or cash availability. Additionally, some organizations set up a **scholarship program** for people in need. Even if the organization's mission has nothing specifically to do with serving the economically disadvantaged, nonprofit organizations are created to provide a service and should be priced accordingly.
2. **Competition.** Membership and program fees should be set so as to be competitive with similar organizations in the area and at the same time be priced so the cost demonstrates there is a real value to being a member or being a part of a program. Some programs may be open to members only, while others may be open to the general public. Some programs may be included as part of a membership fee, while others can cost extra. Often programs that cost extra are listed at a lower rate for members than nonmembers.

3. **Budgetary requirements.** Just as budgetary requirements must be considered when determining the number of members or program participants an organization should have, it must also be considered when setting a price for membership or specific programs. Membership and program fees often make up a substantial portion of an operating budget and are therefore necessary for the overall financial health of the organization.

4. **Tradition.** The organization's history should also be considered in the mix of determining membership and program prices. If an organization has a tradition of setting memberships or program fees at a certain level, the community comes to expect that range of pricing. Pricing can and often does change, but gradual, conservative changes are much easier to accept and deal with than radical, major changes in pricing.

What does a membership campaign consist of?

Many organizations develop a special campaign, referred to as a membership campaign, to recruit members to the organization. This campaign should be designed to stimulate a great deal of enthusiasm and interest in the organization and can last from a few weeks to several months, and even longer.

1. **Special Offers.** Membership campaigns often include special offers during the campaign. These may include a reduced cost for membership, extended membership for a standard cost, additional memberships at a reduced rate (see Figure 6.9), and free or reduced program fees for sign-ups during the campaign. Any innovative special offers that will attract new members to the organization should be considered.

2. **Kick-off.** Effective membership campaigns often have a *kick-off* event, an activity that begins the campaign with a whirl of excitement and activity. The kick-off can be an event that would include information on the organization and special offers involved with the campaign. Door prizes, entertainment, surprises, and free food are all likely to enhance the excitement surrounding the campaign. Local celebrities and the media should be invited along with the members of the organization.

3. **Flyers, Public Service Announcements (PSAs), and Signs.** Attractive, informative flyers should be created and posted strategically throughout the community several weeks prior to the kick-off and the beginning of the campaign. Public service announcements should also be sent to the media prior to the beginning of the campaign. Businesses will often donate space for display and marquee signs to promote the campaign.

4. **Contests.** Introducing contests for the campaign adds excitement and interest, helps create a sense of ownership for staff members, volunteers, and members, and has a strong potential for increasing membership enrollment. Prizes can include days off for staff members and t-shirts for volunteers and members. Grand prizes or drawings for contest participants can include free trips donated by local travel agencies.

Figure 6.9
Reduced Membership Promotional Flyer

Buy One Membership in the Morganfield YMCA and get the Second Membership at 1/2 Price!!

That's right. When you sign up for membership in the Morganfield YMCA, you can bring along a friend for just half price if you both register during the month of June! This 12-month offer is good for current and new members.

Membership includes full use of the facility:

■ Olympic size pool   ■ Giant whirlpool
■ Fitness center   ■ Racquetball courts
■ Youth center   ■ Adult and youth sport leagues
■ Career development center

For more information on this great offer,
contact Darcy Young at 750-9622.

Hurry, offer ends soon!

Special Events

A special event fundraiser is an activity designed with the primary purpose of generating income for an organization and with secondary objectives that could include entertainment, health and fitness, enhanced knowledge and awareness, and fun. Special events have the potential to generate enormous interest in the organization while also developing funds. Criteria for a successful special event include the following (Weis and Gantt 2002):

1. **Safety.** The most important aspect of a special event or any activity in an organization is keeping risks and health hazards to an absolute minimum. For all special events, a conscious effort must be made to follow the guidelines for managing risks listed earlier in Chapter 5, 137-139 and in Chapter 7, 207-212.

2. **Community Need.** The most successful special events are those that fulfill community needs the best. Events that focus on sports, health and fitness, or the arts, as well as any activity that fulfills a community need in a meaningful way—such as an educational event—are sure to succeed.

3. **Creativity and Uniqueness.** Special events should be unique in order to appeal to everyone's interest. For instance, *-thons* have a long and proven history of being successful and a twist on a *–thon* might be to have a *volunteer-a-thon* instead of a *walk-a-thon.* It is a little different than a typical *–thon* and it provides services to the community.

4. **Natural Connection.** Special events that have some kind of a natural connection to the organization can sometimes be easier to implement than others. An example might be a YMCA that develops a bicycle or running race. Health and fitness are two areas that YMCAs typically incorporate in their programs, so they would have access to expertise in those areas as well as access to members with those interests.

5. **Organization and Promotion.** To be successful, special events have to be planned and promoted well, just like any program does. The program development section in Chapter 5 contains detailed steps to follow in developing a program.

6. **Fundraising Potential.** Regardless of how creative or well-planned an event is, it has to have the potential to make money. Corporate and association sponsorships can be solicited to cover many or all costs. It is also important to keep expenses as low as possible, while maintaining a quality event.

Product Sales

The Girl Scouts of America have taken product sales to great heights with their acclaimed Girl Scout cookie campaign that results in tens of millions of dollars for local councils around the country each year. Other organizations are successful selling candy, calendars, popcorn, teddy bears, and fruit, to mention only a few of the items sold each year for nonprofit causes. Selling products can be very successful if a few key factors are incorporated (Weis and Gantt 2002):

- Make safety the number one priority.
- Be certain to have a large and responsible sales force.
- Develop an effective communication system.
- Select products that are popular and easy to sell.
- Provide appropriate and adequate incentives.
- Establish a clear beginning and end date.
- Try to buy products on consignment.
- Develop an effective control system for money.

Product sales also help promote the organization and provide members of the organization an opportunity to develop ownership by assisting the fundraising process.

Residential Campaigns

A number of nonprofit organizations, particularly national health organizations with high visibility, have great success with **residential campaigns**, in which individuals in specific communities are asked to approach their neighbors requesting support for an organization. This type of campaign is highly organized, yet personalized at the same time.

The campaign usually begins with paid or volunteer staff members within the organization calling individuals in various neighborhoods using a specialized phone book that is divided by neighborhoods within communities. The individuals who are called are asked to represent the organization within their neighborhood and are then sent a packet of material that may include the following (Leukemia and Lymphoma Society 2002):

- A letter of explanation describing in detail the residential campaign and th volunteer's role
- Information on the successes of the organization in addressing specific problems
- A list of names and addresses of other individuals in the neighborhood
- A solicitation letter to be left with each individual on the neighborhood list along with a return envelope
- A large, return envelope where all checks can be sent to the organization upon of the campaign

Once an individual has been recruited to coordinate the neighborhood campaign, he or she may be reminded occasionally by the organization about the campaign goal and any deadlines. There is usually a packet or kit goal for each neighborhood that is set at a reasonable level. Residential campaigns designed as such can be very successful, particularly when (1) the organization is recognizable and the purpose desirable; (2) the campaign is well organized; and (3) the solicitation approach is personalized, such as neighbor to neighbor. Residential campaigns result in tens of millions of dollars for nonprofit causes across the country each year.

United Way

Local United Way organizations are designed in part to be umbrella agencies that collect contributions for distribution to other organizations. This money is then **allocated** to organizations based on (1) need, (2) numbers of individuals served, and (3) types of programs. An organization such as a community-based health and wellness center that has a strong capacity for fundraising through membership or program fees may not receive as much United Way support as a Big Brothers Big Sisters organization that provides important services with no membership or program costs to its members.

An organization that is interested in becoming a United Way affiliated agency should review the organization requirements prior to making application to see if it meets the standards and to understand any restrictions. Agencies that apply and become affiliates of the United Way must reapply for support each year. An **allocation committee** made up of local, community volunteers determines the amount of money allocated to each agency. Most United Way funds are generated through a **payroll deduction** process in which individuals designate that a certain amount of money be withheld from their paycheck and contributed to the United Way or a specific organization affiliated with the United Way. This fundraising method has proven to be one of the most successful in history.

Annual and Capital Campaigns

An **annual campaign** is one designed to generate funds for operating expenses, such as special projects or programs, and these funds can be passed on to members in the form of reduced membership and program fees, or in some cases fees may be eliminated (Weis and Gantt 2002).

Annual campaigns are highly organized with a chair, division leaders, team captains, meeting dates, fundraising material and financial goals (see Figure 6.10). One hundred percent of the board of directors should be involved in this campaign, from participating as campaign leaders, to recruiting campaign leaders on or off the board, and giving their own fair share. **Campaign leaders** must be respected members of the community with a commitment to the organization and can be made up of board members and other members of the community in general.

The overall **campaign chair** should be someone who has a great deal of respect from the community, is committed to the purpose of the organization, and is able to organize and motivate others. The chair is sometimes a board member of the organization, but not always.

The community should be divided up into segments, such as small, middle-sized, and large business divisions, an educational division, a professional division, an organizational division, a division that includes city, state, and federal employees, and so on. Each division should have a chair who can organize his or her segment into teams with team captains. Each team is responsible for generating a certain amount of money, and that amount, combined with other teams, is the goal for the division.

A **prospect list** must be established for each division. Special consideration should go to individuals, corporations, and associations with natural ties to the organization, such as board members, staff and volunteer members, members, parents of members, firms represented by members, previous members, previous contributors, community-minded corporations, and service associations. Prospects may also be selected from the Chamber of Commerce list and even from the yellow and white pages, although this should be a lesser priority.

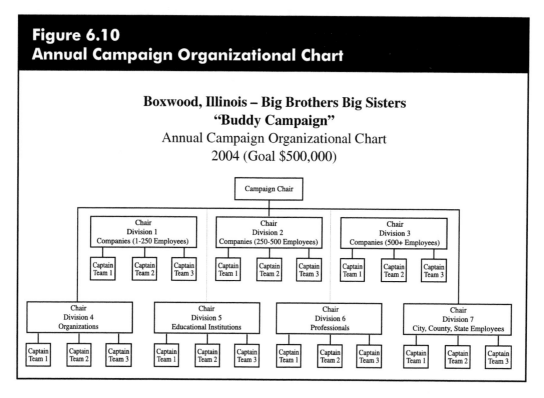

Figure 6.10
Annual Campaign Organizational Chart

Boxwood, Illinois – Big Brothers Big Sisters
"Buddy Campaign"
Annual Campaign Organizational Chart
2004 (Goal $500,000)

The **solicitation process** for an annual campaign should be highly organized, but personable. Telephone calls, face to face meetings, and direct mail contacts between team members and prospects are very important and produce the best results. Often, a campaign will have an appealing **theme** and purpose, such as the "Buddy Campaign" in Figure 6.11, and this theme and purpose will be reflected and explained in the campaign material. This provides some focus for potential prospects and helps assure them that their money is going to make a difference in a specific area within the organization. Meetings should include an informational and inspirational **kick-off** event followed by a number of **update** or **report meetings.** All of these meetings should be informative and inspirational. Although annual campaigns should be planned a year in advance, the actual campaign is relatively brief, lasting from two to four weeks.

Organizational staff members usually play support roles in an annual campaign, developing materials (see Figure 6.11 on the next page), organizing meetings, keeping records, and supporting the volunteers in their fundraising efforts.

A **capital campaign** is designed to generate funds for capital expenditures, such as new buildings, renovations, major equipment purchases, and endowed educational positions (Weis and Gantt 2002). A capital campaign is highly organized, like an annual campaign, and it involves the selection of a chair, division chairs, teams, and team captains. It has a financial goal, campaign materials, and scheduled meeting dates. Unlike an annual campaign, a capital campaign is typically designed to raise larger amounts of money and the campaign period is usually longer. This period can last from several months up to one or two years, and even longer in some circumstances.

Fundraising **consultants** are often hired to coordinate capital campaigns because of their expertise and so that staff members can concentrate on other duties, although the staff should be involved in a support role. The consultant may first conduct a **feasibility study** to determine (1) whether the community believes in the goal the campaign is addressing and (2) whether the community is willing and able to support the campaign. If the feasibility study results are positive, the consultant often serves as the overall advisor for and/or professional coordinator of the campaign. Capital campaigns can result in some great opportunities to serve communities, but they extract a great many resources from the community and should only be considered if real needs exist and if the community is willing to support the campaign.

Corporate and Service Club Support

Whether the support is for a special event, an annual campaign, capital campaign, or some other activity, corporate and club support can be essential. If cultivated effectively, business corporations and clubs, such as the Rotary or Lions Clubs, can become key allies for nonprofit organizations:

1. First of all, most corporations and clubs have a primary interest in the well-being of a community. Their employees and colleagues, along with their families live and work in the communities they are located in, and it is in their best interest to provide support to nonprofit organizations.

2. Another reason corporations and clubs often support nonprofit causes is that this support usually boosts the morale of the employees and members. Supporting

nonprofit causes enhances loyalty and positive feelings among employees and club members.

3. Finally, supporting nonprofit organizations establishes a strong public image and influences public opinion favorably.

When seeking funding support from a corporation or club, it is important to research the organization regarding their work and community involvement. Prior to seeking an interview to present a case for support, a proposal should be carefully prepared listing rea-

Figure 6.11
Flyer for Annual Campaign

Boxwood, Illinois – Big Brothers Big Sisters (BBBS)

"Buddy Campaign 2004"

CAMPAIGN GOAL: $500,000

The Boxwood, Illinois, Big Brothers Big Sisters program matches children from single-parent families with caring, adult mentors for the purpose of friendship and guidance. The organization averages approximately 350 matches each year. The Big Brothers Big Sisters program of Boxwood is affiliated with the National BBBS organization. The Boxwood program has proven to be a deterrent to unacceptable behavior, drugs and alcohol abuse, and school absenteeism. It has fostered positive character development and provided opportunities for young children between the ages of 6 - 17 that might not have them otherwise. Won't you help? BBBS charges no fees to the families who participate, and the organization operates primarily through corporate and private contributions. You and/or your organization can choose to be a "Buddy" at several different levels:

Universal Buddy	$5,000
Galactic Buddy	$2,500
Solar Buddy	$1,000
Super Nova Buddy	$500
Super Buddy	$200
Buddy	$100

Just fill in information below, attach it to your check, and return it to the BBBS Buddy Campaign team member who contacted you. Any amount is greatly appreciated. Thank you so much for being a buddy to children who really need one!

Your Name	Corporation (if applicable)
Address	Phone Number
Amount Contributed	

sons the corporation or club should support one's organization. The funding corporation or club will also want to know what the benefits to its organization will be if it supports the project.

It's a good idea to offer the organization sponsorship at several different levels and to seek an entrée to the organization through a board member or other community leader. Regardless of the results, the organization seeking support should be gracious because organizations that defer support today could be strong allies in the future. Individuals should always be thanked for their support in the most appropriate manner.

Deferred Gifts

People who have pledged support to nonprofit organizations through their wills bequeath billions of dollars to charitable causes each year. This money has been **deferred** to the organization until someone's death. Although this kind of deferred giving program can be very helpful to these organizations, the revocable nature of these gifts places the contributions in an uncertain category. **Deferred planned gifts** involve the transfer of money from a donor to an organization because of its irrevocable status (Wolf 1999).

This kind of deferred giving can take many shapes and forms. For instance, a donor may select the **Charitable Remainder Annuity Trust** plan in which the donor transfers a certain amount of money to a trust that pays the donor a fixed amount of income for life. The donor can also make a stipulation of support for another person or a survivor. The trust principle becomes the property of the nonprofit organization at the time of transfer. Another popular plan is the **Charitable Lead Trust.** This plan is the opposite of the Charitable Remainder Annuity Trust plan. In this plan, the donor makes payments to a nonprofit organization for a set number of years, at which point the organization begins making payments to the donor or other family members. Yet another plan, the **Pooled-Income Fund** plan, involves the donor irrevocably transferring money to a pooled-income fund maintained by a nonprofit organization. This money is invested along with the money from other donors, and the organization agrees to pay the donor income for life from the pooled investment.

A contributor who would like to help an organization but is concerned for his retirement years, may select the **Deferred-Payment-Gift Annuity.** In this plan, the individual makes a financial gift to an organization and the organization agrees to pay the donor a certain amount of income for life, beginning at retirement age or another specified time. Since donors benefit from tax incentives and from the feeling that they have helped the community, and since organizations benefit from the financial aspects, deferred giving is a mutually beneficial process, but it has to be organized and promoted. The first step in organizing a deferred gifts program is to (1) form a committee consisting of an attorney, a banker and/or an accountant, and a marketing specialist. These committee members can be board members or other members of the community, with staff members in a supporting role.

The committee members must then (2) decide the type of deferred gift plans the organization would like to initiate and (3) design marketing material that describes the plan and the ways donors can be involved. (4) A prospect list needs to be developed along the same lines of developing a prospect list for an annual or capital campaign. Once the list is ready, (5) contact should be made in person, over the telephone, and/or through a mail campaign. (6) Seminars describing the plans should also be considered, with the public invited.

Although a deferred gift program usually does not benefit an organization immediately, the long term-benefits can be astounding, and the benefits to donors are significant. Because of the minimal cost invested, the volunteer nature of the process, and the financial potential, seeking deferred giving should be an organizational priority.

Grant Support

Grants from foundations or government agencies can be an important source of restricted funding for nonprofit organizations. Individuals, families, corporations, and communities create foundations to address various needs. In addition to addressing needs, the individual(s) or entity that creates the foundation receives a tax break for the contribution.

Lists of different foundations and a description of what they typically fund can be found in libraries around the country, as well as through such sources as the Foundation Grants Index, the Foundation Directory, online and software programs, and state and regional directories.

Many foundations send notices to select nonprofit organizations informing them of various grant opportunities and describing the application process. Many nonprofit organizations have grant development departments that maintain this information and also provide instructional methods on completing applications and writing proposals for funding. The government is not designed to address actively all of the needs of each individual citizen. Billions of dollars, therefore, are set aside each year for government agencies to provide funding in the form of grants to individuals and organizations that propose to address some of the needs in communities.

To assist in locating these government agencies, the Catalogue of Federal Domestic Assistance maintains information on almost all federally funded grant programs, but the sheer volume of this catalogue may make it an unrealistic resource. A more realistic approach is to check with other nonprofit organizations in a particular area or region to learn what foundations they have applied to with success. Another way is to develop relationships with local, regional, and national political representatives whose job it may be to provide funding for worthwhile projects.

Regarding the application process, most foundations and government agencies have a number of forms that must be filled out exactly as they are requested to be. In completing an application for a grant, it is always important to *follow the directions* just as they are listed. In addition to requiring the completion of forms, some foundations and government agencies will ask for a proposal. Although proposals may vary greatly in length and content, there are some typical sections proposals often include (Weis and Gantt 2002):

1. **Introduction, Abstract, or Summary.** This section is usually brief and to the point. It should include the name of the applicant, the name of the funder from which the money is requested, the amount of money requested, and for what time period. Beginning the content area with detailed information regarding the problem or situation can be a strong start. It is a good idea to describe the program or method that is being proposed to address the problem, along with the program objectives. The program should be innovative and should clearly

address the problem or problems. Information should be provided regarding the credibility of the organization and the credibility of the staff that would be developing the program. This section should be written in clear and concise language.

2. **Problem Statement.** The problem statement often follows the introduction. This section asks for expanded information regarding the problem on a local basis and a description of the constituencies being served. The applicant may include quotes and paraphrases from local experts and officials if they emphasize the importance of the problem. Information can point to community members affected by the problem, and quotes from some of these people can be provided. Incorporating vital statistics is also important. If the problem exists in other areas, regions or localities, this information may also be included. If possible, a connection should be made here with the organization's background and the problem.

3. **Program Objectives.** Program objectives describe *what* is to be accomplished through the program and is therefore an *outcome-based* concept. Objectives should be clear, specific, and measurable and should include established time lines for completion. They should be challenging, yet realistic. The evaluation of the project will assess the achievement of these objectives. Results anticipated beyond the funding period and information regarding the evaluation process may also be mentioned.

4. **Program Description or Methodology.** This section should describe the program activities in detail and answer the question of *how* the objectives will be reached. The program section describes the project staff and often includes resumes from key individuals, particularly the coordinator, attached as appendices. Timelines for activities need to be included and schedules for activities can be a part of the methodology section or attached as appendices.

5. **Evaluation.** The purpose of an evaluation is to determine whether adjustments need to be made to a project (**formative evaluation**) and whether the project was effective in achieving the objectives (**summative** or **final evaluation**). Also, it is often important to provide accountability to funders.

   Evaluations may be done through a number of methods, including surveys, interviews, focus groups, and journals. Pre/post tests can also be administered to participants to determine changes from the beginning of a project to the end. For more detailed information on conducting evaluations, see Chapter 5, "Program Development."

   Specific data, which might come from an educational institute or a health organization, for example, can also be recorded at the beginning of a project and then be recorded again at the end to calculate any significant changes. This section should describe how the results of the evaluation are to be recorded and reported.

6. **Future Funding.** If there is a need for a project to continue, many foundations and governmental sources like to know how the project will be funded in the future. Sometimes this can be accomplished by pulling the project into the

organization's operating budget. Rearranging staff responsibilities and re-prioritizing existing supplies, materials, and other costs might do this.

Another possibility is to institute some program fees, develop special events to support the project, and/or develop corporate sponsorships. Yet another proven method for future funding is to seek additional grant support. There is almost always a way to continue funding a project that should continue.

7. **Budget.** The budget for a project is guided essentially by what is needed for a successful project and by what is available from the funder and other sources. The budget should indicate that all expenses for the project will be met in some way. The income side of the budget should include income that has been confirmed, as well as income that is anticipated. Expenses should be realistic and as minimal as possible without sacrificing quality or important aspects of the project. The budget for a grant includes specific expenses and does not usually include a miscellaneous line. The budget should also include a narrative description.

In all three of the financial areas previously discussed, it is critical that staff, board, and volunteer members follow the guidelines and policies of the organization regarding financial matters, and that the integrity of the individuals involved and that of the organization are always maintained. The **ethical culture** that is described in Chapter 2 of this text is exactly the culture that must exist in all areas of finance. Maintaining openness will result in the community developing a trust for the organization and the individuals who are a part of it. Being able to explain and be accountable for financial activities also leads to community trust and is an integral ally in all financial matters.

For more information about financial management, financial procedures, and financial development in a nonprofit organization, the following references are suggested: *Managing a Nonprofit Organization* by Thomas Wolf, New York: Prentice Hall (1999); and *Achieving Excellence in Fund Raising* by H. A. Rosso & Associates, San Francisco: Jossey-Bass (1991).

■ Summary

This chapter is divided into three major areas regarding fiscal matters: (1) financial management or budgeting, (2) financial statements and procedures, and (3) financial development or fundraising.

Managing finances includes the process of developing a budget, which is a financial plan for an organization. Creating a budget should follow certain steps, such as developing a list of expenses necessary for the organization to operate for a fiscal year. A next logical step in developing a budget should be to determine available resources for the coming year. Once this is done, a comparison of expenses to revenue should be made to determine whether the revenue projections are adequate for the anticipated expenses. Following this, organizational leaders must meet and set program and administrative priorities for the fiscal year. Once these priorities are set, expense and income figures should be placed on a budget sheet and balanced. Following this, the board of directors approves the budget and, along with staff members, monitors, and in some cases adjusts, the budget at specific times in the fiscal year.

Other important budgetary considerations include a project or program budget that allows program leaders to project and calculate expenses and income lines for specific programs. A contingency/reserve fund is necessary so that nonprofit organizations can address unexpected expenses, potential growth, or other concerns and opportunities. Keeping a positive cash flow for expenses is important, and preparing a month-by-month cash-flow analysis is critical in managing a budget.

The term used for financial record keeping is *accounting*. Organizations either use a cash-basis accounting system, in which financial records are made only when cash changes hands, or they use an accrual-based system, in which records are made when money changes hands, and in addition, money owed by an organization and owed to an organization is accounted for as well. Many organizations also employ a modified cash-basis accounting system, in which some records are kept on a cash basis and others on an accrual-based system.

Unrestricted funds are funds that are designated for the sole purpose of operating an organization and are often kept on a single fund budget. Special projects and funds restricted for specific purposes must be noted separately and are often recorded on a multiple fund budget in a separate area from the operating funds.

A balance sheet provides a thorough look at the assets and liabilities of an organization at one particular point in time, usually the end of a fiscal year. An income statement summarizes financial activity over a period of time, usually a month or a year. Both provide valuable analytical information on the current and overall financial status of an organization.

Expenses and income must be controlled carefully. This usually entails having a specific checks and balances system involving at least two individuals within the organization. Bonding, which is a form of insurance, is a necessary process to protect the organization from loss of income through either intentional or unintentional irregularities. Other controls include making sure there is physical protection for records and finances.

Most nonprofit organizations are required to complete a number of forms that verify their tax-exempt status. These organizations must also withhold income taxes and social security from pay and report this amount to the IRS. Prepackaged accounting software is readily available to assist organizations with accounting needs. Some organizations contract accounting procedures to firms that specialize in these procedures.

Modern nonprofit organizations must construct a thorough and comprehensive financial development plan involving a number of revenue producing areas. Many nonprofit organizations require a membership fee to provide funds for operating the organization and providing members with a sense of ownership. Program fees may also be charged for special programs and are designed to cover some of the direct expenses involved.

Special events can also be effective in developing revenue and should be planned as carefully as all other programs. Product sales, if planned correctly, can provide substantial revenue, and United Way affiliation can be a significant source of funds. Annual campaigns provide money for the operating budget and help keep membership and program costs low. Capital campaigns provide much-needed funds for new buildings, renovations, major equipment purchases and other major expenses.

Deferred gifts are mutually beneficial to nonprofit organizations as well as providing tax breaks for the donors, and grant support can infuse funds for special projects and community needs. Corporate and service club support is also mutually beneficial by providing support for organizations and providing a morale boost and good public relations to the corporation or club.

This chapter addressed, in part, the American Humanics Certification Competency Requirements of Fundraising Principles and Practices and Nonprofit Accounting and Financial Management

■ Discussion Questions

1. How are financial budgeting, accounting, and development interrelated? Describe.
2. How is the term *line item* relevant in the budgeting process?
3. What are the steps in developing a budget? List and discuss.
4. How does a program budget fit into the overall budgetary scheme?
5. What is the importance of a contingency/reserve fund? Discuss.
6. What are the steps in a successful cash-flow analysis? Describe.
7. What are the differences between an annual and capital campaign? Discuss.
8. What is the significance of United Way affiliation in fund-raising?
9. How are membership and program fees determined?
10. What are some key elements of a grant proposal?

■ Activities

1. Select a nonprofit organization and develop a financial development plan for one fiscal year. A reasonable financial goal should be used.
2. Using the same organization, analyze its operating budget; its cash-flow projections.
3. Using the sections discussed in this chapter, develop a grant proposal addressing a specific program, and incorporate it in a nonprofit organization.

■ References

Brinckerhoff, P. (1994). *Mission-Based Management: Leading Your Not-For-Profit into the 21st Century*. Dillon, CO: Alpine Guild Books.

Broce, T. (1986). *Fund Raising: The Guide to Raising Money from Private Sources*. Norman, OK: University of Oklahoma Press.

Drucker, P. (1990). *Managing the Nonprofit Organization*. Rockville, MD: Taft Group.

Edginton, C. R., and Ford, P. F. (1985). *Leadership in Recreation and Leisure Service Organizations*. New York: John Wiley and Sons.

Edginton, C. R., Ford, P. F., and Hudson, S. D. (1999). *Leadership in Recreation and Leisure Service Organizations*. Champaign, IL: Sagamore Publishing.

Edginton, S. R., and Edginton, C. R. (1994). *Youth Programs: Promoting Quality Services*. Champaign IL: Sagamore Publishing.

Flannagan, J. (1982). *The Grassroots Fund Raising Book*. Chicago: Contemporary Books.

Hardy, J. M. (1984). *Managing for Impact in Nonprofit Organizations*. Erwin, TN: Essex Press.

Konrad, P., and Novak, A. (2000). *Financial Management for Nonprofits: Keys to Success*. Denver, CO: Regis University, School of Professional Studies.

Marts, A. (1966). *The Generosity of Americans: Its Source, Its Achievements.* Englewood Cliffs, NJ: Prentice-Hall.

Massarsky, C. (1994). *Enterprising Strategies for Generating Revenue/The Jossey-Bass Handbook of Nonprofit Leadership and Management.* Edited by Robert Herman and Associates. San Francisco: Jossey-Bass.

Rosso, H. A. (1996). *Rosso on Fund Raising: Lessons from a Master's Lifetime.* San Francisco: Jossey-Bass.

Rosso, H. A., and Associates (1991). *Achieving Excellence in Fund Raising.* San Francisco: Jossey-Bass.

Seymour, H. J. (1966). *Designs for Fund Raising.* Rockville, MD: Taft Group.

Weis, R., and Gantt, V. (2002). *Leadership and Program Development in Nonprofit Organizations.* Peosta, IA: E. Bowers Publishing.

Wolf, T. (1999). *Managing a Nonprofit Organization.* New York: Prentice Hall.

7 Risk Management and Insurance

Securing adequate insurance, keeping risk to a minimum, and maintaining the highest concern for constituents, staff members, volunteers, and the organization should be the most important objectives of leaders in nonprofit institutions. Risk is inherent in everything we do, and nonprofit organizations are certainly not exempt from this reality, but they need to develop guidelines for understanding and dealing with risk in the most effective ways. Although insurance acquisition is primarily a task for administrators, developing and maintaining an effective risk management plan is the concern of board members, administrators, and program leaders.

It is a generally accepted tenet that no program is totally safe and that risk is an inherent part of doing business. In many parts of the world, program participants often assume a large part of the responsibility for risk. But in the United States, participants are far less likely to accept as much personal responsibility for risk, and this acceptance for responsibility varies from activity to activity and from one age group to another. This translates into the fact that organizations bear varying degrees of responsibility and must be as prepared as possible with adequate insurance coverage and a comprehensive plan for managing risks.

In this chapter we will discuss what types of risk exist within a nonprofit organization, what risk management means, reasons for an organization-wide risk management plan, and ways that plan can be developed. We will also discuss specific risk management guidelines for program activities that involve complex logistics and unusual potential for risk. Finally, we will discuss forms, waivers and releases relevant to risk management and the role insurance plays in providing financial relief for losses.

■ What is Risk and Risk Management?

A **risk** might be considered as any threat to a nonprofit organization's ability to accomplish its mission (Jackson, White, and Herman 1999). Threats could take a number of different forms including potential risk to people, property, income, and reputation in the community. Risk can never be managed away, but organizations can develop a framework and a *culture* for both understanding and addressing risk in the most effective manner.

Maintaining insurance coverage does not eliminate risk; it just transfers some of the financial responsibility for risk to the insurance company in exchange for a premium. Purchasing insurance does not reduce the possibility that an accident or some other mishap will occur; it simply provides a method of payment for any damages or compensation.

Risk management is a plan for dealing with potential threats to individuals, income, property, or reputation. Good risk management plans are carefully undertaken and result in well-thought-out implementation procedures. They should be aimed at protecting people, property, income and the reputation of the organization (Weis and Gantt 2002).

Too often nonprofit organizations delegate risk management to a second or even third level of importance because of the complexities and potential cost involved, when a good risk management plan often impedes other problems and saves money in the long run. The Nonprofit Risk Management Center proposes **ten reasons** why nonprofit organizations need **risk management plans**:

1. Risk management plans help the organization protect clients, staff and volunteers and other individuals in the community from harm.
2. Nonprofit organizations are like any other institutions: they are vulnerable to claims and lawsuits alleging damages and injuries due to operational activities and are not excepted for punishment because of their altruistic mission.
3. Accidents and other adverse situations can often be prevented with a carefully thought out plan.
4. Nonprofit organizations often undertake projects collaboratively with other entities, and it is essential that organizations have a comprehensive plan that protects collaborative partners as well.
5. Part of a risk management plan prepares organizations to forecast, prevent, and cope with difficulties stemming from a crisis in public confidence or negative publicity.
6. Prospective board, staff, and volunteer members will be far more attracted to an organization with an integrated risk management plan in place. All three groups are interested in strategies used to protect members and preserve the organization's assets.
7. A good risk management plan can preserve various categories of assets and enable the organization to concentrate its focus on fulfilling its mission.
8. Although some finances are necessary in funding the risk management plan, it will enable the organization to conserve financial resources in the long run by preventing the loss of finances in unexpected situations.
9. A risk management plan allows the organization to concentrate the majority of its financial resources on realizing its mission, rather than on accidents and other unanticipated incidents.
10. Having an effective plan for managing risks focuses attention on safe and productive operations and allows the organization to offer more programs and activities within the framework of a positive environment.

Another reason to develop effective risk management plans is that the types of legal suits that can be filed against nonprofit organizations is almost without limits, and good risk management plans can prevent many situations that might lead to a lawsuit. Some of the more **common types of lawsuits** against nonprofit organizations are listed below (Herman and Associates 1994):

1. Accidents make up the largest number of lawsuits filed against organizations. When someone causes an automobile accident, for instance, or creates some other dangerous condition that results in an injury, it is referred to as a **tort.** Under tort law, liability is typically based on negligence that implies the person causing harm did not exercise a degree of care that a reasonable person in a

similar situation would exhibit.

2. Oftentimes a negligent act may be an indirect cause of an accident. For instance, an accident might occur while taking children through leadership training at a high ropes-course. The organization may be held liable for a broken limb, based on the fact the ropes-course instructors had not been properly trained. The organization may also be held liable if the instructors had not been properly screened and did not have adequate certification. Improper screening of staff and volunteer members is the basis of hundreds of claims against nonprofit organizations each year.

3. Board members have also been sued if practices based on their policy resulted in negligence and/or injury or some other form of harm. If a member is hurt on the diving board of the local, community YMCA and the policy allows the diving board to be present, then board members as the only body that approved that policy are open to litigation.

4. Unfair employment practices are a large source of litigation. Some areas that employees may recover for include discrimination, wrongful dismissal, sexual harassment, and other employment-related acts.

5. In addition to organizations and directors being sued by parties who allege injury, the government office for fines and penalties can also sue them. Another arm of the government, the Internal Revenue Service, can also file claim against board members for the organization's failure to file tax forms or for breaching other IRS rules. Although board members should certainly take great care in their duties of board service, the number of lawsuits is relatively small and most claims derive from the area of employment.

Different experts in the field of risk management propose various **strategies for managing risk**. For instance, Van der Smissen (1990) suggests three components for managing risks (also mentioned in Chapter 5 in the context of program development):

1. **Identification of Risk.** Each operation, program, or activity presents conditions or situation that might present risks. Both obvious and not so obvious risks must be explored. For example, a service program that involves cleaning up debris along the bank of a lake presents some potential risk of drowning along with the possibility being harmed from dangerous materials.

2. **Evaluation of Risk.** Determining the relative importance of risks can be accomplished by asking the following questions:
   - What is the probability that a risk will result in an accident, injury, illness, or damage?
   - How severe would the loss be if it occurred?

3. **Handling Risk.** There are three basic ways to handle risk:
   - **Prevention (Avoidance).** Matching participants to appropriate experiences is one key to preventing and avoiding risk, as is effective orientation, training, and appropriate supervision.
   - **Risk Reduction** – Providing safety rules and well-thought-out emergency procedures are examples of risk reduction. In the case of the lake clean-up above, following safety procedures regarding how close individuals should

get to the water's edge and providing effective materials such as gloves, orange vests and/or life jackets are ways to reduce risk. Clear communication is also important in risk reduction.

- **Risk Retention or Transfer.** Risk retention or transfer refers to how a loss will be handled should it occur. That is, who is responsible for the loss and who will pay for the loss?

Experts with the Nonprofit Risk Management Center propose four somewhat different strategies for managing risk (1997):

1. **Avoidance.** Most nonprofit organizations will simply not offer a service or conduct an activity if it is considered too risky and will curtail programs or services if risks cannot be managed well. For instance, providing a zip-line at a Boys and Girls Club swimming facility could be great fun, but the inherent risk might far outweigh any benefits.

    A number of nonprofit organizations that transport members or clients are scrutinizing this activity more closely and deciding it may not be cost or risk effective. If the risk outweighs the benefits, but completely stopping an activity impairs the mission of the organization, another technique, modification, can be considered.

2. **Modification.** This implies changing the activity so that it can still be implemented, but within bounds, so the potential for harm is within acceptable limits. Modification might be as simple as screening volunteers more carefully, taking hazardous materials away from a fence next to a YMCA, or removing the diving board from the Salvation Army pool area.

    With the example of transporting clients or members above, some modifications that could keep a program within acceptable limits might include:
    - Making sure driver licenses are up-to-date and that no driver transporting members has an unsafe or unacceptable driving record.
    - Providing drivers with training relevant to safe driving, accident procedures, emergencies, and other proper vehicle operation procedures.
    - Conducting regular vehicle inspections and maintenance, and removing or fixing any unsafe vehicles.
    - Maintaining records on all risk management procedures.

    Modifying activities increases the safety factor throughout operations and activities while still allowing activities to continue within the revised framework. These modifications are a clear message to members and personnel that safety is the number one concern of the organization.

3. **Retention.** If an organization decides that it will retain the risk inherent with a certain procedure, then it must be prepared to handle that threat if it occurs. For instance, if an organization decides not to purchase insurance for the loss of money, then it should consider a contingency fund that could handle financial losses that might occur from theft or some other manner. To retain risk adequately, the organization should project what losses could occur in various areas and decide the extent that those risks could be handled. This type of projection should be ongoing, since potential losses may increase or decrease, as the

case may be, and the organization must stand ready to handle them to whatever extent they may occur.

4. **Sharing.** This involves the transfer of risk or the financial consequences to another institution. Agreements for sharing with such parties may include other nonprofit organizations, insurance companies (through premiums), or through some other contractual agreement. This option is also referred to as "transfer," since it is possible to transfer risk to another party. It is, however, almost impossible to fully transfer the risk of an activity to another party and maintain responsibility for the activity.

For instance, a nonprofit organization has purchased "adequate" fire insurance, and a fire occurs. The insurance may cover the cost of property and injury, but not cover the loss of membership or program fees that the organization could be faced with, nor the serious damage to the organization's reputation for safety and managing risk. In this case, financial loss has not been completely "transferred" and the organization may still retain damage to its reputation.

■ The Process for Developing a Risk Management Plan

Administrative leaders and board members should undertake the development and implementation of risk management plans with input from staff members, volunteers, organizational members and other constituents. Another consideration is to involve a specialist in risk management to provide guidance in the development of a plan. The organization may wish to confer with other specialists as well, such as a human-resources professional who could examine the employee handbook, and an accountant who could help in developing financial and accounting controls. Ideally, representatives from the groups mentioned above would be assimilated into a **risk management project team** or **committee** and this committee would spearhead the plan. Although there are any number of strategies designed to develop good risk management plans, this section will concentrate for the most part on suggestions developed at the Nonprofit Risk Management Center (Jackson, White, and Herman 1997, 1999):

1. Develop risk management goals and a policy statement.
2. Determine responsibility for the risk management program.
3. Use four techniques—avoidance, modification, retention, and sharing—in developing a work plan for the program.
4. Document, implement, and monitor the program.

Step 1. Develop Risk Management Goals and a Policy Statement

The first step in developing a risk management plan is to determine the goals of the plan. The goals are set in collaboration with the chief executive officer and the board of directors along with input from the risk management committee, although *only board members can actually approve the plan.* In addition to setting goals, this group must also design a brief (one or two sentences) risk management policy statement expressing the organization's commitment to managing risk and outlining what individuals throughout the organization can do to support the risk management plan.

One of the first steps in establishing goals is to review reasons that it is important to have a risk management plan. Many of these reasons have been mentioned previously in this chapter and include the desire to reduce accidents, which also lowers insurance rates. Other reasons may include the discussion of preventive activities that can occur before any threat or loss and activities that can occur in response to a threat or loss. Some sample reasons for a plan could include the following:

- Protect members from harm.
- Decrease the number of accidents of employees.
- Reduce insurance costs.
- Provide a healthy, safe, and positive environment.
- Prevent financial loss.
- Respond effectively to accidents and/or injuries.
- Maintain operations in spite of loss.
- Assess insurance coverage.
- Conserve resources by preventing theft.

Based on this kind of list, the risk management committee can develop three or four specific goals for the risk management program:

1. To protect the organization's financial assets.
2. To provide a safe and healthy environment for staff members, volunteers constituents.
3. To develop plans for any crisis that should occur.
4. To confirm that insurance is adequate and cost effective.

After determining the goals of the risk management plan, the next step is to write a **risk management policy.** The risk management policy is extracted from the program goals. The policy should reflect the goals of the program and point to actions that others can take in the risk management efforts. A simulated Scottsdale Salvation Army policy statement is included below:

> *The Scottsdale Salvation Army's number one priority is to protect its people, property, income, and reputation through the practice of effective risk management. The organization's board, staff members, and volunteers are dedicated to maintaining the safety and dignity of all constituents.*

A risk management policy can and should appear on all important documents associated with the organization, and it should be emphasized more than anything else the organization promotes.

Step 2. Determine Responsibility of the Risk Management Program

With consultation from the board of directors, the ED/CEO should assign responsibility for developing and implementing the organization's risk management program. This is where a **Risk Management Project Team** or **Committee**, made up of board members, key staff members, consulting experts, and even organizational members when appropriate, can be invaluable. In addition to key staff, board members and constituents, experts from any appropriate field not already included above should be considered, such as the following:

- insurance
- legal area
- public relations
- safety
- program development
- child care
- geriatric

Of course, the composition of this kind of committee will vary with the type of risk associated with the organization and may change over time as risk changes. The committee should represent a wide range of expertise, and having personal knowledge of some of the risk the organization may face would be a plus.

The Risk Management Committee should consider dividing into subcommittees to address various operational categories. These categories could include; program, finance, building and grounds, governance (board operations), and public relations, to mention several. The subcommittees would then be charged with designing materials for in-service training as well as be responsible for the training, which should be ongoing. The greater the involvement of everyone in risk management training, the greater the possibility that risk management will be understood as the highest priority by all.

Step 3. Develop a Working Plan for the Program

The first step of the committee is to develop an action plan and assign responsibility and completion dates for each part of the plan. Committee and subcommittee tasks are listed next:

- Discuss the four techniques of risk management.
- Indicate key subcommittees and determine responsibilities.
- Begin risk identification and analysis by subcommittee.
- Review, analyze, and consolidate subcommittee reports.
- Set priorities for risk management (top, moderate, low).
- Determine appropriate risk management technique.

A. Discuss the Four Techniques of Risk Management

Determining techniques of risk management provides a framework for the Risk Management Committee to work from. A brief summary of the four steps in the risk management process follows: (1) Recognize and identify risk., (2) Assess and prioritize risk, (3) Select and initiate effective risk management techniques, and (4) Continually monitor and change the risk management program when necessary.

1. **Recognize and Identify Risk**

    One of the first tasks is to pull the Risk Management Committee together for a brainstorming session to determine what can go wrong in the organization. Such a session begins with a discussion of potential threats to people, property, income, and reputation. Many risks are generic in that they are virtually present within any organization. Wet floors around a swimming pool, the potential for break-ins, allegations of improper hiring or firing are typical kinds of threats.

Other threats can be unique to specific organizations, such as sexual abuse within a youth organization, or a malpractice suit against an organization for providing free legal services. The facilitator for such a brainstorming session should be someone with expertise in both facilitation and risk management, when possible.

2. **Assess and Prioritize Risk**

   Once potential risks have been identified, the committee can begin evaluating the risks mentioned and determine the probability of certain risks materializing, how often, and what would happen if they did occur.

   Following this evaluation, the committee (or subcommittees within the committee) can begin assigning a high, moderate, or low grading for risks based on their probability and severity. Once labels of Top, Moderate, or Low are assigned, the committee can look at those risks with a top assessment to determine if the organization should avoid the activity, provide appropriate insurance for the activity, and/or manage the risk in a more effective manner than before. An activity that is placed in a low priority might be postponed until those activities in the top and moderate categories have been attended to.

3. **Select and Initiate Effective Risk Management Techniques**

   The four risk management techniques explained earlier are briefly reviewed below:
   - *Avoidance.* Eliminate all activities that are deemed too risky.
   - *Modification.* Restructure the activity so any threats are within acceptable limits.
   - *Retention.* Accept all risk and prepare for potential consequences.
   - *Sharing* (transfer). Share potential consequences with another entity, such as with insurance.

   This implementation phase is a critical part of risk management. Expectations for the techniques mentioned above should be clear, measurable, and easily observed. This entire process needs to be explained carefully to board, staff, constituents and anyone else who could be affected by the process.

4. **Continually Monitor and Change the Risk Management Program when Necessary**

   This phase of the risk management program is also important because it involves members of the Risk Management Committee evaluating the program and determining if it is having its desired effect. The committee needs to assess whether or not the program is working and if not, it needs to modify the program to become more effective. Monitoring the program requires a structured communication process in which members can interact with each other at scheduled times as well as at impromptu times to assess and make adjustments.

B. Identify Key Subcommittees and Determine Responsibilities

Because of the complex nature of developing a risk management program, sharing the responsibilities with subcommittees simplifies the process. Subdividing tasks by the organization's different operations is one way to address this complexity:
- **Programs.** All identified programs can be assigned to a subcommittee specifi-

Figure 7.1
Risk Management Project Task Worksheet

Organization: Lexington Kentucky Family YMCA
Date: November 15, 2004

Task	Leader	Start/Finish Dates
Risk Identification		11/15 – 12/15
Special Events	Jeffery Howe	
Field Trips	Ann Sakona	
Sports Leagues	Jeremy Fishe	
Fundraising	Roland Gunn	
Administration	Sandy Lynd	
Governance	David Monahan	
Review SubcommitteeFindings	David Monahan	12/15 – 12/31
Establish Priorities	David Monahan	1/10 – 1/30
Evaluate and Select Techniques		
Special Events	Jeffery Howe	
Field Trips	Ann Sakona	
Sports Leagues	Jeremy Fishe	
Fundraising	Roland Gunn	
Administration	Sandy Lynd	
Governance	David Monahan	
Document the Program	Sandy Lynd	3/15 – 3/30

cally established for this operation. Another way to do this would be to have a subcommittee assigned to categories of programs, such as special events, facility based programs, or field trips. Each of these areas can involve unique and significant risk that may need to be addressed.

- **Fundraising activities.** Fundraising activities present different kinds of risks. Controls and security processes for handling money need to be carefully spelled out for all to know and follow. Careful consideration should also be given in developing a system of controls that virtually prohibits any possible impropriety.
- **Administrative operations.** Administrative activities actually have a great potential for threat or loss when areas such as physical facilities, employment practices, office policies and procedures, computer equipment and data, and the accounting and financial operations of the nonprofit organization are considered.

- **Governance (board operations).** The legal and fiduciary responsibilities of a board of directors is significant, and examining the operation of the board, including legal documents, bylaws and articles of incorporation, is all a part of a risk management plan. The procedures for board minutes, orientation programs, and operating policies and procedures should also be a focus of risk management. A Risk Management Project Task Worksheet can be used to assign responsibilities and to track progress. A sample task sheet similar to the one suggested by the Nonprofit Risk Management Center is presented in Figure 7.1.

C. Begin Risk Identification and Analysis by Subcommittee

Subcommittees need to begin analyzing risk potential in the program or operation they are responsible for. Committee members should be exhaustive in their efforts to identify risks. There are a number of tools available to help members identify risks. Several tools are discussed below:

- **Surveys, Checklists and Questionnaires.** Forms that help organizations identify risks are sometimes referred to as **exposure analysis forms**. These forms are developed by insurance companies and businesses specializing in risk management and can be helpful to nonprofit organizations in identifying risks. Risks can sometimes also be determined by focusing on the questions asked with insurance applications.

- **Internal Documents.** Documents and records, including bylaws, employee manuals, the annual audit, policies and procedures manuals, board and committee minutes, annual reports, fundraising materials, marketing flyers, accident reports and other informational documents, can be important clues to risks.

- **Financial Statements and Records.** Financial records, such as annual reports, monthly statements, and audit reports, may be helpful in determining whether there are any threats in financial controls and other risks.

- **Workflow.** Analyzing all of the processes involved with delivering core services will help determine if there are any problem areas. Areas to check include registration procedures, service delivery, complaints, grievance resolutions and the monitoring and supervision of staff and members. Marketing, employment, and fundraising procedures are other areas to be considered.

- **Personal Inspections.** Going over paperwork can assist in determining risks, but walking around and personally examining facility areas, financial safeguard systems, and other potential areas of risk can provide additional knowledge regarding possible losses. Personal examinations should be done at different times of the schedule so that numerous types of activities can be observed and assessed.

- **Interviews.** In addition to surveys and questionnaires, conducting personal interviews can provide an in-depth level of information regarding potential hazards. Interviews should be conducted with those individuals who know more about existing risks than anyone else: staff members, volunteers, constituents, and any other parties that interact with the organization.

- **Loss Histories.** Identifying what kinds of losses have occurred will help to insure that history doesn't repeat itself and that the organization can provide safeguards against any trends with particular situations. It is also a good idea to examine what has happened in similar organizations, a process referred to as **bench-marking.**

D. Review, Analyze and Consolidate Subcommittee Findings

Once the subcommittees have collected their information and recorded it on the Risk Management Project Worksheet (Figure 7.1), the full committee should review the information. A number of mutual risks may be common to most areas, such as child abuse, automobile accidents, or injuries, and these can be consolidated on one worksheet. A separate worksheet can be kept for risks unique to specific areas, such as employment procedures.

E. Set Priorities for Risk Management (top, moderate, low)

After risks have been identified, subcommittees can began an in depth assessment of determining how often risks might occur and how severe the damage would be relevant to each and every risk. Having done this, projections can be made for the chances a loss will occur (*frequency*) and its probable effect (*severity*). **Frequency** indicates the probability a risk will actually occur and how often it might occur. **Severity** measures the probable effect and cost to the organization if the loss occurs. Each risk can then be graded as either high, moderate or low for both frequency and severity (see Figure 7.2 below).

Assigning grades to potential risks can be challenging, to say the least, but looking at past history and assessing current operations can help subcommittee members project the frequency and severity. Looking at each past operation to see if there have been injuries— thefts and fires, for instance—and considering the effects of these losses can help determine the grading of potential losses. Although it is still only a projection of losses, it is a calculated and knowledgeable projection.

Figure 7.2
Risk Identification Grades

	SEVERITY			FREQUENCY		
Risk	**High**	**Moderate**	**Low**	**High**	**Moderate**	**Low**
Special Events		x			x	
Field Trips	x					x
Sports Leagues	x			x		

Once all risks have been graded, they can then be divided into top, moderate, and low priorities. For example, incidents within the category of sports leagues, where there is a high potential for severity along with a high possibility for frequency, would certainly go to a top risk priority level. Something with a more moderate level of frequency and severity, such as a special event, would be listed as a moderate priority, and so on.

Categories that receive the highest priority can be very detrimental to a nonprofit organization. These categories should be looked at closely to see if the organization should avoid the risk altogether or transfer a part of the responsibility of the risk to another party, such as an insurance company. Categories of risk that receive a lower priority for severity and frequency may not require such strong actions, but must still be assessed and evaluated. All three categories require close attention.

F. Determine and Establish Appropriate Risk Management Strategies

Once risks have been identified and prioritized, attention should turn to handling risk through various techniques. Sometimes each area requires a combination of techniques. For instance, field trips would certainly require the purchase of insurance covering travel and incidents that may occur during the trip. A screening and driver training program could also be in place. This would help to insure safety and lower the cost of insurance premiums. Or the organization may wish to contract a part of the responsibility of the field trips to another party, such as a charter bus organization. This would still require some insurance, but some of the responsibility of the trip would have been transferred.

Once strategies have been identified and put in place for top-level risks, attention can be focused on other priorities, and techniques can be put in place for these as well. For instance, special events were assessed at a moderate level for frequency and severity (see Figure 7.2, 205). Checking existing insurance may determine that it is adequate and that no additional insurance is required to satisfy the "severity" grade. Providing adequate staff and volunteer risk management training, along with appropriate waivers (discussed later in this chapter) for participants may be all that is required for this category.

Step 4 – Document, Implement, and Monitor the Program

After techniques for every risk are established, they should then be documented, along with plans to monitor the program. Piecing together worksheets and documents produced during the overall process will result in a Risk Management Manual that would be easy to refer to and use. This type of manual can be invaluable for managing risk effectively and as inexpensively as possible.

A number of items should be considered for inclusion in the manual:
- Risk management policy statement and goals
- Responsibilities of the Risk Management Committee
- Job descriptions for committee members and subcommittee members
- A list of all members including addresses, phones numbers and e-mail addresses
- A synopsis of the work that went into developing the manual
- A list of techniques and monitoring methods for each risk
- Crisis and emergency management plans
- Copies of Risk Management Committee reports
- A summary of the organization's insurance coverage

Putting together a Risk Management Plan and Manual will take some time, but it is an important investment in the long-term well-being of the organization and all of its constituents.

Once strategies have been developed and a document plan exists, the committee must then decide how to implement the plan. Responsibilities, deadlines, and objectives for the plan need to be developed in order for it to be effective. An introduction of the plan and an explanation of the risk management program must be presented to all involved with required training for staff and volunteer members.

The Risk Management Committee must monitor the plan continually through established ways of collecting information, and it must evaluate the effectiveness of the plan. As the organization and the communities they serve change, all aspects of the plan should be reviewed and revised as frequently as is appropriate. This review and revision process should be done as needed, but with a formal review process occurring annually. Good risk management plans become a part of an organization's culture and are an integral part of helping it focus on its mission.

∎ Risk Management Guidelines for Specific Program Activities

Because of the nature of some programs, certain activities may require more specific guidelines. Program activities such as water sports, team sports, some special events, and other programs with complicated logistics seem to take on lives of their own and can be managed more effectively with guidelines tailored to these kinds of activities. In a sense, risk management guidelines for specific program activities become a *plan within a plan*. In other words, guidelines for specific activities fit into the overall risk management plan. Although each of these programs or activities need to be looked at separately, the guidelines included in Figure 7.3 can be beneficial in managing risk for a number of different kinds of program activities (Edginton, Hudson, and Ford 1999).

Each activity should be examined carefully to make sure that all identified risks would be graded low enough to be acceptable or made to be low enough through some modifications (e.g., helmets, gloves, lifeguards, trail guides, and safety equipment). It is also important that personnel have the appropriate credentials and training, that participants are of the right age and skill level, that the facilities and equipment are safe and effective, and that no unavoidable risk exists prior to detailed planning, which will be described below:

I. **General Description.**

  A. **Name of Program or Event**

    Appropriately naming a program helps staff members, volunteers, and participants to begin forming a mental picture of the activities that might occur, including any potential risk. Organizers can begin to brainstorm for potential risks. For instance, a swimming activity may bring to mind images of drowning, hypothermia, or choking. A baseball league will include equipment—such as bats, bases, and fences—that can cause bruises or broken bones. Even something as seemingly harmless as an arts and crafts program might include potentially hazardous materials, such as cutting instruments, electrical tools, and heat from the use of a kiln.

Figure 7.3
Risk Management Guidelines for Specific Activities

    I.   GENERAL DESCRIPTION
          A. Name of Program
          B. Type of Activity
          C. Level of Activity
    II.   DATES AND TIMES
          A. Dates
          B. Times
    III.   GOALS AND OBJECTIVES
          A. Organizational
          B. Activity
    IV.   LOCATION
          A. Site/Area
          B. Weather
          C. Routes
          D. Facilities
    V.   TRANSPORTATION
          A. Mode
          B. Routes/Destinations
    VI.   PARTICIPANTS
          A. Number
          B. Skill Level
          C. Characteristics
    VII. LEADERS
          A. Number/Roles
          B. Qualifications
    VIII. EQUIPMENT
          A. Type and Amount
          B. Control
    IX.   CONDUCTING THE ACTIVITY
          A. Pre-Activity Preparation
          B. Group Control
          C. Teaching/Instruction Strategy
          D. Time Management
    X.   EMERGENCY PREPAREDNESS
          A. Policies
          B. Health Forms
          C. Telephone Numbers

Source: Edginton, Hudson and Ford 1999

B. **Type of Activity**

Determining the kinds of activities that are planned for which program or event will help in designing the appropriate risk management techniques.

C. **Level of Activity**

Using appropriate terms when describing the skill levels associated with each activity is also important. Terms such as *beginners*, *advanced beginners*, *intermediate*, and *expert*. Sometimes activities have their own set of terms in describing skill levels, but the most important rule is to use terms that everyone understands, planners and participants alike.

II. Date(s) and Time(s)

The designation of dates and times is important so that contingency plans can be made for events that will be held out-of-doors, in case of inclement weather. Another consideration is timing: an event held out-of-doors in the summer will have a longer opportunity for daylight than if the same event were held in the winter. It is also important to plan things so that activities do not last so long as to fatigue leaders and participants and so that each group receives adequate break time and adequate refreshment. The possibilities for fatigue and overstimulation should be considered when planning a long event, and adequate downtime and refreshment breaks should be built into the schedule.

III. Goals and Objectives

Listing and understanding goals and objectives is imperative to the overall success of the activity. Understanding purpose gives direction to the activity and some guidelines for what risks might be acceptable or not acceptable. Objectives need to be clearly written with specific, projected outcomes. Objectives should be as inclusive as possible, stating skill, knowledge, emotional, spiritual and/or physical attainment when appropriate. Both leaders and participants should have a good understanding of the objectives.

IV. Location

The selection of a location for a program has a lot to do with the potential risk and the type of risk that may be involved.

A. **Activity Site or Area**

The activity site or area should be described by name and/or details may be listed that allow participants to find the site using a map. Information regarding any special hazards associated with getting to the site or the site itself should be identified in advance. Current, in-depth information should be available regarding an activity site prior to the event, and every attempt should be made to visit a site prior to conducting the activity.

B. **Weather and Climate**

Weather should be assessed carefully prior to an activity, particularly an outdoor activity or one in which travel is involved. Being prepared for a change in weather during an activity is also extremely important. It is far better to be prepared for the worst-case scenario and to operate on the conservative side.

C. **Routes**

Activities that involving travel or moving from one place to another should be precisely described in the program plan, particularly when a trip of several days or more is planned. Emergency escape routes should be considered and communicated along with possible lodging sites, locations for food and liquids, and locations of medical facilities or services.

D. Facilities

Facilities that are to be used for an activity should be fully described. Directions should be provided if the facility is located away from the home organization. All facilities should be carefully inspected, especially those with high potential for risk, such as ropes-courses, swimming pools, gyms, and playing fields. When visiting lakes, streams, and oceans, it is imperative to understand the strength of the currents, the depth of the water, unusual occurrences associated with that particular aquatic area, and the way of the tides. Proper plans for fire emergencies are important for activities within a building. Fire alarms need to be continually tested, and a fire emergency exit plan needs to be established and practiced. Periodic inspections of the building's electrical and gas heat and air-conditioning systems must be a priority. Other equipment that should be formally inspected as the risk management committee dictates includes diving boards, gymnastic equipment, swimming pool chemical and filter systems, and any other equipment or structure that may include a risk.

V. Transportation

A. Mode of Transportation

Transportation plans for activities need to be clearly devised and communicated. If a charter bus is chosen for a ski trip, then the company providing the bus should be carefully checked out for its overall safety record, screening of drivers, training of drivers, and scheduling procedures. An understanding of equipment maintenance records is important. Buses, vans, and cars that are maintained by the home organization must also be properly serviced and documented and drivers should be carefully screened, trained, and monitored.

B. Routes, Distance, and Time

Participants should understand prior to an activity that involves transportation which routes are going to be used, the distance to be traveled, and the time involved, as it can best be projected. Alternative routes and times should be discussed, as should emergency or alternative plans based on possible eventualities. Often, the transportation of participants and staff members is the most dangerous part of an activity, yet it is too often considered as an afterthought. With regard to transportation, the risk management plan for transportation needs to be reviewed and always followed and adhered to.

VI. Participants

A. Number

Most events will have both a maximum and a minimum number of participants set in advance. Minimum numbers are often set so that resources are not spent on events with little interest, and maximum numbers are set to insure quality and often to meet guidelines for space accommodation and safety. Both are valid concerns, but flexibility is important when possible and appropriate.

B. Skill Level

Participants should be aware in advance of what skill levels, if any, correlate with a program activity. In many instances, the terms *beginning*, *novice*, *intermediate*, *advanced*, and *expert level* are assigned to different activities and each will have a different skill requirement and a different risk management strategy.

C. Characteristics

Participant characteristics have to do with specific, individual attributes, such as whether a participant is an adult or a child, male or female, and in some cases, disabled, highly fit or just starting a fitness program. Knowing as many characteristics as possible regarding the participants makes it easier for program staff to assign the right kind of supervision. It also allows the participant a chance to understand more about the challenges of a particular activity. For instance, a ten-mile hike or a climb through a hillside covered with rocks would not work for a novice, but may be fine for an intermediate-level participant. Developing a participant profile helps to prevent mismatching lower level skills or other attributes with an activity that is too challenging.

VII. Leaders

A. Number and Roles

Describing the criteria necessary for activity leaders in the program plan is a wise concept, as is listing the number of leaders required for each activity. Most organizations have a specific proportion of staff to participants that has to be adhered to for quality assurances as well as for effective risk management. Program staff members are usually the most expensive part of a program budget, but usually the more qualified staff an activity has, the better and the safer the event.

B. Qualifications

It is important to maintain a current list of qualifications and years of experience of individual staff members. Hiring standards and requirements for members should be at least as stringent as those of comparable organizations in the region.

VIII. Equipment

A. Type and Amount

Listing the various types of equipment involved in an activity and certifying that the equipment meets acceptable guidelines indicates that activity leaders are making every effort to keep risk to a minimum. Maintaining the right number of tumbling mats, for instance, is important, because having a lesser number could raise a concern for safety.

B. Control of equipment

A system for controlling and maintaining equipment is essential to be certain it is kept clean, dry, and in good condition for the next usage. Equipment should be checked, both when it is returned and when it is checked out again, to maintain the best condition possible and to avoid any surprises during an activity.

IX. **Conduct of the Program Activity**

A. **Pre-Activity Preparations**

Pre-activity meetings should be included in the risk management plan for all activities.

B. **Group Control and Communication**

How communication will occur within a group activity, including roll and attendance keeping, should be included in the risk management plan. This, of course, includes any and all safety instructions, as well as a detailed account of who is responsible to whom and for what.

C. **Teaching Strategy**

Teaching strategies for developing various skills should be documented and notes kept on any variation from non-standard methods, with reasons as to the variation. Teaching strategies affect risk levels, so they need to be understood and documented appropriately.

D. **Time Management Plan**

Setting beginning and ending times and dates for activities, along with times and dates for specific parts of the activity schedule, provides guidance for what is to happen, when it happens, and how long each part takes. This provides the program team valuable information for overall program development and is essential for good risk management.

X. **Emergency Preparedness**

Developing strategies for program emergencies is a critical part of any risk management plan. Plans for fires, storms, floods, first aid, missing persons, transportation breakdowns and other emergency situations should be developed and documented.

Each activity plan should also have a place to include emergency help numbers and emergency numbers for participants in case of an incident. If health forms are necessary, they should be current and attached with the plan. The risk management guidelines for specific programs described in the last section addresses most components of program activities and can be used as standard operating procedures for similar types of activities. Standard operating procedures or guidelines, as such, can be easily inserted in the overall risk management plan. Release forms and waivers will be discussed in the next section.

■ Reports, Forms, Waivers and Releases

There are a number of reports and forms that can help in the planning and organizing of program activities. These forms can be prepared by the administrative and program staff, but they should be reviewed by the organizational legal counsel. Examples of forms include the following (Weis and Gantt 2002):

- **Agreements.** Specific agreements can be developed between collaborating organizations, so that expectations are clear regarding who does what. These kinds of agreements clarify roles and make managing risk much easier.

- **Participation Agreement.** Sometimes called **Assumptions of Risk Agreements**, this document indicates that the participant understands the risks, agrees to abide by safety rules, and agrees to a set behavior code.
- **Accident Reports.** Accident reports should be completed on any injury that occurs and must include a detailed description of what happened, a list of the parties involved, and an account of what was done to alleviate any pain or suffering.
- **Incident Reports** Incidents out of the ordinary that pose potential risk to individuals, property, finances or reputation should be recorded and any disposition noted.
- **Personal Health Forms.** Health forms may be required of all participants within an organization, or they may be required prior to specific activities. Health forms should include relevant information such as the participant's limitations, medications, allergies, disabilities, and health status.
- **Waivers/Releases.** These two terms are interchangeable here, and each implies that the participants agree not to hold the school or agency/organization responsible. This form is only valid when signed by an adult, and parents or guardians **can never sign away the rights of children under the legal age of majority**, as previously mentioned in Chapter 5. Signing such a form for children indicates intent, but does not have a strong legal basis.

Signing a waiver does not preclude suing for negligence. Most U.S. courts have ruled that organizations providing a public service cannot absolve themselves from liability to the public to whom they are providing a service, particularly in cases of negligence. Regardless of this fact, it is important that organizations protect themselves and their members as much as possible by providing waivers to program participants. Waivers indicate that the participant has at least stated that he or she will not hold the organization responsible and understands the risk involved, which may dissuade the participant from legal resolve. Release forms also remind participants of potential risks and make them more alert to hazards associated with activities. They are, therefore, well worth the effort.

■ Insurance

As stated earlier in this chapter, insurance does not eliminate risk; it just transfers some of the financial responsibility for risk to the insurance company in exchange for a premium. Insurance is the typical way of handling risk to prevent excessive or possibly devastating financial loss to an agency or entity (Weis and Gantt 2002). Insurance policies assure the availability of some money to pay for damages and to compensate victims following a loss. Just like businesses for profit, nonprofit organizations are vulnerable to losses stemming from accidents or negligence. Given this vulnerability, it would seem that most nonprofit organizations would be adequately insured, when in fact many organizations carry no insurance or are marginally insured at best. Insurance rates are constantly increasing, and budgets are often tight, so smaller organizations sometimes take their chances that a loss will not be catastrophic.

Although insurance is important, it is not the only mechanism available to a nonprofit organization (Jackson, White, and Herman 1997). Other options include setting aside **re-**

serve funds to pay for potential losses, or establishing a line of credit to cover something that might go wrong down the road. Both of these options need to be calculated with the cost of insurance versus the loss of readily available money through the establishment of a reserve fund, or the loss of money to cover a credit owed.

Insurance is usually divided into two different categories, property and liability (Jackson, White, and Herman 1997). **Property insurance** typically covers tangible assets such as furniture, buildings, computers, documents and equipment. This type of coverage will often replace the losses of the assets mentioned above. It also pays the cost of a temporary office, if one needs to be established, and it covers any loss of income. **Liability insurance** provides protection from claims and lawsuits against the organization. It also provides financial relief if the organization is found to be negligent and that negligence has caused damages to another person or organization. These general liability insurance policies— usually referred to as **commercial general liability (CGL)**—do not cover all losses, particularly those arising from board decisions and the delivery of professional services. These types of claims can generally be protected by purchasing **directors' and officers' (D&O)** policies, which provide financial relief in the event the organization and/or its officers and staff are sued regarding a loss as a result of a board decision or of a service provided.

Because of the many different kinds of insurance needs and the number of insurance policies available, a committee consisting of administrative and program staff members, board members and experts in insurance should be formed to examine the best possible coverage for the organization and its constituents at the most cost effective level. Often, insurance is either mandated by law and/or by the organization's national affiliate. Many times, branches of the same organization or organizations with similar missions and programs will band together to purchase less expensive group insurance policies. In most cases, it is far better to have adequate insurance coverage for all potential losses than to rely on other sources of relief.

■ Summary

A risk could be anything that is deemed a threat to an organization's accomplishing its mission. Threats usually take the form of potential risk to people, property, income, and reputation in the community. Risk can never be fully managed away, but organizations can develop ways to deal with risk effectively. Maintaining insurance transfers some of the financial responsibility for risk to insurance companies in exchange for a premium, but does not eliminate risk.

Risk management is a plan for dealing with potential risks. There are a number of reasons for developing organizational risk management plans, all of which are aimed at protecting individuals, income, property, and reputation.

There are a number of different strategies for managing risk, and they include identifying, evaluating, and handling risk. Experts at the Risk Management Center propose other strategies, including avoidance, modification, retention, and sharing, all of which make it easier for an organization to manage risk.

The development of an organizational risk management plan should be undertaken by a risk management committee made up of board members, staff leaders, constituents, and experts in the field of risk management. Developing a good risk management plan involves four steps:

1. Developing risk management goals and a policy statement.
2. Determining responsibility of the risk management program.
3. Developing a working plan for the program.
4. Documenting implementing, and monitoring the program. Each of these can be subdivided into parts relevant to the overall development of a plan.

Certain program activities may require more specific guidelines. In a sense, these guidelines become a plan within the overall organizational risk management plan. They include a general description and details of the program, including dates, times, goals, objectives, location, transportation, participants, leaders, equipment, activities, and emergency processes. Planning and assessing these details in advance adds a great deal of strength to reducing risks in each program activity.

There are a number of reports and forms that can help to plan and organize program activities and help to minimize risk. These include agreements between collaborating organizations, agreements for program participants, accident and incident reports, personal health forms, and waivers and releases.

Insurance is a way to transfer some of the financial responsibility for risk to the insurance company in exchange for a premium. Insurance is the typical way of handling risk to prevent excessive or possibly devastating financial loss to an agency or entity. Because of the many different kinds of insurance needs and the number of insurance policies, a leadership committee should examine the best possible coverage for the organization.

This chapter addressed, in part, the American Humanics Certification Competency Requirements of Nonprofit Risk Management.

■ Discussion Questions

1. Relying on the textbook's definition of *risk*, describe three key risks involved in a program activity in which you have recently participated.
2. Describe the four broad areas that risk management plans are designed to protect and give examples.
3. In one paragraph, summarize the ten reasons the Nonprofit Risk Management Center describes as important reasons to have a risk management plan.
4. Compare and contrast the strategies for managing risk designed by Van der Smissen and by experts at the Nonprofit Risk Management Center.
5. What sorts of goals should be included in a risk management plan?
6. What is the importance of a policy statement and how could it be used?
7. List and give reasons for including specific members on the risk management team or committee.
8. Discuss the process for determining risk management priorities.
9. Why is it important to have risk management guidelines for specific program activities? Give several examples of how guidelines might help reduce risks.
10. What is the role of insurance in managing risk, and what is the process for determining the right kind of insurance for an organization?

■ Activities

1. Simulate a program activity or develop a service learning project and incorporate the risk management guidelines for specific activities in the development of the program.
2. Contact a nonprofit organization and compare and contrast their risk management plan with the one presented in this chapter. Offer a copy of the results to the organization.
3. Ask insurance company representatives to make a classroom presentation on the types of insurance that they think nonprofit organizations should obtain.

■ References

Christiansen, M. L. (1986). How to avoid negligence suits: reducing hazards to prevent injuries. *Journal of Physical Education, Recreation, and Dance* 57 (2): 46-52.

Edginton, C., Hudson, S., and Ford, P. (1999). *Leadership in Recreation and Leisure Service Organizations*. Champaign, IL: Sagamore Publishing.

Fishman, J. and Schwarz, S. (2000). *Nonprofit Organizations: Cases and Materials*. New York: Foundation Press.

Herman, M. and Head, G. (2002). *Enlightened Risk Taking: A Guide to Strategic Risk Management for Nonprofits*. Washington, DC: Nonprofit Risk Management Center.

Jackson, M., White, L., and Herman, M. (1997). *Mission Accomplished: The Workbook*. Washington, DC: Nonprofit Risk Management Center.

_____ (1999). *Mission Accomplished: A Practical Guide to Risk Management for Nonprofits*. 2nd ed. Washington, DC: Nonprofit Risk Management Center.

Kurtz, D. (1988). *Board Liability: Guide for Nonprofit Directors*. Mt. Kisco, N.Y.: Moyer Bell.

Patterson, J., Tremper, C., and Rypkema, P. (1994). *Staff Screening Tool Kit*. Washington, DC: Nonprofit Risk Management Center.

Tremper, C., (1994). Risk management. In Robert Herman & Associates, eds. *The Jossey-Bass Handbook of Nonprofit Leadership and Management*. San Francisco: Jossey-Bass Publishing.

Tremper, C. and Kostin, G. (1993). *No Surprises: Controlling Risks in Volunteer Programs*. Washington, DC: Nonprofit Risk Management Center.

Tremper, C., Lally, F., and Studebaker, D. (1994). *Insurance Assurance for Volunteers*. Washington, DC: Nonprofit Risk Management Center.

Van der Smissen, B. (1990). *Legal Liability and Risk Management for Public and Private Entities*. Vol. 2. Cincinnati, OH: Anderson.

Weis, R. and Gantt, V. (2002). *Leadership and Program Development in Nonprofit Organizations*. Peosta, IA: E. Bowers Publishing.

Customer Service: Knowing the Vision and Making It Work

As in the for-profit world, nonprofit organizations exist to serve a specific audience (customer, client, patron, or guest) outside the actual organization. The recipient of an organization's service holds the key in determining how successful an organization is in meeting its mission. If a need is not met, the organization will soon cease to exit, or it will have to alter its mission to meet the needs of its customers. This fact is easily seen when an organization first comes into existence. However, as an organization ages, it can begin to believe that its own existence is its mission. In other words, the organization exists because it has a place in the community or society.

Every organization has a second set of customers—an internal audience. This internal audience (internal stakeholders) consists of staff, volunteers, Board members and financial and mission supporters. If this set of customers is ignored or not fully appreciated, the organization will suffer discontent, unusually high turn-over and, often, poor customer service in dealing with its other, primary, mission-dedicated audience.

The goal of every organization, for-profit and nonprofit, should be to provide outstanding customer service. This chapter will explore customer dissatisfaction and satisfaction with regard to both audiences (external and internal) and describe various ways to ensure better customer satisfaction.

What is customer service? According to Davidow and Uttal (1989) **customer service** means providing all "features, acts, and information that augment the customer's ability to realize the potential value of a core product or service" (22). If an agency exists to help people, why should it matter if some people are unhappy as long as some people are helped? Can some unhappy people be expected? Can some unhappy people be tolerated? The answer is, it depends on why they are unhappy. If their unhappiness is a personality flaw, the answer might be that they can be ignored. For any other reason, the answer is that their unhappiness must be examined carefully and judged on the merits of each case.

■ The Nature of Dissatisfaction

Let's look at the general case of dissatisfaction. Customer service survey results concerning dissatisfaction fall into **three** broad **categories**:

1. Unmet expectations
2. Poor quality service, and/or
3. Inadequate or confusing policies

If someone is unhappy for any of these three reasons, the agency must understand why satisfactory service has not been delivered or why the recipient of the service believes it is unsatisfactory. When an agency suspects that some people are unhappy, it should find out why. A survey of people receiving services and delivering services could be distributed and the results analyzed.

Here are some of the statements that an organization might receive on a survey:

- "They promised to help me with my bills, and I haven't heard from them. It has been three weeks."
- "The person I talked to was rude. He told me I needed to get a real job."
- "I talked to three people about how to apply for help with my utility bills. One told me to talk with the utility company; another one told me I had to have my utilities cut off before I could get help; and a third person told me all the money was gone for this month."
- "I have been to every agency in this town. No one cares about me or my kids."
- "I was told to talk with the utility company, and when I did, they said there was nothing they could do without a client number from the agency."
- "I have been sitting here for two hours while they go for coffee, lunch, and have phone calls from boyfriends."
- "The receptionist acted like I didn't know anything after ignoring me when I first arrived. After talking with the director, I was right after all. I was just missing one form and the receptionist had a copy of it."
- "When I walked in, the girl at the desk took one look at what I was wearing, frowned and walked into another office. I waited five minutes before anyone even spoke to me."
- "I saw the guy who seems to be in charge reach into the cash drawer and give a good looking woman $20.00. I never saw him write anything down. When I got up to the counter, they told me there wasn't any more cash for anything. I just wanted a hot meal."
- "My Meals-on-Wheels has been late every day for the past three weeks. Every time, they tell me the truck broke down, had a dead battery, or the driver didn't show up on time."

Does any organization receiving this feedback need to listen, or are these people just trying to get something for nothing?

If a nonprofit agency is seen by those whom it serves as deficient in meeting expectations, delivering service, or developing effective policies, that organization is in deep trouble. This is even true when the need for the organization is great.

■ Typical Customer Expectations

An agency must provide first-class customer service if that agency wants to be admired and respected in its community. What might clients or patrons expect when they ask for help? Regardless of what type of service the nonprofit renders, the recipients of that service want and need to:

- **Feel welcome** – The agency staff should greet people quickly, and give them a smile and warm eye contact. Even when one is talking with another person on the phone or in person, eye contact can be made and a smile offered, which suggests, "I will be with you in a moment." This can be done nonverbally.
- **Receive timely service** – No one should feel as though their requests are getting in the way of more important things. While some people are impatient to the

point of being rude, most clients will understand some delay if they perceive that a person is very busy and they are at least greeted warmly.

- **Feel comfortable** – Staff members should approach customers verbally and nonverbally. They should not stare at them or talk down to them. There is a delicate balance between collecting information from a person, verbally and nonverbally, in order to direct them to the correct service provider, and looking at someone in a judgmental manner. Practice and skill training helps. Smiling, speaking softly or confidentially, and asking questions help most people feel more comfortable.

- **Experience orderly service** – It is important to explain to the person that there is a progression of events he or she will go through to receive service from the agency. Patrons need an overview of the process before being sent to the first step. This process should be repeated at every step or, at least, the person should be asked if he or she has questions about the next step. As the patron prepares to depart the agency, someone should ask whether all the patron's questions and concerns have been addressed. If the answer is "No," any remaining needs must be determined before he or she leaves the agency.

- **Be understood** – The person in charge should ask questions and should never assume that each person is just like the person before. It is essential to listen attentively to the answers given. To be understood is to be seen and treated as an individual, not a member of a group or class.

- **Be respected** – A staff member should take time with each person, answer all their questions as thoroughly as possible, and assure them that the agency wants to help. A smile is again useful in communicating respect.

- **Receive help or assistance** – Each person should leave with some help or a clear set of steps to follow to receive help from another agency. If he or she is not eligible for assistance, they need to know what they might do to receive relief from their problem.

- **Feel important** – Staff members should remember to ask for names and use them when talking to the person or when introducing them to another staff member. Again, every request should be met with a smile or pleasant disposition. To take care of one person at a time and to be efficient, but not dismissive, will help people feel that they are important to the agency.

- **Be appreciated** – This means to treat people as human beings, not numbers, cases or stereotypes. A genuine smile still goes a long way in achieving this goal. Staff should be friendly.

- **Be recognized and remembered** – It is important to spend the effort necessary to keep track of repeat customers. Staff should use names and remember circumstances and past actions taken by the agency. They should ask clients for progress reports, when appropriate. This is not to pry, but to show genuine interest and show them they are remembered.

Can all expectations ever be met? What if client expectations are not consistent with the agency mission? What if the expectations are valid, but the resources to meet the expectations do not exist? Can every need in every community ever be met? How does an agency decide what to do when there appears to be no clear answer?

■ Balancing Agency Mission and Customer Needs

Finding a proper balance between why an organization exists and what community needs it meets is the key to success. How does an organization keep from drifting from its course?

A motivational poster available from Successories posits the understanding of service that should be placed on the wall of every nonprofit agency in the world: "Service is the lifeblood of any organization. Everything flows from it and is nourished by it. Customer service is not a department ... it's an attitude."

Another, often ignored, truth of customer service is that it is a journey *not* a destination. You never get there. There is always a new demand, a new person or a new problem. For this reason it seems better if customer service were replaced with customer satisfaction. Customer service implies that an agency only needs to check itself against its own mission—are we doing what we say we should do? On the other hand, if an agency focuses on customer satisfaction, the shift of focus points to the recipient of the agency's mission. It is, then, much easier to remember that the territory is always changing, always evolving, always different.

In order to gain the best information for an agency with regard to customer satisfaction, one standard needs to be set: *Not One Unhappy Patron.* It must be understood that reaching this standard is the responsibility of everyone—executive director, staff, volunteers and board members. Further, the standard must be the demonstrated attitude of everyone—executive director, staff, volunteers and board members. It is not enough to believe it; it must be acted out at all times for the message to be communicated clearly. The message is "We value everyone we serve and we want to satisfy your needs."

The proper balance can be achieved by taking the knowledge about the nature of customer dissatisfaction and customer satisfaction to construct a plan of action—a plan that considers agency mission and customer needs. Neither can be ignored; neither can be more important than the other. There must be balance. Balance can only be achieved after careful thought, planning, and consideration of all variables.

■ A Plan to Improve Satisfaction

Davidow and Uttal (1989) describe a **six-point plan** for gaining the competitive edge in terms of customer satisfaction from a business point of view. First, let's look at their plan, and then we'll look at specific application of that plan to the nonprofit sector. Here is their plan:

1. **Devise a service strategy.**

   This entails dividing customers into categories of service expectations, finding out what those customers expect, and transforming those expectations to match the services you can deliver. This allows an agency to group services or have people develop expertise to meet needs of people with similar needs. It does not mean that the agency is ready for everything, but that the agency should be prepared to handle satisfactorily many or most of their client's needs quickly and efficiently. It also means the agency will have plans concerning how to

handle the difficult situations or even new situations for which there is no specific plan in place. A service provider might say, "Your question is one I have
never been asked. Let me ask the ED/CEO how I can get the information you
need. Will that be acceptable?"

2. **Get top management to behave like customer service fanatics.**
   Agency heads must set the example for outstanding customer service for all
   internal and external customers. If the ED/CEO acts as though customer satisfaction is the most important activity the agency engages in on a daily basis, it
   will be the most important activity. Customer service is not an activity to be
   effectively delegated to one person or an office. It is everyone's job, all the
   time. Maxwell (2001) contends that "one is too small a number to achieve
   greatness" (1).

3. **Concentrate on motivating and training employees.**
   The first step is to hire the right person(s) in the position to be the initial point of
   contact for all customer service. Next, everyone must be trained. People who
   believe in what they do and are well trained to do it succeed. Freiberg and
   Freiberg put it this way, "Hire for attitude, train for skills" (1996, 64). Even with
   the "right" attitude everyone will benefit from training in customer service skills.

4. **Design services that make good customer service possible.**
   For any nonprofit, the key is always to keep in touch with the service provided
   by the agency. There should be constant review of who should be served, why
   and how. The type of services that will most often be needed should be anticipated and a system designed to meet that need efficiently and effectively. Step 1
   is very critical to achieving this step in the plan. If step 1 is well executed, step
   2 will be relatively easy.

5. **Invest in service infrastructure.**
   The agency should make it easy for employees to serve. It should create and
   maintain effective networks of people who can help deliver the services consistent with the agency mission, ensure that necessary facilities and resources exist
   to get the job done well, and arrange access to the necessary information needed
   to support the service mission of the agency. Today, information technology is
   not a luxury; it is a necessity. Computer hardware and software must be sufficient to do the job today and tomorrow. A key is to play for the future, not the
   past, staying ahead rather than trying always to catch up. The American Red
   Cross needs local, regional, and national network connections, while a local
   food bank may not have the same needs. The infrastructure should match the
   needs of the clients.

6. **Monitor achievement of customer service goals.**
   Agencies should measure the success of customer service by asking those who
   receive the service whether they are satisfied. If expectations are unrealistic,
   those receiving services must be educated to limits of the agency's resources.
   At the same time, what is unrealistic today may be imperative tomorrow. For
   this reason, measurement of achievement of customer service goals is central to
   knowing how well an agency is doing today and is the next step in going back to

step 1 of the plan to make adjustments for tomorrow and beyond. Above all, Freiberg and Freiberg (1996) suggest that data like this be used to reveal agency accomplishments and as a basis for honoring those who have excelled.

■ Developing Key Relationships

Building Loyal Relationships with External Customers

Heil, Parker and Stephens (1999) write about **rules for building loyal customer relationships**. Building a relationship from the beginning is always better than trying to recover from bad service. How does an agency build loyal customers when it opens its doors? A nonprofit agency needs to create a **response path** (a way of doing business) that is intended and designed in such a way that service can be provided by the agency to the customers who need the service. Service provided to ensure that an agency has a reason for existing is not justified. Service provided to meet customer needs is the only justifiable reason for existence. Here is how to create an appropriate **response path**:

1. *Decide that the agency's service will be personal.* Train the staff and volunteers to look at each service opportunity as a unique situation with common elements. Use the common elements to construct a response path that will assure that all people are served efficiently and fairly, but a path that allows for individual difference.

2. *Build a response path on the assumption that the agency has no average clients.* Get to know each client and respond to that client's need. As mentioned above, serve individuals.

3. *Create a response path that makes the agency available to clients when they need help the most.* This may mean serving people outside "normal" business hours. If an agency exists to serve, it needs to serve others, not itself.

4. *Promote and display a response path that involves every member of the agency – ED/CEO, staff and volunteers.* If an organizational member is not building positive relationships with clients, he or she is creating negative moments for the clients. Everyone in an agency has some contact with clients. There is no such thing as a neutral contact with a customer.

5. *Carry out the response path in such a way that everyone can leave the agency happy and have his or her needs met.* Put people first—internal and external clients. Budgets are important and necessary, but most nonprofits exist to serve people. Programs are convenient and efficient ways to serve several people at once, but if they are not meeting needs, they might benefit from revision or replacement.

6. *Execute a response path with efficiency.* Show customers that their time is as valuable as any other person's. Efficiency should never take the place of meeting needs. Sometimes "quickly" is not efficient. Take the necessary time but do not waste time.

7. *Create a response path that is reviewed, critiqued, and revised regularly, so that it is responsive to changing client needs.* If something does not work, find out what is wrong and fix it. When a program is working, examine it to see if it

could be more beneficial at other times, with other audiences, or combined with other programs from other nonprofits.

8. *Provide a response path that will assure people that their legitimate needs will be met, that someone will work with them until the agency has exhausted its options and available resources.* Meet needs; don't just deliver services. Be persistent; don't give up at the first obstacle. Be assertive; don't accept the first rejection.

9. *Carry out the response path so that no one is taken for granted.* No matter how many times a service provider has dealt with a specific problem, it may be the first time for the service recipient. Be patient. Find out whether there are complicating problems or mitigating circumstances. Do not assume; verify perceptions and preliminary conclusions.

10. *Perform all agency activities so that the community knows that the agency is a part of the community—a responsible citizen.* Don't insulate the agency from other agencies that help people. Help the United Way with its work for the community of nonprofit agencies. Help them raise funds for all agencies receiving funds from the United Way. Take part in community-wide activities—parades, festivals and community service projects.

Creating a Motivational Environment for Employees

In the second half of their book, Heil, Parker and Stephens (1999) develop **rules for building the kind of working environment that motivates staff and volunteers to develop a customer service mindset.** In order for people to serve others consistently with conviction and enthusiasm, they must believe that the organization they work for treats them as well as it does those being served by the agency's mission. For a time, anyone can deliver a caring attitude when he or she believes that what is being done is important; eventually that caring attitude will fade if the atmosphere in the agency does not support a caring attitude. In short, it is not enough to provide a valuable and needed service; all agencies must  "walk their talk" with clients **and** service providers (staff and volunteers). Here are some suggestions for developing a supportive climate for staff and volunteers (the second set of agency customers).

1. *Create and adjust the agency way of doing things so that everyone's best efforts are encouraged.* Two critical ingredients in doing this involve the promotion and support for teamwork and the empowerment of staff and volunteers to use their knowledge and motivation to maximum benefit for the organization. Maxwell (2001) refers to this as the law of the big picture and suggests a method of assessing what an organization does. The six components can serve to guide

an organization through the process of monitoring its activity to see that everything is being done for the *right* reasons and to the *right* end.

His suggestions are:

    a. LOOK UP at the big picture
    b. SIZE UP the situation
    c. LINE UP needed resources
    d. CALL UP the right players
    e. GIVE UP personal agendas
    f. STEP UP to a higher level.

(Maxwell 20-24)

These six points for analysis should be employed continuously to test the validity of what any organization does and how it does it. This is even more crucial for nonprofit organizations than for others.

2. ***Check and re-check the agency mission to see that it is and continues to be commendable.*** Blanchard, Carlos and Randolph (1996) contend that "the kind of thinking that led to past success will not lead to future success" (2). A mission rarely examined or questioned is a mission that will soon fail to guide an agency to success. Freiberg and Freiberg (1996) advocate examining mission as a way to preserve what the agency values.

3. ***Establish, discuss and symbolize the agency's core values.*** Make every effort to share these core values with all external and internal customers. Maxwell (2001) asserts that shared values give definition to a team. In addition, vision gives team members (staff and volunteers) direction and confidence. A vision apart from core values is doomed to fail. Most people remember what they see or are able to visualize. For that reason, symbols that can be associated with core values help to unify people and efforts with the agency.

4. ***Be truthful and real in everything done in the agency, by the agency and for the agency.*** Give people accurate information and expect appropriate results. Blanchard, Carlos and Randolph (1996) make two salient observations: (1) a key to empowerment is to share information with everyone (29); and (2) people with information are compelled to act responsibly, but people without information cannot act responsibly (34). Maxwell (2001) puts it this way, "interaction fuels action" (193).

5. ***Ensure that every person associated with the agency, in any and all roles, has something meaningful to do.*** Having the correct body count is of little value if the important and necessary work is not getting done. The cost and reward for having the wrong people in place versus having the right people in place is pictured by Maxwell (2001) in the following formulas:

The Wrong Person in the Wrong Place	=	Regression
The Wrong Person in the Right Place	=	Frustration
The Right Person in the Wrong Place	=	Confusion
The Right Person in the Right Place	=	Progression
The Right People in the Right Places	=	Multiplication

(Maxwell 33)

An agency can explode in its service to the community when it gets the right people in the right places doing the right things. This tends to happen when people have meaningful work to do, when they know why they are doing it and they know where to get the support they need to change the things that should be changed to keep the organizational vision vital and dynamic.

6. *Hold everyone accountable for what they do.* Extend and enhance their accountability in reasonable ways, not just by adding more work. Every nonprofit agency should promote continuous learning. Freiberg and Freiberg (1996) contend that people stay fresh and grow when they "learn like crazy" (112).

7. *Demonstrate to everyone inside and outside the organization that cooperation is more valuable than is competition.* Exhibit the motto, "One for all and all for one."

8. *Remove any and all evidence of bureaucracy from the minds and actions of everyone in the agency.* The "organizational caste system" has destroyed too many otherwise "good" organizations. Maxwell (2001) puts it this way, "the goal is more important than the role" (15). The true mark of an organizational leader (ED/CEO) is not how many symbols (big office, reserved parking, private bathroom or a special uniform) he or she can claim. The true mark comes from teaching others things they can do to become less dependent on you (Blanchard, Carlos and Randolph 1996, 64).

9. *Foster a caring, supportive and optimistic environment for all staff and volunteers.* This does not mean an environment without discipline or clear expectations for performance. It means an environment where people are free to act and are accountable for results (Blanchard, Carlos and Randolph 1996, 90). A person not willing to be held accountable is a person who needs to find new employment.

10. *Act in accord with the truism that trust is built one person at a time.* No ED/CEO can build trust with his or her staff except by doing it one person at a time. Trust is often built when people are free to learn without being punished for mistakes. An organization where people trust each other is an organization where people might be heard to say, "Every 'mistake' is an opportunity to increase competence" (Blanchard, Carlos and Randolph 1996, 78). Investing in people is never a cost; it always returns compounded rewards.

■ How to Assure Satisfaction

Attitude

One of the most successful customer-satisfaction-centered organizations in the history of the United States is the Disney organization. All employees of Disney are trained, trained and trained in the Disney Way. The Disney Way is a product of extensive observation and study. Connellan (1997) discusses the **seven keys** to **Disney's success** in the area of customer satisfaction:

1. The competition is anyone your guests compare you with.
2. Always pay fantastic attention to every detail.

3. Everyone must walk the talk.
4. Everything must walk the talk, even the bathrooms.
5. Guests are best heard through many ears.
6. Recognize, reward and celebrate.
7. Everyone makes a difference.

Zsa Zsa Gabor, whose movie and television career spanned the 60s and 70s and who was known for having extensive interest in men and being married many times, is reputed to have said, "To have twenty lovers in one year is easy. To have one lover for twenty years is difficult." The wisdom of her observation can be applied to customer service. Many agencies find it easy to build short-term relationships with clients and funding sources. What is difficult is sustaining long-term relationships with both clients and supporters. If a client is helped by an agency, why not keep track of that person? If need more help becomes necessary, it should be provided. If the person does not need help, perhaps he or she knows of someone else who does. In other words, the person can be drawn into the vision of the organization. This is a similar concept to one employed by Habitat for Humanity—anyone who has a home built for them has to do some of the work. If people who are helped by an agency are drawn into the vision of that agency, they should find it easier to have a sustained relationship.

This can also be true for funding sources. An agency begins by showing a need. Then it reports what the funds were used for, demonstrates a continuing need, documents the recurrent value of the funds, and always recognizes the growing value of the sustained relationship between the agency and the funding source: they are growing together.

Action

How can an agency deliver service that satisfies clients, patrons, guests or customers? The research in this area points to four variables: **sensitivity**; **sincerity**; a warm, **positive attitude**; and **effective interaction skills** as judged by the recipient of the service. Anyone can improve with respect to any or all four variables. Here is **how a successful service provider behaves**:

- Smiles often, having a cheerful outlook and a positive attitude toward people.
- Genuinely enjoys working with and for other people.
- Puts the person receiving service on "center stage" rather than trying to be there too.
- Has high energy and enjoys a fast pace of activity.
- Acts like a human-relations professional.
- Enjoys new experiences and demands and is willing to demonstrate flexibility.
- Allows guests to be right, even on those occasions when they are not.
- Controls his or her anger, even when the client is out of line.
- Apologizes for a mistake, even if he or she didn't make it.
- Enjoys helping others.
- Listens actively.

A person always needs to ask, "How would I feel if I were treated this way?" That is always a good starting point. However, each person also needs to ask, "How do I think others would feel if they were treated this way?" George Washington Carver is reputed to have observed that, "When you can do the common things of life in an uncommon way, you will command the attention of the world." In fact, satisfactory customer service is just doing common things uncommonly well. If an agency wants to **keep** its **customers happy**, here are **10 sure-fire ways** to do just that:

1. Always be pleasant to customers, even if they are not pleasant to you.
2. Smile even during those times when you don't feel like it.
3. Go "above and beyond" to care for every customer.
4. Welcome customer suggestions about how you could improve your service.
5. Graciously receive and handle any and all complaints or problems.
6. Roll with the punches, accepting bad news or harried schedules with calm and a smile.
7. Strive to provide service that exceeds what customers expect from you and your agency.
8. Offer suggestions and/or guidance when a customer asks for your thoughts, but be sure not to exceed the authority of your position.
9. Carefully and thoroughly explain what the customer needs to know and how to do what he or she needs to do to receive full service from your agency.
10. Follow through to ensure that your commitments to customers are honored. If they are not, do what you can to correct the situation by finding out if the reason for the breakdown could have been avoided by greater care on your part.

Moments of Truth

Every organization lives and dies in terms of its *moments of truth*. Moments of truth are those moments when a person makes a qualitative judgment about an agency or organization. It can be when they conclude that they are not being treated with respect. It can be when someone goes beyond what they expect in terms of meeting their needs. It can be when a program is canceled and there is no public notification. It can be when an agency finally starts a program to meet a longstanding need in the community.

If the moment of truth is positive, the long-term result will be positive. An agency would do well to collect positive moments of truth and share them with important stakeholders. Unfortunately, people who experience the positive moment of truth often fail to share the experience. They tend to assume that a positive experience should be expected and is deserved.

If the moment of truth is negative, the long-term result will be negative, and its impact will be multiplied many times over. The negative moment of truth will be shared with anyone who will listen. As with most things in human nature, bad news spreads further and more quickly than does good news.

■ Summary

Customer service or customer satisfaction is about keeping people happy by meeting or exceeding their expectations for service. For nonprofit agencies, this is as important, or more important, than it is for for-profit organizations. It is not a question of making a profit; it is a question of reason for being. If a nonprofit is organized to serve people, and the people being served are not having their needs met, the agency has little reason to exist.

Concerns can come from those being served (external stakeholders) or those providing the service (internal stakeholders).

Typically, one or more of three areas of concern are involved when clients become dissatisfied: unmet expectations, poor quality service, and/or inadequate or confusing policies. None of these concerns can go without being addressed.

One way to reduce dissatisfaction, according to Davidow and Uttal (1989) is to apply a six-point plan to establish and adjust customer satisfaction efforts. They suggest devising a service strategy; getting everyone to behave like customer service fanatics; motivating and training employees in customer service skills; designing services that make good customer service possible; investing in service infrastructure; and monitoring achievement of customer service goals.

In order to be perceived as providing outstanding customer service, an agency must have staff and volunteers who help clients feel welcome, receive timely service, feel comfortable, experience orderly service, be understood, be respected, receive help or assistance, feel important, be appreciated, and be recognized and remembered. The goal is to have not one unhappy customer.

Heil, Parker and Stephens (1999) offer ten rules for building loyal customer relationships. Those ten rules are listed and amplified.

They also propose ten rules for developing a working environment that helps staff and volunteers deliver outstanding customer service. Those rules are discussed and enhanced with information from John Maxwell and others.

This chapter also explores some successes in customer service drawn from the Disney Way. Finally, the chapter ends with some suggestions as to how a person should behave in the presence of others, if the desire is to be perceived as one who believes in customer satisfaction.

This chapter addressed, in part, the American Humanics Certification Competency Requirements of Communication Skills, Personal Attributes, General Nonprofit Management, Nonprofit Marketing and Nonprofit Program Planning.

■ Discussion Questions

1. Why should a client's wants (not needs) be considered when assessing the success of a nonprofit agency?
2. What is the role of client needs in assessing the success of an agency?
3. Discuss the difference between external and internal organizational customers.
4. Discuss ways to find out whether an agency's services are being delivered well and whether the service is being well received by customers.
5. How do leadership qualities influence an agency's delivery of effective customer service?
6. Why is it important for an agency to have loyal clients or service recipients?
7. Why is it important for an agency to provide a supportive working environment for staff and volunteers?
8. What are five things all nonprofit agencies should do to provide appropriate and effective customer service?

9. What is the limit, if any, on a nonprofit agency's participation in the community it serves?
10. Discuss the role of core values in an agency's performance of its mission.
11. Discuss what is required for outstanding customer service.
12. Discuss what should be done if customer needs and agency mission conflict.

■ Activities

1. Visit a local nonprofit service provider. Present yourself as a person desiring to learn more about the service or services they provide. After your visit, write a 2-5-page paper assessing the quality of the agency's service based solely on the way you were treated and the information you received. Use principles from this chapter as the criteria for your evaluation.
2. Interview someone who has worked at Disneyland or Disney World and ask them to describe how the Disney organization goes about establishing their "service" culture. Another option would be to invite someone from Disney to speak to the whole class on the subject of the Disney service culture.
3. Spend an entire day (8-10 hours) living and acting as a customer service person. Do everything possible to be of service to everyone who crosses your path.
4. Do a World Wide Web search to find 10-15 statements from famous people about service to others or customer service.
5. Design an orientation program for volunteers to teach them the core values of the nonprofit for which you work (create your own nonprofit or choose an existing agency from your community).
6. Work in groups to develop motivational sayings using the four letters: TEAM (e.g., **T**ogether **E**veryone **A**chieves **M**ore).

■ References

Blanchard, K., Carlos, J. P., and Randolph, A. (1996). *Empowerment Takes More than a Minute*. San Francisco, CA: Berrett-Koehler Publishers.

Connellan, T. K. (1997). *Inside the Magic Kingdom: Seven Keys to Disney's Success*. Austin, TX: Bard Press.

Davidow, W. H., and Uttal, B. (1989). *Total Customer Service: The Ultimate Weapon*. New York: HarperCollins.

Freiberg, K., and Freiberg, J. (1996). *NUTS!: Southwest Airlines' Crazy Recipe for Business and Personal Success*. Austin, TX: Bard Press.

Heil, G., Parker, T., and Stephens, D. C. (1999). *One Size Fits One: Building Relationships One Customer and One Employee at a Time*. 2nd ed. New York: John Wiley and Sons.

Maxwell, J. C. (2001). *The 17 Indisputable Laws of Teamwork*. Nashville, TN: Thomas Nelson.

Wood, J. T. (1995). *Relational communication: Continuity and change in personal relationships*. Belmont, CA: Wadsworth.

9 Career Development and Exploration: Now and the Future

The purpose of life is not to be happy. It is to be useful, to be honorable, to be compassionate, to have it make some difference that you have lived and lived well. — Ralph Waldo Emerson

The need for qualified professionals in the nonprofit sector is growing at an incredible rate and is expected to continue for several years. Working in a nonprofit organization and developing programs that enhance people's lives is one of the most important and exhilarating careers available. Deciding which organization to work with, and then obtaining a position with that organization, however, can sometimes be confusing and frustrating (Weis 1996).

This chapter helps anyone to assess his or her interests and skills relevant to nonprofit organizations and to learn about specific nonprofit organizations. It also demonstrates processes for developing effective résumés, refining networking skills, writing compelling cover letters, developing dynamic interviewing skills and learning strategies for assessing job offers. There are two critical aspects of career development and exploration. One centers on individual needs for a clear career plan and a view toward the future. The other revolves around organizational needs for specific and general skills and knowledge. In addition, this chapter will explore both individual and organizational issues related to career preparation and planning, as well as how to look to the future and be prepared to alter career paths, both for individuals and for an organization. Finally, this chapter's content can also assist students and current agency employees in organizing professional development strategies to meet short-term and long-term career goals.

What a person values largely determines how he or she will approach career development and career options. Is salary more important than what is being done? Is making a difference in the life of just one person enough? Is helping people more important than the pay scale? Arthur Ashe, tennis professional and founder of the Arthur Ashe Institute for Urban Health, put the issue in these words: "From what we get, we can make a living; what we give, however, makes a life."

The one preeminent word in finding and excelling in a career is: **connectedness**. A person must know or discover the connections between and among the following four areas:

1. Abilities – These are the things a person does well, one's natural skills. They could include the ability to talk with anyone, the ability to help people avoid conflict, the ability to show compassion for people who are hurting, the ability to run fast, or the ability to speak in public with little fear of failure.

2. **Interests** – These are the things a person enjoys doing. These items could include enjoying working outdoors, working with one's hands, working alone, working with people, working in stressful situations, working in a highly predictable position, or working at night.

3. **Learned skills** – These are the things a person has learned to do well. They could include anything from the abilities list that does not come naturally. A person can learn public speaking skills, learn to show compassion, or learn to help people manage conflict. In addition, people can learn budgeting skills, programming skills, fundraising skills or other technical skills.

4. **Interaction styles** – This refers to the way people like to communicate, the way they like for others to communicate with them. The consequences of a person's style determine how effective a person is as judged by others.

All four of these areas, along with all written correspondence, the résumé, networking contacts and interview content must be connected in order to *tell your story*. All the steps and materials prepared to support all applications for employment must be connected to each other. It is in this **connectedness** that an applicant gains power over those who see each step as an individual activity.

Abilities provide the natural base for any career. They set the stage for success. What a person cannot do limits options just as what a person can do creates options. A person with no compassion for the plight of the poor is ill advised to look at careers in the nonprofit sector. It should also be noted that because a person is good at something does not mean he or she would be happy doing that for a career. A person who runs fast may not like training well enough to commit to the preparation necessary to become an Olympic class athlete. For that reason, abilities must be combined with other qualities to determine the best career match for each person.

Interests should drive a person's search for a challenging career path. The other three factors are very important, but if a person has little genuine interest in an area of work, there will be little real reward. A statement attributed to Confucius offers sage advice: "Choose a job you love, and you will never work a day in your life."

Learned skills emerge from the knowledge of what a person **needs** to be able to do in order to combine natural abilities and interests to insure greater chances of success in a desired career. These skills are learned through career-related experience and specific, focused training.

Interaction styles reflect how a person prefers to communicate and interact with others. It is clear to anyone who has lived more than a few years that not everyone likes to give and receive information in the same way. Some people find teasing to be a sign that they are liked by others, but some are offended by any teasing. Some people desire the blunt, straightforward presentation of messages. Some people want messages presented diplomatically and indirectly. There are several tools for assessing interaction styles and the implications of each style. Some of those tools are discussed later in this chapter.

■ The Career Decision Process

It is important to understand the decision-making process relevant to career planning and to develop a strategy for making effective decisions. The *Flowchart for Career Planning* in Figure 9.1 can assist anyone in making informed career decisions. In order to minimize the confusion and frustration, substantial career research is required. There are two major areas in which to develop and assimilate information for an effective career decision. The *Self-assessment Profile* area should include information regarding abilities, values and lifestyle, interests, and interaction style. The *Organizational Exploration* area should include information on professional settings and qualifications for positions in various nonprofit organizations. See **Appendix A** for an extensive list of national nonprofit organizations.

It is also important to select someone who is knowledgeable in career planning to assist in the assessment process. This individual should be an academic advisor; a counse-

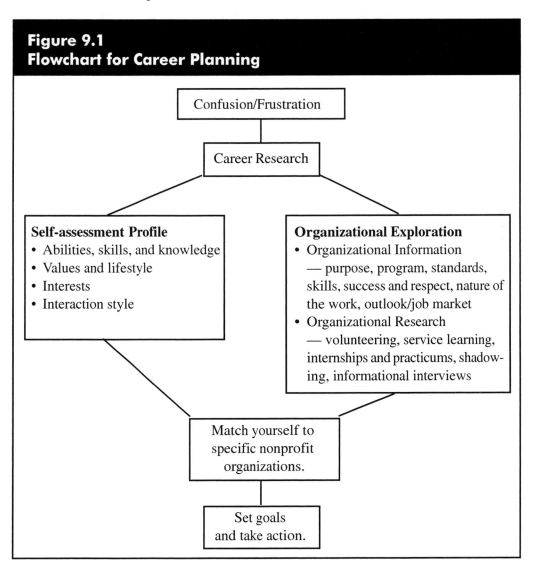

Figure 9.1
Flowchart for Career Planning

Confusion/Frustration

Career Research

Self-assessment Profile
- Abilities, skills, and knowledge
- Values and lifestyle
- Interests
- Interaction style

Organizational Exploration
- Organizational Information
  — purpose, program, standards, skills, success and respect, nature of the work, outlook/job market
- Organizational Research
  — volunteering, service learning, internships and practicums, shadowing, informational interviews

Match yourself to specific nonprofit organizations.

Set goals and take action.

lor with career services; a coordinator of youth, human service, or service learning programs; or any individual who is skilled in the area of career development. For students, the chair of an academic department or dean of an academic college should be contacted for suggestions on the appropriate advisor. For nonprofit professionals, it would be wise to contact a person who has been successful in nonprofit work. It is critical to choose a person who will take the necessary time to advise, review drafts of written work, and assist in planning for interviews.

Using the *Flowchart for Career Planning* reduces confusion and frustration, provides a structure for career research and allows for informed decisions based on specific goals and clear action steps. The process works. As stated earlier, the two major stages in the career research process are the self-assessment profile and organizational exploration.

Self-assessment Profile

Like anything worthwhile, choosing a career path requires a good deal of time and commitment. Self-assessment processes can be useful in determining the right career path. Many of the following assessments can be taken at college and university career planning and placement centers, or at student development offices. Some of the more popular and useful self-assessment processes include the following:

A. **Personality Mosaic** – Based on the work of psychologist and vocational counselor, John Holland, the Personality Mosaic is an assessment tool that takes approximately an hour to complete. It takes about thirty minutes to complete its ninety questions and another thirty minutes to interpret the results.

Holland theorizes that there are six major personality types, or a combination of two or more types, and the Personality Mosaic provides a profile of a person based on these results. The Personality Mosaic is a simple assessment, and students generally report the instrument is accurate based on personal observation.

The assessment is included in the career handbook *Coming Alive from Nine to Five* by Betty Neville Michelozzi. (Check college or university libraries before purchasing a copy.)

B. **Strong-Campbell Interest Inventory (SCCI)** – The SCCI is also based on the work of John Holland. It contains over three hundred items requiring a "like," "indifferent" or "dislike" response. These items are then divided into groups of professional occupations, academic disciplines, activities, amusements, and types of people.

The individual results are compared to successful individuals in over seventy occupations. Occupations are grouped into the same six categories used by the Personality Mosaic: Realistic, Investigative, Artistic, Social, Enterprising, and Conventional. Because individual responses are mailed to a testing firm for computerized results, an appointment with the campus career counselor for an interpretation of the results is generally necessary

C. **Discover** - This is a computer-based planning and information system that includes an interest inventory and activities to help identify individual abilities, experience, and values. These variables are then considered relevant to various occupations. The Discover system also contains modules on exploring various occupations, making educational choices, planning careers and making career transitions.

    D. Personal Profile (DiSC) – The DiSC is an interaction styles analysis tool. It is available through Inscape Publishing. This and other tools can be obtained from a number of independent consultants. One of these is Resources Unlimited (online at www.resourcesunlimited.com).

        By choosing (from several sets of adjectives) the adjective which is most like you when you interact with people in a given situation and the adjective which is least like you in the same situation, a profile is shaped. That profile then suggests the consequences of your style of interaction. The profiles allow a person to see not only the consequences of his or her interaction style, but also allows for an understanding of the consequences of another's style, when the two are working together or in a relationship.

    E. Myers-Briggs Type Indicator (MBTI) – The MBTI is an excellent assessment that places individuals in one of sixteen different personality types based on responses to various questions. The MBTI then describes different variables involved, for each personality type, with respect to activities such as choosing a major, studying, playing and relaxing.

        The MBTI includes a list of careers most often chosen by individuals from each of the sixteen personality types, along with a list of careers chosen the least by each personality type.

    Each of the assessment tools above can provide valuable information for self-assessment. The results from each assessment should be discussed with someone who is experienced and competent in interpreting the results. Additional self-assessment activities designed specifically for individuals seeking a career in nonprofit organizations are located in **Appendix B.** The more self-knowledge a person is able to assemble, the better prepared that person is to tell his or her story. Everyone works best in a situation where there is a match between the person and the organization.

Organizational Exploration

    There are a number of effective ways to research and assimilate career information for youth, human service, and other nonprofit organizations. The exploration process that follows concentrates on direct, experience-based techniques for gathering information regarding various careers in nonprofit organizations.

    As the examination of different kinds of organizations begins, it is important for students or nonprofit professionals to have some sense of who they are and the kinds of professional goals each hopes to accomplish. Exploring various organizations can help in understanding their purpose and the kinds of activities professional staff members engage in on a daily basis. First-hand exploration will provide opportunities to see how organizations really operate. This section of the flowchart concentrates on processes for researching organizational information and activities.

    Organizational Information

    A. Purpose – One of the most important aspects of any organization is its purpose

– what the organization stands for. The purpose of each organization varies, but generally speaking, all are designed to enhance the quality of life for specific individuals in specific communities through some sort of program or process. Identifying with the purpose of an organization is one of the essential elements of being comfortable and successful with a career within that organization.

B. Programs – Nonprofit organizations will have a number of programs designed to achieve their purpose. It is equally important to have an idea of the kinds of programs organizations implement to determine whether they are the kinds of programs that would be interesting and challenging to work with.

C. Standards, qualifications, and skills – One should be aware of what an organization expects in the area of educational requirements, certifications, skills and experience in order to prepare to be a viable candidate for a position. One should also be aware of these expectations because the standards and qualifications an organization maintains provide an indication of the level of quality of the organization.

D. Success and respect – Organizations that are consistently successful in achieving their goals in an effective and professional manner maintain a high level of respect in the community. This is an important consideration for employment.

E. Nature of work – Being aware of an organization's mission and programs and having an awareness of the work that individuals do daily to help the organization achieve its mission is essential.

F. Outlook/job market – According to news reports, government and organizational reports, the need for professionals in the youth and human service field increases substantially each year. It is important, however, to research the need for specific positions in certain nonprofit organizations as well as in specific geographical areas.

After information about what the organization claims to do is collected, it is time to get information about how the organization actually works on a day-to-day basis. This is best done by hands-on contact with the organization. The following suggestions help conduct the most important organizational exploration.

Organizational Research

A. Volunteering – Volunteering in a nonprofit organization has numerous benefits. Most importantly, a service is provided to a population in the community who needs assistance. At the same time it's also one of the most direct and effective methods of gaining information relevant to a particular organization. Volunteer opportunities can usually be found through the campus volunteer center or student development office. Included in Appendix A are the names, addresses, phone numbers, and mission statements of a number of national nonprofit organizations. Contacting the national number will help one learn whether there is a local affiliate.

B. Service learning – More and more campuses are developing service learning course work, in which students work in community service projects that incorporate learning objectives. Information can be obtained from an academic counselor or the office of academic affairs to determine which courses these might be. Service learning is a structured and effective way to provide service, learn course content, and receive college credit.

C. **Internships and practicums** – Internships and practicums are an excellent way to learn about an organization. It's a good idea to select an organization that could be of interest as a career choice to initiate an internship or practicum.

D. **Shadowing** – Another way to gain information about an organization is to follow one or several of the employees around for a day or more. This can be an excellent way to determine what individuals do on a daily basis, without a large commitment of time. Organizational leaders are usually willing to accommodate these kinds of requests.

E. **Informational interviews** – It can be helpful to contact an organizational leader and request an interview to obtain information regarding the organization prior to getting involved. Informational interviews are generally more successful when they are done in person, but a phone interview can also be effective if a personal interview is not possible. Potential questions for an interview are listed below:

- What is the mission of the organization?
- Could you tell me a little about the programs?
- How successful has the organization been in accomplishing goals?
- How did you become interested in this field?
- What do you like best about your job? Least?
- What sort of qualities and qualifications do you look for when hiring employees?
- What is the outlook for employment within this organization?

NOTE: After the interview, a thank you note should be sent to the person who granted the interview.

Match and Act

Once an individual's interests and skills have been assessed and specific nonprofit organizations have been researched carefully, it is time to choose target organizations, set goals and design a plan of action. Which organizations are the best matches for your interests and skills? Which organization missions best match your values and style of interaction? What is the best way to approach each organization chosen? Can others help in the process? What is next?

The most important document for career planning is the résumé. What should go in a résumé? How should it look?

The résumé is a one- or two-page summary of educational, service, and work history. In conjunction with the cover letter, it is the document employers typically use to determine whether an individual's qualifications match those of a specific position in their organization. It will determine whom they invite for interviews.

Generally, there are two types of résumés: a chronological résumé, in which various activities are listed by date, with the most recently held position listed first; and a functional résumé, in which skills and supporting activities are presented in segments (there is no emphasis on dates). Since it is the most commonly used, this text concentrates on the preparation of a chronological résumé.

■ The Résumé

Résumés should be divided into three main sections: header information, basic information, and support information. There should be a good deal of white space in the margins to allow an interviewer to make notes. The paper should be white, gray, or off-white and at least fifty percent rag content. This is not the time to use cheap paper. These sections should be included in the résumé in the order they are listed (Figure 9.2). A sample of an effective résumé is included as Figure 9.5, 247 and should be referred to periodically as various sections of a résumé are discussed.

HEADER INFORMATION

Header information is contact information. It must be correct and current. One should

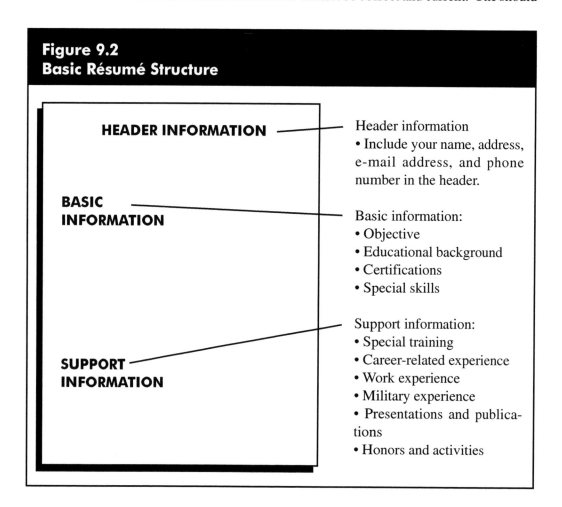

Figure 9.2
Basic Résumé Structure

HEADER INFORMATION

BASIC INFORMATION

SUPPORT INFORMATION

Header information
• Include your name, address, e-mail address, and phone number in the header.

Basic information:
• Objective
• Educational background
• Certifications
• Special skills

Support information:
• Special training
• Career-related experience
• Work experience
• Military experience
• Presentations and publications
• Honors and activities

never list a phone number that will not be regularly answered or does not have an answering machine or voice mail. If an e-mail address is listed, messages should be checked two to three times a day.

The perception of a person's professionalism starts at the top. Font size and style for contact information must be professional. Very large fonts and very graphic or ornate styles detract from the message of a professional image. People who read résumés will be helpful in affirming this advice.

BASIC INFORMATION

This may be the most important section of the résumé because it is what employers see first. The quality and impact of this section may determine whether an employer continues reviewing a résumé further. Research indicates that a résumé will receive a twenty-second glance to see if it deserves further attention (Dawson and Dawson 1996).

Career Objective

The career objective should be listed immediately after the heading of a résumé. If an internship is the objective, rather than a job, the phrase "Internship Objective" can be substituted for this heading. The career objective is important because it enables employers to see the focus of professional intentions and a summary of an individual's strengths. This helps employers identify whether an applicant is truly interested in their field or just applying randomly.

If a person has five or more years of professional experience, career summary can replace career objective. A career summary includes what the professional has been doing and for how long, and it lists some demonstrated personal qualities that would make them attractive to an employer.

Career objectives are frequently made up of two or three phases that form one cohesive statement regarding the career direction someone is interested in pursuing. For the purpose of this discussion, the objective statement is broken down into three sections.

- **First section of the career objective – field-focused phrase**
    The first section of the career objective is most effective when it is focused

---

Figure 9.3
Sample Starters for Field-Focused Objectives

To obtain a position in a health and wellness organization ...
To obtain a position in a performing arts organization ...
To obtain a position in a child care organization ...
To obtain a position in an educational organization ...
To obtain a position in a therapeutic recreational organization ...
To obtain a position in a career development organization ...
To obtain a position in a crime prevention organization ...
To obtain a position in an outdoor recreational organization ...
To obtain a position in an outdoor camping organization ...

on a particular field. A **field-focused** objective is directed toward a specific segment of organizations, and this adds clarity to a résumé. For instance, if someone is interested in working for a youth and human service organization, then the initial portion could be written thus: To *obtain a position in a youth or human service organization.* When they see an indication of the field of interest, employers are much more likely to be interested in a résumé with a field listed that is related to their work. Other sample starters for field-focused objectives are listed in Figure 9.3, 239.

- **Second section of the career objective – skills-related phrase**

  The next section of the career objective statement is specific to the skills an individual brings to the organization. Skills listed here should be ones that have been developed, or are being developed, and should be relevant for the organizations that will receive the résumé. These are skills that occur naturally or have been developed in the classroom, in class projects, during practicums, or internships, or in some other manner. Prospective employers expect college graduates to have acquired skills at a level of expertise required for an entry-level position.

  The skills listed below are ones important to most nonprofit organizations, although the relative importance of each skill varies with each organization and position:

advising	evaluation	program development
analysis	facilitation	problem-solving
communication	financial development	public relations
conflict resolution	financial management	supervising/teaching
counseling	leadership	team development
cultural diversification	marketing	therapeutic assessment

Two or three skills should be listed in the career objective statement. These skills should be realistic and relevant to the job that is being sought. The most important skill should be listed first, and so on. Skills can be listed in several different ways. For instance, it is acceptable to list skills simply by stating: *. . where skills in communication and leadership ... .*

If these skills have been developed significantly through class projects, class projects or some other means, it sounds stronger to include the word "proven" in the statement. For example: *... where proven skills in communication, program development, and leadership ... .*

- **Third section of the career objective – the "why" phrase**

  The third and last section of the statement should be written so there is an implied benefit to prospective employers. The last part of the objective should be stated positively, assertively and in a manner that indicates the organization will be benefited by hiring the applicant. For example: *... can be utilized to assist the organization.*

When these three parts of the career statement are written together, the objective will look something like this:

CAREER OBJECTIVE	To obtain a position in a youth or human service organization where proven skills in communication, program development and leadership can be utilized to assist the organization.

This objective focuses on a particular field, briefly summarizes the applicant's strengths relevant to a prospective employer's needs, and indicates that the applicant wants to make a difference in the employer's organization. The career objective is the first area that prospective employers see, and it provides them with some idea of the applicant's professional intentions, skills, and abilities to organize concepts on paper.

Education

Educational experiences should be included in the basic information portion of the résumé. The following areas are suggested for the education section:

- The institution being attended (or graduated from)
- Location of the institution (city and state only)
- The degree that is being sought or has been acquired
- The date of graduation (or anticipated date of graduation)
- Major and minor fields of study
- Overall grade point average and/or the grade point average in a major – if the GPA is above 3.0 on a 4.0 scale (most career counselors recommend including these averages if they are above a 3.0).
- Any academic honors that are outstanding (for example, graduating magna cum laude or being selected senior of the year in a department).

Although special honors are also included in the Honors/Activities section of the résumé, it is important to list them here as well because it will attract attention sooner and provide more reason to consider a candidacy. Samples of how educational experiences should be listed follow:

If someone has graduated from one institution, here is how it should be listed on a résumé:

EDUCATION	**Murray State University**, Murray, KY Bachelor of Science, May 2004 Health major, Human Services minor GPA 3.93/4.00 GPA in major: 4.00/4.00 Graduated Magna Cum Laude

If a student is graduating in the near future:

EDUCATION	**Missouri Valley College**, Marshall, MO
	Bachelor of Arts, Expected in May 2005
	Health major, Human Services minor
	GPA 3.50/4.00
	GPA in major: 3.65/4.00

If the applicant has attended two different schools:

EDUCATION	**University of Houston**, Houston, TX
	Bachelor of Science, May 2004
	Education major
	GPA 3.21/4.00
	Perry Community College, Perry, KY
	Associates degree, May 2001
	Social Services emphasis

If the applicant has two degrees from the same institution:

EDUCATION	**Clemson University**, Clemson, SC
	Master of Arts in Recreation, May 2004
	Bachelor of Science, May 2000
	Recreation Major

Certifications

Being certified in areas of proficiency relevant to nonprofit organizations is important and should be included on the résumé. Often, certification in various areas is required for a particular job, and prospective employers always look upon this favorably when choosing employees. A list of example certifications is included below:

- American Humanics National Certification
- American Red Cross Basic Life Support (CPR)
- American Red Cross Advanced Lifesaving and Water Safety
- Certified North Carolina Emergency Medical Technician
- State of California Provisional Certification, Grades K-12
- Certified Therapeutic Recreation Specialist
- American Canoe Association Certification

Certifications should be included on the résumé as follows:

| **CERTIFICATIONS:** | American Humanics National Certification
American Red Cross Basic Life Support (CPR)

Since certification is so important to some agencies, it is never too late to become certified in a certain area if it is important or required for a position.

Special Skills

Skills that have been acquired in areas such as computer technology, foreign language, or program development may be included in a special skills section immediately following the certification section. Some examples of special skills are listed below:

- Knowledge of IBM personal computer
- Familiar with WordPerfect and Microsoft Word
- Experience with Power Point and Excel
- Proficient in written and spoken Spanish
- Experience in administering the following tests:
    (List appropriate tests)
- Proficient in program promotion

Special skills should be included on the résumé as follows:

| **SPECIAL SKILLS:** | Familiar with Microsoft Word
Proficient in written and spoken Spanish

Figure 9.4
Common Action Verbs Used in Résumés

Accelerated	Created	Initiated	Reported
Accomplished	Designed	Inspected	Researched
Acquired	Developed	Maintained	Reviewed
Administered	Directed	Managed	Scheduled
Analyzed	Distributed	Minimized	Selected
Appointed	Edited	Modified	Serviced
Arranged	Engineered	Monitored	Started
Assisted	Equipped	Operated	Supervised
Attended	Established	Organized	Surveyed
Combined	Evaluated	Originated	Taught
Completed	Expanded	Planned	Tested
Composed	Facilitated	Prepared	Trained
Conducted	Generated	Presented	Used
Constructed	Guided	Produced	Worked
Controlled	Helped	Recorded	Wrote
Coordinated	Implemented		

SUPPORT INFORMATION

This section should include support information regarding any special training, career-related experience, work experience, military experience, presentations and publications, and honors and activities. All entries should reflect achievements and accomplishments to the degree possible. It is a good idea to show potential employers what to expect, based on past performance and accomplishments.

When listing various experiences, each descriptive statement should begin with an action verb (see Figure 9.4). Each statement should describe an aspect of an experience and should express a level of responsibility, skill, initiative and/or success. Two to four statements for each experience, beginning with the most important to the least important should also be included.

Special Training

This section should include specific knowledge and skill areas that have been acquired through workshops, seminars, special projects, conferences or lecture series. Special training in customer relations, leadership, public relations, finance, first aid, risk management, computer technology. Any area relevant to a field of interest should be included. Each descriptive phrase should begin with an action verb. For example:

> **SPECIAL TRAINING:** **American Red Cross, Tempe, AZ**
> **Disaster Relief Workshop, Spring 2003**
> **Student participant:**
> - Attended lectures on community disaster preparedness and relief strategies
> - Participated in simulated community- wide disaster preparedness and relief activities
> - Awarded competency certificates in disaster preparedness and relief strategies

Career-related Experience

Career-related experiences are those experiences that relate to future professional directions and include experiences from class projects, internships, service learning and volunteer work, and part-time or summer jobs. An example is listed below:

> **CAREER-RELATED**   **YMCA Camp Lakewood, Potosi, MO**
> **EXPERIENCE:**   **Youth Agency Intern/Leadership**
> **Development Coordinator, Summer 2003**
> - Planned and implemented leadership programs for over 500 campers
> - Coordinated the activities of counselors in the delivery of leadership programs
> - Developed evaluation processes to assess camper satisfaction and skill development

Work Experience

Jobs held during the collegiate experience may not be directly related to future professional experiences, but they do represent responsibility and should be included in the résumé. An example is listed below:

> **WORK EXPERIENCE: Red Lobster Restaurant, Shreveport, LA,**
> **Cashier, Summer 2002**
> - Provided customer service and handled financial transactions
> - Initiated and developed a customer assessment process that provided important service information

Military

Military experience may be directly related to a future career direction. It is important to include on a résumé, even if it is not directly related to current career plans:

> **MILITARY**   **U.S. Army, Ft. Monmouth, NJ**
> **EXPERIENCE:**   **Specialist, 4th Class, 1998-2001**
>
> - Supervised a staff of six in the development of monthly newsletters
> - Created a special section advising service men and women of educational opportunities in the community

Presentations and Publications

Presenting formally, conducting research and/or being published indicates a high level of achievement and should be included on the résumé following work experience. For example:

> **PRESENTATIONS:**   Smart, Amy S. (2003). **The Implications of Service Projects for Student Development in Higher Education.** Presented at the American Humanics Management Institute, Orlando, FL.
>
> **PUBLICATIONS:**   Smart, Amy S. (2004). A comparison of the grades of students involved in service learning projects with those not involved. *Journal of Leadership for Youth and Human Services*, 8: 4.

Honors and Activities

Employers want to know about student activities beyond the classroom and if those activities have been successful. Listed below are areas from which activities and honors should be considered:

- Social and service organizations
- Student government
- Student organizations
- Class projects
- Dean's list
- Service awards
- Leadership roles
- Academic activities and awards
- Athletic activities and awards
- Service and volunteer activities

Honors and activities should not be repeated if they appear elsewhere in the résumé. The ones included in this section should be listed in the order of importance, as indicated in the example below:

HONORS AND ACTIVITIES:	Girl Scouts of the U.S.A. – Gold Award
	Dean's List – six semesters
	American Humanics Senior of the Year
	All-Greek 4.0 Award
	Social Work Club
	Alpha Delta Pi Social Sorority

Personal information should not be included in the résumé. A person can unwittingly supply information that is not required or is illegal for the potential employer to ask about. While personal information can be used to establish connection with the interviewer, it can also give the person a reason for disqualification. Most often a résumé is used to knock people out of consideration. The reviewer is looking for a reason to reduce the pile of résumés.

There is also no need to take up space on the résumé to tell the reader that "references are available upon request." This is understood. Use the space for positive information that will increase the value of the résumé to the organization.

Developing a résumé is challenging, but it is an important step in starting a career. Once a résumé is developed, keeping it updated is much easier. The same basic format used for the **Sample Résumé** in Figure 9.5 can be used over and over again, although the "Career-related Experience" section should be renamed "Professional Experience." Various skills, experiences, and certifications will change and will need to be updated as well.

■ Networking

With the self-assessment profile and organizational exploration complete and the résumé in-hand, it is time to consider the most critical step of making productive use of the network to take the next step in the career process. A personal network is crucial.

Often college students are selected for a position from campus interviews or internships, but most individuals must establish a networking and job search campaign to connect with individuals in organizations. Establishing a system of friends, family, and professional acquaintances for encouragement and guidance is of critical importance. Since over sev-

Figure 9.5
Sample Résumé — page 1

AMY S. SMART

Present Address	*Permanent Address*
1405 Sycamore St.	1721 Quarry Lane
Murray, KY 42071	Bath, ME 24112
(270) 759-1833	(213) 475-4678
e-mail: amy.smart@murraystate.edu	

CAREER OBJECTIVE: To obtain a position in a youth or human service organization where proven skills in communication, program development, and leadership will be utilized to assist the organization.

EDUCATION:

Murray State University, Murray, KY
Degree: Bachelor of Science, May 2003
Major: Recreation
Minor: Youth and Human Services

Grade Point Average: 3.93/4.00
Grade Point Average in Major: 4.00/4.00

Graduated Magna Cum Laude

CERTIFICATION:

American Humanics National Certification
American Red Cross Basic Life Support (CPR)

SPECIAL SKILLS: Familiar with Power Point and EXCEL

SPECIAL TRAINING:

Murray Family YMCA, Murray, KY
Risk Management Workshop, Fall 2000
Student Participant

- Attended lectures on all aspects of reducing and managing health and safety risks
- Participated in simulated high-risk scenarios and developed risk management plan

CAREER-RELATED EXPERIENCE:

Camp Wyman, Eureka, MO
Human Services Internship, Summer 2001
Leadership-Challenge Coordinator

- Developed leadership-challenge programs for 500 inner-city children
- Directed the activities of support staff and counselors in delivery of services
- Designed Leadership-Challenge Program Manual as a guide for future staff

Figure 9.5
Sample Résumé — page 2

AMY S. SMART

CAREER
RELATED
EXPERIENCE:

Camp Wyman, Eureka, MO
Human Services Internship, Summer 2001
Leadership-Challenge Coordinator

- Developed leadership-challenge programs
  for 500 inner-city children
- Directed the activities of support staff and counselors
  in delivery of services
- Designed Leadership-Challenge Program Manual as a guide
  for future staff

Boy Scout National Museum, Murray, KY
Recreation Internship, Summer 1999
Challenge Course Coordinator

- Planned and implementing team-building
  activities related to high ropes challenge course
- Developed team-building activities to enhance high ropes
  experience
- Supervised all part-time and full-time challenge course leaders

WORK
EXPERIENCE:

Office of Alumni Affairs, Murray, KY
Murray State University, 2000-2003
Student Worker

- Coordinated alumni-faculty scholarship meetings
- Organized functions and meetings involving the Board of
  Trustees and the Alumni

PRESENTATIONS:

Smart, Amy S. (2003). **The Implications of Service Projects**
for Student Development in Higher Education. Presented at
The American Humanics Management Institute, Orlando, Florida.

HONORS AND
ACTIVITIES:

American Humanics Senior of the Year
Dean's List – six semesters
All Greek 4.0 Award
Sigma Delta Honorary Fraternity
American Humanics Student Recruitment – Chair
Girl Scouts of the U.S.A., 4-H, and YMCA – Volunteer
Recreation Club
Alpha Delta Pi Social Sorority

enty-five percent of all positions are not advertised, it is very important that anyone seeking employment should focus the greatest effort in the area where the unadvertised positions can be found: the network. Networking, simply stated, means using every contact the candidate knows and everyone each contact knows to find the hidden jobs. The following step-by-step approach to networking and job seeking can be helpful:

Step 1 – Understand and Prepare for the Task Ahead

Networking is the process of developing individual connections within professional settings, and promoting your potential as an effective candidate for vacancies. Networking helps people to get to know someone as a professional candidate so they can support that candidate for a position within their organization or someone else's organization. Networking is not actually applying for a job, but campaigning for a position that may be open sometime in the future. Candidates must be prepared for a job search that can be long, frustrating, and expensive. Finding a job is a full-time job.

Step 2 – Develop a List of People and Services

Developing a list of people and services with potential for providing ideas, strategies or leads on career opportunities can be very helpful. The following list of people should be considered for contact:

Category I – People

- Faculty members
- American Humanics Campus/Executive Directors
- Organizational leaders
- Boards of directors members
- Friends and classmates
- Family members
- Former employers
- College and university administrators
- Networking contacts generated from other persons listed above

Category II – Services and Lists

- University/College career planning and placement office
- Organizational vacancy lists (YMCA, Boys and Girls Clubs, etc.)
- Chamber of Commerce
- United Way
- Professional placement services
- Association Directories
- The Internet (Hot Jobs, etc.)
- Newspaper – Classified Ads

Step 3 – Organize a Networking Notebook

One of the most important tools a job candidate can have is a networking notebook, designed to keep records of all the people and organizations contacted during a job search. The notebook can be of immense help in organizing the job search and for future job searches in the years to come. It is also useful when memory fails. Record important data, such as who has been called, who has a résumé, who has provided other contacts, etc.

A thick, lined, spiral notebook can be divided into categories of **People** and **Services** (listed in Step 2). Record keeping should include names, addresses, e-mail addresses, phone numbers, dates, and information on the results of the contact. A loose-leaf, three-ring binder could be used since it makes it easy to move information around to generate a section of "hot" prospects. However, it is easy to lose sheets. This is not good.

Step 4 – Making the Connection

Once the networking notebook is organized, contacts should be made with those individuals or services that are most likely to have information on available professional opportunities. Introductory phone calls should be made explaining that you are beginning a career search and would like to meet with them to get some ideas on a career direction. Sending résumés prior to meeting can be helpful, but it is essential that you take copies of your résumé with you and that you share them with any and all network contacts. Face-to-face meetings are generally best, but a phone or e-mail meeting can also be helpful. A candidate should try to get the names and addresses of at least three people who might be helpful in the job search, and these names and addresses should be recorded in the networking notebook. A thank-you note should always be sent to the contact person after the meeting.

Step 5 – Developing a Support System

Since job searches can be long, frustrating and expensive, it is important to develop a support system from the outset. A candidate must realize that the process can be daunting and that determination is essential. Temporary jobs are sometimes necessary and should be selected with flexibility, so interviews can be scheduled when needed. Family members and friends should be informed of the situation and recruited for support and encouragement. Faculty members, college administrators, career advisors and organizational leaders should also be recruited into the support group. It is important to remain focused and to recognize that the process is normal and that we all survive it.

■ References

Successful organizations carefully screen potential employees by reviewing letters of recommendation and calling references. Potential references should always be asked whether they are willing to be a reference and whether they are willing to write a letter of recommendation. It is necessary to provide each person who agrees to be a reference with a copy of your résumé. It is very appropriate to draft a letter describing how the person knows you, items from your résumé that are related to the job for which you are applying, and personal characteristics that the potential employer can expect from you as an employee. This reduces the risk that a reference might produce a negative response, and it increases **connectedness**.

References may come from a number of areas, including these:

Professors	Advisors
Employers	Administrators
Co-workers	Organizational leaders
Coaches	

Figure 9.6
Sample Cover Letter

2207 Carol Drive
Murray, KY 42071
(270) 371-9897

August 30, 2003

Mr. Brad Simmons
Executive Director
Wilmington YMCA
Wilmington, NC 47501

Dear Mr. Simmons:

I would like to submit my résumé for your consideration for the position of Program Coordinator, which I recently saw advertised in the YMCA Vacancy List. I graduated in May of this year from Murray State University with a major in Therapeutic Recreation and a minor in Youth and Human Services. I am very interested in working for a youth and human service organization.

I believe my educational and career-related experience is ideally suited for this position. As an intern for the YMCA of Jeffersonville, Indiana, I was responsible for supervising the Counselors-In-Training (CIT) program. This program was so successful that I was asked to write the operating manual for the CIT program. I have also had successful program and supervisory experience with the Murray Family YMCA and the American Humanics program at Murray State University (MSU). As the Program Chair For College Day, I successfully organized fellow students in the planning and implementation of a complete day of activities for 8th grade students on the MSU campus. I was recently honored for my accomplishments by being selected the American Humanics Student of the Year. The enclosed résumé lists my qualifications in more detail.

I am very interested in making a career with the YMCA. I am certainly interested in being considered for this position and working with the Wilmington YMCA. Thank you for your consideration, and I look forward to hearing from you in the near future.

Sincerely,

Jeffrey A. Student

Enclosure

Thank you notes or letters should **always** be sent to individuals who agree to serve as a reference. It is never a waste of time to send a thank you note. A handwritten note is best, but a typed one is better than nothing.

The names of references are never included on résumés, but a list of references should be a part of every job search toolkit. One should provide a list of references with name, address, phone number and the nature of their relationship to the applicant. Four or five is enough. No more than one personal reference is necessary. Most employers are interested in professional associations.

■ Cover Letters

The cover letter has several purposes. It serves as a letter of introduction for a résumé, informs individuals in organizations which position a candidate is interested in and provides insight regarding a candidate's experiences and skills. Cover letters should be written specifically for the position that is being applied for. In other words, it should reflect the educational and career-related experiences a candidate has had that are relevant to a particular position.

The cover letter is the first document a prospective employer reads, and it should be well written and error free. There are three main paragraphs that make up the content of the cover letter.

In the first paragraph a candidate should:

- Explain that the résumé is being submitted for review.
- Describe the specific position being applied for.
- Identify oneself in terms of the position.
- Indicate interest in the organization.

The second paragraph is generally the most detailed of the three paragraphs and describes:

- Career-related and educational experiences relevant to the position (taken from the résumé).
- Levels of responsibility, leadership, initiative and successes a candidate may have had with these experiences.

The third paragraph is the concluding paragraph and should:

- Reiterate interest in this type of organization.
- Thank the individual reviewing the material.

The cover letter should include the return address, e-mail address (if applicable), telephone number, and the date as well as the name, title and address of the person to whom the letter is directed. A salutation (greeting) should be used before jumping to the body of the letter. See Figure 9.6, 251 for a sample cover letter.

Tips for Cover Letters

- The same quality and color of paper should be used for the cover letter and the résumé.
- Take every opportunity to **connect** the content of the résumé with the cover letter content.
- The cover letter and résumé should be sent as soon as a position becomes vacant

or a network lead is received.

- Contacting the individual to whom the cover letter and résumé were sent will help insure receipt of the material. This should be done within seven to ten days after the material was sent.
- If possible, set a specific date and time to contact the person to arrange an interview.

∎ Interviewing

The purpose of creating effective cover letters and résumés is to be offered an interview for a position that is of interest. With practice an interview can be as natural as having a conversation with a friend. Without practice an interview can be a professionally devastating experience. A person should prepare for an interview as she or he would for an important exam.

There are two main goals of an interview:

1. First, members of the selection committee or the interviewer want to see if a candidate is as promising in person as he or she seems to be on paper. Interviewers generally take note of dress and appearance, body language and voice, and even a candidate's handshake. As a matter of fact, the first few minutes of an interview are very important in establishing a positive impression. Interviewers are trying to determine whether a candidate seems like someone who can do the job and is someone they might like to work with.

2. An interview also provides the candidate with a chance to discover whether the position and the people who work for the organization are right for him or her. A candidate should ask questions that will help determine if this position is the right position at the right time. The interview is a two-way street. It is just as important for the candidate to be comfortable with the situation and the personnel as it is for the others to be comfortable with the candidate.

Preparation

One of the biggest mistakes most people make is not preparing adequately for the interview. The more an individual knows about the position, the organization, the people who work there, his or her own personal goals and interests, and the interview process, the better chance the individual has of making a positive impression that will result in a job offer. Use of a library or the Internet to research an organization before going for an interview will help to fill in the gaps.

Exploring the Position

Some information regarding the position is already available if the response was to a vacancy notice. Good organizations have clear and comprehensive job descriptions for each position and are usually willing to share these with candidates. A request can be made for a clarification of the job description from the interviewer(s). Asking for more information lets employers know that a candidate is interested in a position, and it provides the candidate with valuable information.

Exploring the Organization

It is important to find out as much as possible about the organization and the people who work there to assist a candidate in deciding whether the organization is worthy of individual commitment. It is also important to gather information about an organization to be knowledgeable in the decision-making process and to indicate to employers that a candidate is taking the position seriously enough to spend time researching the organization. There are several ways to gather information regarding a specific organization:

- Ask for and review a copy of the organization's annual report to get an idea of its goals, programs, and level of support and success.
- Contact the local United Way and ask for information about the organization.
- Contact someone who has received services from or has worked for the organization in the past, and ask his or her opinion of the organization.

Common Interview Considerations

Making the cut to the interview is a major accomplishment in and of itself. It is normal to be nervous at an interview. One of the best ways to calm down before and during an interview is to breathe deeply and slowly. If perspiration under stressful conditions is a concern, bring a handkerchief to the interview. Be aware of nervous habits (like running fingers through the hair or clicking a pen) and eliminate these practices from the interview. Throughout the interview, interviewers need to know that the candidate is enthusiastic about the organization (without being overly zealous) and excited to be considered for the position.

The following categories of information can be helpful in making the interview process a success.

A. **Dress** – Dress should almost always be conservative. Men should wear suits or sport coats and be conservative with the length of their hair and facial hair. Women should wear business suits or a skirt and blouse, and be conservative with make-up, jewelry, lotions and perfumes. This is not the time to express a rebellious side or a creative flare.

B. **Interview Etiquette** – Copies of résumés should be brought to the interview for everyone, even though they may already have copies. Candidates should arrive at the interview fifteen to twenty minutes early. The following etiquette is suggested:

- Shake hands firmly (without excessive force) with each person involved in the interview.
- Always make eye contact when speaking with someone.
- Sit straight (yet comfortably) in a chair, and occasionally lean forward when emphasizing important points.
- Speak clearly and distinctly.
- Always express respect for the interviewers and the organization.

C. **Questions That May be Asked** - There is no rule on the number of questions that screening committee members can ask, so a candidate should be prepared to answer almost anything. Employers will sometimes present questions based on a specific problem scenario and ask how it can be solved. It is important to answer questions honestly, clearly, and as intelligently as possible. The following are standard questions asked in interviews.

- Tell me a little about yourself.
- Why do you want to work for this organization?
- What experience have you had that prepares you for this position?
- In what areas would you need to improve to be successful in this position?
- Describe a problem you've had in a career-related situation and tell us how you solved it?
- What would you hope to accomplish in this position?
- Why should we hire you for this position rather than someone else?
- What would you like to be doing professionally five years from now?

The first question in the list above is the most common and potentially the most deadly question asked in an interview. It is easily answered. It is an opportunity to focus the rest of the interview. It is an opportunity often squandered. An answer for this question should be practiced over and over. The question should be answered with a two- to four-minute response containing the following items:

- **The candidate's early history** (especially anything that relates to the position being applied for, such as interests and skills developed or nurtured)
- **Education** (with special focus on job related aspects – internships, etc.)
- **A brief description of career-related experience** (as much as possible, connect to the position being applied for)
- **How that experience qualifies the candidate for the position** (explain why you are a good match for the job)
- **Close the answer with a thank you for the opportunity to interview** (if it is the first or second question asked).

Too many people give their whole life history or say, "There isn't much to tell." Neither response gets jobs. A carefully thought-out answer **connects** the interviewee's training and experience with the job qualifications.

D. **Questions a Candidate May Wish to Ask. –** It is important for a candidate to ask good questions in order to have as much information as possible and to express a sense of knowledge and organization to the screening committee. The following questions should be considered during the interview:

- Why is this position open?
- What were the strong points of the person who last held the position?
- What exactly would be my responsibilities in this position?
- Who will be my supervisor?
- Could you describe his/her/your leadership style?
- Will I be supervising anyone, and if so, whom?
- Would you explain what a typical day would be like?
- What kind of person are you looking for?
- Would I have some flexibility to create new programs?
- Do you anticipate any changes for the organization in the future?
- What resources are available to me to do my job?
- Is further training and/or education available?
- How and when will I be evaluated?

• When can I expect to hear from you?

Questions regarding salary and benefits should never be mentioned in a first interview, unless the subject is introduced by someone else. There will be an appropriate time to do this.

E. **Practice, Practice, Practice** – No one ever did anything well without a lot of practice, and interviewing is no exception. Simulated interviews with a teacher or administrator can be very helpful. **Appendix C** contains an *interview simulation critique form*, which is useful in practice.

F. **Following the Interview** – A thank-you letter should be sent to the screening committee chair immediately following the interview. If the screening committee does not make contact within the designated time frame, a phone call may be appropriate.

■ Assessing Job Offers

An effective networking and job search campaign eventually culminates in job offers. The tendency for many people is to accept the first offer they receive. But accepting an offer without carefully evaluating it could be a major mistake. One should create a list of all the important variables to consider in choosing a position, and then assign weight to each variable in keeping with one's own values and the values of those affected by this choice. As offers come in, each offer can be objectively evaluated in light of the list. This process will produce a better decision. There are several areas to resolve before a job offer is finalized:

• **Salary and Benefits** – Key benefits often included in a traditional benefits package include health insurance, life insurance, vacation and sick leave, a pension plan, tax shelters, and continued training and educational opportunities. Other benefits may include dental care, eye care, day care, and discounted or free facility use, if a facility is involved. When discussing benefits such as health or life insurance, candidates should ask what percentage of the costs they must pay versus what the employer pays.

• **Salary Negotiation** – If the demands of the job appear to outmatch the salary, or if the candidate thinks that the organization should offer more money for his or her skills and experience, the candidate may decide to negotiate for a higher salary. This can be done by explaining that he or she will accept the position at the salary offered, but that a higher salary (specific) would be more desirable for whatever the reason. Another option is to explain to the employer that the offer is appreciated, but it can only be accepted at a higher salary (again, be specific). This second option is obviously a risky strategy, and the candidate should be prepared for the possibility that the offer will be withdrawn.

Responding to Job Offers

Once a job has been offered and accepted, it is wise to send an acceptance letter. Acceptance letters are important because they provide written documentation regarding the acceptance of the job offer. They also provide an opportunity for clarification of the job offer. Besides, following up with a written letter of acceptance is the expected and courteous thing to do.

If a decision is made to turn down a job offer, it is also important to send a letter of rejection. This letter expresses consideration to the employer, and it helps keep the door open for future possibilities.

∎ Professional Development
Training and Education

One of the most important aspects of developing professionally is to involve oneself in as many training and educational opportunities as possible. Good organizations offer numerous in-service training workshops or provide opportunities to attend training workshops elsewhere. Good organizations also encourage employees to continue their formal education, and some even pay for all or part of advanced educational pursuits. In the final analysis, training and education are not job benefits; they are personal necessities. They must be pursued, whether the organization provides them or they come at personal expense.

Professional Associations

Professional associations can be extremely helpful. They frequently offer support through a number of educational and informational workshops. They can also be helpful for career advancement opportunities. A person is not a professional if he or she is not connected with other professionals. Again, professional associates are not an option; they are a necessity.

Community Responsibility

Nonprofit leaders should always strive to have the best organization, with the best programs, and the best support systems possible. Of equal importance, leaders should strive to have the best relationships with colleagues, organizational members, volunteers, and other community members.

Leaders should also become involved in as many activities sponsored by the organization as possible. Most organizations are like big families. It is important for leaders to get to know and understand people in the organization.

Becoming involved with other organizations as a volunteer or as an interested community member is a good idea. "Practice what you preach" helps leaders remember to offer assistance to organizations other than their own. It is rewarding and fun, and it will ultimately benefit one's organization and career as well.

Just as it is important to continue learning and growing professionally, it's also important to balance professional pursuits with personal activities and responsibilities. Reserving quality time for oneself, family and friends is important. It helps to provide the support and strength needed to be a successful, professional leader.

An appropriate concluding statement for this chapter is found in another of those Successories motivational posters: "Great achievements are not born from a single vision but from the combination of many distinctive viewpoints. Diversity challenges assumptions, opens minds and unlocks potential to solve any problem we may face."

A wise person will spend five percent of every day preparing for the next step in his or her career—promotion, new employer, career change or retirement. Abraham Lincoln reportedly passed along this insight: "I do not think much of a man who is not wiser today than he was yesterday." To be totally content with today is to be foolish. The wise person positions himself or herself for the next bend in the road. A curve in a person's career path is not a disaster unless he or she fails to make the turn.

■ A Final Thought

Here are **20 suggestions for personal success** adapted from a list by H. Jackson Brown, Jr.:

- Enjoy your work and work to make a difference in the lives of others.
- Be cheerful as you work to exceed the expectations of others.
- Do everything in your life with enthusiasm.
- Always forgive yourself.
- Forgive others.
- Be grateful and say "Thank You" often.
- Never, ever give up.
- Treat others as you think they wish to be treated.
- Practice constant personal improvement.
- Set the highest standards of quality for yourself and others.
- Look for happiness in your relationships with others.
- Be fair to everyone.
- Establish honesty as your best policy.
- Stay busy; don't wait for orders to do what needs to be done.
- Be strong and courageous.
- Act rather than react.
- Don't blame anyone for your own actions or the actions of others.
- Be mindful of others.
- Serve those you love and who love you.
- Do everything to bring honor and glory to those you love.

■ Summary

Success in career planning begins with a through knowledge of self. Without self-knowledge and understanding, planning a career and find a job is confusing and frustrating. The *Flowchart for Career Planning* reduces the confusion. The process begins with the construction of a *Self-assessment Profile,* ideally using more than one assessment tool. The next step involves organizational exploration by first collecting information about the purpose and scope of the organization. Then, one must do organizational research, which includes collecting data from volunteering, service learning experiences, internships, staff shadowing or informational interviews.

With a specific direction in mind and potential target organizations chosen, the next step is résumé construction. This is usually the most important step in the process. A résumé is a one- to two-page document providing a summary of education and experience. An effective résumé helps to get an interview. It must be error-free and completed before any other steps are taken.

The next step is personal and professional networking. This involves using contacts to locate potential positions and developing leads for open positions. Each person needs a copy of the résumé.

References need to be contacted based on their knowledge of the candidate's work experience and training. It is helpful for each reference to receive a résumé and a draft of a letter that they might be comfortable sending on behalf of the candidate. References often come from a person's professional network.

With a résumé constructed and contacts from networking activities in place, cover letters can be constructed to convey to potential employers how the candidate can meet the needs of the targeted organizations. These letters are specific but contain three basic paragraphs: a personal introduction of the candidate; an indication of which position is of interest and how the candidate qualifies for that position; and an expression of interest in moving forward with the employment process, along with a thank you for the agency's consideration. This too must be carefully written and error-free.

If all goes well, the next step is the interview. If effective preparation occurs, an interview can be an enjoyable experience. For all candidates, the same rules apply: Carefully collect background information on the target organization; prepare answers to commonly asked questions; select questions to be answered by organizational members; dress appropriately; control nervous habits; and give people a firm handshake.

A successful interview frequently results in a job offer. One should not accept the first offer unless it meets all the requirements of a dream job. It is good to be knowledgeable regarding job market conditions, salary ranges and benefits packages for positions of interest. It is essential to be realistic and to be prepared to negotiate for the things most important for a reasonable career progression.

The last section of this chapter discussed the role of professional development in the life of nonprofit staff members. Candidates should take every opportunity to gain additional educational credentials, acquire new skills and up-date old skills. In addition, he or she should seek every occasion to work with appropriate professional associations and community projects in order to expand network contacts for that next job search.

This chapter addressed, in part, the American Humanics Certification Competency Requirements of Employability Skills and Career Development and Exploration.

■ Discussion Questions

1. Discuss the implications for any society of the Ralph Waldo Emerson quote at the beginning of this chapter.
2. Discuss the benefits of the ***Flowchart for Career Planning***.
3. What is the difference between "abilities" and "learned skills"? Is this difference important?
4. Discuss the value of self-assessment. How can others help in the process?
5. Discuss the skills necessary for most careers in nonprofit.
6. Discuss what can be done to develop each of the skills mentioned in response to question #3.
7. Discuss the role of an interview in the employment process from the point of view of the employer and that of the potential employee.
8. How can any and all work experience be valuable for any career path?
9. Why is professional development important in career success?

■ Activities

1. Write a 2-5-page paper describing your ideal or dream career.
2. In groups of 3-6 people, discuss the most important factors in accepting an initial employment position after receiving a bachelor's degree. Do any of those factors change if you are considering the first position after receiving a master's degree?
3. Choose a nonprofit organization in the community and plan and secure permission for a day of *shadowing*.
4. Write a 2-page paper about the charity established by Arthur Ashe in 1992, two months before his death.
5. Write a personal vision statement for seven years from now, fifteen years from now, and thirty years from now. Consider changes in your personal life and economic conditions.
6. Create a *networking* list of 15-20 individuals or organizational contacts.
7. Participate in a simulated interview (in-class or with the Career Services Office on campus).

■ References

Dawson, K. M. and Dawson, S. N. (1996). *Job Search: The Total System.* 2nd ed. New York: John Wiley & Sons.

Hirsch, A. S. (1999). *Interviewing.* 3rd ed. New York: John Wiley & Sons.

Kennedy, J. (2000). *Job Interviews for Dummies.* New York: John Wiley & Sons.

Michelozzi, B. N., (1992). *Coming Alive from Nine to Five.* Mountain View, CA: Mayfield Printing Company.

Lowe, D. (2002). *Networking for Dummies.* New York: John Wiley & Sons.

Weis, R. (1996). *A Lifetime of Making a Difference.* Kansas City, MO: Clevenger & Company Publishers.

Appendix A
Directory of National
Nonprofit Organizations

4-H

History

An informal organization established by Congress in 1914, the Cooperative Extension Service is a partnership of U.S. Department of Agriculture. 4-H is one of the extension's educational youth programs. Since 1914, 4-H has reached more than 40 million youth from all states, including about four-and-a-half million boys and girls enrolled today.

Purpose

To help youth acquire knowledge, develop life skills, and form attitudes that will enable them to become self-directing, productive, and contributing members of society.

Programs

Cooperative Extension Service
Expanded Food and Nutrition Programs
Agriculture and Science Project
Home Environment Project

Leadership Programs
Honor Club
Public Speaking
Safety and Health Programs

Career Opportunities

Camp Managers
Camp Instructors
Medical Technicians
Home Economics
Recreation
Asst. Director for Youth Development

County Extension Agents
4-H Specialists
Extension Associates
Agriculture
Education
Management

Contact

Local offices are located in most counties with state offices based in state universities. Check the Internet for the latest news.

7100 Connecticut Avenue
Chevy Chase, MD 20815-4999

Phone: 301-961-2800

In Kentucky, use these numbers:
Phone: 859-257-5961
Fax: 859-257-7180

http://shelley.ca.uky.edu:80/adcollege/4-H/
http://www.fourhcouncil.edu/

ALANON/ALATEEN

History

Al-Anon was founded in 1951 to help relatives and friends of individuals with an alcohol problem. They currently have 30,000 regional groups.

Purpose

To share experiences, strength, and hope with others; discuss difficulties; learn effective ways to cope with problems; encourage one another; and help each other understand the principles of the Al-Anon program.

Programs

Help Line
National Drug Prevention Program
Support Groups

Career Opportunities

Accounting   Literature
International Services Archivist   Clerical

Contact

Local offices are located in most cities. Check the Internet for the latest news.

1600 Corporate Landing Pkwy.   Phone: 757-499-1443
Virginia Beach, VA 23454   Fax: 757-563-1655

http://www.al-anon-alateen.org

Alcoholics Anonymous

History

AA was founded in 1935 by a New York stockbroker and an Ohio surgeon, both of whom had been "hopeless" drunks. It has grown from two members to more than 2,000,000. There are now 89,000 small groups.

Purpose

To stay sober and help other alcoholics to achieve sobriety.

Programs

TV or radio programs
AA Grapevine

Support Groups
Information dissemination

Career Opportunities

Therapy
Counseling
(Few paid positions)

Administrative
Research

Contact

Local groups are located in most communities. Check the Internet for the latest news.

475 Riverside Drive
New York, NY 10115

Phone: 212-870-3400
Fax: 212-870-3003

http://www.aa.org

Alzheimer's Association

History

It was founded in 1980 by seven independent caregiver groups of dedicated family members. It is officially known as the Alzheimer's Disease and Related Disorders Association. The Association works through a network of more than 221 local chapters, more than 2,000 support groups and 35,000 volunteers nationwide.

Purpose

To lead in promoting awareness of Alzheimer's Disease and serving the diverse needs of the more than 400,000 affected persons and their families.

Programs

Adult Day Care Programs
Support Systems
Memory Walk
Safe Return

Respite Care Programs
Research Programs
National Education Conference
AA Newsletter

Career Opportunities

Fundraising
Accounting
Administration

Medical and Scientific Affairs
Management Information
Publicity

Contact

Local offices are located in many cities. Check the Internet for the latest news.

919 North Michigan Ave., Suite 1000
Chicago, IL 60611-1676

Phone: 312-335-8700
800-272-3900
Fax: 312-335-1110

http://www.alz.org

American Association for Higher Education

History

It was founded in 1870. More than 7,800 educators are members today.

Purpose

To clarify and help resolve critical issues in post-secondary education through conferences, publications and special projects.

Programs

Educational Assistant Programs
Training Programs
Support of Academic Alliance

Career Opportunities

Clerical
Human Resources

Development Officer
Fundraising

Contact

Local chapters are located at many colleges and universities. Check the Internet for the latest news.

1 Dupont Circle NW, Suite 360	Phone:	202-293-6440
Washington, DC 20036	Fax:	202-293-0073

http://www.ahe.org

American Cancer Society

History

In 1913, ten physicians and five laymen founded the American Society for the Control of Cancer. It was later named the American Cancer Society, Inc. The national ACS consists of 57 divisions and more than 3,400 units.

Purpose

To disseminate knowledge concerning the symptoms, treatment and prevention of cancer; to investigate conditions under which cancer is found, and to compile statistics in regard thereto.

Programs

Service Programs:
—Community Connection
—Transportation
—Home Care Items

Rehabilitation Programs:
—Reach to Recovery
—Laryngectomy Rehabilitation
—Look Good...Feel Better
—Children's camps

Patient and Family Education Programs:
—I Can Cope
—Anti-tobacco Programs

Group Support Programs

Career Opportunities

Management
Community Services
Public Education

Patient Services
Research
Fundraising

Contact

Local offices are located in most cities. Check the Internet for the latest news.

1599 Clifton Road NE
Atlanta, GA 30329

Phone: 404-320-3333
          800-227-2345
Fax: 404-325-1467

http://www.cancer.org

American Foundation for the Blind

History

Founded in 1921, the American Foundation for the Blind is recognized in the United States as Helen Keller's cause.

Purpose

To enable people who are blind or visually impaired to achieve equality of access and opportunity that will ensure freedom of choice in their lives.

Programs

Education Programs   Guide Dog Schools
Research   Client Assistance
Books on Tape

Career Opportunities

Medical
Fundraising
Research   Administrative
Dog Training   Readers

Contact

Local offices are located in many cities. Check the Internet for the latest news.

11 Penn Plaza, Suite 300	Phone:	212-505-7600
New York, NY 10001		800-232-5463
	Fax:	212-502-7777

http://gopher.afb.org.5005/1/

American Lung Association

History

The National Association for the Study and Prevention of Tuberculosis was formed in 1904 by a group of doctors and concerned citizens dedicated to the elimination of tuberculosis. Its best-known funding program has been Christmas Seals. As tuberculosis was brought under control, the organization expanded its work to fight other lung diseases and pollution and adopted the name American Lung Association. More than 8,700 medical professionals take part in its medical programs today.

Purpose

To promote pulmonary health through research, education and patient assistance.

Programs

Medical Research Programs
School Health Education Programs:
—Lungs Are for Life
—Open Airways for Schools

Environmental Health Programs
Lung Disease Education Programs:
—Better Breathers Club
—Camp Superkids
—Alpha 1 Support Groups

Smoking Cessation/Intervention Programs:
—Freedom-from-Smoking Clinics
—In Control
—Healthy Beginnings
—Coping Without Smoking

Career Opportunities

Health Education Director
Communications Director
Development Director
Fundraising

Volunteer Coordinator
Clerical
Executive Director

Contact

Local offices are located in many cities. Check the Internet for the latest new.

4100 Churchman Ave.
Louisville, KY 40215

Phone: 800-LUNG-USA
Fax: 270-363-0222

http://www.kylung.org

American Red Cross

History

In 1859, Henri Dunant, a Swiss banker, visited the battlefields of Solferino, in Italy. After seeing thousands of wounded and dying victims, he organized a group of peasant women to assist him in rescue operations. This was the first mission in what was to become the Red Cross Movement. In 1863, the International Committee of Red Cross formed. A few years later, Clara Barton founded the American Red Cross through her experience in the Civil War and the Franco-Prussian War. Today there are 2,817 chapters, 56 blood service regions, 277 field stations on military bases and in hospitals, three operation headquarters, and one national headquarters.

Purpose

The American Red Cross is a humanitarian organization whose volunteers provide relief to victims of disasters and help people prevent, prepare for and respond to emergencies.

Programs

Disaster

Tissue Services

HIV/AIDS Education

International Services

…and many others

Blood Services

Health and Safety Services

Military and Social Services

Youth Services

Career Opportunities

Finance

Biomedical Services

International Services

Accounting

Public Support

Human Resources

Health and Safety

Corporate Planning and Evaluation

Contact

Local offices are located in most cities. Check the Internet for the latest news.

431 18th St. NW
Washington, DC 20006

Phone: 202-737-8300
              800-842-2200
Fax: 202-639-3711

http://www.redcross.org

America's Second Harvest

History

In 1979 the organization was given the name America's Second Harvest. However the food bank concept began in the late 1960s in Phoenix, Arizona. The organization's goal is to end hunger. It is America's largest charitable hunger-relief organization distributing 1.8 billion bounds of donated food and grocery products annually.

Purpose

America's Second Harvest mission is to feed hungry people by soliciting and distributing food and grocery products through a nationwide network of certified affiliate food banks and food rescue programs and to educate the public about the nature of and solutions to the problem of hunger in America.

Programs

Community Kitchen
Disaster Relief
Fresh Food Initiative
Production Alliance

Kids Cafe
Seafood Initiative
Pallet for the Hungry
Relief Fleet

Career Opportunities

Associate Director
Partner Relations Coordinator
Chef Instructor
Catering Manager
Brown Bag Manager

Food Procurement Manager
Business Manager
Kitchen Supervisor
Capital Campaign Officer
Office Assistant

Contact

Local offices are located in most counties with state offices based in state universities. Check the Internet for the latest news.

35 E. Wacker Drive, #200   Phone: 1-800-771-2303
Chicago, IL 60601   1-312-263-2303

http://www.secondharvest.org

The Arc of the United States

History

The Arc was founded in 1950 by a small group of parents and other concerned individuals. The association worked to change the public perception of children with mental retardation and educate parents and others regarding the potential of people with mental retardation.

Purpose

The Arc of the United States works to include all children and adults with cognitive, intellectual, and developmental disabilities in every community.

Programs

Citizen Advocacy and Self Advocacy
Recreational Activities
Employment

Career Opportunities

Volunteer Work

Contact

1010 Wayne Avenue, Suite 650   Phone: 301-565-3842
Silver Spring, MO 20910

http://www.thearc.org

Big Brothers Big Sisters of America

History

The Big Brothers Big Sisters movement began at the turn of the century, when citizens in many American cities organized programs to stop the rising tide of juvenile delinquency. By 1917, the Big Brothers and Big Sisters Federation formed. It existed until 1937. In 1945, a national federation for Big Brothers agencies, Big Brothers of America, was formed. Big Sisters International, Inc. was formed in 1970. In 1977, the two national organizations merged to create today's Big Brothers Big Sisters of America. Today, over 500 agencies located throughout the United States help more than 75,000 children.

Purpose

To make a positive difference in lives of children and youth, primarily through a professionally supported one-to-one relationship with a caring adult, and to assist children in achieving their highest potential as they grow to become responsible men and women.

Programs

Mentoring
EMPOWER

Career Opportunities

Office Manager	Executive Director
Support Staff	Caseworkers
Field Managers	Finance
Marketing	Supervisor/Program Directors

Contact

Local offices are located in many cities. Check the Internet for the latest news.

230 North 13th St.	Phone: 215-567-7000
Philadelphia, PA 19107	Fax: 215-567-0394

http://www./bbbsa.org/   http://www.bbbsa@aol.com/

Boy Scouts of America

History

The Boy Scouts of America was founded in 1910 by William D. Boyce, after he had been impressed by the young British Scout who had helped him find his way out of a dense London fog. The organization now serves more than four million members in programs ranging from Tiger Cubs for six-year-old boys to Eagle Scouts for older teens and with special programs for handicapped people of any age.

Purpose

To serve others by helping to instill values in young people and, in other ways, to prepare them to make ethical choices over their lifetime in achieving their full potential.

Programs

Trail Boss
Boy Scouting
Learning for Life

Cub Scouting
Exploring

Career Opportunities

Public Relations
Sales
Service
Sociology
Management

Administration
Finance
Psychology
Human Relations

Contact

Local offices are located in many cities. Check the Internet for the latest news.

1325 W. Walnut Hill Lane	Phone: 972-580-2000
Irving, TX 75038	Fax: 972-580-2502

http://www.scouting.org

Boys and Girls Club of America

History

In 1860, three ladies invited a group of street boys into their home. They saw a positive influence on the boys' behavior and extended their hospitality several more times. Along With others, the ladies resolved themselves to finding a facility where boys could go regularly. They called it Dashaway Club, which was the first Boys Club. Although this particular club was discontinued the following year, the idea grew. In 1897, the first building was planned specifically for a boys club in Fall River, Massachusetts. The movement then spread westward. There are now 1,460 Boys and Girls Club facilities that help more than 1.84 million young people.

Purpose

To help youth of all backgrounds, with special concern for those from disadvantaged circumstances, develop the qualities needed to become responsible citizens and leaders.

Programs

National Association of Keystone Clubs
Young Artists Program
National Photography Contest
Sectional Tournaments and Contests Programs

SMART Moves
Feed the Children
A Helping Hand

Career Opportunities

Educational Director
Social Recreation Director
Executive Director
Aquatics Director
Camp Director
Assistant Executive Director

Physical Education Director
Group Club Supervisor
Guidance Counselor
Industrial Arts Instructor
Program Director

Contact

Local offices are located in many cities. Check the Internet for the latest news.

1230 West Peachtree St. NW
Atlanta, GA 30309

Phone: 404-815-5700
Job Line: 404-815-5828
Fax: 404-815-5757

http://www.bgca.org

Camp Fire Boys and Girls

History

This organization was founded in 1910 as Camp Fire Girls by Luther Halsey Gulick, M.D., and his wife, Charlotte Vetter Gulick. It was the first national, nonsectarian organization for girls in the United States. In the 1970s, membership was expanded to include boys, and the name was changed to Camp Fire Boys and Girls. Each year, Camp Fire Boys and Girls serves more than 400,000 young children across the United States.

Purpose

To provide, through a program of informal education, opportunities for youth to realize their potential and to function effectively as caring, self-directed individuals, responsible to themselves and others; and, as an organization, to seek to improve those conditions in society which affect youth.

Programs

A Gift of Peace   Club Program
Teens in Action   Teen Campaign on Suicide Awareness
Teen Parent Program   Special Saturday Club

Career Opportunities

Executive Directors   Camp Administrators

Contact

Local offices are located in many cities. Check the Internet for the latest news.

4601 Madison Ave.   Phone: 816-756-1950
Kansas City, MO 64122-1278   Fax: 916-756-0258

http://www.campfire.org

Catholic Charities USA

History

The Catholic Charities USA was founded in 1910. The Catholic Charities Association has more than 1,400 local organizations with more then 300,00 staff members and volunteers, which serve nearly 10 million people in need.

Purpose

The purpose of the organization is for thousands of concerned volunteers and independent social service agencies to work together to reduce poverty, support families, and build communities in the United States.

Programs

Counseling
Health Services
Adoption Services
Refugee Resettlement
Residential Care

Education and Family Support
Housing
Neighborhood Support
Pregnancy Services

Career Opportunities

Administration
Development
Facilities and Services
Training and Convening

Communications
Disaster Response
Social Services

Contact

Local offices are located in many cities. Check the Internet for the latest news.

1731 King Street, Suite 200
Alexandria, VA 22314

Phone: 703-549-1390
Fax: 703-549-1656

http://www.catholiccharitiesusa.org

Chamber of Commerce

History

The beginnings of the Chamber of Commerce movement can be traced back almost 6,000 years to the city of Mari, in Mesopotamia. The modern movement began in 1599, when merchants in Marseilles, France, formed an independent voluntary organization to represent commercial interests of the port. During the eighteenth century, chambers were established in many cities in France, England and Ireland. The first American Chamber of Commerce was organized in 1768 in New York, and five years later, businessmen from Charleston, South Carolina, united to form their Chamber of Commerce. Today there are more than 2,700 local, state and regional Chambers and American Chambers abroad, comprised of 1,100 trade and professional associations and more than 39,000 business members. It is estimated that approximately six million persons may be involved with Chambers of Commerce.

Purpose

To promote development of a community by pulling together its various elements: business, professional, industrial and artistic.

Programs

Communications
Growth/Recruitment
Convention Center

Small Business Assistance
Promotion of Tourism
Housing Bureau

Career Opportunities

Tourism Sales
Sales Manager
Executive Director
Marketing Director

Convention Planning
Administrative Assistant
Director of Public Relations
Business Services

Contact

Most communities have Chambers of Commerce. Check the Internet for latest news.

American Chamber of
Commerce Executives.
4232 King St
Alexandria, VA 22302-1507

Phone: 703-998-0072
Fax: 703-931-5624

http://www.acce.org

Co-ette Club

History

The Co-ette Club was founded in 1914 in Detroit, where it currently operates. It consists of 35 local groups with membership limited to 35 per chapter.

Purpose

To stress involvement in national and local charitable, civic, educational, and cultural causes.

Programs

Charity
Civic Events
Cultural Events
Educational Events

Career Opportunities

No paid positions.

Contact

Located only in Detroit.

Council on International Educational Exchange

History

Founded in 1947, the Council on International Educational Exchange now has 276 members.

Purpose

To develop and administer a wide variety of study, work, travel and volunteer service programs for American and international students at secondary, undergraduate, graduate and professional programs.

Programs

Council Travel   Volunteer Service
Work Abroad Program   Summer Study Abroad Program

Career Opportunities

Program Coordinators   Administrative

(To qualify, applicants must have worked or studied abroad, have good language skills and have two to five years of experience.)

Contact

Check the Internet for the latest news.

633 3rd Avenue   Phone: 212-822-2600
New York, NY 10017   Fax: 212-822-2699

http://www.info@councilexchange.org

Cystic Fibrosis Foundation

History

CFF was established in 1955 to raise money for research to find a cure for cystic fibrosis and to improve the quality of life for 30,000 children and young adults with the disease. Today it supports 12 CF research centers and finances 114 CF centers nationwide. There are currently 10 chapters across the country.

Purpose

To raise money for research to find a cure for cystic fibrosis and to improve the quality of life for those with the disease.

Programs

Research   Medical Care
Financial Assistance   GREAT STRIDES Walk-a-Thon

Career Opportunities

Medical   Research
Financial   Fundraising
Pharmacy   Communications

Contact

Local offices are located in many cities, especially at larger hospitals. Check the Internet for the latest news.

6931 Arlington Rd., 2nd Floor   Phone: 800-FIGHTCF
Bethesda, MD 20814   Fax: 301-951-6378

http://www.cff.org

Ducks Unlimited

History

Ducks Unlimited was founded in 1937 and currently has 500,000 members in 3,500 regional groups.

Purpose

To fulfill the annual life cycle needs of North American waterfowl by protecting, enhancing, restoring and managing important wetlands.

Programs

Rehabilitation Work Programs   Monitoring Programs

Career Opportunities

Biologist   Administrative
Engineering Technician   Support Staff
Fundraising

Contact

Local offices are located in many cities and rural areas. Check the Internet for the latest news.

1 Waterfowl Way   Phone: 901-758-3825
Memphis, TN 38120   Fax: 901-758-3850

http://www.ducks.org

Easter Seal Society

History

The Easter Seal Society, founded in 1922, serves a large number of children with special needs. More than 8,000 children and young adults benefit from their services annually.

Purpose

ESS is dedicated to helping children with physical disabilities achieve their full individual potential and future independence.

Programs

Camping
Financial Assistance
Integrated Preschools
Family Education Workshops

Parent-to-Patient Link
Respite Care
Parent Delegates

Career Opportunities

Nursing
Medical
Fundraising

Research
Administrative

Contact

Local offices are located in many cities. Check the Internet for the latest news.

230 W. Monroe Street
Suite 1800
Chicago, IL 60606

Phone: 312-726-6200
Fax: 312-726-1494

http://www.easterseals.org

Family Career and Community Leaders of America

History

FCCLA was founded in 1945 for home economics students in junior and senior high schools of the United States, Puerto Rico and the Virgin Islands. Its current membership is 250,000 with 10,000 local chapters.

Purpose

To prepare young men and women in high school for careers related to home economics, family life and consumer education; to promote personal growth and leadership development through home economics education.

Programs

STAR events
Chapter projects
Community projects

Home projects
School projects
Youth for Understanding

Career Opportunities

Clerical
Membership Services Assistant
Computer Services
Program Manager
Program Coordinator
Teacher/Chapter Adviser

Administrative
Accountant
Meetings Manager
Adult/Chapter Relations Coordinator
Communications
Youth/Program Assistant

Contact

Local chapters are located in many high schools and colleges. Check the Internet for the latest news.

1910 Association Dr.
Reston, VA 22091

Phone: 703-620-0215
Fax: 703-860-2713

http://www.fcclainc.org

Fellowship of Christian Athletes

History

The Fellowship of Christian Athletes was founded in 1954. Currently there are more than 5,000 clubs with an estimated 250,000 – 400,000 athletes involved.

Purpose

To present to athletes and coaches, and all whom they influence, the challenge and adventure of receiving Jesus Christ as Savior and Lord, serving him in their relationships and in the fellowship of the church.

Programs

Rallies   Retreats
Camps   Sports Clinics
School Assemblies

Career Opportunities

Development/Public Relations   Camp Coordinators
Administrative/Executive Directors   Ministry Services
Finance   Publications
Data Processing

Contact

Local chapters are located in many cities and schools. Check the Internet for the latest news.

8701 Leeds Rd.   Phone: 816-921-0909
Kansas City, MO 64129   Fax: 816-921-8755

http://www.fca.org

FFA

History

Organized under the provisions of the Smith-Hughes Act of 1917, FFA's first national convention was held in 1982. Its current membership is 428,000 members with 52 state chapters and 7,300 local chapters.

Purpose

To motivate and vitalize the systematic instruction offered to students of vocational agriculture and to provide training and farm citizenship.

Programs

Vocational Agriculture Programs   Community Programs

Career Opportunities

Chief Operative Officer   National Adviser
National Executive Secretary   Team Leader
Administration Specialist   Co-team Leader
Clerical   Membership Services Specialist
Marketing Consultant   Management Information Systems Director
Distribution Resources Specialist   Partner Development Specialist
Teacher Services Specialist   Student Services Specialist
Alumni Services Specialist   Conference Program Director

Contact

Local chapters are located in many schools and colleges. Check the Internet for the latest news.

5632 Mt. Vernon Memorial HWY   Phone: 703-360-3600
P.O. Box 15160
Alexandria, VA 22309-0160

http://www.ffa.org

Fine Arts

History

Artists appear in the earliest recorded history and were the actual historians. Ancient cave drawings depict musicians and dancers. Jubal, the first maker and player of the pipes, is mentioned early in Genesis in the Bible; young David's harp skills were sought as therapy for the mentally disturbed King Saul, and his poetry is loved by millions. Today's arts include avenues unheard of only a few decades ago. Applications beyond pure visual and performance art are almost constantly developing.

Career Opportunities

Art Therapist*

Dance Therapist*

Graphic Designer

Symphony Conductor

Community Theater Director

Theater Director

Creative Arts Project Planner

Museum Curator

Concert Promoter

Artist Manager

Fundraiser

Music Therapist*

Performer

Program Planner

Community Band Director

Puppet Therapist

Skit Writer

Teacher

Civic Auditorium Manager

Fine Arts Center Director

Agent

Marketing Specialist

*Some career paths require special certification.

Contact

There are many local, state and national associations for the arts, which may be contacted through universities or specific disciplines. Most community arts groups are nonprofit organizations that may not be registered with any national agency. Job seekers are advised not to overlook such prospective employers as may be found through newspaper announcements, networking and Chamber of Commerce directories.

Future Business Leaders of America

History

FBLA was founded in 1942. Its current membership is 300,000 members with 12,000 local chapters.

Purpose

To promote competent, aggressive business leadership, establish career goals, encourage scholarships, promote efficient money management, and develop character and self-confidence.

Programs

Skills Competition   National Student Award
Educational Programs

Career Opportunities

Communications Specialist   Conference Assistant
Receptionist   Membership Coordinator
Executive Assistant   Membership Director
Conference Director   Publications Coordinator
Resource Center Coordinator   Mail Room Clerk

Contact

Local chapters are located in many schools and universities. Check the Internet for the latest news.

1912 Association Dr.	Phone: 703-860-3334
Reston, VA 22091	Fax: 703-758-0749

http://fbla-pbl.org

Girl Scouts of the U.S.A.

History

The organization was founded in 1812 by Juliette Gordon Lowe. The first club was formed with 18 girls. Today, it has nearly three million members throughout the United States.

Purpose

To inspire girls with the highest ideals of character, conduct, patriotism and service so that they may become happy and resourceful citizens.

Programs

Daisy Girl Scouts
Junior Girl Scouts
Senior Girl Scouts

Brownie Girl Scouts
Cadette Girl Scouts

Career Opportunities

Marketing and Sales
Fund Development
Communication Services
Human Resources
Program Specialist

Finance Services
Information Systems and Services
Legal Services
Field Director

Contact

Local offices are located in many cities. Check the Internet for the latest news.

420 5th Ave.
New York, NY 10018

Phone: 212-852-8000
Fax: 212-852-6517

http://www.gsusa.org/

Girls Incorporated

History

The first Girls Club was founded in Waterbury, Connecticut, in 1854. The early clubs were safe havens and social and educational centers for the young women who worked in northeastern mill town during the Industrial Revolution. In 1990, the membership voted to change its name to Girls Incorporated. Girls Incorporated has grown to have over 200 centers in 121 cities. They serve a quarter of a million girls and young women, ages six to eighteen.

Purpose

The purpose of Girls Incorporated is to empower girls to be self-sufficient, personally fulfilled, and economically independent.

Programs

Friendly PEERsuasion
Going Places
Teen Connections

Preventing Adolescent Pregnancy
Operation SMART
Sporting Chance

Career Opportunities

Administrative Services
Communication Services

Program Services

Contact

Local offices are located in many cities. Check the Internet for the latest news.

120 Wall Street
New York, NY 10016

Phone: 212-509-2000
Fax: 212-509-8708

http://www.girlsinc.org

Goodwill Industries International

History

In the late 1890's, Methodist Minister Edgar J. Helms found ways to help his community's immigrant, jobless poor. His church's "industrial school" offered skills training. A job placement service developed in 1896. In 1902, a new facility was built and Goodwill Industries was truly born. The words "Goodwill Industries" were first used in Brooklyn, New York. During the 1930's, Goodwill Industries redirected its mission to helping people with disabilities. Today, there are 183 Goodwill organizations. In 1993, they served more than 123,000 people with disabilities and special needs in the United States. They also served approximately 40,000 outside the United States and Canada.

Purpose

To achieve the full participation in society of people with disabilities and other individuals with special needs by expanding their opportunities and occupational capabilities through a network of autonomous, nonprofit, community-based organizations providing services throughout the world in response to local needs.

Programs

Employment & Training Services   Second-hand Retail Stores
Recycling Services

Career Opportunities

Rehabilitation   Vocational Training
Accounting   Retailing
Industrial Operations   Marketing and Sales

Contact

Local offices are located in many cities. Check the Internet for the latest news.

9200 Rockville Pike   Phone: 301-530-6500
Bethesda, MD 20814   Fax: 301-530-1516

http://www.goodwill.org/

Habitat for Humanity International

History

Founded in 1976 by Millard and Linda Fuller, Habitat for Humanity International (HFHI) is a nonprofit, ecumenical Christian housing ministry.

Purpose

HFHI seeks to eliminate poverty housing and homelessness from the world, and to make decent shelter a matter of conscience and action. HFHI invites people from all walks of life to work together in partnership to help build houses with families in need. HFHI has built more than 40,000 houses around the world, providing some 250,000 people with safe, decent, affordable housing.

Career Opportunities

International Services
Accounting
Project Management

Contact

Local offices are located in many cities. Check the Internet for the latest news.

121 Habitat Street	Phone:	912-924-6935 or
Americus, GA 31709		800-HABITAT
	Fax:	912-924-0641

http://www.habitat.org/

Hospice

History

The first modern hospice was founded in London in 1968. Cicely Saunders, the founder, believed that institutions were ignoring the special needs of the dying. The first American hospice was started in New Haven, Connecticut, in 1974. Now more than 1,800 hospices are serving people.

Purpose

To provide special care for dying people and their families.

Programs

Support Groups
Health Care Programs

Career Opportunities

Medical	Counseling
Nursing	Physical Therapy

Contact

Local offices are located in many hospitals. Check the Internet for the latest news.

1700 Diagonal Rd. Suite 625	Phone:	800-658-8898
Alexandria, VA 22314	Fax:	703-525-5762

http://www.nhpco.org

The Humane Society of the United States

History

The Humane Society was founded in 1954. It maintains a regional office, an educational division, a team of investigators, legislative experts and an animal-control academy. There are more than a million members involved.

Purpose

To make the world safe for animals through legal, educational, legislative and investigative means.

Programs

Educational   Wildlife Experts
Research   HSUS News
HSUS Adopt-a-Teacher

Career Opportunities

Human Resources   Accounting
Financial   Secretarial/Administrative
Program Coordinators   Executive Directors
Public Relations   Development Department
Marketing

Contact

Local offices are located in many cities. Check the Internet for the latest news.

2100 L Street NW   Phone: 202-452-1100
Washington, DC 20037   Fax: 301-258-3079

http://www.hsus.org

Junior Achievement

History

Junior Achievement was founded in 1919. By 1994, 55,000 children participated in the organization.

Purpose

To provide young people with practical, economic education programs and experiences in the competitive private enterprise system through a partnership with the business and education communities.

Programs

Project Business
GLOBE

Applied Economics
Business Basics

Career Opportunities

Field Services
Communications and Marketing
Management

Research and Development
Human Resources

Contact

Local contacts may be made through schools, businesses and local offices. Check the Internet for the latest news.

One Education Way
Colorado Springs, CO 80906

Phone: 719-540-8000
Fax: 719-540-9151

http://www.ja.org

Juvenile Diabetes Foundation

History

The Juvenile Diabetes Foundation was founded in 1970. Since then, it has given more than $155 million to diabetes research around the world.

Purpose

To support research in the cause, cure, treatment and prevention of diabetes and its complications.

Programs

Walk for the Cure   Promise Ball
Patient Camps

Career Opportunities

Fundraising   Research
Medical   Administrative

Contact

Local offices are located in many cities. Check the Internet for the latest news.

120 Wall Street	Phone: 212-785-9500
New York, NY 10005	800-JDF-CURE
	Fax: 212-785-9595

http://www.jdrf.org

Leukemia and Lymphoma Society of America

History

It was established in 1949 as the de Villiers Foundation, in memory of Robert Roesler de Villiers, a young man who died of leukemia. In 1967, it was renamed the Leukemia Society of America. It now has 57 chapters, with branch offices in 33 states and the District of Columbia.

Purpose

It is dedicated to eradicating leukemia and its related cancers and improving the lives of patients and their families.

Programs

Research Programs   Patient Aid
Public and Professional Education   Community Service

Career Opportunities

Accounting   Public Relations
Communications   Administration
Research   Marketing
Finance
Medical

Contact

Local offices may be found through larger hospitals. Check the Internet for the latest news.

1311 Mamaroneck Avenue   Phone: 800-9554LSA
3rd floor
White Plains, NY 10605

http://www.leukemia/lempfomo.org

Little League Baseball Inc.

History

In 1939, Carl E. Stotz wanted to form a baseball league for young boys in Williamsport, Pennsylvania. Today, it is organized in all U.S. states and territories, and 29 foreign countries.

Purpose

To teach the game and sportsmanship to youngsters and provide a pastime for the player's entire family.

Programs

Local, State, National and International Games
World Series

Career Opportunities

Clerical   Financial Officer
Coordinators   Merchandising
Insurance   Accounting

Contact

Local organizations are active in most communities. Check the Internet for the latest news.

P.O. Box 3485   Phone: 570-326-1921
Williamsport, PA 17701   Fax: 570-326-1074

http://www.littleleague.org

March of Dimes

History

The March of Dimes has been dedicated to saving babies from birth defects and other infant health problems for more than sixty years. Since 1958, the March of Dimes has been funding cutting-edge research and innovative programs to save babies. It provides care for victims of polio, while aggressively working to develop vaccines against it. It represents the first large-scale, nationwide biomedical initiative led by a charitable organization.

Purpose

The March of Dimes researchers, volunteers, educators, outreach workers and advocates work together to give all babies a fighting chance against threats to their health, such as prematurity, birth defects and low birth weight.

Programs

Global Health Newsletter   RIDE
Walk America   Golf Tournaments
Mothers March   Jail and Bail

Career Opportunities

Assistant Director   Program Coordinator
Senior Designer   Special Events
Manager

Contact

1275 Mamaroneck Avenue   Phone: 212-558-5300
White Plains, NY 10605

http://www.modimes.org

National Collegiate Athletic Association

History

It was founded in 1906 and reorganized in 1973 into three divisions, each with national championship competition. It has established 73 national championships in 21 sports. Today, nearly 1,000 education institutions are members of NCAA.

Purpose

To supervise regional and national collegiate athletics contests, adopt and enforce eligibility rules, and publish rule books for collegiate sports.

Programs

College Athletics   Statistics Services
National Youth Sports   Research
Life Skills Program   Youth Educational through Sports (YES)

Career Opportunities

Administrative   Research
Executive Director   Championship Staff
Sports Scientists   Professional Development
Education   Public Information
Marketing and Broadcasting   Finance
Compliance Services   Enforcement and Eligibility Appeals
Legislative Services   Publishing

Contact

Check the Internet for the latest news.

P.O. Box 6222   Phone: 317-917-6222
Indianapolis, IN 46206-6222   Fax: 317-917-6888

http://www.ncaa.org

National Gardening Association

History

Founded in 1972, the National Gardening Association currently has 250,000 members.

Purpose

To promote environmental responsibility and create partnerships that restore and enhance communities by donating tools and seeds and teaching youth the joys of gardening.

Programs

Technical Assistance
Educational

Grants
Publications

Career Opportunities

Personnel
Clerical
Youth Garden Grants Director
Research Director
Advertising
Artist

Building/Grounds
Accounting
Marketing
Professional Development Coordinator
Editors
Horticulturist

Contact

Check the Internet for the latest news.

180 Flynn Ave.
Burlington, VT 05401

Phone:　802-863-1308
Fax:　　802-863-5962

http://www.nationalgardeing.com

National Geographic Society

History

Founded in January 1888 by thirty-three men from occupations ranging from explorer to meteorologist, the National Geographic Society now has a membership of nearly eleven million. Designed to increase geographic knowledge, National Geographic now issues four monthly publications in addition to books, atlases, maps, videos and documentary films.

Purpose

To disseminate information about the physical and social world by publicizing research of various natures in terms understood by lay people.

Programs

Map-making   Publication
Education   Seminars

Career Opportunities

Cartographer   Photographer
Administrator   Editor
Program Planner   Publisher

Contact

Check the Internet for the latest news.

1145 17th St. NW   Phone: 202-857-7000
Washington, DC 20036   Fax: 202-775-6141

http://www.nationalgeographic.com

National Teenage Republican Headquarters

History

It was founded in 1965 and currently has 100,000 members.

Purpose

To educate teens in principles of free enterprise, constitutional government and patriotism. To promote involvement of teenagers in the U.S. political process.

Programs

Training
Community Service Projects

Sub-teenage Republican (STARS)

Career Opportunities

Membership Coordinator
Administrative
Fundraising

Clerical

Contact

Local chapters may be found at many schools and colleges. Check the Internet for the latest news.

10620C Crestwood Dr.
P.O. Box 1896
Manassas, VA 20101-1896

Phone: 703-368-4214
Fax: 703-368-0830

http://www.teenagerepublicans.org

National Wildlife Federation

History

Founded in 1936 as a nationwide network of grass-roots conservationists, the NWF now has a budget of $103 million and a staff of more than 500 professionals working throughout the United States and territories.

Purpose

To educate, inspire and assist individuals and organizations of diverse cultures to conserve wildlife and other natural resources and to protect the Earth's environment in order to achieve a peaceful, equitable and sustainable future.

Programs

Naturequest   Naturelink
Naturescope   Wildlife Camp & Teen Adventure
Conservation Summits   Washington Action Workshop
Animal Tracks

Career Opportunities

Conservationists   Public Relations
Administrative   Researchers
Writers
Artists

Contact

Local offices are located in most cities. Check the Internet for the latest news.

11100 Wildlife Center Dr.	Phone:	800-822-9919
Reston, VA 20192	Fax:	202-790-4040

http://www.nwf.org/nwf/

Parks and Outdoor Recreation

History

America's parks include vast national acreage (such as Yellowstone National Park, established in 1872) and small town centers that provide little more than picnic table and softball parks. Wildlife and ecology programs have grown as the public has become more and more involved in conservation issues, and governmental and private agencies have proliferated.

Purpose

To provide recreational and conservation opportunities on local, state and national levels; to preserve natural resources.

Programs

Ecology   Wildlife Preservation
Community Recreation   State Parks

Career Opportunities

Recreation Director   Forest Ranger
Pool Manager   Trail Guide
Program Director   Finance
Landscape Designer   Ecologist
Veterinarian   Biologist
Marine Specialist   Writer
Firefighter   Administrative Managers
Volunteer Coordinator   Law Enforcement

Contact

Check the Internet for the latest news. Local, state and national parks may be contacted for career opportunities. The following agencies are suggested contacts: U.S. Fish & Wildlife Service, National Wildlife Refuges, National Park Service, U.S. Forest Service, Bureau of Land Management, Army Corps of Engineers, Bureau of Reclamation – all are based in Washington, DC; Tennessee Valley Authority (400 West Summit Hill Drive, Knoxville, TN 37902, phone 615-632-4409); individual state and municipal parks departments; and private organizations, many of which may be found in this book.

Peace Corps

History

The Peace Corps began as President John F. Kennedy sought to bring peace and prosperity to the world by sending American volunteers into third-world countries to teach their citizens how to use their own resources to support themselves. The first workers left for Ghana in August 1961. Today, nearly 6,000 volunteers work in 91 countries. While most volunteers are recent college graduates, many retired people are now opting to spend a few years in Peace Corps service.

Purpose

To aid less fortunate countries in their struggle to gain independence and prosperity by teaching their people basic skills and self-reliance.

Programs

Agriculture and Forestry
Fisheries
Master's Internationalist Program
Medical/Nursing
Special Education
"Life After Peace Corps"

Adult Education
Language Skills
Nutrition Programs
Public Health
Home Economics

Career Opportunities

Entering Peace Corps workers in almost any field are volunteers. Some administrative positions may be available through the national and regional offices, such as the following:

Recruiter
Program Coordinator
Clerical

Office Administrator
Investigator

Contact

There are currently sixteen regional offices. Check your local phone directory for the nearest office. The Peace Corps maintains several websites on the Internet.

1111 20th St.
Washington, DC 20526

Phone: 703-235-9191
        800-424-8580

http://www.peacecorps.gov

Special Olympics

History

In the early 1960's, Eunice Kennedy Shriver held day camps for people with mental retardation. Mrs. Shriver organized the first National Games in 1968 at Chicago's Soldier Field, and Special Olympics Inc., was established. Today ninety percent of U.S. communities and more than 140 countries around the world are involved with Special Olympics.

Purpose

To provide year-round sports training and athletic competition in a variety of Olympic-type sports for children and adults with mental retardation, giving them continuing opportunities to develop physical fitness, demonstrate courage, experience joy, and participate in a sharing of gifts, skills and friendship with their families, other Special Olympics athletes and the community.

Programs

Recycle for Gold
Unified Sports
Senior Sports

Standard Special Olympics
Motor Activity Training

Career Opportunities

Telemarketing
Mail
Recreation
Administrative

Management
Fundraising
Public Relations

Contact

Local offices are located in most cities. Check the Internet for the latest news.

1325 G Street NW
Washington, DC 20005

Phone: 202-628-3630
Fax: 202-824-0200

http://www.specialolympics.org

St. Jude Children's Research Hospital

History

Entertainer Danny Thomas once prayed to St. Jude Thaddeous, the patron saint of the hopeless, to "show me my way in life and I will build you a shrine." As his career prospered, he remembered his pledge and sought a way to fulfill it. The idea of creating a unique research hospital devoted to curing catastrophic diseases in children began to take shape, and he nearly single-handedly raised money to build the hospital. However, the larger problem of continued funding was bigger than one man could solve. That's why in 1957, he and other Arabic-speaking leaders founded the American Lebanese Syrian Associated charities specifically to raise operating funds for this research hospital, which opened in 1962. Today, it has grown to be America's seventh largest health-care charity. More than 5,000 patients are seen annually at no cost to their families.

Purpose

To save children's lives by finding the causes and cures for fatal diseases in children.

Programs

Math-a-thons	Bike-a-thons
Radiothons	Special Television Programming
Patient Care	Family Support Groups

Career Opportunities

Research	Medical
Physicians	Scientists
Executive Director	Board of Governors
Fundraising	Administration

Contact

Check the Internet for the latest news.

332 N. Lauderdale	Phone:	901-495-3306
Memphis, TN 38101-0318		902-495-3300
	Fax:	901-495-3103

http://www.stjude.org

Student Affairs Offices on College and University Campuses

History

To promote retention, welfare, and growth and development in all dimensions of student life, including educational, vocational, social-cultural, civility and tolerance, psychological, values clarification, and physical. Student Affairs' offices also provide a variety of educational and administrative services, programs and activities in support of each university's strategic plan.

Programs

Judicial Affairs
Learning Center
Counseling and Testing
Women's Center
National Student Exchange
Educational Talent Search
Upward Bound
Health Services
Campus Recreation
Special Events

African-American Student Services
Ethnic Programs
Student Financial Aid
Career Services
School Relations
Veterans Affair
Admissions
Student Government Association
Student Organizations
Homecoming

Career Opportunities

Admission Counselor
Residence Hall Director
Academic Advisor
International Student Advisor
Greek Affair Coordinator
Coordinator of Intramural Sports Programs
Director of Health Education Programs
Coordinator for Sexual Assault Prevention
Career Development and Planning

Dean of Students
Director of Volunteer Programs
Director of Enrollment Services
Campus Life Coordinator
Director of Family Programs
Student Activities Director
Financial Aid Advisor
Multicultural Affairs

Contact

All colleges and universities have Student Affairs offices. The professional association to which many administrators belong is:

National Association of Student Personnel Administrators
1875 Connecticut Ave. Suite 418
Washington, DC. 20009
http://www.naspa.org

Therapeutic Recreation

History

Therapeutic recreation has been recognized as a professional field only in the last half of the twentieth century, but its evolution began centuries ago. The Menninger Clinic in Topeka, Kansas, began using recreation activities in an attempt to reduce tension and anxiety in disturbed patients in the 1930s, and penal institutions have long used such sports as boxing and baseball to channel aggressive tendencies and promote physical well-being among their inmates. Today, most hospitals and clinics hire certified recreation therapists (CRT) as part of their health care teams.

Career Opportunities

Recreation therapists must meet national certification requirements and should plan their college course work at an accredited institution.

Setting

Hospitals

Nursing Homes

Prisons

Goodwill Industries

Rehabilitation Centers

Residential Treatment Centers

Freelance Recreation Therapists

Contact

For openings, contact organizations in the area where you wish to live or work. You might also try contacting the following:

American Therapeutic Recreation Association
753 St. Michael's Dr.
Mitchellville, MD 20716

United Way of America

History

United Way originated in Denver in 1887, when four clergymen organized a single fundraising effort to support community organizations. The idea of united fundraising spread to other areas of the community. As of 1993, there were approximately 2,200 United Way organizations in communities throughout the United States and Canada.

Purpose

To increase the organized capacity of people to care for one another.

Programs

United Way Management Training Program
Children's Program
Homeless Family Prevention Project

Child Care Programs
Priority Program Fund

Career Opportunities

Resource Development
Administrative Services
Social Work
Agency Relations
Social Planning

Community Planning
Communication
Fund Distribution
Management

Contact

Local offices are located in many cities. Check the Internet for the latest news.

701 N. Fairfax St.
Alexandria, VA 22314-2045

Phone: 703-836-7100
Fax: 703-683-7840

http://www.unitedway.org

Volunteers of America

History

The Volunteers of America organization was founded in 1896. Today, there are five regional groups and fifty-four local chapters.

Purpose

To provide social services for the homeless, disabled, senior citizens, etc.

Programs

Substance Abuse Programs   Meals on Wheels
Elderly, Youth, Family Programs   Programs for Disabled

Career Opportunities

Fundraising Officer   Social Services
Executive Director   Program Director
Accountant   Human Resources

Contact

Local offices are located in many cities. Check the Internet for the latest news.

320 Hammond Highway   Phone: 504-835-3005
Metairie, LA 70002   Fax: 504-835-0409

http://www.com.neworleans

World Vision

History

It was founded in 1950 and now has more than 5,100 projects in over 85 countries.

Purpose

To provide emergency relief for victims of national and man-made disasters and also to convey Christian love in action and Christian witness in deeds and words.

Programs

Emergency Relief   Disaster Aid Funds

Career Opportunities

Financial Assistant   Fundraising
Marketing Personnel   Communications
Data Processing Specialist   Clerical
Coordinator

Contact

Check the Internet for the latest news.

> P.O. Box 9716   Phone: 253-815-1000
> Federal Way, WA 98063   800-423-4200

http://www.worldvision.org

YMCA

History

In 1844, George Williams organized prayer and Bible studies for the shopmen at the store where he worked in London. The idea spread to nearby firms and the Young Men's Christian Association was formed June 6, 1844. By 1852, the first YMCA in the United States was formed in Boston. Today, YMCA is at work in more than 2,000 locations.

Purpose

To put Christian principles into practice through programs that build healthy body, mind, and spirit for all.

Programs

YMCA Youth Development Programs
Youth Fitness Programs
Aerobics
Family Programs

Teen Esteem
Aquatics
Youth Overnights
Day Camps

Career Opportunities

Marketing and Communications
Fundraising
Juvenile Justice
Physical Education Directors
Residence Managers

Finance
General Directors
Program Directors
Camp Directors
Executive Directors

Contact

Local offices are located in many cities. Check the Internet for the latest news.

101 N. Wacker Dr., 14th Floor
Chicago, IL 60606

Phone: 800-872-9622
Fax: 312-977-9063

http://www.ymca.net

YMCA Leaders Club

History

YMCA was founded in 1844 by George Williams. The Leaders Club is a program of the YMCA.

Purpose

To provide young men and women, ages 12-18, with values and well-rounded training in physical education, health, personal growth, education and leadership skills.

Programs

Service Projects
Volunteer Work

Social Activities

Career Opportunities

Marketing
Fund Raising
Camp Directors
Finance
Executive Directors

Communication
Juvenile Justice
Residence Managers
Program Directors

Contact

101 N. Wacker Dr., 14th Floor
Chicago, IL 60606

Phone: 312-977-0031
         800-872-9622
Fax: 312-977-9063

http://www.ymca.net

YMCA Youth Sports

History

George Williams founded YMCA in 1844. Seven years later, YMCA Youth Sports was added.

Purpose

To stress the value of teamwork and cooperation, fair play, and leadership development.

Programs

Soccer	Gymnastics
Basketball	Baseball
Softball	Volleyball

Career Opportunities

Physical Education	Program Director
Marketing	Communications
Fundraising	Camp Director
Juvenile Justice	Finance
Executive Director	

Contact

Local programs may be found at community YMCA. Check the Internet for the latest news.

101 N. Wacker Dr., 14th Floor	Phone:	800-USA-YMCA
Chicago, IL 60606	Fax:	312-977-9063

http://www.ymca.net

Young Life

History

It was founded in 1941 by a young minister, Jim Rayburn, who saw the need to reach out to young people with the message of Jesus Christ. Today, it operates several resorts for teenagers in the western United States and Canada.

Purpose

To introduce Jesus Christ's love to students who otherwise would not be exposed to such a message.

Programs

Camps
Leadership Training
Campaigns

Career Opportunities

Clergyman
Fundraising
Accountant

Contact

Local offices are located in many cities. Check the Internet for the latest news.

420 N. Cascade Ave.   Phone: 719-473-4262
Colorado Springs, CO 80903   Fax: 719-381-1750

http://www.younglife.org

Youth Section, Democratic Socialists of America

History

It was founded in 1982. Today, there are 40 local chapters with a total of 1,500 members.

Purpose

To protect and expand rights of workers, women, minorities and all people; to encourage democratic social planning; and to achieve a more equitable distribution of the nation's wealth.

Programs

Conferences
Publications

Career Opportunities

Advertising
Administrative
Publications

Contact

Check the Internet for the latest news.

180 Varick St.	Phone: 212-727-8610
New York, NY 10014	Fax: 212-727-8616

YWCA

History

The Young Women's Christian Association began its work in the United States in the mid-1850s. Today, there are community and student YWCAs in all fifty states, with some 400 associations operating at 4,000 locations.

Purpose

To empower women and to eliminate racism.

Programs

Community and Leadership Programs   Youth Development Programs
Family Life Programs   Empowerment Programs
Health Promotion Programs

Career Opportunities

Executive Director   Business Manager
Branch Director   School-age Program Director
Association Network Specialist

Contact

Local offices are located in many cities. Check the Internet fort the latest news.

350 5th Ave.	Phone:	212-273-7800
Empire State Building		800-YWCA-US1
New York, NY 10118	Fax:	212-465-2281

http://www.ywca.org

B

Appendix B
Self-assessment Activities
Career Planning in a
Nonprofit Organization

Self-assessment Profile

Interests

It is important to have interests similar to the activities, programs and goals of a particular organization. On a separate sheet of paper, list 10 different activities or goals you are interested in doing in the context of a professional setting. These activities or goals may deal with issues such as substance abuse prevention, career planning, recreation, education, sports, the environment, fitness and health or something else. Once the list is made, prioritize these activities or goals below in the order of importance from 1 to 10; then set the list aside.

1.

2.

3.

4.

5.

6.

7.

8.

9.

10.

Values

What aspects of life are important to you and what principles guide your life? Just as it is important to express interests through a career, it is equally important to choose an organization with values similar to your own. Use the *Values Inventory* below to help rank values most important to you. Number each item in the order of priority to you, with 1 being the most important and 30 being the least important. Two spaces are available to fill in additional values. After this is finished, set the list aside for later.

—Integrity

—Enjoying the environment

—Making a lot of money

—Working with people

—Being close to your family

—Organizing activities/programs

—Helping special populations

—Working with money

—Living a long, healthy life

—Having a meaningful relationship with God

—Growing personally and professionally

—Having job security

—Living with meaning and purpose

—Being respected for achievements

—_____
(fill in with your own value)

—Having the chance to be creative

—Autonomy at work

—Being the leader

—Having fun

—Planning and developing programs

—Working in crisis situations

—Helping others develop skills

—Determination

—Working in a relaxed environment

—Traveling

—Working with children

—Having a financially comfortable life

—Maintaining close friends

—Having equal opportunities for all

—_____
(fill in with your own value)

Skills and Knowledge Exercise

Based on both classroom achievements and life experiences, write a brief reaction statement to each sentence under the three categories of skills; then put this exercise away for future analysis.

Human Relations Skills

1.   I relate well to other people.

2.   I communicate my ideas and feelings effectively to others.

3.   I am a good listener, and I understand others well.

4.   I can motivate and inspire others when I believe in something.

5.   I can lead activities, yet I am also a good team player.

6.   I can be effective in public speaking and presentations.

7.   I communicate ideas well in writing.

Conceptual Skills

1.   I have been successful at visualizing how a program should be planned.

2.   I am able to assess problem areas and develop effective strategies to address these problems.

3.   I can assimilate information and make good, effective decisions.

4.   I am often creative in how I address problems and opportunities.

5.   I would rather plan and implement someone else's programs instead of my own.

6.   I am looking forward to developing my own programs when I begin working in an organization.

7.   I enjoy creating something from scratch.

Technical Skills

1. I like to organize programs and activities.

2. I have some experience with financial development, and I am familiar with budgeting and other financial processes.

3. I have had some success in supervising others as part of a program development team.

4. I am knowledgeable in the areas of promotion and marketing, and I enjoy this aspect of program development.

5. I have had experience in most areas of program development.

6. I am competent in program development.

7. I understand the way in which conceptual and human relations skills interrelate with technical aspects of program development.

Personal Epitaph

How do you want to be remembered? In the space below, describe the way in which you hope to be remembered at the end of your life. Describe your personal, family and community relationships as you hope they would have been. Then describe your professional activities and accomplishments. Be as specific and detailed as possible with your descriptions.

Once you have completed the entire Self-assessment Profile, review each section; then discuss the results with a faculty member, campus administrator or nonprofit leader.

C Appendix C
Interview Simulation
Critique Form

Interview Simulation Critique Form

Your name _____

Interviewer's name _____

Date____/____/____

Score the interview on each item
by rating him/her with a score from 1-5.

	1 Least Satisfactory	2	3	4	5 Most Satisfactory
Appearance	☐	☐	☐	☐	☐
Communication Skills *Verbal*	☐	☐	☐	☐	☐
Nonverbal	☐	☐	☐	☐	☐
Listening/Understanding	☐	☐	☐	☐	☐
Preparation	☐	☐	☐	☐	☐
Answered questions effectively	☐	☐	☐	☐	☐

Enthusiasm _____

_____

Strengths _____

_____

Areas of Improvement _____

_____

Overall Impression _____

_____

Additional Comments _____

_____

_____

D Appendix D
Sample Organizational
Chart

Sample Organizational Chart

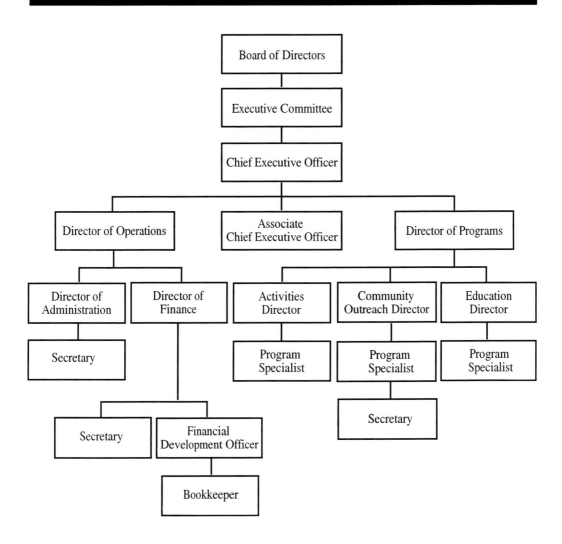

Index